The Comic Tradition in America

An Anthology
Edited with Foreword
and Notes by
Kenneth S. Lynn

W · W · NORTON & COMPANY
New York · London

W. W. Norton & Company, Inc., 500 Fifth Avenue, New York, N.Y. 10110

ISBN 0-393-00447-3

PRINTED IN THE UNITED STATES OF AMERICA

8 9 0

For
Armand Schwab, Jr.
and
Andrew S. Crichton

Contents

Foreword

This book is a critical anthology of American humor. In putting it together, I have tried first of all to follow the simple principle that a story which didn't amuse me didn't get in. No other attribute, not notoriety nor historical importance nor representativeness, was regarded as sufficient qualification in itself for inclusion. The laughter of the editor has been the *sine qua non,* and you will look in vain in these pages for Petroleum V. Nasby, Josh Billings and many another "phunny phellow" whom I find dull.

With the notable exception of Benjamin Franklin, the selections are all drawn from what seems to me the great age of American humor, the nineteenth century. The thread of laughter in America, of the wilderness tough, the Yankee farmer, the Negro slave, can be traced from our own time far back into the seventeenth century and can be picked up again, after a transatlantic leap, in the England and Scotland and Africa of a still more remote time. But it was in the nineteenth century that the comic expression of the popular mind was transmuted into print: an oral tradition became the raw material of a literary art, and Simon Suggs, Major Jack Downing, and Uncle Remus were born. No pre-Revolutionary writer—except Franklin—had fully realized what sort of comic concoction might be brewed out of the roots of folk humor, while in the twentieth century every strain of American humor has had its flavor diluted by the mass media. The end product is, of course, television, wherein the jokes of the Negro, the Jew, the Irishman, and the frontiersman have all been suburbanized into what may very well be the most pallid vernacular humor in history.

But I do not mean to stress unduly the popular origins of American humor. On the contrary, I would prefer to play down this aspect of our comic tradition, if only to counteract what seems to me an over-emphasis by some scholars. The anxiety of many intellectuals of the 1920s to establish contact with what Van Wyck Brooks had called a usable past, and the fascination of the New Deal generation with popular culture, undoubtedly inspired a rewarding interest in the history of American folk humor. (Constance Rourke's sensitive studies are a good example.) But in the process of rediscovering such fabulous creatures as Davy Crockett, we have tended to assume that such masters of the vernacular art as T. B. Thorpe, George Washington Harris, and above all, Mark Twain, were no more self-conscious than the oral tradition on which they drew, thereby denying them the sophistication and the dedicated craftsmanship which are the most conspicuous qualities of their writing. Furthermore, the emphasis on folk humor has obscured the fact that a thoroughly native, thoroughly American humor which has very little connection with either the language or the forms of the oral tradition is a vital part of our literary heritage, and that one of the most significant links between the important writers of our national past has been a willingness to experiment with the comic as a means of expressing their personal vision of life.

A word about the title. I am aware that the term "tradition" has been terribly overworked, particularly by historians of American civilization. Yet I hope that this anthology will demonstrate that a meaningful tradition of American humor does exist, that a vague term is, after all, definable. The central theme of the tradition, as I see it, has been a quixotic comedy of illusion and disillusion, under which may be subsumed such recurring situations as the masquerade, the innocent abroad, and the war between the sexes. Significantly, these are the situations with which the darkest books in American literature are concerned; in viewing tragic emotion under a comic light, the humorists of our past have been able to transform violence and suffering into occasions of pleasure. In a day when American humor seems determined to gloss over reality rather than to transform it, the triumph of our comic tradition seems worth recalling.

K. S. L.

The Comic Tradition in America

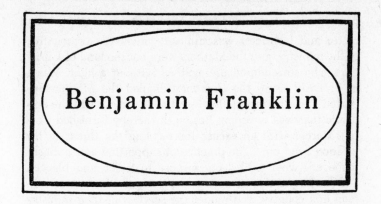

Benjamin Franklin

The first of the series of letters which Franklin contributed to the *New-England Courant* under the *nom de plume* of Silence Dogood appeared in the issue of April 2, 1722. Published by Franklin's older brother, the *Courant* spoke for those Anglicans and deists (and possibly some Puritan saints as well) who longed for the sophisticated tone of London life. James Franklin's newspaper gave them a reasonable facsimile, in the form of imitations of Sir Roger de Coverley. Letters to the editor from local wits who signed themselves Tabitha Talkative, Ichabod Henroost, Fanny Mournful (or Silence Dogood) satirized Bostonian foibles in what they dearly hoped was the true *Tatler* or *Spectator* manner. The fun seemed harmless, especially since James Franklin promised not to print anything that would reflect on the clergy, but in fact it was dynamite.

As Bergson points out, comedy stands midway between life and the "disinterestedness" of most art in that it "accepts social life as a natural environment" and even has a "scarcely conscious intention to correct and instruct." Just as the *Tatler's* announced purpose was to expose the "false arts of life," so the provincial imitator had, as Benjamin Franklin confessed in the *Courant's* pages, "a natural inclination to observe and reprove the faults of others." In the Boston of the 1720s, however, the role of social corrector and instructor was still very much the prerogative of the ministry, and the Mathers were not the kind of Christians who surrendered prerogatives without a fight. When in its early issues the *Courant* ridiculed the Mather-supported idea that inoculation for smallpox might halt the epidemic that was sweeping Boston, it thereby furnished Cotton Mather with an excuse for meeting the threat to his position head on: "The practice of supporting and publishing every week a libel on purpose to lessen and blacken and burlesque the virtuous and principal ministers of religion in a country, and render the services of their ministry despicable, even detestable, to the people, is a wickedness that was never known before in any country, Christian, Turkish or Pagan, on the face of the earth." The battle was protracted, but the outcome was inevitable. In June of 1722 James Franklin was jailed for three weeks for contempt of the government; the following January he was accused of mocking religion and forbidden to publish his newspaper except under the supervision of the Secretary of the Province. It was at this point that the indentured younger brother became the ostensible publisher, but the subterfuge was short-lived. In September of 1723 the *Courant* advertised for a "likely lad for an apprentice"—the younger Franklin, it seems, had run off to seek his fortune. Not quite three years later the *Courant* folded.

But if the Mathers thus held onto their prerogative, they were nevertheless powerless to exercise it effectively. In the second volume of *The New England Mind,* Professor Perry Miller has demonstrated that by the end of the first quarter of the eighteenth century Boston was a very different society from what it had been fifty years before, and that the ministerial leadership had lost contact with the reality of the new age. Certainly this was Franklin's view of the situation. In Number IV of the Dogood letters, he suggested that Harvard College, the great training ground of the ministry, was producing only conceited blockheads, and in Number IX he wondered why it was that moral hypocrites could easily deceive the ministers long after the people had seen through their masquerade. For a moralist, such ignorance on the part of the learned leaders of society constituted an intolerable state of affairs, and even at sixteen years of age Franklin was a moralist. All his thinking life he adhered to the belief of his youth that "the happiness or real good of men consists in right action, and right action cannot be produced without right opinion . . . [therefore] it behoves us, above all things in this world, to take care that our opinions of things be according to the nature of things." But those who were officially charged with this care no longer understood the nature of things, and so in the spring of 1722 Benjamin Franklin slipped the first of the Dogood letters under the door of his brother's printing house.

The letters make evident a cheerful affection for improper Bostonians; Franklin knew, as the author of *Pamela* did not, that "to be proud of one's virtue is like poisoning one's self with the antidote." But it was precisely because he knew raffish Boston so well that he could be quite clear in his mind that "the good of man is not natural and sensual, but rational and moral," and the comedy of the Dogood letters is always directed toward that revelation. Franklin's genial cynicism conceals the high seriousness of a moral teacher. The sharp edge of the humor in this early work is occasionally blunted by amateurish writing, but Boston would have to wait for Jonathan Edwards to come out of the Connecticut Valley before religion would regain its power to instruct the community with a greater effectiveness than Silence Dogood's.

What is most significant about this story of the Dogood letters is that it reveals the relationship of American humor to American religion. The invention of Silence Dogood filled a moral vacuum created by the blindness of the clergy; in a period of religious declension, the humorist took over from the minister. This was the first time in American history that such a thing had happened, but it was not the last. Franklin is not the only American humorist who was a minister *manqué*, a Puritan in reverse, whose humor was at once irreverent and more serious than the churches. At the heart of the laughter of Mark Twain, Ring Lardner, and Sinclair Lewis, there is a raging Puritanical didacticism that few contemporary sermons could match.

The style of the Dogood letters reveals the relation of Franklin's humor to religion in another way. The letters were consciously modeled on Addison, whom Franklin greatly admired. But whereas Addison's prose is, in the words of Dr. Johnson, "the model of the middle style . . . always equable, and always easy," Franklin's style constantly sacrifices urbanity for the sake of the homely, specific image or the vivid detail. Franklin tried to imitate the polish of Addison, but he could not escape the fact that he had been raised on the earthiness of Bunyan. As a humorist Franklin was a secular priest, and Silence Dogood speaks in a voice that mixes the accents of the *Spectator* papers and *Pilgrim's Progress*.

To the Editor of the New-England Courant

No XIII

SIR,

IN Persons of a contemplative Disposition, the most indifferent Things provoke the Exercise of the Imagination; and the Satisfactions which often arise to them thereby, are a certain Relief to the Labour of the Mind (when it has been intensely fix'd on more substantial Subjects) as well as to that of the Body.

IN one of the late pleasant Moon-light Evenings, I so far indulg'd in my self the Humour of the Town in walking abroad, as to continue from my Lodgings two or three Hours later than usual, & was pleas'd beyond Expectation before my Return. Here I found various Company to observe, and various Discourse to attend to. I met indeed with the common Fate of *Listeners*, who *hear no good of themselves*, but from a Consciousness of my Innocence, receiv'd it with a Satisfaction beyond what the Love of Flattery and the Daubings of a Parasite could produce. The Company who rally'd me were about Twenty in Number, of both Sexes; and tho' the *Confusion of Tongues* (like that of *Babel*) which always happens among so many impetuous Talkers, render'd their Discourse not so intelligible as I could wish, I learnt thus much, That one of the Females pretended to know me, from some Discourse she had heard at a certain House before the Publication of one of my Letters; adding, *That I was a Person of an ill Character, and kept a criminal Correspondence with a Gentleman who assisted me in Writing.* One of the Gallants clear'd me of this random Charge, by saying, *That tho' I wrote in the Character of a Woman, he knew me to be a Man; But,* continu'd he, *he has more need of endeavouring a Reformation in himself, than spending his Wit in satyrizing others.*

I HAD no sooner left this Set of Ramblers, but I met a Crowd of *Tarpolins* and their Doxies, link'd to each other by the Arms, who ran (by their own Account) after the Rate of *Six Knots an Hour,* and bent their Course towards the *Common.* Their eager and amorous Emotions of Body, occasion'd by taking their Mistresses *in Tow,* they call'd *wild Steerage:* And as a Pair of them happen'd to trip and come to the Ground, the Company were call'd upon to *bring to,* for that *Jack* and *Betty* were *founder'd.* But this Fleet were not less comical or irregular in their Progress than a Company of Females I soon after came up with, who, by throwing their Heads to the Right and Left, at every one who pass'd by them, I concluded came out with no other Design than to revive the Spirit of Love in Disappointed Batchelors, and expose themselves to Sale to the first Bidder.

BUT it would take up too much Room in your Paper to mention all the Occasions of Diversion I met with in this Night's Ramble. As it grew later, I observed, that many pensive Youths with down looks and a slow Pace, would be ever now and then crying out on the Cruelty of their Mistresses; others with a more rapid Pace and chearful Air, would be swinging their Canes, and clapping their Cheeks, and whispering at certain Intervals, *I'm certain I shall have her! This is more than I expected! How charmingly she talks!* &c.

UPON the whole I conclude, That our *Night-Walkers* are a Set of People, who contribute very much to the Health and Satisfaction of those who have been fatigu'd with Business or Study, and occasionally observe their pretty Gestures and Impertinencies. But among Men of Business, the *Shoemakers,* and other Dealers in Leather, are doubly oblig'd to them, inasmuch as they exceedingly promote the Consumption of their Ware: And I have heard of a *Shoemaker,* who being ask'd by a noted Rambler, *Whether he could tell how long her Shoes would last;* very prettily answer'd, *That he knew how many Days she might wear them, but not how many Nights; because they were then put to a more violent and irregular Service than when she employ'd her self in the common Affairs of the House.*

I am, Sir,
Your Humble Servant,
SILENCE DOGOOD

From the satirical essays he wrote on holding the empire together to the jokes he told at the Constitutional Convention, a good deal of Franklin's humor was political. As the crisis between England and America deepened in consequence of the passage of the Stamp Act, Franklin sent a letter to a London newspaper. In a brilliant exploitation of the resources of frontier humor, Franklin used the tall-tale technique, not to befuddle and mislead the English, as the Mississippi river-boat men would do sixty-five years later with Mrs. Trollope, but to promote better understanding between the mother country and her American colonies.

To the Editor of a Newspaper

Monday, May 20 [1765]

SIR,

In your Paper of Wednesday last, an ingenious Correspondent that calls himself THE SPECTATOR, and dates from *Pimlico,* under the Guise of Good Will to the Newswriters, whom he calls an "useful Body of Men in this great City," has, in my Opinion, artfully attempted to turn them & their Works into Ridicule, wherein if he could succeed, great Injury might be done to the Public as well as to those good People.

Supposing, Sir, that the *"We hears"* they give us of this & t'other intended Voyage or Tour of this & t'other great Personage, were mere Inventions, yet they at least offer us an innocent Amusement while we read, and useful Matter of Conversation when we are dispos'd to converse.

Englishmen, Sir, are too apt to be silent when they have nothing to say; too apt to be sullen when they are silent; and, when they are sullen, to hang themselves. But, by these *We hears,* we are supplied with abundant funds of Discourse, we discuss the Motives for such Voyages, the Probability of their being undertaken, and the Practicality of their Execution. Here we display our Judgment in Politics, our Knowledge of the Interests of Princes, and our Skill in Geography, and (if we have it) show our Dexterity moreover in Argumentation. In the mean time, the tedious Hour is kill'd, we go home pleas'd with the Applauses we have receiv'd from others, or at least with those we secretly give to ourselves: We sleep soundly, & live on, to the Comfort of our Families. But, Sir, I beg leave to say, that all the Articles of News that seem improbable are not mere Inventions. Some of them, I can assure you on the Faith of a Traveler, are serious Truths. And here, quitting Mr. Spectator of Pimlico, give me leave to instance the various numberless Accounts the Newswriters have given us, with so much honest Zeal for the welfare of *Poor Old England,* of the establishing Manufactures in the Colonies to the Prejudice of those of this Kingdom. It is objected by superficial Readers, who yet pretend to some Knowledge of those Countries, that such Establishments are not only improbable, but impossible, for that their Sheep have but little Wooll, not in the whole sufficient for a Pair of Stockings a Year to each Inhabitant; and that, from the Universal Dearness of Labour among them, the Working of Iron and other Materials, except in some few coarse Instances, is impracticable to any Advantage.

Dear Sir, do not let us suffer ourselves to be amus'd with such groundless Objections. The very Tails of the American Sheep are so laden with Wooll, that each has a little Car or Waggon on four little Wheels, to support & keep it from trailing on the Ground. Would they caulk their Ships, would they fill their Beds, would they even litter their Horses with Wooll, if it were not both plenty and cheap? And what signifies Dearness of Labour, when an English Shilling passes for five and Twenty? Their engaging 300 Silk Throwsters here in one Week, for New York, was treated as a Fable, because, forsooth, they have "no Silk to throw." Those who made this Objection, perhaps did not know, that at the same time the Agents from the King of Spain were at Quebec to contract for 1000 Pieces of Cannon to be made there for the Fortification of Mexico, and at N York engaging the annual Supply of woven Floor-Carpets for their West India Houses, other Agents from the Emperor of China were at Boston treating about an Exchange of raw Silk for Wooll, to be carried in Chinese Junks through the Straits of Magellan.

And yet all this is as certainly true, as the Account said to be from Quebec, in all the Papers of last Week, that the Inhabitants of Canada are making Preparations for a Cod and Whale Fishery this "Summer in the upper Lakes." Ignorant People may object that the upper Lakes are fresh, and that Cod and Whale are Salt Water Fish: But let them know, Sir, that Cod, like other Fish when attack'd by their

Enemies, fly into any Water where they can be safest; that Whales, when they have a mind to eat Cod, pursue them wherever they fly; and that the grand Leap of the Whale in that Chase up the Fall of Niagara is esteemed, by all who have seen it, as one of the finest Spectacles in Nature. Really, Sir, the World is grown too incredulous. It is the Pendulum ever swinging from one Extream to another. Formerly every thing printed was believed for just the very same Reason. Wise Men wonder at the present Growth of Infidelity. They should have consider'd, when they taught People to doubt the Authority of Newspapers and the Truth of Predictions in Almanacks, that the next Step might be a Disbelief in the well vouch'd Accts of Ghosts Witches, and Doubts even of the Truths of the Creed!

Thus much I thought it necessary to say in favour of an honest Set of Writers, whose comfortable Living depends on collecting & supplying the Printers with News at the small Price of Sixpence an Article, and who always show their Regard to Truth, by contradicting in a subsequent Article such as are wrong,—for another Sixpence,—to the great Satisfaction & Improvement of us Coffee-house Students in History & Politics, and the infinite Advantage of all future Livies, Rapins, Robertsons, Humes, and McAulays, who may be sincerely inclin'd to furnish the World with that *rara Avis,* a true History. I am Sir, your humble Servant.

A TRAVELLER.

In *American Humor,* Constance Rourke says of the mythological figure of the Yankee peddler that his distinguishing mark was his ability to disguise himself. By the terms of this definition Benjamin Franklin was the greatest Yankee peddler of them all. For not only was Franklin a writer, a scientist, an inventor, a philosopher, a diplomat, and a printer, but he was also a master of many disguises; indeed, his being a master-of-all-trades was in part made possible by his amazing versatility as an actor. When, for example, Franklin enjoined himself to "imitate Jesus and Socrates," he was perfectly serious, and the diffident manner he subsequently put on was a triumphantly successful masquerade. The Yankee peddler looms up again and again in the American imagination, but Benjamin Franklin is his most memorable incarnation.

One of the best illustrations of his acting talent is the story of his career in France as the agent of the American Revolutionary cause. When he arrived in Paris in December of 1776 he found that the French were enchanted by the idea of a Pennsylvania never seen on land or sea, where dwelt a race of simple, peace-loving Quakers who farmed the land and talked philosophy. Because he was from Philadelphia, the French assumed that Franklin must be such a man. Recognizing that the role was the perfect disguise for the agent of a revolution, Franklin did nothing to disabuse French expectations.

But if Franklin was perfectly content to wear a benevolent expression on his face and an outlandish fur cap on his head so long as it aided the American cause, he did not allow the pious disguise to cramp his personal life. He established himself at Passy in a magnificent house with a cellar that boasted over a thousand bottles of vintage wines. And there were other indulgences; as John Adams wrote in a sternly disapproving tone, Franklin "at the age of seventy-odd had neither lost his love of beauty nor his taste for it."

To some people, this story is neither funny nor patriotically inspiring, but rather a chilling piece of hypocrisy. Yet if it is undeniable that there is something slightly sinister about Franklin's talent for disguise, what saves him is that, unlike many other Americans who have cashed in on appearances, he never confused his disguise with the reality of himself. As the "Dialogue Between Franklin and the Gout" makes clear, the mask of piety did not blind him to his own faults and weaknesses. At Passy he must have enjoyed the colossal joke he had put over on the French, but he was also capable of laughing at himself.

Dialogue Between Franklin and the Gout

Franklin. Eh! O! Eh! What have I done to merit these cruel sufferings?

Gout. Many things; you have ate and drank too freely, and too much indulged those legs of yours in their indolence.

Franklin. Who is it that accuses me?

Gout. It is I, even I, the Gout.

Franklin. What! my enemy in person?

Gout. No, not your enemy.

Franklin. I repeat it,—my enemy; for, you would not only torment my body to death, but ruin my good name; you reproach me as a glutton and a tippler; now, all the world that knows me will allow that I am neither the one nor the other.

Gout. The world may think as it pleases; it is always very complaisant to itself, and sometimes to its friends; but I very well know that the quantity of meat and drink proper for a man, who takes a reasonable degree of exercise, would be too much for another, who never takes any.

Franklin. I take—Eh! O!—as much exercise—Eh!—as I can, Madam Gout. You know my sedentary state; and, on that account, it would seem, Madam Gout, as if you might spare me a little, seeing it is not altogether my own fault.

Gout. Not a jot; your rhetoric and your politeness are thrown away; your apology avails nothing. If your situation in life is a sedentary one, your amusements, your recreations, at least, should be active. You ought to walk or ride; or, if the weather prevents that, play at billiards. But let us examine your course of life. While the mornings are long, and you have leisure to go abroad, what do you do? Why, instead of gaining an appetite for breakfast by salutary exercise, you amuse yourself with books, pamphlets or news-papers, which commonly are not worth the reading. Yet you eat an inordinate breakfast: four dishes of tea, with cream, and one or two buttered toasts, with slices of hung beef, which I fancy are not things the most easily digested. Immediately afterward, you sit down to write at your desk, or converse with persons who apply to you on business. Thus the time passes till one, without any kind of bodily exercise. But all this I could pardon, in regard, as you say, to your sedentary condition. But what is your practice after dinner? Walking in the beautiful gardens of those friends with whom you have dined would be the choice of men of sense; yours is to be fixed down to chess, where you are found engaged for two or three hours! This is your perpetual recreation, which is the least eligible of any for a sedentary man, because, instead of accelerating the motion of the fluids, the rigid attention it requires helps to retard the circulation and obstruct internal secretions. Wrapt in the speculations of this wretched game, you destroy your constitution. What can be expected from such a course of living, but a body replete with stagnant humors, ready to fall a prey to all kinds of dangerous maladies, if I, the Gout, did not occasionally bring you relief by agitating those humors, and so purifying or dissipating them? If it was in some nook or alley in Paris, deprived of walks, that you played a while at chess after dinner, this might be excusable; but the same taste prevails with you in Passy, Auteuil, Montmartre, or Sanoy, places where there are the finest gardens and walks, a pure air, beautiful women, and most agreeable and instructive conversation; all which you might enjoy by frequenting the walks. But these are rejected for this abominable game of chess. Fie, then, Mr. Franklin! But amidst my instructions, I had almost forgotten to administer my wholesome corrections; so take that twinge,—and that!

Franklin. O! Eh! O! O-o-o-o! As much instruction as you please, Madam Gout, and as many reproaches; but pray, Madam, a truce with your corrections!

Gout. No, sir, no,—I will not abate a particle of what is so much for your good,—therefore——

Franklin. O! E-h-h-h!—It is not fair to say I take no ex-

ercise, when I do very often, going out to dine and returning in my carriage.

Gout. That, of all imaginable exercises, is the most slight
and insignificant, if you allude to the motion of a carriage
suspended on springs. By observing the degree of heat obtained by different kinds of motion, we may form an esti-
mate of the quantity of exercise given by each. Thus, for
example, if you turn out to walk in winter with cold feet,
in an hour's time you will be in a glow all over; ride on
Horseback, the same effect will scarcely be perceived by
four hours' round trotting; but, if you loll in a carriage,
such as you have mentioned, you may travel all day, and
gladly enter the last inn to warm your feet by a fire. Flatter
yourself, then, no longer, that half an hour's airing in your
carriage deserves the name of exercise. Providence has appointed few to roll in carriages, while He has given to all
a pair of legs, which are machines infinitely more commo-
dious and serviceable. Be grateful, then, and make a proper
use of yours. Would you know how they forward the circulation of your fluids, in the very action of transporting
you from place to place;—observe, when you walk, that all
your weight is alternately thrown from one leg to the other;
this occasions a great pressure on the vessels of the foot,
and repels their contents; when relieved by the weight being thrown on the other foot, the vessels of the first are allowed to replenish, and, by a return of the weight, this repulsion again succeeds; thus accelerating the circulation of
the blood. The heat produced in any given time depends
on the degree of this acceleration; the fluids are shaken,
the humors attenuated, the secretions facilitated, and all
goes well; the cheeks are ruddy, and health is established.
Behold your fair friend at Auteuil;* a lady who received
from bounteous nature more really useful science than half
a dozen such pretenders to philosophy as you have been
able to extract from all your books. When she honors you
with a visit it is on foot. She walks all hours of the day,
and leaves indolence and its concomitant maladies, to be endured by her horses. In this see at once the preservative of

* Madame Helvétius

her health and personal charms. But, when you go to Auteuil, you must have your carriage, though it is no further from Passy to Auteuil than from Auteuil to Passy.

Franklin. Your reasonings grow very tiresome.

Gout. I stand corrected. I will be silent, and continue my office; take that, and that!

Franklin. O! O-o-o! Talk on, I pray you!

Gout. No, no; I have a good number of twinges for you to-night, and you may be sure of some more to-morrow.

Franklin. What, with such a fever! I shall go distracted. O! Eh! Can no one bear it for me?

Gout. Ask that of your horses; they have served you faithfully.

Franklin. How can you so cruelly sport with my torments?

Gout. Sport! I am very serious. I have here a list of offences against your own health distinctly written, and can justify every stroke inflicted on you.

Franklin. Read it, then.

Gout. It is too long a detail; but I will briefly mention some particulars.

Franklin. Proceed. I am all attention.

Gout. Do you remember how often you have promised yourself, the following morning, a walk in the grove of Boulogne, in the garden de la Muette, or in your own garden, and have violated your promise, alleging, at one time, it was too cold, at another too warm, too windy, too moist, or what else you pleased; when in truth it was too nothing but your insuperable love of ease?

Franklin. That, I confess, may have happened occasionally, probably ten times in a year.

Gout. Your confession is very far short of the truth; the gross amount is one hundred and ninety-nine times.

Franklin. Is it possible?

Gout. So possible, that in fact; you may rely on the accuracy of my statement. You know Mr. Brillon's gardens, and what fine walks they contain; you know the handsome flight of an hundred steps, which lead from the terrace above to the lawn below. You have been in the practice of visiting this amiable family twice a week, after dinner, and it is a maxim of your own that "a man may take as much exercise in walking a mile, up and down stairs, as in ten on level ground." What an opportunity was here for you to have had exercise in both these ways! Did you embrace it, and how often?

Franklin. I cannot immediately answer that question.

Gout. I will do it for you; not once.

Franklin. Not once?

Gout. Even so. During the summer you went there at six o'clock. You found the charming lady, with her lovely children and friends, eager to walk with you and entertain you with their agreeable conversation; and what has been your choice? Why, to sit on the terrace, satisfying yourself with the fine prospect, and passing your eye over the beauties of the garden below, without taking one step to descend and walk about them. On the contrary, you call for tea and chess-board; and lo! you are occupied in your seat till nine o'clock, and that besides two hours' play after dinner; and then, instead of walking home, which would have bestirred you a little, you step into your carriage. How absurd to suppose that all this carelessness can be reconcilable with health, without my interposition!

Franklin. I am convinced now of the justness of poor Richard's remark, that "Our debts and our sins are always greater than we think for."

Gout. So it is. You philosophers are sages in your maxims, and fools in your conduct.

Franklin. But do you charge, among my crimes, that I return in a carriage from Mr. Brillon's?

Gout. Certainly; for, having been seated all the while, you cannot object the fatigue of the day, and cannot want, therefore, the relief of a carriage.

Franklin. What, then would you have me do with my carriage?

Gout. Burn it, if you choose; you would at least get heat out of it once in this way. Or, if you dislike that proposal, here's another for you: observe the poor peasants, who work in the vineyards and grounds about the villages of Passy, Auteuil, Chaillot, &c.; you may find every day, among these deserving creatures, four or five old men and women, bent and perhaps crippled by weight of years, and too long and too great labor. After a most fatiguing day, these people have to trudge a mile or two to their smoky huts. Order your coachman to set them down. This is an act that will be good for your soul; and, at the same time, after your visit to the Brillons, if you return on foot, that will be good for your body.

Franklin. Ah! how tiresome you are!

Gout. Well, then, to my office; it should not be forgotten that I am your physician. There!

Franklin. O-o-o-o! what a devil of a physician!

Gout. How ungrateful you are to say so! is it not I who, in the character of your physician, have saved you from the palsy, dropsy, and apoplexy? one or other of which would have done for you long ago, but for me.

Franklin. I submit, and thank you for the past, but entreat the discontinuance of your visits for the future; for, in my mind, one had better die than be cured so dolefully. Permit me just to hint that I have also not been unfriendly to *you.* I never feed physician or quack of any kind, to enter the list against you; if, then, you do not leave me to my repose, it may be said you are ungrateful too.

Gout. I can scarcely acknowledge that as any objection. As to quacks, I despise them; they may kill you, indeed, but cannot injure me. And, as to regular physicians, they are at last convinced that the gout, in such a subject as you are, is no disease, but a remedy; and wherefore cure a remedy?—but to our business,—there!

Franklin. O! O!—for Heaven's sake leave me; and I promise faithfully never more to play at chess, but to take exercise daily, and live temperately.

Gout. I know you too well. You promise fair; but, after a few months of good health, you will return to your old habits; your fine promises will be forgotten, like the forms of the last year's clouds. Let us, then, finish the account, and I will go. But I leave you with an assurance of visiting you again at a proper time and place; for my object is your good, and you are sensible now that I am your *real friend.*

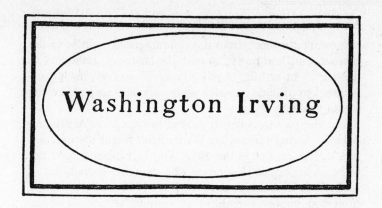

Washington Irving

Like Franklin, Irving began his career as a humorist by satirizing the contemporary manners of his home town. But the humor of Irving's Jonathan Oldstyle has none of Silence Dogood's sure sense of right opinion and right action. Franklin's spectator judged Boston from a clearly defined point of view, but Jonathan Oldstyle has no philosophy which he does not eventually betray. To his shifting, nervous eye, no values are sacred; everything in life is a joke. As Irving scholar William Leonard Hedges has observed, Oldstyle's instability undoubtedly reflects some sort of personal insecurity in the author—his scatter-shot wit seems to have been an anxious defense against a world in which Irving felt out of place.

Thus the commercial life of New York, as symbolized by his father's hardware business, was to Irving "a sordid, dusty, soul-killing way of life," and the law, which he tried for a time, was full of "technical rubbish and dull routine." To escape both occupations, he learned to be ill; he read incessantly and compulsively; his dreams became more real to him than reality. He was drawn to Europe, because there it was possible "to wander," as he would write in *The Sketch Book*, "over the scenes of renowned achievement, —to tread, as it were, in the footsteps of antiquity,—to loiter about the ruined castle,—to meditate on the falling tower,

—to escape, in short, from the commonplace realities of the present, and lose myself among the shadowy grandeurs of the past." In writing *A History of New York,* Irving attempted to provide America with a similar escape from the sordid present.

But the past in America proved to be a joke. Across the Atlantic, Irving's friend Sir Walter Scott might discover heroes in history, but in the New World, Ivanhoe turned out to be an inglorious Dutchman who swindled Indians out of real estate. In America the past was not so much an escape from commonplace realities as another version of them. Since, therefore, the past couldn't be celebrated, it must be spoofed; by writing a mock history, Irving could still have the last laugh on a past which mocked his hunger for romantic associations.

Largely because the *History* contains a satirical characterization of Thomas Jefferson (as William the Testy), some critics have taken it as a pro-Federalist document, but this is to ignore the true nature of the book's satire, which is psychological, not political. The businessman, the soldier, and the explorer are made to look as foolish as the Republican politician, because it is the threatening image of a certain male type, the energetic doer, the man of affairs, whom Irving's humor is really concerned to reduce to a harmless figure of fun.

From *A History of New York*
by Diedrich Knickerbocker

Book VI

CONTAINING THE SECOND PART OF THE REIGN OF
PETER THE HEADSTRONG, AND HIS GALLANT ACHIEVE-
MENTS ON THE DELAWARE

Chapter VIII

*Containing the Most Horrible Battle Ever Recorded in
Poetry or Prose; With the Admirable Exploits of Peter
the Headstrong*

"Now had the Dutchmen snatched a huge repast," and
finding themselves wonderfully encouraged and animated
thereby, prepared to take the field. Expectation, says
the writer of the Stuyvesant manuscript—Expectation now
stood on stilts. The world forgot to turn round, or rather
stood still, that it might witness the affray; like a round-
bellied alderman, watching the combat of two chivalrous
flies upon his jerkin. The eyes of all mankind, as usual in
such cases, were turned upon Fort Christina. The sun, like
a little man in a crowd at a puppet-show, scampered about
the heavens, popping his head here and there, and endeav-
oring to get a peep between the unmannerly clouds that
obtruded themselves in his way. The historians filled their
ink-horns—the poets went without their dinners, either that
they might buy paper and goose-quills, or because they
could not get anything to eat. Antiquity scowled sulkily out
of its grave, to see itself outdone—while even Posterity stood
mute, gazing in gaping ecstasy of retrospection on the
eventful field.

The immortal deities, who whilom had seen service at
the "affair" of Troy—now mounted their feather-bed clouds,

and sailed over the plain, or mingled among the combatants in different disguises, all itching to have a finger in the pie. Jupiter sent off his thunderbolt to a noted coppersmith, to have it furbished up for the direful occasion. Venus vowed by her chastity to patronize the Swedes, and in semblance of a blear-eyed trull paraded the battlements of Fort Christina, accompanied by Diana, as a sergeant's widow, of cracked reputation. The noted bully, Mars, stuck two horse-pistols into his belt, shouldered a rusty firelock, and gallantly swaggered at their elbow, as a drunken corporal—while Apollo trudged in their rear, as a bandy-legged fifer, playing most villainously out of tune.

On the other side, the ox-eyed Juno, who had gained a pair of black eyes over night, in one of her curtain lectures with old Jupiter, displayed her haughty beauties on a baggage-wagon—Minerva, as a brawny gin-suttler, tucked up her skirts, brandished her fists, and swore most heroically, in exceeding bad Dutch (having but lately studied the language), by way of keeping up the spirits of the soldiers; while Vulcan halted as a club-footed blacksmith, lately promoted to be a captain of militia. All was silent awe, or bustling preparation: war reared his horrid front, gnashed loud his iron fangs, and shook his direful crest of bristling bayonets.

And now the mighty chieftains marshalled out their hosts. Here stood stout Risingh, firm as a thousand rocks —incrusted with stockades, and intrenched to the chin in mud batteries. His valiant soldiery lined the breastwork in grim array, each having his mustachios fiercely greased, and his hair pomatumed back, and queued so stiffly, that he grinned above the ramparts like a grisly death's head.

There came on the intrepid Peter—his brows knit, his teeth set, his fists clenched, almost breathing forth volumes of smoke, so fierce was the fire that raged within his bosom. His faithful squire Van Corlear trudged valiantly at his heels, with his trumpet gorgeously bedecked with red and yellow ribbons, the remembrances of his fair mistresses at the Manhattoes. Then came waddling on the sturdy chivalry of the Hudson. There were the Van Wycks, and the Van Dycks, and the Ten Eycks—the Van Nesses, the Van Tassels, the Van Grolls; the Van Hoesens, the Van Giesons, and the Van Blarcoms—the Van Warts, the Van Winkles, the Van Dams; the Van Pelts, the Van Rippers, and the Van Brunts. There were the Van Hornes, the Van Hooks, the Van Bunschotens; the Van Gelders, the Van Arsdales, and the Van Bummels; the Vander Belts, the Vander Hoofs, the Vander Voorts, the Vander Lyns, the Vander Pools, and the Vander Spiegles—then came the Hoffmans, the Hooghlands, the Hoppers, the Cloppers, the Ryckmans, the Dyckmans, the Hogebooms, the Rosebooms, the Oothouts, the Quackenbosses, the Roerbacks, the Garrebrantzes, the Bensons, the Brouwers, the Waldrons, the Onderdonks, the Varra Vangers, the Schermerhorns, the Stoutenburghs, the Brinkerhoffs, the Bontecous, the Knickerbockers, the Hockstrassers, the Ten Breecheses, and the Tough Breecheses, with a host more of worthies, whose names are too crabbed to be written, or if they could be written, it would be impossible for man to utter—all fortified with a mighty dinner, and, to use the words of a great Dutch poet,

"Brimful of wrath and cabbage."

For an instant the mighty Peter paused in the midst of his career, and mounting on a stump, addressed his troops in eloquent Low Dutch, exhorting them to fight like *duyvels*, and assuring them that if they conquered, they should get plenty of booty—if they fell, they should be allowed the satisfaction, while dying, of reflecting that it was in the service of their country—and after they were dead, of seeing their names inscribed in the temple of renown, and handed down, in company with all the other great men of the year, for the admiration of posterity.—Finally, he swore to them, on the word of a governor (and they knew him too well to doubt it for a moment), that if he caught any mother's son of them looking pale, or playing craven, he would curry his hide till he made him run out of it like a snake in spring time. Then lugging out his trusty sabre, he brandished it three times over his head, ordered

Van Corlear to sound a charge, and shouting the words
"St. Nicholas and the Manhattoes!" courageously dashed
forwards. His warlike followers, who had employed the interval in lighting their pipes, instantly stuck them into their
mouths, gave a furious puff, and charged gallantly under
cover of the smoke.

The Swedish garrison, ordered by the cunning Risingh
not to fire until they could distinguish the whites of their
assailants' eyes, stood in horrid silence on the covert-way,
until the eager Dutchmen had ascended the glacis. Then
did they pour into them such a tremendous volley, that
the very hills quaked around, and were terrified even unto
an incontinence of water, insomuch that certain springs
burst forth from their sides, which continue to run unto the
present day. Not a Dutchman but would have bitten the
dust beneath that dreadful fire, had not the protecting Minerva kindly taken care that the Swedes should, one and
all, observe their usual custom of shutting their eyes and
turning away their heads at the moment of discharge.

The Swedes followed up their fire by leaping the coun-
terscarp, and falling tooth and nail upon the foe with furious outcries. And now might be seen prodigies of valor,
unmatched in history or song. Here was the sturdy Stoffel
Brinkerhoff brandishing his quarter-staff, like the giant
Blanderon his oak tree (for he scorned to carry any other
weapon), and drumming a horrific tune upon the hard
heads of the Swedish soldiery. There were the Van Kort-
landts, posted at a distance, like the Locrian archers of
yore, and plying it most potently with the longbow, for
which they were so justly renowned. On a rising knoll were
gathered the valiant men of Sing-Sing, assisting marvel-
lously in the fight, by chanting the great song of St. Nicholas; but as to the Gardeniers of Hudson, they were absent
on a marauding party, laying waste the neighboring watermelon patches.

In a different part of the field were the Van Grolls of
Antony's Nose, struggling to get to the thickest of the fight,
but horribly perplexed in a defile between two hills, by reason of the length of their noses. So also the Van Bunschotens

of Nyack and Kakiat, so renowned for kicking with the left foot, were brought to a stand for want of wind, in consequence of the hearty dinner they had eaten, and would have been put to utter rout but for the arrival of a gallant corps of voltigeurs, composed of the Hoppers, who advanced nimbly to their assistance on one foot. Nor must I omit to mention the valiant achievements of Antony Van Corlear, who, for a good quarter of an hour, waged stubborn fight with a little pursy Swedish drummer; whose hide he drummed most magnificently, and whom he would infallibly have annihilated on the spot, but that he had come into the battle with no other weapon but his trumpet.

But now the combat thickened.—On came the mighty Jacobus Varra Vanger and the fighting men of the Wallabout; after them thundered the Van Pelts of Esopus, together with the Van Rippers and the Van Brunts, bearing down all before them—then the Suy Dams, and the Van Dams, pressing forward with many a blustering oath, at the head of the warriors of Hell-gate, clad in their thunder and lightning gaberdines; and lastly, the standard-bearers and body-guard of Peter Stuyvesant, bearing the great beaver of the Manhattoes.

And now commenced the horrid din, the desperate struggle, the maddening ferocity, the frantic desperation, the confusion and self-abandonment of war. Dutchman and Swede commingled, tugged, panted, and blowed. The heavens were darkened with a tempest of missives. Bang! went the guns—whack! went the broadswords—thump! went the cudgels—crash! went the musket-stocks—blows—kicks—cuffs—scratches—black eyes and bloody noses swelling the horrors of the scene! Thick thwack, cut and hack, helter-skelter, higgledy-piggledy, hurly-burly, head over heels, rough and tumble!—Dunder and blixum! swore the Dutchmen—splitter and splutter! cried the Swedes—Storm the works! shouted Hardkoppig Peter—Fire the mine! roared stout Risingh—Tanta-rarra-ra! twanged the trumpet of Antony Van Corlear—until all voice and sound became unintelligible—grunts of pain, yells of fury, and shouts of triumph mingling in one hideous clamor. The earth shook as if struck with a paralytic stroke—trees shrunk aghast, and withered at the sight—rocks burrowed in the ground like rabbits—and even Christina creek turned from its course, and ran up a hill in breathless terror!

Long hung the contest doubtful, for though a heavy shower of rain, sent by the "cloud-compelling Jove," in some measure cooled their ardor, as doth a bucket of water thrown on a group of fighting mastiffs, yet did they but pause for a moment, to return with tenfold fury to the charge. Just at this juncture a vast and dense column of smoke was seen slowly rolling toward the scene of battle. The combatants paused for a moment, gazing in mute astonishment, until the wind, dispelling the murky cloud, revealed the flaunting banner of Michael Paw, the Patroon of Communipaw. That valiant chieftain came fearlessly on at the head of a phalanx of oyster-fed Pavonians and a corps de reserve of the Van Arsdales and Van Bummels, who had remained behind to digest the enormous dinner they had eaten. These now trudged manfully forward, smoking their pipes with outrageous vigor, so as to raise the awful cloud that has been mentioned; but marching exceedingly slow, being short of leg, and of great rotundity in the belt.

And now the deities who watched over the fortunes of the Nederlanders having unthinkingly left the field, and stepped into a neighboring tavern to refresh themselves with a pot of beer, a direful catastrophe had well nigh ensued. Scarce had the myrmidons of Michael Paw attained the front of battle, when the Swedes, instructed by the cunning Risingh, levelled a shower of blows full at their tobacco-pipes. Astounded at this assault, and dismayed at the havoc of their pipes, these ponderous warriors gave way, and like a drove of frightened elephants broke through the ranks of their own army. The little Hoppers were borne down in the surge: the sacred banner emblazoned with the gigantic oyster of Communipaw was trampled in the dirt: on blundered and thundered the heavy-sterned fugitives, the Swedes pressing on their rear and applying their feet *a parte poste* of the Van Arsdales and the Van Bummels with a vigor that prodigiously accelerated their movements —nor did the renowned Michael Paw himself fail to receive divers grievous and dishonorable visitations of shoe-leather.

But what, oh Muse! was the rage of Peter Stuyvesant, when from afar he saw his army giving way! In the transports of his wrath he sent forth a roar, enough to shake the very hills. The men of the Manhattoes plucked up new courage at the sound; or rather, they rallied at the voice of their leader, of whom they stood more in awe than of all of the Swedes in Christendom. Without waiting for their aid, the daring Peter dashed sword in hand into the thickest of the foe. Then might be seen achievements worthy of the days of the giants. Wherever he went, the enemy shrank before him; the Swedes fled to right and left, or were driven, like dogs, into their own ditch; but as he pushed forward singly with headlong courage, the foe closed behind and hung upon his rear. One aimed a blow full at his heart; but the protecting power which watches over the great and good turned aside the hostile blade and directed it to a side-pocket, where reposed an enormous iron tobacco-box, endowed, like the shield of Achilles, with supernatural powers, doubtless from bearing the portrait of the blessed St. Nicholas. Peter Stuyvesant turned like an angry bear upon the foe, and seizing him as he fled, by an immeasurable queue, "Ah, whoreson caterpillar," roared he, "here's what shall make worms' meat of thee!" So saying, he whirled his sword, and dealt a blow that would have decapitated the varlet, but that the pitying steel struck short and shaved the queue forever from his crown. At this moment an arquebusier levelled his piece from a neighboring mound, with deadly aim; but the watchful Minerva, who had just stopped to tie up her garter, seeing the peril of her favorite hero, sent old Boreas with his bellows, who, as the match descended to the pan, gave a blast that blew the priming from the touch-hole.

Thus waged the fight, when the stout Risingh, surveying the field from the top of a little ravelin, perceived his troops banged, beaten, and kicked by the invincible Peter. Drawing his falchion and uttering a thousand anathemas, he strode down to the scene of combat with some such thundering strides as Jupiter is said by Hesiod to have taken, when he strode down the spheres to hurl his thunderbolts at the Titans.

When the rivals came face to face, each made a prodigious start in the style of a veteran stage-champion. Then did they regard each other for a moment with the bitter aspect of two furious ram-cats on the point of a clapperclawing. Then did they throw themselves into one attitude, then into another, striking their swords on the ground, first on the right side, then on the left—at last at it they went, with incredible ferocity. Words cannot tell the prodigies of strength and valor displayed in this direful encounter— an encounter compared to which the far-famed battles of Ajax with Hector, of Æneas with Turnus, Orlando with Rodomont, Guy of Warwick with Colbrand the Dane, or of that renowned Welsh knight, Sir Owen of the Mountains with the giant Guylon, were all gentle sports and holiday recreations. At length the valiant Peter, watching his opportunity, aimed a blow, enough to cleave his adversary to the very chine; but Risingh, nimbly raising his sword, warded it off so narrowly, that glancing on one side, it shaved away a huge canteen in which he carried his liquor; thence pursuing its trenchant course, it severed off a deep coat pocket, stored with bread and cheese—which provant rolling among the armies, occasioned a fearful scrambling between the Swedes and Dutchmen, and made the general battle to wax more furious than ever.

Enraged to see his military stores laid waste, the stout Risingh, collecting all his forces, aimed a mighty blow full at the hero's crest. In vain did his fierce little cocked hat oppose its course. The biting steel clove through the stubborn ram beaver, and would have cracked the crown of any one not endowed with supernatural hardness of head; but the brittle weapon shivered in pieces on the skull of Hardkoppig Piet, shedding a thousand sparks, like beams of glory, round his grizzly visage.

The good Peter reeled with the blow, and turning up his eyes beheld a thousand suns, besides moons and stars,

dancing about the firmament—at length, missing his footing, by reason of his wooden leg, down he came on his seat
of honor with a crash which shook the surrounding hills,
and might have wrecked his frame, had he not been received into a cushion softer than velvet, which Providence,
or Minerva, or St. Nicholas, or some cow, had benevolently
prepared for his reception.

The furious Risingh, in spite of the maxim, cherished by
all true knights, that "fair play is a jewel," hastened to take
advantage of the hero's fall; but, as he stooped to give a
fatal blow, Peter Stuyvesant dealt him a thwack over the
sconce with his wooden leg, which set a chime of bells ringing triple bob majors in his cerebellum. The bewildered
Swede staggered with the blow, and the wary Peter seizing a pocket pistol, which lay hard by, discharged it full
at the head of the reeling Risingh. Let not my reader mistake; it was not a murderous weapon loaded with powder
and ball; but a little sturdy stone pottle charged to the
muzzle with a double dram of true Dutch courage, which
the knowing Antony Van Corlear carried about him by way
of replenishing his valor; and which had dropped from his
wallet during his furious encounter with the drummer. The
hideous weapon sang through the air, and true to its course
as was the fragment of rock discharged at Hector by bully
Ajax, encountered the head of the gigantic Swede with
matchless violence.

This heaven-directed blow decided the battle. The ponderous pericranium of General Jan Risingh sank upon his
breast; his knees tottered under him; a deathlike torpor
seized upon his frame, and he tumbled to the earth with
such violence, that old Pluto started with affright, lest he
should have broken through the roof of his infernal palace.

His fall was the signal of defeat and victory—the Swedes
gave way—the Dutch pressed forward; the former took to
their heels, the latter hotly pursued.—Some entered with
them, pell-mell, through the sally-port—others stormed the
bastion, and others scrambled over the curtain. Thus in a
little while the fortress of Fort Christina, which, like another Troy, had stood a siege of full ten hours, was car-

ried by assault, without the loss of a single man on either side. Victory, in the likeness of a gigantic ox-fly, sat perched upon the cocked hat of the gallant Stuyvesant; and it was declared, by all the writers whom he hired to write the history of his expedition, that on this memorable day he gained a sufficient quantity of glory to immortalize a dozen of the greatest heroes in Christendom.

When Irving sailed for Europe in 1815 the family hardware business was prospering; he was confident that there would be enough money for him to lead a life of leisurely sensibility. But in England he found that his brother Peter, who was stationed there as the family's business agent, had fallen ill. Perforce, Irving had to step in. The long-averted commercial career was now a sickening reality: "There it was, day after day; work hard all day and then to bed late, a troubled sleep, for three hours perhaps, and then wake up; thump, thump, thump, at the heart comes the care."

During this period his mother, his father, and one of his sisters died; in 1818 the family firm went bankrupt. "I underwent ruin," Irving cried, "in all its bitterness and humiliation—in a strange land—among strangers. I went through the horrible ordeal of Bankruptcy. It is true I was treated with indulgence—even with courtesy; for they perceived that I was a mere nominal party in the concern—But to me it was a cruel blow—I felt cast down—abased—I had lost my *cast*. . . . I shut myself up from society—and would see no one." Irving was now neurasthenic, infected with what he described as "a melancholy that corrodes the spirits & seems to rust all the springs of mental energy." His anodyne in this major crisis, as in all the minor ones of his life, was reverie. He read the novels of Scott; he plunged into the fairy-tale world of German folklore; he wandered through English country churchyards and stood brooding in the Poet's Corner of Westminster Abbey. He also wrote "Rip Van Winkle."

The story is Irving's finest fantasy of escape from responsibility. When Rip, fleeing the scolding of wife—who operates in the story as the outraged voice of the gospel of work—strolls off into the woods and falls asleep, he is transported into a dream world of eternal play, where all of life is a game of ninepins. The modulation from the dream into the lean, hustling America of twenty years after is brought off with great skill and psychological accuracy. Yet even in this waking world of nightmare there is an avenue of escape from the necessity for competing in the business race, for the story of Rip Van Winkle, composed in a time of personal crisis, is Irving's projection of a most profoundly felt wish. In a letter to Sir Walter Scott, Irving admitted that "My whole course of life has been desultory, and I am unfitted for any periodically recurring task, or any stipulated labor of body and mind." Rip Van Winkle is similarly unfitted, but it is all right; Rip is permitted to live lazily and happily ever after because there is still one escape route open: in twenty years Rip has become old, and is no longer expected to labor. When Irving was twenty years old he assumed the mask of Jonathan Oldstyle; at twenty-four he became the old bachelor of the *Salmagundi* papers; "Rip Van Winkle" is supposedly one of the posthumous papers of old Diedrich Knickerbocker. Again and again in the course of his writing career Irving slipped behind the mask of an old man, and the same was true of his personal life. Describing his life, Irving once wrote, "My summer is nearly over—the shadows of autumn begin to come—the leaves of past pleasure are strewn around me—the joys of youth, how have they passed away—friendships faded—loves untimely fallen—hopes blighted—what fruit is there to repay this ill-spent summer?" When he wrote that valedictory, Irving was not quite forty. The image of old Rip Van Winkle, arrived at "that happy age when a man can be idle with impunity," represented for Irving some sort of culmination of a dream.

In his response to his hero, Irving has not been alone. A secret hankering for idleness on the part of a people publicly committed to the competitive struggle of the Ameri-

can Way has made Irving's story so famous that it has
passed out of the realm of fiction and become a part of
our comic folklore. Americans have never gone in much for
plotting to overthrow social controls, but the impulse to
walk out on them, to secede from them, has been persistent, both in our history and our literature. Rip Van Winkle,
ducking out on Dame Van Winkle and strolling off into the
woods, is a prophetic figure. Undergoing a series of meta-
morphoses, he reappears again and again in the course of
nineteenth-century American literature. He shows up as
Natty Bumppo, and again as Huck Finn; his spirit can be
detected in the author of *Walden*. The wish to become Rip
Van Winkle has been one of the great American dreams.

Rip Van Winkle
A Posthumous Writing of Diedrich Knickerbocker

Whoever has made a voyage up the Hudson must remember the Kaatskill mountains. They are a dismembered
branch of the great Appalachian family, and are seen away
to the west of the river, swelling up to a noble height, and
lording it over the surrounding country. Every change of
season, every change of weather, indeed, every hour of the
day, produces some change in the magical hues and shapes
of these mountains, and they are regarded by all the good
wives, far and near, as perfect barometers. When the
weather is fair and settled, they are clothed in blue and
purple, and print their bold outlines on the clear evening
sky; but sometimes, when the rest of the landscape is cloud-
less, they will gather a hood of gray vapors about their
summits, which, in the last rays of the setting sun, will glow
and light up like a crown of glory.

At the foot of these fairy mountains, the voyager may
have descried the light smoke curling up from a village,
whose shingle-roofs gleam among the trees, just where the
blue tints of the upland melt away into the fresh green of

the nearer landscape. It is a little village, of great antiquity, having been founded by some of the Dutch colonists in the early times of the province, just about the beginning of the government of the good Peter Stuyvesant, (may he rest in peace!) and there were some of the houses of the original settlers standing within a few years, built of small yellow bricks brought from Holland, having latticed windows and gable fronts, surmounted with weathercocks.

In that same village, and in one of these very houses (which, to tell the precise truth, was sadly time-worn and weather-beaten), there lived, many years since, while the country was yet a province of Great Britain, a simple, good-natured fellow, of the name of Rip Van Winkle. He was a descendant of the Van Winkles who figured so gallantly in the chivalrous days of Peter Stuyvesant, and accompanied him to the siege of Fort Christina. He inherited, however, but little of the martial character of his ancestors. I have observed that he was a simple, good-natured man; he was, moreover, a kind neighbor, and an obedient, hen-pecked husband. Indeed, to the latter circumstance might be owing that meekness of spirit which gained him such universal popularity; for those men are most apt to be obsequious and conciliating abroad, who are under the discipline of shrews at home. Their tempers, doubtless, are rendered pliant and malleable in the fiery furnace of domestic tribulation; and a curtain-lecture is worth all the sermons in the world for teaching the virtues of patience and long-suffering. A termagant wife may, therefore, in some respects be considered a tolerable blessing; and if so, Rip Van Winkle was thrice blessed.

Certain it is, that he was a great favorite among all the good wives of the village, who, as usual with the amiable sex, took his part in all family squabbles; and never failed, whenever they talked those matters over in their evening gossipings, to lay all the blame on Dame Van Winkle. The children of the village, too, would shout with joy whenever he approached. He assisted at their sports, made their playthings, taught them to fly kites and shoot marbles, and told them long stories of ghosts, witches, and Indians. Whenever he went dodging about the village, he was surrounded by a troop of them, hanging on his skirts, clambering on his back, and playing a thousand tricks on him with impunity; and not a dog would bark at him throughout the neighborhood.

The great error in Rip's composition was an insuperable aversion to all kinds of profitable labor. It could not be from the want of assiduity or perseverance; for he would sit on a wet rock, with a rod as long and heavy as a Tartar's lance, and fish all day without a murmur, even though he should not be encouraged by a single nibble. He would carry a fowling-piece on his shoulder for hours together, trudging through woods and swamps, and up hill and down dale, to shoot a few squirrels or wild pigeons. He would never refuse to assist a neighbor even in the roughest toil, and was a foremost man at all country frolics for husking Indian corn, or building stone fences; the women of the village, too, used to employ him to run errands, and to do such little odd jobs as their less obliging husbands would not do for them. In a word, Rip was ready to attend to anybody's business but his own; but as to doing family duty, and keeping his farm in order, he found it impossible.

In fact, he declared it was of no use to work on his farm; it was the most pestilent little piece of ground in the whole country; everything about it went wrong, and would go wrong, in spite of him. His fences were continually falling to pieces; his cow would either go astray, or get among the cabbages; weeds were sure to grow quicker in his fields than anywhere else; the rain always made a point of setting in just as he had some out-door work to do; so that though his patrimonial estate had dwindled away under his management, acre by acre, until there was little more left than a mere patch of Indian corn and potatoes, yet it was the worst conditioned farm in the neighborhood.

His children, too, were as ragged and wild as if they belonged to nobody. His son Rip, an urchin begotten in his own likeness, promised to inherit the habits, with the old clothes, of his father. He was generally seen trooping like a colt at his mother's heels, equipped in a pair of his father's cast-off galligaskins, which he had much ado to hold up with one hand, as a fine lady does her train in bad weather.

Rip Van Winkle, however, was one of those happy mortals, of foolish, well-oiled dispositions, who take the world easy, eat white bread or brown, whichever can be got with least thought or trouble, and would rather starve on a penny than work for a pound. If left to himself, he would have whistled life away in perfect contentment; but his wife kept continually dinning in his ears about his idleness, his carelessness, and the ruin he was bringing on his family. Morning, noon, and night, her tongue was incessantly going, and everything he said or did was sure to produce a torrent of household eloquence. Rip had but one way of replying to all lectures of the kind, and that, by frequent use, had grown into a habit. He shrugged his shoulders, shook his head, cast up his eyes, but said nothing. This, however, always provoked a fresh volley from his wife; so that he was fain to draw off his forces, and take to the outside of the house—the only side which, in truth, belongs to a henpecked husband.

Rip's sole domestic adherent was his dog Wolf, who was as much hen-pecked as his master; for Dame Van Winkle regarded them as companions in idleness, and even looked upon Wolf with an evil eye, as the cause of his master's going so often astray. True it is, in all points of spirit befitting an honorable dog, he was as courageous an animal as ever scoured the woods; but what courage can withstand the ever-during and all-besetting terrors of a woman's tongue? The moment Wolf entered the house his crest fell, his tail drooped to the ground, or curled between his legs, he sneaked about with a gallows air, casting many a sidelong glance at Dame Van Winkle, and at the least flourish of a broomstick or ladle he would fly to the door with yelping precipitation.

Times grew worse and worse with Rip Van Winkle as years of matrimony rolled on; a tart temper never mellows with age, and a sharp tongue is the only edged tool that grows keener with constant use. For a long while he used to console himself, when driven from home, by frequenting a kind of perpetual club of the sages, philosophers, and other idle personages of the village, which held its sessions on a bench before a small inn, designated by a rubicund portrait of His Majesty George the Third. Here they used to sit in the shade through a long, lazy summer's day, talking listlessly over village gossip, or telling endless sleepy stories about nothing. But it would have been worth any statesman's money to have heard the profound discussions that sometimes took place, when by chance an old newspaper fell into their hands from some passing traveller. How solemnly they would listen to the contents, as drawled out by Derrick Van Bummel, the schoolmaster, a dapper learned little man, who was not to be daunted by the most gigantic word in the dictionary; and how sagely they would deliberate upon public events some months after they had taken place.

The opinions of this junto were completely controlled by Nicholas Vedder, a patriarch of the village, and landlord of the inn, at the door of which he took his seat from morning till night, just moving sufficiently to avoid the sun and keep in the shade of a large tree; so that the neighbors could tell the hour by his movements as accurately as by a sun-dial. It is true he was rarely heard to speak, but smoked his pipe incessantly. His adherents, however (for every great man has his adherents), perfectly understood him, and knew how to gather his opinions. When anything that was read or related displeased him, he was observed to smoke his pipe vehemently, and to send forth short, frequent, and angry puffs; but when pleased, he would inhale the smoke slowly and tranquilly, and emit it in light and placid clouds; and sometimes, taking the pipe from his mouth, and letting the fragrant vapor curl about his nose, would gravely nod his head in token of perfect approbation.

From even this stronghold the unlucky Rip was at length routed by his termagant wife, who would suddenly break in upon the tranquillity of the assemblage and call the members all to naught; nor was that august personage, Nicholas Vedder himself, sacred from the daring tongue of this terrible virago, who charged him outright with encouraging her husband in habits of idleness.

Poor Rip was at last reduced almost to despair; and his only alternative, to escape from the labor of the farm and clamor of his wife, was to take gun in hand and stroll away into the woods. Here he would sometimes seat himself at the foot of a tree, and share the contents of his wallet with Wolf, with whom he sympathized as a fellow-sufferer in persecution. "Poor Wolf," he would say, "thy mistress leads thee a dog's life of it; but never mind, my lad, whilst I live thou shalt never want a friend to stand by thee!" Wolf would wag his tail, look wistfully in his master's face; and if dogs can feel pity, I verily believe he reciprocated the sentiment with all his heart.

In a long ramble of the kind on a fine autumnal day, Rip had unconsciously scrambled to one of the highest parts of the Kaatskill mountains. He was after his favorite sport of squirrel-shooting, and the still solitudes had echoed and re-echoed with the reports of his gun. Panting and fatigued, he threw himself, late in the afternoon, on a green knoll, covered with mountain herbage, that crowned the brow of a precipice. From an opening between the trees he could overlook all the lower country for many a mile of rich woodland. He saw at a distance the lordly Hudson, far, far below him, moving on its silent but majestic course, with the reflection of a purple cloud, or the sail of a lagging bark, here and there sleeping on its glassy bosom, and at last losing itself in the blue highlands.

On the other side he looked down into a deep mountain glen, wild, lonely, and shagged, the bottom filled with fragments from the impending cliffs, and scarcely lighted by the reflected rays of the setting sun. For some time Rip lay musing on this scene; evening was gradually advancing; the mountains began to throw their long blue shadows over the valleys; he saw that it would be dark long before he could reach the village, and he heaved a heavy sigh when he thought of encountering the terrors of Dame Van Winkle.

As he was about to descend, he heard a voice from a distance, hallooing, "Rip Van Winkle, Rip Van Winkle!"

He looked round, but could see nothing but a crow wing-ing its solitary flight across the mountain. He thought his fancy must have deceived him, and turned again to de-scend, when he heard the same cry ring through the still evening air: "Rip Van Winkle! Rip Van Winkle!"—at the same time Wolf bristled up his back, and giving a low growl, skulked to his master's side, looking fearfully down into the glen. Rip now felt a vague apprehension stealing over him; he looked anxiously in the same direction, and perceived a strange figure slowly toiling up the rocks, and bending under the weight of something he carried on his back. He was surprised to see any human being in this lonely and unfrequented place; but supposing it to be some one of the neighborhood in need of his assistance, he has-tened down to yield it.

On nearer approach he was still more surprised at the singularity of the stranger's appearance. He was a short, square-built old fellow, with thick bushy hair, and a grizzly beard. His dress was of the antique Dutch fashion,—a cloth jerkin strapped round his waist—several pair of breeches, the outer one of ample volume, decorated with rows of but-tons down the sides, and bunches at the knees. He bore on his shoulder a stout keg, that seemed full of liquor, and made signs for Rip to approach and assist him with the load. Though rather shy and distrustful of this new ac-quaintance, Rip complied with his usual alacrity; and mu-tually relieving one another, they clambered up a narrow gully, apparently the dry bed of a mountain torrent. As they ascended, Rip every now and then heard long, rolling peals, like distant thunder, that seemed to issue out of a deep ra-vine, or rather cleft, between lofty rocks, toward which their rugged path conducted. He paused for an instant, but sup-posing it to be the muttering of one of those transient thun-der-showers which often take place in mountain heights, he proceeded. Passing through the ravine, they came to a hollow, like a small amphitheatre, surrounded by perpen-dicular precipices, over the brinks of which impending trees shot their branches, so that you only caught glimpses of the azure sky and the bright evening cloud. During the whole time Rip and his companion had labored on in silence; for though the former marvelled greatly what could be the object of carrying a keg of liquor up this wild mountain, yet there was something strange and incomprehensible about the unknown, that inspired awe and checked familiarity.

On entering the amphitheatre, new objects of wonder presented themselves. On a level spot in the centre was a company of odd-looking personages playing at ninepins. They were dressed in a quaint, outlandish fashion; some wore short doublets, others jerkins, with long knives in their belts, and most of them had enormous breeches, of similar style with that of the guide's. Their visages, too, were peculiar: one had a large beard, broad face, and small piggish eyes; the face of another seemed to consist entirely of nose, and was surmounted by a white sugar-loaf hat, set off with a little red cock's tail. They all had beards, of various shapes and colors. There was one who seemed to be the commander. He was a stout old gentleman, with a weather-beaten countenance; he wore a laced doublet, broad belt and hanger, high-crowned hat and feather, red stockings, and high-heeled shoes, with roses in them. The whole group reminded Rip of the figures in an old Flemish painting, in the parlor of Dominie Van Shaick, the village parson, and which had been brought over from Holland at the time of the settlement.

What seemed particularly odd to Rip was, that, though these folks were evidently amusing themselves, yet they maintained the gravest faces, the most mysterious silence, and were, withal, the most melancholy party of pleasure he had ever witnessed. Nothing interrupted the stillness of the scene but the noise of the balls, which, whenever they were rolled, echoed along the mountains like rumbling peals of thunder.

As Rip and his companion approached them, they suddenly desisted from their play, and stared at him with such fixed, statuelike gaze, and such strange, uncouth, lacklustre countenances, that his heart turned within him, and his knees smote together. His companion now emptied the contents of the keg into large flagons, and made signs to him to wait upon the company. He obeyed with fear and trembling; they quaffed the liquor in profound silence, and then returned to their game.

By degrees Rip's awe and apprehension subsided. He even ventured, when no eye was fixed upon him, to taste the beverage, which he found had much of the flavor of excellent Hollands. He was naturally a thirsty soul, and was soon tempted to repeat the draught. One taste provoked another; and he reiterated his visits to the flagon so often that at length his senses were overpowered, his eyes swam in his head, his head gradually declined, and he fell into a deep sleep.

On waking, he found himself on the green knoll whence he had first seen the old man of the glen. He rubbed his eyes—it was a bright sunny morning. The birds were hopping and twittering among the bushes, and the eagle was wheeling aloft, and breasting the pure mountain breeze. "Surely," thought Rip, "I have not slept here all night." He recalled the occurrences before he fell asleep. The strange man with a keg of liquor—the mountain ravine—the wild retreat among the rocks—the woe-begone party at ninepins —the flagon—"Oh! that flagon! that wicked flagon!" thought Rip,—"what excuse shall I make to Dame Van Winkle?"

He looked round for his gun, but in place of the clean, well-oiled fowling-piece, he found an old firelock lying by him, the barrel incrusted with rust, the lock falling off, and the stock worm-eaten. He now suspected that the grave roisters of the mountain had put a trick upon him, and, having dosed him with liquor, had robbed him of his gun. Wolf, too, had disappeared, but he might have strayed away after a squirrel or partridge. He whistled after him, and shouted his name, but all in vain; the echoes repeated his whistle and shout, but no dog was to be seen.

He determined to revisit the scene of the last evening's gambol, and if he met with any of the party, to demand his dog and gun. As he rose to walk, he found himself stiff in the joints, and wanting in his usual activity. "These mountain beds do not agree with me," thought Rip, "and if this frolic should lay me up with a fit of the rheumatism, I shall have a blessed time with Dame Van Winkle." With some difficulty he got down into the glen: he found the gully up which he and his companion had ascended the preceding evening; but to his astonishment a mountain stream was now foaming down it, leaping from rock to rock, and filling the glen with babbling murmurs. He, however, made shift to scramble up its sides, working his toilsome way through thickets of birch, sassafras, and witch-hazel, and sometimes tripped up or entangled by the wild grape-vines that twisted their coils or tendrils from tree to tree, and spread a kind of network in his path.

At length he reached to where the ravine had opened through the cliffs to the amphitheatre; but no traces of such opening remained. The rocks presented a high, impenetrable wall, over which the torrent came tumbling in a sheet of feathery foam, and fell into a broad deep basin, black from the shadows of the surrounding forest. Here, then, poor Rip was brought to a stand. He again called and whistled after his dog; he was only answered by the cawing of a flock of idle crows, sporting high in air about a dry tree that overhung a sunny precipice; and who, secure in their elevation, seemed to look down and scoff at the poor man's perplexities. What was to be done? the morning was passing away, and Rip felt famished for want of his breakfast. He grieved to give up his dog and gun; he dreaded to meet his wife; but it would not do to starve among the mountains. He shook his head, shouldered the rusty firelock, and, with a heart full of trouble and anxiety, turned his steps homeward.

As he approached the village he met a number of people, but none whom he knew, which some what surprised him, for he had thought himself acquainted with every one in the country round. Their dress, too, was of a different fashion from that to which he was accustomed. They all stared at him with equal marks of surprise, and whenever they cast their eyes upon him, invariably stroked their chins. The constant recurrence of this gesture induced Rip, involuntarily, to do the same, when, to his astonishment, he found his beard had grown a foot long!

He had now entered the skirts of the village. A troop of strange children ran at his heels, hooting after him, and pointing at his gray beard. The dogs, too, not one of which he recognized for an old acquaintance, barked at him as he passed. The very village was altered; it was larger and more populous. There were rows of houses which he had never seen before, and those which had been his familiar haunts had disappeared. Strange names were over the doors —strange faces at the windows—everything was strange. His mind now misgave him; he began to doubt whether both he and the world around him were not bewitched. Surely this was his native village, which he had left but the day before. There stood the Kaatskill mountains—there ran the silver Hudson at a distance—there was every hill and dale precisely as it had always been. Rip was sorely perplexed. "That flagon last night," thought he, "has addled my poor head sadly!"

It was with some difficulty that he found the way to his own house, which he approached with silent awe, expecting every moment to hear the shrill voice of Dame Van Winkle. He found the house gone to decay—the roof fallen in, the windows shattered, and the doors off the hinges. A half-starved dog that looked like Wolf was skulking about it. Rip called him by name, but the cur snarled, showed his teeth, and passed on. This was an unkind cut indeed. "My very dog," sighed poor Rip, "has forgotten me!"

He entered the house, which, to tell the truth, Dame Van Winkle had always kept in neat order. It was empty, forlorn, and apparently abandoned. This desolateness overcame all his connubial fears—he called loudly for his wife and children—the lonely chambers rang for a moment with his voice, and then all again was silence.

He now hurried forth, and hastened to his old resort, the village inn—but it too was gone. A large rickety wooden building stood in its place, with great gaping windows, some of them broken and mended with old hats and petticoats, and over the door was painted, "The Union Hotel, by Jonathan Doolittle." Instead of the great tree that used to shelter the quiet little Dutch inn of yore, there now was reared a tall naked pole, with something on the top that looked like a red nightcap, and from it was fluttering a flag, on which was a singular assemblage of stars and stripes; —all this was strange and incomprehensible. He recognized on the sign, however, the ruby face of King George, under which he had smoked so many a peaceful pipe; but even this was singularly metamorphosed. The red coat was changed for one of blue and buff, a sword was held in the hand instead of a sceptre, the head was decorated with a cocked hat, and underneath was painted in large characters, GENERAL WASHINGTON.

There was, as usual, a crowd of folk about the door, but none that Rip recollected. The very character of the people seemed changed. There was a busy, bustling, disputatious tone about it, instead of the accustomed phlegm and drowsy tranquillity. He looked in vain for the sage Nicholas Vedder, with his broad face, double chin, and fair long pipe, uttering clouds of tobacco-smoke instead of idle speeches; or Van Bummel, the schoolmaster, doling forth the contents of an ancient newspaper. In place of these, a lean, bilious-looking fellow, with his pockets full of hand-bills, was haranguing vehemently about rights of citizens —elections—members of congress—liberty—Bunker's Hill —heroes of seventy-six—and other words, which were a perfect Babylonish jargon to the bewildered Van Winkle.

The appearance of Rip, with his long, grizzled beard, his rusty fowling-piece, his uncouth dress, and an army of women and children at his heels, soon attracted the attention of the tavern-politicians. They crowded round him, eying him from head to foot with great curiosity. The orator bustled up to him, and, drawing him partly aside, inquired "On which side he voted?" Rip stared in vacant stupidity. Another short but busy little fellow pulled him by the arm, and, rising on tiptoe, inquired in his ear, "Whether he was Federal or Democrat?" Rip was equally at a loss to comprehend the question; when a knowing, self-important old gentleman, in a sharp cocked hat, made his way through

the crowd, putting them to the right and left with his
elbows as he passed, and planting himself before Van
Winkle, with one arm akimbo, the other resting on his cane,
his keen eyes and sharp hat penetrating, as it were, into
his very soul, demanded, in an austere tone, "What brought
him to the election with a gun on his shoulder, and a mob
at his heels; and whether he meant to breed a riot in
the village?"—"Alas! gentlemen," cried Rip, somewhat dismayed, "I am a poor quiet man, a native of the place, and
a loyal subject of the King, God bless him!"

Here a general shout burst from the by-standers—"A
tory! a tory! a spy! a refugee! hustle him! away with him!"
It was with great difficulty that the self-important man in
the cocked hat restored order; and, having assumed a tenfold austerity of brow, demanded again of the unknown
culprit, what he came there for, and whom he was seeking?
The poor man humbly assured him that he meant no harm,
but merely came there in search of some of his neighbors,
who used to keep about the tavern.

"Well—who are they?—name them."

Rip bethought himself a moment, and inquired, "Where's
Nicholas Vedder?"

There was a silence for a little while, when an old man
replied, in a thin piping voice, "Nicholas Vedder! why, he
is dead and gone these eighteen years! There was a wooden
tombstone in the churchyard that used to tell all about him,
but that's rotten and gone too."

"Where's Brom Dutcher?"

"Oh, he went off to the army in the beginning of the
war; some say he was killed at the storming of Stony Point
—others say he was drowned in a squall at the foot of
Antony's Nose. I don't know—he never came back again."

"Where's Van Bummel, the schoolmaster?"

"He went off to the wars too, was a great militia general, and is now in congress."

Rip's heart died away at hearing of these sad changes in
his home and friends, and finding himself thus alone in the
world. Every answer puzzled him too, by treating of such
enormous lapses of time, and of matters which he could

not understand: war—congress—Stony Point;—he had no courage to ask after any more friends, but cried out in despair, "Does nobody here know Rip Van Winkle?"

"Oh, Rip Van Winkle!" exclaimed two or three, "oh, to be sure! that's Rip Van Winkle yonder, leaning against the tree."

Rip looked, and beheld a precise counterpart of himself, as he went up the mountain; apparently as lazy, and certainly as ragged. The poor fellow was now completely confounded. He doubted his own identity, and whether he was himself or another man. In the midst of his bewilderment, the man in the cocked hat demanded who he was, and what was his name.

"God knows," exclaimed he, at his wit's end; "I'm not myself—I'm somebody else—that's me yonder—no—that's somebody else got into my shoes—I was myself last night, but I fell asleep on the mountain, and they've changed my gun, and everything's changed, and I can't tell what's my name, or who I am!"

The by-standers began now to look at each other, nod, wink significantly, and tap their fingers against their foreheads. There was a whisper, also, about securing the gun, and keeping the old fellow from doing mischief, at the very suggestion of which the self-important man in the cocked hat retired with some precipitation. At this critical moment a fresh, comely woman pressed through the throng to get a peep at the gray-bearded man. She had a chubby child in her arms, which, frightened at his looks, began to cry. "Hush, Rip," cried she, "hush, you little fool; the old man won't hurt you." The name of the child, the air of the mother, the tone of her voice, all awakened a train of recollections in his mind. "What is your name, my good woman?" asked he.

"Judith Gardenier."

"And your father's name?"

"Ah, poor man, Rip Van Winkle was his name, but it's twenty years since he went away from home with his gun, and never has been heard of since,—his dog came home without him; but whether he shot himself, or was carried away by the Indians, nobody can tell. I was then but a little girl."

Rip had but one question more to ask; but he put it with a faltering voice:

"Where's your mother?"

"Oh, she too had died but a short time since; she broke a bloodvessel in a fit of passion at a New England peddler."

There was a drop of comfort, at least, in this intelligence. The honest man could contain himself no longer. He caught his daughter and her child in his arms. "I am your father!" cried he—"Young Rip Van Winkle once—old Rip Van Winkle now!—Does nobody know poor Rip Van Winkle?"

All stood amazed, until an old woman, tottering out from among the crowd, put her hand to her brow, and peering under it in his face for a moment, exclaimed, "Sure enough! it is Rip Van Winkle—it is himself! Welcome home again, old neighbor. Why, where have you been these twenty long years?"

Rip's story was soon told, for the whole twenty years had been to him but as one night. The neighbors stared when they heard it; some were seen to wink at each other, and put their tongues in their cheeks: and the self-important man in the cocked hat, who when the alarm was over, had returned to the field, screwed down the corners of his mouth, and shook his head—upon which there was a general shaking of the head throughout the assemblage.

It was determined, however, to take the opinion of old Peter Vanderdonk, who was seen slowly advancing up the road. He was a descendant of the historian of that name, who wrote one of the earliest accounts of the province. Peter was the most ancient inhabitant of the village, and well versed in all the wonderful events and traditions of the neighborhood. He recollected Rip at once, and corroborated his story in the most satisfactory manner. He assured the company that it was a fact, handed down from his ancestor the historian, that the Kaatskill mountains had always been haunted by strange beings. That it was affirmed that the great Hendrick Hudson, the first discoverer of the river and country, kept a kind of vigil there every twenty years, with his crew of the *Half-moon;* being permitted in this way to revisit the scenes of his enterprise, and keep a guardian eye upon the river and the great city called by his name. That his father had once seen them in their old Dutch dresses playing at ninepins in a hollow of the mountain; and that he himself had heard, one summer afternoon, the sound of their balls, like distant peals of thunder.

To make a long story short, the company broke up and returned to the more important concerns of the election. Rip's daughter took him home to live with her; she had a snug, well-furnished house, and a stout, cheery farmer for a husband, whom Rip recollected for one of the urchins that used to climb upon his back. As to Rip's son and heir, who was the ditto of himself, seen leaning against the tree, he was employed to work on the farm; but evinced an hereditary disposition to attend to anything else but his business.

Rip now resumed his old walks and habits; he soon found many of his former cronies, though all rather the worse for the wear and tear of time; and preferred making friends among the rising generation, with whom he soon grew into great favor.

Having nothing to do at home, and being arrived at that happy age when a man can be idle with impunity, he took his place once more on the bench at the inn-door, and was reverenced as one of the patriarchs of the village, and a chronicle of the old times "before the war." It was some time before he could get into the regular track of gossip, or could be made to comprehend the strange events that had taken place during his torpor. How that there had been a revolutionary war,—that the country had thrown off the yoke of old England,—and that, instead of being a subject of His Majesty George the Third, he was now a free citizen of the United States. Rip, in fact, was no politician; the changes of states and empires made but little impression on him; but there was one species of despotism under which he had long groaned, and that was—petticoat government. Happily that was at an end; he had got his neck out of the yoke of matrimony, and could go in and out whenever he pleased, without dreading the tyranny of Dame Van Winkle. Whenever her name was mentioned, however, he shook his head, shrugged his shoulders, and cast up his eyes; which might pass either for an expression of resignation to his fate, or joy at his deliverance.

He used to tell his story to every stranger that arrived at Mr. Doolittle's hotel. He was observed, at first, to vary on some points every time he told it, which was, doubtless, owing to his having so recently awaked. It at last settled down precisely to the tale I have related, and not a man, woman, or child in the neighborhood but knew it by heart. Some always pretended to doubt the reality of it, and insisted that Rip had been out of his head, and that this was one point on which he always remained flighty. The old Dutch inhabitants, however, almost universally gave it full credit. Even to this day they never hear a thunder-storm of a summer afternoon about the Kaatskill, but they say Hendrick Hudson and his crew are at their game of ninepins; and it is a common wish of all hen-pecked husbands in the neighborhood, when life hangs heavy on their hands, that they might have a quieting draught out of Rip Van Winkle's flagon.

"The creations of American literature," Anthony Trollope observed, "generally are no doubt more given to the speculative—less given to the realistic—than are those of English literature. On our side of the water we deal more with beef and ale, and less with dreams. Even with the broad humor of Bret Harte, even with the broader humor of Artemus Ward and Mark Twain, there is generally present an undercurrent of melancholy, in which pathos and satire are intermingled. There was a touch of it even with . . . the kindly Washington Irving." This observation is extremely perspicacious. In the history of drama and fiction the comic characters have traditionally been "low" characters, and hence realistic rather than romantic. But as Trollope points out, American humorists have dealt with dreams, so that although their characters are oftentimes drawn with realistic detail, they move and have their being in a weird world.

"Adventure of the German Student" takes us deep inside a dream world. In *Tales of a Traveller,* in which this story figures, we are handed on from one narrator to another, and thereby led further and further away from reality, until finally we encounter the man with the haunted head: "He was an old gentleman, one side of whose face was no match for the other. The eye-lid drooped and hung down like an unhinged window-shutter. Indeed, the whole side of his head was dilapidated, and seemed like the wing of a house shut up and haunted." The story he tells is a nightmare of sexual horror; not until the end are we made aware that it was all a hoax. But why should Irving wish us to dismiss with a laugh the trauma of a young man who suddenly discovers that the bride of his dreams is a corpse? One of the letters Irving wrote on his first trip to Europe is possibly of some significance with regard to this question: "You can't imagine how many narrow escapes I have every day, from falling in love. How often in walking the street, do I see a fair nymph before me tripping along in airy movements. Her form of the greatest symmetry, while the zephyrs are continually betraying:

> the alluring line of grace
> That leads the eye a wanton chase
> And lets the fancy rove.

I hurry after her to catch a nearer view, to feast my eyes with the bright vision before it disappears. The sound of my steps calls her attention, she turns her face towards me —the charm is broken—and all admiration and enthusiasm is dissipated. I see a wide mouth, small black eyes, cheeks highly rouged and hair greased with ancient oil and from the forehead to the chin till it resembles the head dress of a Medusa!" The bantering tone of a gay (and, as it turned out, perennial) bachelor scarcely conceals an overwhelming revulsion.

Sexual insecurity, however, is not the only uncertainty driving Irving to such macabre humor. In both the story and the letter the woman operates as the symbol of Europe. The nervous tension between attraction and repulsion toward her which racks both Irving and the protagonist of his story represents the American innocent's historic unsureness of attitude toward the alluring corruptions of the Old World. Masculine-feminine ambivalence mirrors a cultural drama in which the American traveler abroad is torn between his eagerness to be taken in and his fear of what will happen to him if he is.

Adventure of the German Student

On a stormy night, in the tempestuous times of the French revolution, a young German was returning to his lodgings, at a late hour, across the old part of Paris. The lightning gleamed, and the loud claps of thunder rattled through the lofty narrow streets—but I should first tell you something about this young German.

Gottfried Wolfgang was a young man of good family. He had studied for some time at Göttingen, but being of a visionary and enthusiastic character, he had wandered into those wild and speculative doctrines which have so often bewildered German students. His secluded life, his intense application, and the singular nature of his studies, had an effect on both mind and body. His health was impaired; his imagination diseased. He had been indulging in fanciful speculations on spiritual essences, until, like Swedenborg, he had an ideal world of his own around him. He took up a notion, I do not know from what cause, that there was an evil influence hanging over him; an evil genius or spirit seeking to ensnare him and ensure his perdition. Such an idea working on his melancholy temperament, produced the most gloomy effects. He became haggard and desponding. His friends discovered the mental malady preying upon him, and determined that the best cure was a change of scene; he was sent, therefore, to finish his studies amidst the splendors and gayeties of Paris.

Wolfgang arrived at Paris at the breaking out of the revolution. The popular delirium at first caught his enthusiastic mind, and he was captivated by the political and philosophical theories of the day: but the scenes of blood which followed shocked his sensitive nature, disgusted him with society and the world, and made him more than ever a recluse. He shut himself up in a solitary apartment in the *Pays Latin,* the quarter of students. There, in a gloomy street not far from the monastic walls of the Sorbonne, he pursued his favorite speculations. Sometimes he spent hours together in the great libraries of Paris, those catacombs of departed authors, rummaging among their hoards of dusty and obsolete works in quest of food for his unhealthy appetite. He was, in a manner, a literary ghoul, feeding in the charnel-house of decayed literature.

Wolfgang, though solitary and recluse, was of an ardent temperament, but for a time it operated merely upon his imagination. He was too shy and ignorant of the world to make any advances to the fair, but he was a passionate admirer of female beauty, and in his lonely chamber would often lose himself in reveries on forms and faces which he had seen, and his fancy would deck out images of loveliness far surpassing the reality.

While his mind was in this excited and sublimated state, a dream produced an extraordinary effect upon him. It was of a female face of transcendent beauty. So strong was the impression made, that he dreamt of it again and again. It haunted his thoughts by day, his slumbers by night; in fine, he became passionately enamoured of this shadow of a dream. This lasted so long that it became one of those fixed ideas which haunt the minds of melancholy men, and are at times mistaken for madness.

Such was Gottfried Wolfgang, and such his situation at the time I mentioned. He was returning home late one stormy night, through some of the old and gloomy streets of the *Marais,* the ancient part of Paris. The loud claps of thunder rattled among the high houses of the narrow streets. He came to the Place de Grève, the square where public executions are performed. The lightning quivered about the pinnacles of the ancient Hôtel de Ville, and shed flickering gleams over the open space in front. As Wolfgang was crossing the square, he shrank back with horror at finding himself close by the guillotine. It was the height of the reign of terror, when this dreadful instrument of death stood ever ready, and its scaffold was continually running with the blood of the virtuous and the brave. It had that very day been actively employed in the work of carnage, and there it stood in grim array, amidst a silent and sleeping city, waiting for fresh victims.

Wolfgang's heart sickened within him, and he was turning shuddering from the horrible engine, when he beheld a shadowy form, cowering as it were at the foot of the steps which led up to the scaffold. A succession of vivid flashes of lightning revealed it more distinctly. It was a female figure, dressed in black. She was seated on one of the lower steps of the scaffold, leaning forward, her face hid in her lap; and her long dishevelled tresses hanging to the ground, streaming with the rain which fell in torrents. Wolfgang paused. There was something awful in this solitary monument of woe. The female had the appearance of being above the common order. He knew the times to be full of vicissitude, and that many a fair head, which had once been pillowed on down, now wandered houseless. Perhaps this was some poor mourner whom the dreadful axe had rendered desolate, and who sat here heart-broken on the strand of existence, from which all that was dear to her had been launched into eternity.

He approached, and addressed her in the accents of sympathy. She raised her head and gazed wildly at him. What was his astonishment at beholding, by the bright glare of the lightning, the very face which had haunted him in his dreams. It was pale and disconsolate, but ravishingly beautiful.

Trembling with violent and conflicting emotions, Wolfgang again accosted her. He spoke something of her being exposed at such an hour of the night, and to the fury of such a storm, and offered to conduct her to her friends. She pointed to the guillotine with a gesture of dreadful signification.

"I have no friend on earth!" said she.

"But you have a home," said Wolfgang.

"Yes—in the grave!"

The heart of the student melted at the words.

"If a stranger dare make an offer," said he, "without danger of being misunderstood, I would offer my humble dwelling as a shelter; myself as a devoted friend. I am friendless myself in Paris, and a stranger in the land; but if my life could be of service, it is at your disposal, and should be sacrificed before harm or indignity should come to you."

There was an honest earnestness in the young man's manner that had its effect. His foreign accent, too, was in his favor; it showed him not to be a hackneyed inhabitant of Paris. Indeed, there is an eloquence in true enthusiasm that is not to be doubted. The homeless stranger confided herself implicitly to the protection of the student.

He supported her faltering steps across the Pont Neuf, and by the place where the statue of Henry the Fourth had been overthrown by the populace. The storm had abated, and the thunder rumbled at a distance. All Paris was quiet; that great volcano of human passion slumbered for a while, to gather fresh strength for the next day's eruption. The student conducted his charge through the ancient streets of the *Pays Latin*, and by the dusky walls of the Sorbonne, to the great dingy hotel which he inhabited. The old portress who admitted them stared with surprise at the unusual sight of the melancholy Wolfgang with a female companion.

On entering his apartment, the student, for the first time, blushed at the scantiness and indifference of his dwelling. He had but one chamber—an old-fashioned saloon—heavily carved, and fantastically furnished with the remains of former magnificence, for it was one of those hotels in the quarter of the Luxembourg palace, which had once belonged to nobility. It was lumbered with books and papers, and all the usual apparatus of a student, and his bed stood in a recess at one end.

When lights were brought, and Wolfgang had a better opportunity of contemplating the stranger, he was more that ever intoxicated by her beauty. Her face was pale, but of a dazzling fairness, set off by a profusion of raven hair that hung clustering about it. Her eyes were large and brilliant, with a singular expression approaching almost to wildness. As far as her black dress permitted her shape to be seen, it was of perfect symmetry. Her whole appearance was highly striking, though she was dressed in the simplest style. The only thing approaching to an ornament which she wore, was a broad black band round her neck, clasped by diamonds.

The perplexity now commenced with the student how to dispose of the helpless being thus thrown upon his protection. He thought of abandoning his chamber to her, and seeking shelter for himself elsewhere. Still he was so fascinated by her charms, there seemed to be such a spell upon his thoughts and senses, that he could not tear himself from her presence. Her manner, too, was singular and unaccountable. She spoke no more of the guillotine. Her grief had abated. The attentions of the student had first won her confidence, and then, apparently, her heart. She was evidently an enthusiast like himself, and enthusiasts soon understand each other.

In the infatuation of the moment, Wolfgang avowed his passion for her. He told her the story of his mysterious dream, and how she had possessed his heart before he had even seen her. She was strangely affected by his recital, and acknowledged to have felt an impulse towards him equally unaccountable. It was the time for wild theory and wild actions. Old prejudices and superstitions were done away; everything was under sway of the "Goddess of Reason." Among the rubbish of the old times, the forms and ceremonies of marriage began to be considered superfluous bonds for honorable minds. Social compacts were the vogue. Wolfgang was too much of a theorist not to be tainted by the liberal doctrines of the day.

"Why should we separate?" said he: "our hearts are united; in the eye of reason and honor we are as one. What need is there of sordid forms to bind high souls together?"

The stranger listened with emotion: she had evidently received illumination at the same school.

"You have no home nor family," continued he; "let me be everything to you, or rather let us be everything to one another. If form is necessary, form shall be observed—there is my hand. I pledge myself to you forever."

"Forever?" said the stranger, solemnly.

"Forever!" repeated Wolfgang.

The stranger clasped the hand extended to her: "Then I am yours," murmured she, and sank upon his bosom.

The next morning the student left his bride sleeping, and sallied forth at an early hour to seek more spacious apartments suitable to the change in his situation. When he returned, he found the stranger lying with her head hanging over the bed and one arm thrown over it. He spoke to her, but received no reply. He advanced to awaken her from her uneasy posture. On taking her hand, it was cold—there was no pulsation—her face was pallid and ghastly. In a word, she was a corpse.

Horrified and frantic, he alarmed the house. A scene of confusion ensued. The police was summoned. As the officer of police entered the room, he started back on beholding the corpse.

"Great heaven!" cried he, "how did this woman come here?"

"Do you know anything about her?" said Wolfgang eagerly.

"Do I?" exclaimed the officer: "she was guillotined yesterday."

He stepped forward; undid the black collar round the neck of the corpse, and the head rolled on the floor!

The student burst into a frenzy. "The fiend! the fiend has gained possession of me!" shrieked he: "I am lost forever."

They tried to soothe him, but in vain. He was possessed with the frightful belief that an evil spirit had reanimated the dead body to ensnare him. He went distracted, and died in a mad-house.

Here the old gentleman with the haunted head finished his narrative.

"And is this really a fact?" said the inquisitive gentleman.

"A fact not to be doubted," replied the other. "I had it from the best authority. The student told it me himself. I saw him in a mad-house in Paris."

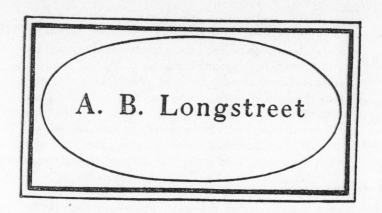

A. B. Longstreet

Starting about 1830, a sea change took place in south-western humor. The jokes and anecdotes which had been told around campfires on every American frontier for two hundred years, which had been retold on river boats and elaborated in backwoods cabins and lonely forts, began to be written down.

The men who put the comic stories of the American folk on paper hardly thought of themselves as professional writers of fiction, but it would be a mistake to assume—as some historians of American humor apparently do—that they were rough-hewn frontier types who had somehow learned to write the English language. On the contrary, they were self-conscious, sophisticated, well-educated men, in general identified with the Whig party—which in the South was the party of the big planters—and conservative in religion. They came in contact with the ragged edge of American culture because most of them were either lawyers or newspaper editors who traveled into the back country to talk to people as a part of their job. The speech of the bear hunter or the piney-woods farmer, with its grotesque vocabulary, its leisurely pace, its digressiveness, was taken in by these travelers in all its flavor. The experience was not unlike that enjoyed by Fielding, whose vocation as a circuit justice took him out of the polite world of Eton and Leyden where he had been educated, and exposed him to what Professor Maynard Mack has called the "vivid and barbarous life of country inns and alehouses"—a life which forms the basis of both *Joseph Andrews* and *Tom Jones*. No more than Fielding is to be identified with his materials, are the southwestern humorists to be confused with the men they described, who were a good deal more vividly barbarous than even the inmates of eighteenth-century English alehouses. The gentlemen authors of southwestern humor viewed the source of their inspiration from above; indeed, one of the main motives for their putting into print the stories they had heard was that as conservatives they had a stake in portraying the antics of the unwashed democracy as a comic spectacle. The feeling of superiority on the part of the laugher to the object of his amusement lies, as Bergson says, at the heart of laughter, and it is no accident that gentlemen began to convert the oral tradition of frontier humor into a written literature during the first administration of Andrew Jackson.

The most representative, and one of the best, of these humorists was Augustus Baldwin Longstreet. Born in Augusta, Georgia, he grew up in comfortable circumstances, his father, William Longstreet, having made a good deal of money speculating in land. Before being sent to Yale, Longstreet was educated in private schools, and after college he attended Tapping Reeve's famous law school in Connecticut.

It was from his father that Longstreet inherited his notorious temper. In addition to land speculating, the senior Longstreet fancied himself an inventor and did not tolerate jokes about his ability. When an actor in a local theater sang a song one night which made light of one of his inventions, William Longstreet, who was in the audience, got up out of his seat, blind with rage, and strode out of the theater. The habit of angry withdrawal he passed on to his son. Gus Longstreet's secessionist tendencies were conspicuously evinced in his support of Calhoun, whose education he had aped and whom he idolized, in the Nullification crisis, but as early as 1824 he had run for Congress on a

States' Rights platform, only to withdraw from the race when his wife's mother and his child died. In 1832 he planned to run for representative to the state legislature, but withdrew when delegates to the nominating convention turned out to include Unionists (anti-States' Righters). This pattern of vindictive withdrawal is discernible throughout his life. All during his later years as president of various institutions, he was constantly holding above his trustees' heads the threat that he would resign. Even as a tottering old man, he threatened to walk out on his family.

A complex, twisted personality, Longstreet was famous for his droll stories and his ability as a mimic. Yet he was never easy to be with; a pronounced physical ugliness was matched by a sneering, arrogant manner. His political withdrawals invariably had no effect, a fact which served only to increase his bitterness and frustration. In his later years as a Methodist minister and a college president he savagely squelched reminders that he was the well-known author of a series of humorous sketches of frontier life—not because he was ashamed of them, as certain critics have suggested, but because he was enraged that he should be remembered chiefly for what seemed to him such a trivial aspect of his career.

His first sketches appeared in a newspaper in Milledgeville, Georgia, until Longstreet himself bought a paper. In 1833 Georgia had gone Unionist more strongly than ever before; Longstreet, never a man to shun unpopular causes, decided to go into the newspaper business to defend his principles. Purchasing a paper in Augusta, he renamed it the *States Rights Sentinel*. In the two and a half years before he characteristically sold out, Longstreet wrote editorials that screamed political and moral outrage. As a kind of emotional release from his editorializing Longstreet contributed to the paper a series of humorous stories about Georgia life, culled from his immense fund of backwoods lore. Yet if the stories are to be understood as comic relief from the portentous editorials, they nevertheless have to be understood as coming from the same pen which endorsed the temperance movement, advocated States' Rights and

celebrated slavocracy, which saw corruption everywhere
and used words like "filth" and "poison" to describe the
body politic of the United States.

Like the editorials, the stories take a high moral line.
Longstreet would not become a Methodist minister until the
end of the 1830s, but as a writer he was forever sermon-
izing, whether in his humor or in his political diatribes. His
literary model was Addison, which is to say that the official
aim of *Georgia Scenes* (the sketches were collected in book
form in 1835) is moral and the superficial tone of the prose
is optimistic. However, when juxtaposed with the editorials,
the Addisonianism of the stories is at once exposed as a
cover-up for a tremendous uneasiness. *Georgia Scenes* is full
of sickening violence and appalling cruelty; men writhe in
agony to the tune of raucous laughter. By containing the
humor of the frontier within a frame of correct and elevated
diction, by holding the dog-eat-dog ethics of the backwoods within a matrix of moralistic Addisonian prose,
Longstreet endeavors to control and direct the fearfully ex-
plosive force of the new democracy, but it is a control
which is perilously maintained, not least because Longstreet
himself seems curiously attracted by the violence. Poe, who
reviewed the book for the *Southern Literary Messenger,*
cut through its bland surfaces at once. A dealer in horrors himself, he understood the true nature of Longstreet's
stories. "Perhaps never in our lives," said Poe, "have we
laughed as immoderately over any book as over the one
before us now." In particular, he praised Longstreet's "de-
lineation of Southern bravado." What, in sum, was the
cause of Poe's immoderate amusement was that here was a
book which made a joke out of the very sort of nightmarish
violence which was Poe's fearful obsession.

Longstreet's most memorable comic creation, the miserable clay-eater, Ransy Sniffle, is not only the country
cousin of Poe's sadists, but the prototype of Flem Snopes.
Just as the tension of Faulkner's humor derives from the
fact that he converts the tragedy of an all-conquering evil
into comedy, so Longstreet makes us laugh at the triumph
of ugliness and hate.

Georgia Theatrics

If my memory fail me not, the 10th of June, 1809, found me, at about eleven o'clock in the forenoon, ascending a long and gentle slope in what was called "The Dark Corner" of Lincoln. I believe it took its name from the moral darkness which reigned over that portion of the county at the time of which I am speaking. If in this point of view it was but a shade darker than the rest of the county, it was inconceivably dark. If any man can name a trick or sin which had not been committed at the time of which I am speaking, in the very focus of all the county's illumination (Lincolnton), he must himself be the most inventive of the tricky and the very Judas of sinners. Since that time, however (all humor aside), Lincoln has become a living proof "that light shineth in darkness." Could I venture to mingle the solemn with the ludicrous, even for the purposes of honorable contrast, I could adduce from this county instances of the most numerous and wonderful transitions from vice and folly to virtue and holiness which have ever, perhaps, been witnessed since the days of the apostolic ministry. So much, lest it should be thought by some that what I am about to relate is characteristic of the county in which it occurred.

Whatever may be said of the moral condition of the Dark Corner at the time just mentioned, its natural condition was anything but dark. It smiled in all the charms of spring; and spring borrowed a new charm from its undulating grounds, its luxuriant woodlands, its sportive streams, its vocal birds, and its blushing flowers.

Rapt with the enchantment of the season and the scenery around me, I was slowly rising the slope, when I was startled by loud, profane, and boisterous voices, which seemed to proceed from a thick covert of undergrowth about two hundred yards in the advance of me and about one hundred to the right of my road.

"You kin, kin you?"

"Yes, I kin, and am able to do it! Boo-oo-oo! Oh, wake snakes, and walk your chalks! Brimstone and—fire! Don't hold me, Nick Stoval! The fight's made up, and let's go at it—My soul if I don't jump down his throat, and gallop every chitterling out of him before you can say 'quit'!"

"Now, Nick, don't hold him! Jist let the wild-cat come, and I'll tame him. Ned'll see me a fair fight! Won't you, Ned?"

"Oh yes; I'll see you a fair fight, blast my old shoes if I don't!"

"That's sufficient, as Tom Haynes said when he saw the elephant. Now let him come!"

Thus they went on, with countless oaths interspersed which I dare not even hint at, and with much that I could not distinctly hear.

In mercy's name! thought I, what band of ruffians has selected this holy season and this heavenly retreat for such pandemoniac riots! I quickened my gait, and had come nearly opposite to the thick grove whence the noise proceeded, when my eye caught, indistinctly and at intervals, through the foliage of the dwarf-oaks and hickories which intervened, glimpses of a man, or men, who seemed to be in a violent struggle; and I could occasionally catch those deep-drawn, emphatic oaths which men in conflict utter when they deal blows. I dismounted, and hurried to the spot with all speed. I had overcome about half the space which separated it from me, when I saw the combatants come to the ground, and, after a short struggle, I saw the uppermost one (for I could not see the other) make a heavy plunge with both his thumbs, and at the same instant I heard a cry in the accent of keenest torture, "Enough! My eye's out!"

I was so completely horror-struck that I stood transfixed for a moment to the spot where the cry met me. The accomplices in the hellish deed which had been perpetuated had all fled at my approach—at least, I supposed so, for they were not to be seen.

"Now, blast your corn-shucking soul!" said the victor (a youth about eighteen years old) as he rose from the ground—"come cutt'n' your shines 'bout me agin, next time I come to the court-house, will you? Get your owl eye in agin if you can!"

At this moment he saw me for the first time. He looked excessively embarrassed, and was moving off, when I called to him, in a tone emboldened by the sacredness of my office and the iniquity of his crime, "Come back, you brute, and assist me in relieving your fellow-mortal, whom you have ruined forever!"

My rudeness subdued his embarrassment in an instant; and, with a taunting curl of the nose, he replied, "You needn't kick before you're spurr'd. There a'n't nobody there, nor ha'n't been nother. I was jist seein' how I could 'a' fout." So saying, he bounded to his plough, which stood in the corner of the fence about fifty yards beyond the battle-ground.

And, would you believe it, gentle reader? his report was true. All that I had heard and seen was nothing more nor less than a Lincoln rehearsal, in which the youth who had just left me had played all the parts of all the characters in a court-house fight.

I went to the ground from which he had risen, and there were the prints of his two thumbs, plunged up to the balls in the mellow earth, about the distance of a man's eyes apart; and the ground around was broken up as if two stags had been engaged upon it.

The Fight

In the younger days of the Republic there lived in the county of —— two men who were admitted on all hands to be the very *best men* in the county, which in the

Georgia vocabulary means they could flog any other two men in the county. Each, through many a hard-fought battle, had acquired the mastery of his own battalion; but they lived on opposite sides of the court-house and in different battalions, consequently they were but seldom thrown together. When they met, however, they were always friendly; indeed, at their first interview they seemed to conceive a wonderful attachment to each other, which rather increased than diminished as they became better acquainted; so that, but for the circumstance which I am about to mention, the question, which had been a thousand times asked, "Which is the best man, Billy Stallions (Stallings) or Bob Durham?" would probably never have been answered.

Billy ruled the upper battalion and Bob the lower. The former measured six feet and an inch in his stockings, and, without a single pound of cumbrous flesh about him, weighed a hundred and eighty. The latter was an inch shorter than his rival, and ten pounds lighter; but he was much the more active of the two. In running and jumping he had but few equals in the county; and in wrestling, not one. In other respects they were nearly equal. Both were admirable specimens of human nature in its finest form. Billy's victories had generally been achieved by the tremendous power of his blows, one of which had often proved decisive of his battles; Bob's by his adroitness in bringing his adversary to the ground. This advantage he had never failed to gain at the onset, and when gained he never failed to improve it to the defeat of his adversary. These points of difference have involved the reader in a doubt as to the probable issue of a contest between them. It was not so, however, with the two battalions. Neither had the least difficulty in determining the point by the most natural and irresistible deductions *a priori;* and though, by the same course of reasoning, they arrived at directly opposite conclusions, neither felt its confidence in the least shaken by this circumstance. The upper battalion swore "that Billy only wanted one lick at him to knock his heart, liver, and lights out of him, and if he got two at him

he'd knock him into a cocked hat." The lower battalion re-
torted "that he wouldn't have time to double his fist before
Bob would put his head where his feet ought to be; and
that, by the time he hit the ground, the meat would fly
off his face so quick that people would think it was shook
off by the fall." These disputes often led to the *argumen-
tum ad hominem,* but with such equality of success on
both sides as to leave the main question just where they
found it. They usually ended, however, in the common way
—with a bet; and many a quart of old Jamaica (whiskey
had not then supplanted rum) was staked upon the issue.
Still, greatly to the annoyance of the curious, Billy and
Bob continued to be good friends.

Now, there happened to reside in the county just alluded to a little fellow by the name of Ransy Sniffle; a
sprout of Richmond, who, in his earlier days, had fed copi-
ously upon red clay and blackberries. This diet had given
to Ransy a complexion that a corpse would have disdained
to own, and an abdominal rotundity that was quite unpre-
possessing. Long spells of fever and ague, too, in Ransy's
youth, had conspired with clay and blackberries to throw
him quite out of the order of nature. His shoulders were
fleshless and elevated; his head large and flat; his neck slim
and translucent; and his arms, hands, fingers, and feet were
lengthened out of all proportion to the rest of his frame.
His joints were large and his limbs small; and as for flesh,
he could not, with propriety, be said to have any. Those
parts which nature usually supplies with the most of this
article—the calves of the legs, for example—presented in
him the appearance of so many well-drawn blisters. His
height was just five feet nothing; and his average weight
in blackberry season, ninety-five. I have been thus particular in describing him, for the purpose of showing what a
great matter a little fire sometimes kindleth. There was
nothing on this earth which delighted Ransy so much as a
fight. He never seemed fairly alive except when he was wit-
nessing, fomenting, or talking about a fight. Then, indeed,
his deep-sunken gray eyes assumed something of a living
fire, and his tongue acquired a volubility that bordered

upon eloquence. Ransy had been kept for more than a year in the most torturing suspense as to the comparative manhood of Billy Stallings and Bob Durham. He had resorted to all his usual expedients to bring them in collision, and had entirely failed. He had faithfully reported to Bob all that had been said by the people in the upper battalion "agin him," and "he was sure Billy Stallings started it. He heard Billy say himself to Jim Brown that he could whip him, *or any other man in his battalion*"; and this he told to Bob, adding, "Dod darn his soul, if he was a little bigger, if he'd let any man *put upon* his battalion in such a way!" Bob replied, "If he (Stallings) thought so, he'd better come and try it." This Ransy carried to Billy, and delivered it with a spirit becoming his own dignity and the character of his battalion, and with a coloring well calculated to give it effect. These and many other schemes which Ransy laid for the gratification of his curiosity entirely failed of their object. Billy and Bob continued friends, and Ransy began to lapse into the most tantalizing and hopeless despair, when a circumstance occurred which led to a settlement of the long-disputed question.

It is said that a hundred game-cocks will live in perfect harmony together if you do not put a hen with them; and so it would have been with Billy and Bob had there been no women in the world. But there were women in the world, and from them each of our heroes had taken to himself a wife. The good ladies were no strangers to the prowess of their husbands, and, strange as it may seem, they presumed a little upon it.

The two battalions had met at the court-house upon a regimental parade. The two champions were there, and their wives had accompanied them. Neither knew the other's lady, nor were the ladies known to each other. The exercises of the day were just over, when Mrs. Stallings and Mrs. Durham stepped simultaneously into the store of Zephaniah Atwater, from "down East."

"Have you any Turkey red?" said Mrs. S.

"Have you any curtain calico?" said Mrs. D. at the same moment.

"Yes, ladies," said Mr. Atwater, "I have both."

"Then help me first," said Mrs. D., "for I'm in a hurry."

"I'm in as great a hurry as she is," said Mrs. S., "and I'll thank you to help me first."

"And pray, who are you, madam?" continued the other.

"Your betters, madam," was the reply.

At this moment Billy Stallings stepped in. "Come," said he, "Nancy, let's be going; it's getting late."

"I'd 'a' been gone half an hour ago," she replied, "if it hadn't 'a' been for that impudent hussy."

"Who do you call an impudent hussy, you nasty, good-for-nothing, snaggle-toothed gaub of fat, you?" returned Mrs. D.

"Look here, woman," said Billy. "Have you got a husband here? If you have, I'll lick him till he learns to teach you better manners, you *sassy* heifer you!"

At this moment something was seen to rush out of the store as if ten thousand hornets were stinging it, crying, "Take care—let me go—don't hold me—where's Bob Durham?" It was Ransy Sniffle, who had been listening in breathless delight to all that had passed.

"Yonder's Bob, setting on the court-house steps," cried one. "What's the matter?"

"Don't talk to me!" said Ransy. "Bob Durham, you'd better go long yonder and take care of your wife. They're playing h—l with her there in Zeph Atwater's store. Dod etarnally darn my soul, if any man was to talk to my wife as Bill Stallions is talking to yours, if I wouldn't drive blue blazes through him in less than no time!"

Bob sprang to the store in a minute, followed by a hundred friends; for a bully of a county never wants friends.

"Bill Stallions," said Bob, as he entered, "what have you been saying to my wife?"

"Is that your wife?" inquired Billy, obviously much surprised and a little disconcerted.

"Yes, she is; and no man shall abuse her, I don't care who he is."

"Well," rejoined Billy, "it ain't worth while to go over it;

I've said enough for a fight, and if you'll step out we'll set-tle it."

"Billy," said Bob, "are you for a fair fight?"

"I am," said Billy. "I've heard much of your manhood, and I believe I'm a better man than you are. If you will go into a ring with me we can soon settle the dispute."

"Choose your friends," said Bob; "make your ring, and I'll be in with mine as soon as you will!"

They both stepped out, and began to strip very deliber-ately, each battalion gathering round its champion, except Ransy, who kept himself busy in a most honest endeavor to hear and see all that transpired in both groups at the same time. He ran from one to the other in quick succession; peeped here and listened there; talked to this one, then to that one, and then to himself; squatted under one's legs and another's arms; and, in the short interval between stripping and stepping into the ring, managed to get him-self trod on by half of both battalions. But Ransy was not the only one interested upon this occasion; the most in-tense interest prevailed everywhere. Many were the con-jectures, doubts, oaths, and imprecations uttered while the parties were preparing for the combat. All the knowing ones were consulted as to the issue, and they all agreed, to a man, in one of two opinions—either that Bob would flog Billy, or Billy would flog Bob. We must be permitted, how-ever, to dwell for a moment upon the opinion of Squire Thomas Loggins, a man who, it was said, had never failed to predict the issue of a fight in all his life. Indeed, so un-erring had he always proved in this regard that it would have been counted the most obstinate infidelity to doubt for a moment after he had delivered himself. Squire Loggins was a man who said but little, but that little was always delivered with the most imposing solemnity of look and cadence. He always wore the aspect of profound thought, and you could not look at him without coming to the con-clusion that he was elaborating truth from its most intricate combinations.

"Uncle Tommy," said Sam Reynolds, "you can tell us all about it if you will; how will the fight go?"

The question immediately drew an anxious group around the squire. He raised his teeth slowly from the head of his walking-cane, on which they had been resting, pressed his lips closely and thoughtfully together, threw down his eyebrows, dropped his chin, raised his eyes to an angle of twenty-three degrees, paused about half a minute, and replied, "Sammy, watch Robert Durham close in the beginning of the fight, take care of William Stallions in the middle of it, and see who has the wind at the end." As he uttered the last sentence he looked slyly at Bob's friends and winked very significantly; whereupon they rushed, with one accord, to tell Bob what Uncle Tommy had said. As they retired, the squire turned to Billy's friends and said, with a smile, "Them boys think I mean that Bob will ship."

Here the other party kindled into joy, and hastened to inform Billy how Bob's friends had deceived themselves as to Uncle Tommy's opinion. In the meantime the principals and seconds were busily employed in preparing themselves for combat. The plan of attack and defence, the manner of improving the various turns of conflict, "the best mode of saving wind," etc., etc., were all discussed and settled. At length Billy announced himself ready, and his crowd were seen moving to the centre of the Court-house Square, he and his five seconds in the rear. At the same time Bob's party moved to the same point, and in the same order. The ring was now formed, and for a moment the silence of death reigned through both battalions. It was soon interrupted, however, by the cry of "Clear the way!" from Billy's seconds, when the ring opened in the centre of the upper battalion (for the order of march had arranged the centre of the two battalions on opposite sides of the circle), and Billy stepped into the ring from the east, followed by his friends. He was stripped to the trousers, and exhibited an arm, breast, and shoulders of the most tremendous portent. His step was firm, daring, and martial; and as he bore his fine form a little in advance of his friends an involuntary burst of triumph broke from his side of the ring, and at the same moment an uncontrollable thrill of awe ran along the whole curve of the lower battalion.

"Look at him!" was heard from his friends; "just look at him!"

"Ben, how much you ask to stand before that man two seconds?"

"Pshaw, don't talk about it! Just thinkin' about it's broke three o' my ribs a'ready!"

"What's Bob Durham going to do when Billy lets that arm loose upon him?"

"God bless your soul, he'll think thunder and lightning a mint-julep to it!"

"Oh, look here, men, go take Bill Stallions out o' that ring, and bring in Phil Johnson's stud-horse, so that Durham may have some chance! I don't want to see the man killed right away."

These and many other like expressions, interspersed thickly with oaths of the modern coinage, were coming from all points of the upper battalion, while Bob was adjusting the girth of his pantaloons, which walking had discovered not to be exactly right. It was just fixed to his mind, his foes becoming a little noisy, and his friends a little uneasy at his delay, when Billy called out, with a smile of some meaning, "Where's the bully of the lower battalion? I'm getting tired of waiting."

"Here he is!" said Bob, lighting as it seemed from the clouds into the ring, for he had actually bounded clear of the head of Ransy Sniffle into the circle. His descent was quite as imposing as Billy's entry, and excited the same feelings, but in opposite bosoms.

Voices of exultation now rose on his side.

"Where did he come from?"

"Why," said one of his seconds (all having just entered), "we were girting him up, about a hundred yards out yonder, when he heard Billy ask for the bully, and he fetched a leap over the court-house and went out of sight; but I told them to come on, they'd find him here."

Here the lower battalion burst into a peal of laughter, mingled with a look of admiration which seemed to denote their entire belief of what they had heard.

"Boys, widen the ring, so as to give him room to jump."

"Oh, my little flying wild-cat, hold him if you can! and, when you get him fast, hold lightning next."

"Ned, what do you think he's made of?"

"Steel springs and chicken-hawk, God bless you!"

"Gentlemen," said one of Bob's seconds, "I understand it is to be a fair fight—catch as catch can, rough and tumble; no man touch till one or the other halloos."

"That's the rule," was the reply from the other side.

"Are you ready?"

"We are ready."

"Then blaze away, my game-cocks!"

At the word, Bob dashed at his antagonist at full speed, and Bill squared himself to receive him with one of his most fatal blows. Making his calculation from Bob's velocity of the time when he would come within striking distance, he let drive with tremendous force. But Bob's onset was obviously planned to avoid this blow; for, contrary to all expectations, he stopped short just out of arm's reach, and before Billy could recover his balance Bob had him "all under-hold." The next second, sure enough, "found Billy's head where his feet ought to be." How it was done no one could tell; but, as if by supernatural power, both Billy's feet were thrown full half his own height in the air, and he came down with a force that seemed to shake the earth. As he struck the ground, commingled shouts, screams, and yells burst from the lower battalion, loud enough to be heard for miles. "Hurrah, my little hornet!" "Save him!" "Feed him!" "Give him the Durham physic till his stomach turns!" Billy was no sooner down than Bob was on him, and lending him awful blows about the face and breast. Billy made two efforts to rise by main strength, but failed. "Lord bless you, man, don't try to get up! *Lay* still and take it! You *bleege* to have it!"

Billy now turned his face suddenly to the ground, and rose upon his hands and knees. Bob jerked up both his hands and threw him on his face. He again recovered his late position, of which Bob endeavored to deprive him as before; but, missing one arm, he failed, and Billy rose. But he had scarcely resumed his feet before they flew up as

before, and he came agin to the ground. "No fight, gentlemen!" cried Bob's friends; "the man can't stand up! Bounc-
ing feet are bad things to fight in." His fall, however, was
this time comparatively light; for, having thrown his right
arm round Bob's neck, he carried his head down with him.
This grasp, which was obstinately maintained, prevented
Bob from getting on him, and they lay head to head, seeming, for a time, to do nothing. Presently they rose, as if
by mutual consent; and as they rose a shout burst from
both battalions. "Oh, my lark!" cried the east, "has he foxed
you? Do you begin to feel him! He's only beginning to fight;
he ain't got warm yet."

"Look yonder!" cried the west. "Didn't I tell you so? He
hit the ground so hard it jarred his nose off. Now ain't he a
pretty man as he stands? He shall have my sister Sal, just
for his pretty looks. I want to get in the breed of them
sort o' men, to drive ugly out of my kinfolks."

I looked, and saw that Bob had entirely lost his left ear
and a large piece from his left cheek. His right eye was a
little discolored, and the blood flowed profusely from his
wounds.

Bill presented a hideous spectacle. About a third of his
nose, at the lower extremity, was bit off, and his face was
so swelled and bruised that it was difficult to discover in it
anything of the human visage, much more the fine features
which he carried into the ring.

They were up only long enough for me to make the fore-
going discoveries, when down they went again, precisely
as before. They no sooner touched the ground than Bill relinquished his hold upon Bob's neck. In this he seemed to
all to have forfeited the only advantage which put him
upon an equality with his adversary. But the movement
was soon explained. Bill wanted this arm for other purposes
than defence; and he had made arrangements whereby he
knew that he could make it answer these purposes; for
when they rose again he had the middle finger of Bob's
left hand in his mouth. He was now secure from Bob's
annoying trips; and he began to lend his adversary tremendous blows, every one of which was hailed by a shout

from his friends: "Bullets!" "*Hoss*-kicking!" "Thunder!"
"That'll do for his face; now feel his short ribs, Billy!"

I now considered the contest settled. I deemed it impossible for any human being to withstand for five seconds the loss of blood which issued from Bob's ear, cheek, nose, and finger, accompanied with such blows as he was receiving. Still he maintained the conflict, and gave blow for blow with considerable effect. But the blows of each became slower and weaker after the first three or four; and it became obvious that Bill wanted the room which Bob's finger occupied for breathing. He would therefore, probably, in a short time, have let it go, had not Bob anticipated his politeness by jerking away his hand and making him a present of the finger. He now seized Bill again, and brought him to his knees, but he recovered. A third effort, however, brought him down, and Bob on top of him. These efforts seemed to exhaust the little remaining strength of both; and they lay, Bill undermost and Bob across his breast, motionless and panting for breath. After a short pause Bob gathered his hand full of dirt and sand and was in the act of grinding it in his adversary's eyes when Bill cried, "Enough!" Language cannot describe the scene that followed—the shouts, oaths, frantic gestures, taunts, replies, and little fights—and therefore I shall not attempt it. The champions were borne off by their seconds and washed; when many a bleeding wound and ugly bruise was discovered on each which no eye had seen before.

Many had gathered round Bob, and were in various ways congratulating and applauding him, when a voice from the centre of the circle cried out, "Boys, hush, and listen to me!" It proceeded from Squire Loggins, who had made his way to Bob's side, and gathered his face up into one of its most flattering and intelligible expressions. All were obedient to the squire's command. "Gentlemen," continued he, with a most knowing smile, "is—Sammy Reynolds—in—this—company—of—gentlemen?"

"Yes," said Sam, "here I am."

"Sammy," said the squire, winking to the company and drawing the head of his cane to his mouth with an arch smile as he closed, "I—wish—you—to tell—Cousin—Bobby—and—these—gentlemen here present—what—your—Uncle—Tommy—said—before—the—fight—began?"

"Oh, get away, Uncle Tom," said Sam, smiling (the squire winked), "you don't know nothing about *fighting*." (The squire winked again.) "All you know about it is how it'll begin, how it'll go on, how it'll end; that's all. Cousin Bob, when you are going to fight again, just go to the old man, and let him tell you all about it. If he can't, don't ask nobody else nothing about it, I tell you."

The squire's foresight was complimented in many ways by the bystanders; and he retired, advising "the boys to be at peace, as fighting was a bad business."

Durham and Stallings kept their beds for several weeks, and did not meet again for two months. When they met, Billy stepped up to Bob and offered his hand, saying, "Bobby, you've *licked* me a fair fight; but you wouldn't have done it if I hadn't been in the wrong. I oughtn't to have treated your wife as I did; and I felt so through the whole fight; and it sort o' cowed me."

"Well, Billy," said Bob, "let's be friends. Once in the fight, when you had my finger in your mouth, and was pealing me in the face and breast, I was going to halloo; but I thought of Betsy, and knew the house would be too hot for me if I got whipped when fighting for her, after always whipping when I fought for myself."

"Now that's what I always love to see," said a bystander. "It's true I brought about the fight, but I wouldn't have done it if it hadn't 'a' been on account of *Miss* (Mrs.) Durham. But dod etarnally darn my soul if I ever could stand by and see any woman put upon, much less *Miss* Durham! If Bobby hadn't been there I'd 'a' took it up myself, be darned if I wouldn't, even if I'd 'a' got whipped for it! But we're all friends now." The reader need hardly be told that this was Ransy Sniffle.

Thanks to the Christian religion, to schools, colleges, and benevolent associations, such scenes of barbarism and cruelty as that which I have been just describing are now of rare occurrence, though they may still be occasionally met with in some of the new counties. Wherever they prevail, they are a disgrace to that community. The peace-officers who countenance them deserve a place in the Penitentiary.

The Horse-Swap

During the session of the Supreme Court in the village of ——, about three weeks ago, when a number of people were collected in the principal street of the village, I observed a young man riding up and down the street, as I supposed, in a violent passion. He galloped this way, then that, and then the other; spurred his horse to one group of citizens, then to another; then dashed off at half-speed, as if fleeing from danger; and, suddenly checking his horse, returned first in a pace, then in a trot, and then in a canter. While he was performing these various evolutions he cursed, swore, whooped, screamed, and tossed himself in every attitude which man could assume on horseback. In short, he cavorted most magnanimously (a term which, in our tongue, expresses all that I have described, and a little more), and seemed to be setting all creation at defiance. As I like to see all that is passing, I determined to take a position a little nearer to him, and to ascertain, if possible, what it was that affected him so sensibly. Accordingly I approached a crowd before which he had stopped for a moment, and examined it with the strictest scrutiny. But I could see nothing in it that seemed to have anything to do with the cavorter. Every man appeared to be in good humor, and all minding their own business. Not one so much as noticed the principal figure. Still he went on. After a semicolon pause, which my appearance seemed to produce (for he eyed me closely as I approached), he fetched a whoop, and swore that "he could out-swap any live man, woman, or child that ever walked these hills, or that ever straddled horseflesh since the days of old daddy Adam."

"Stranger," said he to me, "did you ever see the *Yellow Blossom* from Jasper?"

"No," said I, "but I have often heard of him."

"I'm the boy," continued he; "perhaps a *leetle*, jist a *leetle* of the best man at a horse-swap that ever trod shoe-leather."

I began to feel my situation a little awkward, when I was relieved by a man somewhat advanced in years, who stepped up and began to survey the Yellow Blossom's horse with much apparent interest. This drew the rider's attention, and he turned the conversation from me to the stranger.

"Well, my old coon," said he, "do you want to swap *hosses?*"

"Why, I don't know," replied the stranger; "I believe I've got a beast I'd trade with you for that one, if you like him."

"Well, fetch up your nag, my old cock; you're jist the lark I wanted to get hold of. I am perhaps a *leetle*, jist a *leetle*, of the best man at a horse-swap that ever stole *cracklins* out of his mammy's fat gourd. Where's your *hoss?*"

"I'll bring him presently; but I want to examine your horse a little."

"Oh, look at him," said the Blossom, alighting and hitting him a cut—"look at him! He's the best piece of *hoss*-flesh in the thirteen united univarsal worlds. There's no sort o' mistake in little Bullet. He can pick up miles on his feet, and fling 'em behind him as fast as the next man's *hoss*, I don't care where he comes from. And he can keep at it as long as the sun can shine without resting."

During this harangue little Bullet looked as if he understood it all, believed it, and was ready at any moment to verify it. He was a horse of goodly countenance, rather expressive of vigilance than fire; though an unnatural appearance of fierceness was thrown into it by the loss of his ears, which had been cropped pretty close to his head. Nature had done but little for Bullet's head and neck; but he managed, in a great measure, to hide their defects by bowing perpetually. He had obviously suffered severely for corn; but if his ribs and hip-bones had not disclosed the fact, *he*

never would have done it; for he was in all respects as
cheerful and happy as if he commanded all the corn-cribs
and fodder-stacks in Georgia. His height was about twelve
hands; but as his shape partook somewhat of that of the
giraffe, his haunches stood much lower. They were short,
strait, peaked, and concave. Bullet's tail, however, made
amends for all his defects. All that the artist could do to
beautify it had been done; and all that horse could do to
compliment the artist, Bullet did. His tail was nicked in
superior style, and exhibited the line of beauty in so many
directions that it could not fail to hit the most fastidious
taste in some of them. From the root it dropped into a
graceful festoon, then rose in a handsome curve, then resumed its first direction, and then mounted suddenly upward like a cypress knee to a perpendicular of about two
and a half inches. The whole had a careless and bewitching inclination to the right. Bullet obviously knew where
his beauty lay, and took all occasions to display it to the
best advantage. If a stick cracked, or if any one moved suddenly about him, or coughed, or hawked, or spoke a little
louder than common, up went Bullet's tail like lightning;
and if the *going up* did not please, the *coming down* must
of necessity, for it was as different from the other movement
as was its direction. The first was a bold and rapid flight
upward, usually at an angle of forty-five degrees. In this
position he kept his interesting appendage until he satisfied
himself that nothing in particular was to be done; when he
commenced dropping it by half inches, in second beats,
then in triple time, then faster and shorter, and faster and
shorter still, until it finally died away imperceptibly into
its natural position. If I might compare sights to sounds, I
should say its *settling* was more like the note of a locust
than anything else in nature.

Either from native sprightliness of disposition, from uncontrollable activity, or from an unconquerable habit of removing flies by the stamping of the feet, Bullet never stood
still, but always kept up a gentle fly-scaring movement of
his limbs, which was peculiarly interesting.

"I tell you, man," proceeded the Yellow Blossom, "he's

the best live hoss that ever trod the grit of Georgia. Bob Smart knows the hoss. Come here, Bob, and mount this hoss, and show Bullet's motions." Here Bullet bristled up, and looked as if he had been hunting for Bob all day long, and had just found him. Bob sprang on his back. "Boooo-oo-ool!" said Bob, with a fluttering noise of the lips, and away went Bullet as if in a quarter race, with all his beauties spread in handsome style.

"Now fetch him back," said Blossom. Bullet turned and came in pretty much as he went out.

"Now trot him by." Bullet reduced his tail to *customary*, sidled to the right and left airily, and exhibited at least three varieties of trot in the short space of fifty yards.

"Make him pace!" Bob commenced twitching the bridle and kicking at the same time. These inconsistent movements obviously (and most naturally) disconcerted Bullet; for it was impossible for him to learn from them whether he was to proceed or stand still. He started to trot, and was told that wouldn't do. He attempted a canter, and was checked again. He stopped, and was urged to go on. Bullet now rushed into the wide field of experiment, and struck out a gait of his own that completely turned the tables upon his rider, and certainly deserved a patent. It seemed to have derived its elements from the jig, the minuet, and the cotillion. If it was not a pace, it certainly had pace in it, and no man would venture to call it anything else; so it passed off to the satisfaction of the owner.

"Walk him!" Bullet was now at home again, and he walked as if money were staked on him.

The stranger, whose name I afterwards learned was Peter Ketch, having examined Bullet to his heart's content, ordered his son Neddy to go and bring up Kit. Neddy soon appeared upon Kit, a well-formed sorrel of the middle size, and in good order. His *tout-ensemble* threw Bullet entirely in the shade, though a glance was sufficient to satisfy any one that Bullet had the decided advantage of him in point of intellect.

"Why, man," said Blossom, "do you bring such a hoss

as that to trade for Bullet? Oh, I see, you've no notion of trading!"

"Ride him off, Neddy!" said Peter. Kit put off at a handsome lope.

"Trot him back!" Kit came in at a long, sweeping trot, and stopped suddenly at the crowd.

"Well," said Blossom, "let me look at him; maybe he'll do to plough."

"Examine him," said Peter, taking hold the bridle close to the mouth; "he's nothing but a tacky. He ain't as *pretty* a horse as Bullet, I know, but he'll do. Start 'em together for a hundred and fifty *mile*, and if Kit ain't twenty mile ahead of him at the coming out, any man may take Kit for nothing. But he's a monstrous mean horse, gentlemen; any man may see that. He's the scariest horse, too, you ever saw. He won't do to hunt on, nohow. Stranger, will you let Neddy have your rifle to shoot off him? Lay the rifle between his ears, Neddy, and shoot at the blaze in that stump. Tell me when his head is high enough."

Ned fired and hit the blaze, and Kit did not move a hair's-breadth.

"Neddy, take a couple of sticks, and beat on that hogshead at Kit's tail."

Ned made a tremendous rattling, at which Bullet took fright, broke his bridle, and dashed off in grand style, and would have stopped all further negotiations by going home in disgust, had not a traveller arrested him and brought him back; but Kit did not move.

"I tell you, gentlemen," continued Peter, "he's the scariest horse you ever saw. He ain't as gentle as Bullet, but he won't do any harm if you watch him. Shall I put him in a cart, gig, or wagon for you, stranger? He'll cut the same capers there he does here. He's a monstrous mean horse."

During all this time Blossom was examining him with the nicest scrutiny. Having examined his frame and limbs, he now looked at his eyes.

"He's got a curious look out of his eyes," said Blossom.

"Oh yes, sir," said Peter, "just as blind as a bat. Blind

horses always have clear eyes. Make a motion at his eyes, if you please, sir."

Blossom did so, and Kit threw up his head rather as if something pricked him under the chin than as if fearing a blow. Blossom repeated the experiment, and Kit jerked back in considerable astonishment.

"Stone-blind, you see, gentlemen," proceeded Peter; "but he's just as good to travel of a dark night as if he had eyes."

"Blame my buttons," said Blossom, "if I like them eyes!"

"No," said Peter, "nor I neither. I'd rather have 'em made of diamonds; but they'll do—if they don't show as much white as Bullet's."

"Well," said Blossom, "make a pass at me."

"No," said Peter, "you made the banter, now make your pass."

"Well, I'm never afraid to price my hosses. You must give me twenty-five dollars boot."

"Oh, certainly; say fifty, and my saddle and bridle in. Here, Neddy, my son, take away daddy's horse."

"Well," said Blossom, "I've made my pass, now you make yours."

"I'm for short talk in a horse-swap, and therefore always tell a gentleman at once what I mean to do. You must give me ten dollars."

Blossom swore absolutely, roundly, and profanely that he never would give boot.

"Well," said Peter, "I didn't care about trading; but you cut such high shines that I thought I'd like to back you out, and I've done it. Gentlemen, you see I've brought him to a back."

"Come, old man," said Blossom, "I've been joking with you. I begin to think you do want to trade; therefore, give me five dollars and take Bullet. I'd rather lose ten dollars any time than not make a trade, though I hate to fling away a good hoss."

"Well," said Peter, "I'll be as clever as you are. Just put the five dollars on Bullet's back, and hand him over; it's a trade."

Blossom swore again, as roundly as before, that he would not give boot; and, said he, "Bullet wouldn't hold five dollars on his back, nohow. But, as I bantered you, if you say an even swap, here's at you."

"I told you," said Peter, "I'd be as clever as you; therefore, here goes two dollars more, just for trade sake. Give me three dollars, and it's a bargain."

Blossom repeated his former assertion; and here the parties stood for a long time, and the bystanders (for many were now collected) began to taunt both parties. After some time, however, it was pretty unanimously decided that the old man had backed Blossom out.

At length Blossom swore he "never should be backed out for three dollars after bantering a man"; and, accordingly, they closed the trade.

"Now," said Blossom, as he handed Peter the three dollars, "I'm a man that, when he makes a bad trade, makes the most of it until he can make a better. I'm for no rues and after-claps."

"That's just my way," said Peter; "I never goes to law to mend my bargains."

"Ah, you're the kind of boy I love to trade with. Here's your hoss, old man. Take the saddle and bridle off him, and I'll strip yours; but lift up the blanket easy from Bullet's back, for he's a mighty tender-backed hoss."

The old man removed the saddle, but the blanket stuck fast. He attempted to raise it, and Bullet bowed himself, switched his tail, danced a little, and gave signs of biting.

"Don't hurt him, old man," said Blossom, archly; "take it off easy. I am, perhaps, a leetle of the best man at a horse-swap that ever catched a coon."

Peter continued to pull at the blanket more and more roughly, and Bullet became more and more *cavortish*, insomuch that, when the blanket came off, he had reached the *kicking* point in good earnest.

The removal of the blanket disclosed a sore on Bullet's back that seemed to have defied all medical skill. It measured six full inches in length and four in breadth, and had as many features as Bullet had motions. My heart sickened at the sight; and I felt that the brute who had been riding him in that situation deserved the halter.

The prevailing feeling, however, was that of mirth. The

laugh became loud and general at the old man's expense, and rustic witticisms were liberally bestowed upon him and his late purchase. These Blossom continued to provoke by various remarks. He asked the old man "if he thought Bullet would let five dollars lie on his back." He declared most seriously that he had owned that horse three months, and had never discovered before that he had a sore back, "or he never should have thought of trading him," etc., etc.

The old man bore it all with the most philosophic composure. He evinced no astonishment at his late discovery, and made no replies. But his son Neddy had not disciplined his feelings quite so well. His eyes opened wider and wider from the first to the last pull of the blanket, and when the whole sore burst upon his view, astonishment and fright seemed to contend for the mastery of his countenance. As the blanket disappeared, he stuck his hands in his breeches pockets, heaved a deep sigh, and lapsed into a profound reverie, from which he was only roused by the cuts at his father. He bore them as long as he could; and, when he could contain himself no longer, he began, with a certain wildness of expression which gave a peculiar interest to what he uttered: "His back's mighty bad off; but dod drot my soul if he's put it to daddy as bad as he thinks he has, for old Kit's both blind and *deef*, I'll be dod drot if he ein't!"

"The devil he is!" said Blossom.

"Yes, dod drot my soul if he ein't!" You walk him, and see if he ein't. His eyes don't look like it; but he's *jist as leve go agin the* house with you, or in a ditch, as anyhow. Now you go try him." The laugh was now turned on Blossom, and many rushed to test the fidelity of the little boy's report. A few experiments established its truth beyond controversy.

"Neddy," said the old man, "you oughtn't to try and make people discontented with their things. Stranger, don't mind what the little boy says. If you can only get Kit rid of them little failings you'll find him all sorts of a horse. You are a *leetle* the best man at a horse-swap that ever I got hold of but don't fool away Kit. Come, Neddy, my son, let's be moving; the stranger seems to be getting snappish."

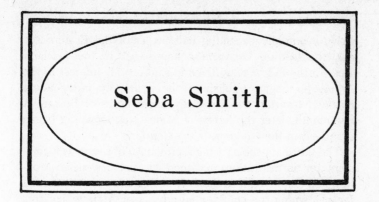

Seba Smith

A log cabin in a little town his father helped to found "away down East in the state of Maine" was the birthplace of Seba Smith. Like Andrew Jackson, to whom he would gaily dedicate his first book, Smith had a meager schooling; throughout most of his boyhood he was variously employed as a farm hand, a grocery boy, and a helper in a foundry. Yet by the time he was twenty-three he had managed to learn enough Greek and Latin to pass the entrance requirements for Bowdoin College and was admitted to the class of 1818.

In Horatio Bridge's *Personal Recollections of Hawthorne*, Bowdoin in its early days is described as being divided into two camps, the Peucinian and the Athenean, both of them literary societies. To the former belonged the professors and the more serious students (including Henry Wadsworth Longfellow); the latter attracted the more unruly undergraduates (including Nathaniel Hawthorne). That Seba Smith chose the Peucinian is only one indication of the conservatism that marked him all his life, a conservatism that sprang out of his deep attachment to the old, sometimes bizarre ways of the country and small-town people in his native state.

After graduating first in his class Smith went to Portland to teach in a private school, then drifted into newspaper work, eventually becoming half owner of the *Eastern Argus*, the leading Democratic newspaper in the Portland area. In the fall of 1829, having sold out his interest in the *Argus*, he began publishing the politically independent *Portland Courier*, the first daily paper north of Boston. A few months later the letters of Major Jack Downing began to appear in the columns of the *Courier*.

The satiric device of using a provincial observer as a commentator on institutions and men was not new when Montesquieu employed it in the *Lettres Persanes;* and in making Jack Downing the confidential adviser of Andrew Jackson, Smith had both Sancho Panza and Gil Blas as examples of the comic potential of this situation. Yet there was an originality in Downing's letters: the down-East personality of the hero. Royall Tyler's characterization of Jonathan in *The Contrast* (1787) had been skillfully executed, but by 1830 the stage Yankee had long since degenerated into a burlesque. The farmers' almanacs had caught some of the Yankee's taciturnity, shrewdness, and sly, understated wit, but no other writer before Smith had been able to free himself so completely from the self-conscious quaintness that mars so much New England humor. Lowell's Hosea Biglow owes a good deal to Jack Downing, as does Haliburton's Sam Slick.

In addition to Smith's seminal contribution to the development of the figure of the Yankee, he demonstrated to later writers the diverse literary possibilities of New England country life. The Downing letters showed that the down-East dialect did not simply furnish the writer with an excuse to show how ludicrously he could misspell, but was the rich, regional language of a vividly individualistic people. Mrs. Stowe's *Oldtown Folks*, Sarah Orne Jewett's *Country of the Pointed Firs*, and Robert Frost's *North of Boston* contain more accomplished New England portraits than Smith was capable of, but they hang in the same regional gallery with his sketches of the inhabitants of Downingville.

While the character of Jack Downing made a wonderfully effective political interpreter, the major was at first as politically independent as the *Courier*. Even in the famous letter which satirized Andrew Jackson's acceptance of a Harvard honorary degree, a basic sympathy with the President is evident. In the middle 1830s, however, Smith came to fear Jackson's bold use of the executive power, and his letters became both more concerned with national affairs and more overtly anti-administration. The change in the nature of the letters was, however, scarcely noticed. For by 1834 or 1835 Smith's hero had become such an astoundingly popular character that Jack Downings had sprung up all over the country, and just as the Whigs had bribed Davy Crockett to become the conservative answer to Old Hickory, so a great many of the pseudo-Downings were simply mouthpieces for Whig propaganda.

The best of Smith's imitators was Charles Augustus Davis, a New York iron merchant with bookish friends, particularly among the Whiggish *Knickerbocker Magazine* set, and a certain literary talent for the light touch. Although not directly involved in politics, he was strongly interested in the Whig cause—in the diary of the New York businessman, Philip Hone, Davis is mentioned as being present at a dinner given for Daniel Webster by a small group of influential New York Whigs. Seeing the possibilities for political satire in the Downing letters, Davis calmly appropriated Smith's character, the one exquisite difference being that he signed his letters "J. Downing, Major." Almost from the beginning, Davis's Downing concentrated on Jackson's war with Nicholas Biddle on the bank issue, while Downingville was almost forgotten. Gifted with a keener sense of humor than Smith, Davis quickly achieved great popularity. But like all the other imitations, his chief character was a stage Yankee—a New York gentleman's idea of the comic down-Easter. If his hero made brighter, sharper remarks than Smith's, he lacked the tangy Maine flavor of the original Major Jack Downing.

In which Major Downing shakes hands for the President at Philadelphia, while on the grand tour down East.

To Uncle Joshua Downing, Post Master, up in Downingville, in the State of Maine. This to be sent by my old friend, the Editor of the Portland Courier, with *care and speed.*

Philadelphia, June 10, 1833.

DEAR UNCLE JOSHUA,—We are coming on full chisel. I've been trying, ever since we started, to get a chance to write a little to you; but when we've been on the road I couldn't catch my breath hardly long enough to write my name, we kept flying so fast; and when we made any stop, there was such a jam round us there wasn't elbow room enough for a miskeeter to turn round without knocking his wings off.

I'm most afraid now we shall get to Downingville before this letter does, so that we shall be likely to catch you all in the suds before you think of it. But I understand there is a *fast mail* goes on that way, and I mean to send it by that, so I'm in hopes you'll get it time enough to have the children's faces washed and their heads combed, and the gals get on their clean gowns. And if Sargent Joel *could* have time enough to call out my old Downingville Company and get their uniforms brushed up a little, and come down the road as fur as your new barn to meet us, there's nothing that would please the President better. As for the victuals, most any thing wont come amiss; we are as hungry as bears after travelling a hundred miles a day. A little fried pork and eggs, or a pot of baked beans and an Indian pudding would suit us much better than the soft stuff they give us here in these great cities.

The President wouldn't miss seeing you for any thing in

the world, and he will go to Downingville if he has legs and arms enough left when he goes to Portland to carry him there. But for fear any thing should happen that he shouldn't be able to come, you had better meet us in Portland, say about the 22nd, and then you can go up to Downingville with us, you know.

This travelling with the President is capital fun after all, if it wasn't so plaguy tiresome. We come into Baltimore on a Rail Road, and we flew over the ground like a harrycane. There isn't a horse in this country that could keep up with us, if he should go upon the clean clip. When we got to Baltimore, the streets were filled with folks as thick as the spruce trees down in your swamp. There we found Black Hawk, a little, old, dried up Indian king.—And I thought the folks looked at him and the prophet about as much as they did at me and the President. I gave the President a wink that this Indian fellow was taking the shine off of us a little, so we concluded we wouldn't have him in our company any more, and shall go on without him.

I cant stop to tell you in this letter how we got along to Philadelphy, though we had a pretty easy time some of the way in the steam-boats. And I cant stop to tell you of half of the fine things I have seen here. They took us up into a great hall this morning as big as a meeting-house, and then the folks begun to pour in by thousands to shake hands with the President; federalists and all, it made no difference. There was such a stream of 'em coming in that the hall was full in a few minutes, and it was so jammed up round the door that they couldn't get out again if they were to die. So they had to knock out some of the windows and go out t'other way.

The President shook hands with all his might an hour or two, till he got so tired he couldn't hardly stand it. I took hold and shook for him once in awhile to help him along, but at last he got so tired he had to lay down on a soft bench covered with cloth and shake as well as he could, and when he couldn't shake he'd nod to 'em as they come along. And at last he got so beat out, he couldn't only wrinkle his forward and wink. Then I kind of stood behind him and reached my arm round under his, and shook for him about a half an hour as tight as I could spring. Then we concluded it was best to adjourn for to-day."

And I've made out to get away up into the garret in the tavern long enough to write this letter. We shall be off tomorrow or next day for York, and if I can possibly get breathing time enough there, I shall write to you again.

Give my love to all the folks in Downingville, and believe me your loving neffu,

MAJOR JACK DOWNING

In which cousin Nabby describes the unutterable disappointment at Downingville because the President didn't come, and tells what a terrible pucker ant Keziah was in about it.

GREAT UPROAR IN DOWNINGVILLE

Letter from Major Downing's Cousin Nabby to the editor of the Portland Courier.

RESPECTABLE SIR:—As cousin Jack is always so mity budge in writing letters to you, and as he and the President has showed us a most provoking trick and run off like a stream of chalk back to Washington without coming here, after they had promised over and over again that they would come, and we had got all slicked up and our clean gownds on, and more good victuals cooked, than there ever was in all Downingville before, I say, Mr. Editor, I declare it's tu bad; we are all as mad as blazes about it, and I mean to write and tell you all about it, if I live, and if cousin Jack dont like it he may lump it, so there now.

Ye see cousin Jack writ to us that he and the President and some more gentlemen should be here the 4th of July, and we must spring to it and brush up and see how smart we could look and how many fine things we could show to the President. This was a Saturday before the 4th of July come a Thursday. The letter was to Uncle Joshua, the Post Master. Most all the folks in Downingville were at the Post Office waiting when the mail come in, for we expected to hear from Jack.

Uncle Joshua put on his spettacles and opened the mail and hauled out the papers and letters in a bunch. In a minute I see one to uncle Joshua with the President's name on the outside; so I knew it was from Jack, for the President always puts his name on Jack's letters. We all cried out to Uncle Joshua to open it and let us know what was in it. But he's such a provoking odd old man he wouldn't touch it till he got every one of the papers and letters sorted and put up in his arm chair, and took out his tobacker box and took a chaw of tobacker, and then he broke open the seal and sot and chawed and read to himself. We all stood tip-toe with our hearts in our mouths, and he must needs read it over to himself three times, chawing his old quid and once in awhile giving us a knowing wink, before he would tell us what was in it.—And he wouldn't tell us arter all, but says he, you must all be ready to put the best side out Thursday morning; there'll be business to attend to, such as Downingville never see before.

At that we all cut and run, and such a hubbub as we were in from that time till Thursday morning I guess you never see. Such a washing and scrubbing and making new clothes and mending old ones and baking and cooking. Every thing seemed to be in a clutter all over the neighborhood. Sargent Joel flew round like a ravin-distracted rooster. He called out his company every morning before sun-rise and marched 'em up and down the road three hours every day. He sent to the store and got a whole new set of buttons and had 'em sowed on to his regimental coat, and had a new piece of red put round the collar. And had his trowses washed and his boots greesed, and looked as though he might take the shine off of most any thing. But the greatest rumpus was at uncle Joshua's; for they said the President must stay there all night. And ant Keziah was in such a pucker to have every thing nice, I didn't know but she would fly off the handle.

She had every part of the house washed from garret to cellar, and the floors all sanded, and a bunch of green bushes put into all the fire places. And she baked three ovens full of dried punkin pies, besides a few dried huckleberry pies, and cake, and a great pot of pork and beans. But the worst trouble was to fix up the bed so as to look nice; for ant Keziah declared the President should have as good a night's lodging in her house as he had in New York or Boston. So she put on two feather beds on top the straw bed, and a bran new calico quilt that she had made the first summer after she was married and never put it on a bed before. And to make it look as nice as the New York beds, she took her red silk gown and ripped it up and made a blanket to spread over the top. And then she hung up some sheets all round the bed-room, and the gals brought in a whole handful of roses and pinks and pinned 'em up round as thick as flies in August.

After we got things pretty much fixed, uncle Joshua started off to meet cousin Jack and the President, and left Sargent Joel to put matters to rights, and told us we must all be ready and be paraded in the road by nine o'clock Thursday morning. Well Thursday morning come, and we all mustered as soon as it was daylight and dressed up. The children were all washed and had their clean aprons on and their heads combed and were put under the care of the schoolmarm to be paraded along with her scholers.

About eight o'clock all the village got together down the road as fur as uncle Joshua's new barn; and Sargent Joel told us how to stand, as he said, in militery order. He placed Bill Johnson and cousin Ephraim out a little ways in front with each of 'em a great long fowling piece with a smart charge in to fire a salute, and told 'em as soon as the President hove in sight to let drive, only be careful and pint their guns up so as not to hurt any body. Then come Sargent Joel and his company; and then come the schoolmarm and the children; and then come all the women and gals over sixteen with ant Keziah at their head; and then come all the men in town that owned horses riding on horseback; and all the boys that Sargent Joel didn't think was large enough to walk in the profession got up and sot on the fences along by the side of the road.

There we stood till about nine o'clock, when sure enough we saw somebody come riding out of the woods down the hill. The boys all screamed ready to split their throats hoorah for Jackson, and Bill Johnson fired off his gun. Cousin Ephraim, who aint so easy fluttered, held on to his and didn't fire, for he couldn't see any body but uncle Joshua on his old grey horse. Along came uncle Joshua on a slow trot, and we looked and looked, but couldn't see any body coming behind him.

Then they all begun to look at one another as wild as hawks and turn all manner of colors. When uncle Joshua got up so we could see him pretty plain he looked as cross as a thunder cloud. He rid up to Sargent Joel, and says he, you may all go home about your business, and put away your knick-nacks, for Jack and the President are half way to Washington by this time.

My stars! what a time there was then. I never see so many folks boiling over mad before. Bill Johnson threw his gun over into the field as much as ten rods, and hopped up and down and struck his fists together like all possessed. Sargent Joel marched back and forth across the road two or three times, growing redder and redder, till at last he drew out his sword and fetched a blow across a hemlock stump and snapped it off like a pipe stem. Ant Keziah fell down in a conniption fit; and it was an hour before we could bring her tu and get her into the house.—And when she come to go round the house and see the victuals she had cooked up, and go into the bed-room and see her gown all cut up, she went into conniption fits again and had 'em half the night. But she's better to day, and has gone to work to try to patch up her gown again.

I thought I would jest let you know about these things, and if you are a mind to send word on to cousin Jack and the President, I'm willing. You may tell 'em there aint five folks in Downingville that would hoorah for Jackson now, and I don't believe there's one that would vote for him unless 'tis uncle Joshua, and he wouldn't if he wasn't afraid of losing the post office.

But there, uncle Joshua has called to me and says he wont keep the mail open another minute for my letter, so I must prescribe myself your respected friend.

NABBY DOWNING

In Which Major Downing tells about going to Cambridge and making the President a Doctor of Laws.

On board the Steam-boat, going from Providence to York, July 2, 1833.

To my old friend, the Editor of the Portland Courier, in the Mariners' Church building, second story, eastern end, Fore street, away down east, in the State of Maine.

My dear Friend.—We are driving back again full chisel, as fast as we come on when we were on the Rail Road between Washington and Baltimore. And we've been drivin so fast on a round turn in all the places where we've been, and have had so much shaking hands and eating and one thing another to do, that I couldn't get time to write to you at half the places where I wanted to, so I thought I'd set down now, while the President's laid down to rest him awhile, and tell you something about Cambridge and Lowell. Ye see when we were at Boston they sent word to us to come out to Cambridge, for they wanted to make the President a Doctor of Laws. What upon arth a Doctor of Laws was, or why they wanted to make the President one, I couldn't think. So when we come to go up to bed I asked the Gineral about it. And says I, Gineral, what is it they want to do to you out to Cambridge? Says he they want to make a Doctor of Laws of me. Well, says I, but what good will that do? Why, says he, you know Major Downing, there's a pesky many of them are laws passed by Congress, that are rickety things. Some of 'em have very poor constitutions, and some of 'em haven't no constitutions at all. So that it is necessary to have somebody there to doctor 'em up a little, and not let 'em go out into the world where they would stan a chance to catch cold and be sick, without they had good constitutions to bear it. You know, says he, I have had to doctor the Laws considerable ever since I've been at Washington, although I wasn't a regular bred Doctor. And I made out so well about it, that these Cambridge folks think I better be made into a regular Doctor at once, and there'll be no grumbling and disputing about my practice. Says he, Major, what do you think of it? I told him I thought it was an excellent plan; and asked him if he didn't think they would be willing, bein I'd been round in the military business considerable for a year or two past, to make me a Doctor of War. He said he didn't know, but he thought it would be no harm to try 'em. But says he, Major, I feel a little kind of streaked about it after all; for they say they will go to talking to me in Latin, and although I studied it a little once, I don't know any more about it now than the man in the moon. And how I can get along in that case I don't know. I told him my way, when any body talked to me in a lingo that I didn't understand, was jest to say nothing, but look as knowing as any of 'em, and then they ginerally thought I knew a pesky sight more than any of 'em. At that the Gineral fetched me a slap on my shoulder, and haw hawed right out. Says he, Major Downing, you are the boy for me; I don't know how I should get along in this world if it wasn't for you.

So when we got ready we went right to Cambridge as bold as could be. And that are Cambridge is a real pretty place; it seems to me I should like to live in them Colleges as well as any place I've seen. We went into the Libry, and I guess I stared a little, for I didn't think before there was half so many books in the world. I should think there was

near about enough to fill a meetin house. I don't believe
they was ever all read or ever will be to all ages.

When we come to go in to be made Doctors of, there
was a terrible crowding round; but they give us a good
place, and then sure enough they did begin to talk in Latin
or some other gibberish; but whether they were talking to
the Gineral, or who 'twas, I couldn't tell. I guess the Gineral was a little puzzled. But he never said a word, only
once in a while bowed a little. And I spose he happened
sometimes to put in the bows in the wrong place, for I
could see some of the sassy students look up one side once
in a while, and snicker out of one corner of their mouths.
Howsomever the Gineral stood it out like a hero, and got
through very well. And when 'twas over, I stept up to Mr.
Quincy and asked him if he wouldn't be so good as to make
me a Doctor of War, and hinted to him a little about my
services down to Madawasca and among the nullifiers. At
that he made me a very polite bow, and says he, Major
Downing, we should be very happy to oblige you if we
could, but we never give any degrees of war here; all our
degrees are degrees of peace. So I find I shall have to prac-
tise war in the natural way, let nullification, or what will,
come. After 'twas all over we went to Mr. Quincy's and
had a capital dinner. And on the whole had about as good
a visit to Cambridge as most any where.

I meant to a told you considerable about Lowell, but
the steam-boat goes so fast, I shant have time to. We went
all over the Factories; and there! I wont try to say one
word about 'em, for I've been filled with such a wonder-
ment ever since, that my ideas are all as big as hay stacks,
and if I should try to get one of 'em out of my head, it
would tear it all to pieces. It beat all that ever I heard of
before, and the Gineral said it beat all that ever he heard
of. But what made the Gineral hold his head up and feel
more like a soldier, than he had before since he was at
New Orleans, was when we marched along the street by
them are five thousand gals, all dressed up and looking as
pretty as a million of butterflies. The Gineral marched along
as light as a boy, and seems to me I never see his eyes

shine so bright afore. After we got along about to the middle of 'em, he whispered to me, and says he, Major Downing, is your Cousin Nabby here among 'em; if she is, I must be introduced to her. I told him she was not; as they were expecting us to come to Downingville, she staid to home to help get ready. Well, says he, if any thing should happen that we can't go to Downingville, you must send for your Cousin Nabby and Uncle Joshua to come on to Washington to see me. I will bear all the expenses, if they will only come, says he; these northern gals are as much afore our southern and western gals as can be, and I've thought of your Cousin Nabby a great deal lately—he looked as though he was going to say something more, but Mr. Van Buren and the rest of 'em crowded along up so near that it broke off, and we had to go along.

I see we've got most to York, and shall have to go ashore in a few minutes, so I cant write any more now, but remain your sincere and loving friend,

MAJOR JACK DOWNING

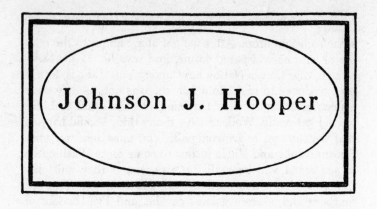

Johnson J. Hooper

Many theorists of humor have noted that in tragedy the audience tends to identify with one or more of the actors, whereas in comedy the audience is rather callously indifferent: a pratfall is funny only if you do not empathize with the victim. If, therefore, there is in the very nature of comedy a general connection between laughter and cruelty, it must also be said that nowhere is the connection more evident than in American humor. Efforts have been made to explain away this fact by assigning the coarseness and violence of our comic tradition to the grotesque taste of the frontiersman, now happily a thing of the past. But the sadism of the animated cartoons, in which laughter is evoked by the electrocution, flagellation, or mangling of animals dressed up as human beings, is proof enough that as a people we still retain our peculiar sense of fun; and the fact that the most important literary outlet for southwestern humor in the nineteenth century was a magazine published and sold in New York City suggests that the appetite for cruel comedy was never confined to the frontier.

The name of the magazine was the *Spirit of the Times,* a "Chronicle of the Turf, Agriculture, Field Sports, Literature and the Stage," as its subtitle grandiosely announced. Established in 1831, the magazine by the middle 1840s was selling more than forty thousand copies a week. The editor who achieved this huge circulation was William T. Porter, a native of Vermont, who had been brought up on large estates where he had acquired a lasting interest in horse racing, cockfighting, and other sports. As editor of the *Spirit*, Porter published original stories, but he also personally combed through the exchanges from newspapers all over the country for stories that he could reprint. In this way he gave encouragement and a national audience to writers who might otherwise have never achieved more than local fame, while at the same time he influenced the main development of American literature by bringing the best examples of regional humor to the attention of the urban literati.

The key role that Porter played in the growth of southwestern humor as a literary art is illustrated by the career of Johnson J. Hooper. In 1842 Hooper became the editor of a Whig newspaper called the *East Alabamian,* in Chambers County, Alabama. Seeking, like Longstreet, to vary the diet of his editorials, he put into the paper, in the summer of 1843, a funny story he had written. Porter apparently read not only such papers as the New Orleans *Delta,* the St. Louis *Reveille,* and the Louisville *Courier,* but the *East Alabamian* as well, for in September of 1843 the *Spirit* reprinted Hooper's story, with a prefatory note stating that "this Hooper is a clever man, and we must enlist him among the correspondents of the 'Spirit of the Times.' " Thus overnight Hooper left the ranks of purely local funnymen, of which there were hundreds, particularly in the South and West, to become a nationally read humorist. It was because of Porter's recognition of his talent that Hooper was encouraged to go on as a writer and eventually to create the remarkable Captain Simon Suggs of the Tallapoosa Volunteers, who with the single exception of Sut Lovingood is the most notable comic character to come out of southwestern humor before the Civil War.

Comic characters run to types, and the most popular characters of southwestern humor are the confidence man and the would-be military hero. Simon Suggs is the confidence man par excellence; his whole ethical system is summed up in his favorite aphorism, "It is good to be shifty in a new country." So memorable was Hooper's characterization that Joseph G. Baldwin named one of the con men who populate his *Flush Times of Alabama and Mississippi* Simon Suggs, Jr., and Twain paid Hooper the compliment of appropriating Simon's conning of the camp meeting for one of the episodes in *Huckleberry Finn*.

Simon is also the funniest of the would-be military heroes. *Georgia Scenes* had included a scene about a militia muster (the author was not Longstreet, but his friend Oliver Hillhouse Prince), which Poe praised and Thomas Hardy would pre-empt for his novel, *The Trumpet Major*, but which seems somewhat ordinary today. Longstreet's fellow Georgian and fellow editor, William T. Thompson, invented the humorous character, Major Jones, an officer of militia in a small Georgia town, whose ignorance and naïveté led him into a series of embarrassing scrapes and misunderstandings. But Major Jones is an obvious variation on Fielding's Partridge and his buffoonery quickly palls. What makes for the terrific comic energy of Simon Suggs is that Hooper was able to break free of existing literary models and build his comic type out of new American materials.

The distance that is discernible in Longstreet's *Georgia Scenes* between the superior author and his "low" subject is evident in Hooper's book as well. *Some Adventures of Simon Suggs* is cast in the form of a political campaign biography, and a comparison in the opening chapter of Andrew Jackson's face to the Devil's emphasizes the fact that the book is the creation of a Whig editor who regarded his satirization of a would-be military hero from the backwoods as a commentary on the Democratic party. Yet if Hooper looked down on the antics of Simon Suggs as a comic spectacle, he also identified with his protagonist in certain situations. The sexual license that so often flourished in the ecstatic atmosphere of the camp meeting and the displacement of the educated ministry by irresponsible demagogues were aspects of southern religion that appalled Hooper. Suggs may be an uncouth, unlettered, Jacksonian militarist, but when he exposes the gullibility, prurience, and hypocrisy of the camp meeting, Hooper is clearly sympathetic with his hero.

Simon Suggs Attends a Camp-Meeting

Captain Suggs found himself as poor at the conclusion of the Creek war as he had been at its commencement. Although no "arbitrary," "despotic," "corrupt," and "unprincipled" judge had fined him a thousand dollars for his proclamation of martial law at Fort Suggs, or the enforcement of its rules in the case of Mrs. Haycock; yet somehow—the thing is alike inexplicable to him and to us—the money which he had contrived, by various shifts, to obtain, melted away and was gone forever. To a man like the Captain, of intense domestic affections, this state of destitution was most distressing. "He could stand it himself—didn't care a d—n for it, no way," he observed, "but the old woman and the children; *that* bothered him!"

As he sat one day, ruminating upon the unpleasant condition of his "financial concerns," Mrs. Suggs informed him that "the sugar and coffee was nigh about out," and that there were not "a dozen j'ints and middlins, *all put together,* in the smoke-house." Suggs bounced up on the instant, exclaiming, "D—n it! *somebody* must suffer!" But whether this remark was intended to convey the idea that he and his family were about to experience the want of the necessaries of life; or that some other, and as yet unknown, individual should "suffer" to prevent that prospective exigency, must be left to the commentators, if perchance any of that—genious class of persons should hereafter see proper to write notes for this history. It is enough for us that we give all the facts in this connection, so that ignorance of the subsequent conduct of Captain Suggs may not lead to an erroneous judgment in respect to his words.

Having uttered the exclamation we have repeated—and

perhaps, hurriedly walked once or twice across the room —Captain Suggs drew on his famous old green-blanket overcoat, and ordered his horse, and within five minutes was on his way to a camp-meeting, then in full blast on Sandy Creek, twenty miles distant, where he hoped to find amusement, at least. When he arrived there, he found the hollow square of the encampment filled with people, listening to the mid-day sermon, and its dozen accompanying "exhortations." A half-dozen preachers were dispensing the word; the one in the pulpit, a meek-faced old man, of great simplicity and benevolence. His voice was weak and cracked, notwithstanding which, however, he contrived to make himself heard occasionally, above the din of the exhorting, the singing, and the shouting which were going on around him. The rest were walking to and fro (engaged in the other exercises we have indicated), among the "mourners" —a host of whom occupied the seat set apart for their especial use—or made personal appeals to the mere spectators. The excitement was intense. Men and women rolled about on the ground, or lay sobbing or shouting in promiscuous heaps. More than all, the negroes sang and screamed and prayed. Several, under the influence of what is technically called "the jerks," were plunging and pitching about with convulsive energy. The great object of all seemed to be, to see who could make the greatest noise—

"And each—for madness ruled the hour—
Would try his own expressive power."

"Bless my poor old soul!" screamed the preacher in the pulpit; "ef yonder aint a squad in that corner that we aint got one outen yet! It'll never do"—raising his voice—"you must come outen that! Brother Fant, fetch up that youngster in the blue coat! I see the Lord's a-workin' upon him! Fetch him along—glory—yes!—hold to him!"

"Keep the thing warm!" roared a sensual seeming man, of stout mould and florid countenance, who was exhorting among a bevy of young women, upon whom he was lavishing caresses. "Keep the thing warm, breethring!—come to the Lord, honey!" he added, as he vigorously hugged one of the damsels he sought to save.

"Oh, I've got him!" said another in exulting tones, as he led up a gawky youth among the mourners—"I've got him —he tried to git off, but—ha! Lord!"—shaking his head as much as to say, it took a smart fellow to escape him—"ha! Lord!"—and he wiped the perspiration from his face with one hand, and with the other, patted his neophyte on the shoulder—"he couldn't do it! No! Then he tried to argy wi' me—but bless the Lord!—he couldn't do that nother! Ha! Lord! I tuk him, fust in the Old Testament—bless the Lord! —and I argyed him all thro' Kings—then I throwed him into Proverbs,—and from that, here we had it up and down, kleer down to the New Testament, and then I begun to see it work him!—then we got into Matthy, and from Matthy right straight along to Acts; and *thar* I throwed him! Y-e-s—L-o-r-d!"—assuming the nasal twang and high pitch which are, in some parts, considered the perfection of rhetorical art—"Y-e-s—L-o-r-d! and h-e-r-e he is! Now g-i-t down thar," addressing the subject, "and s-e-e ef the L-o-r-d won't do somethin' f-o-r you!" Having thus deposited his charge among the mourners, he started out, summarily to convert another soul!

"Gl-o-ree!" yelled a huge, greasy negro woman, as in a fit of the jerks, she threw herself convulsively from her feet, and fell "like a thousand of brick," across a diminutive old man in a little round hat, who was speaking consolation to one of the mourners.

"Good Lord, have mercy!" ejaculated the little man earnestly and unaffectedly, as he strove to crawl from under the sable mass which was crushing him.

In another part of the square a dozen old women were singing. They were in a state of absolute ecstasy, as their shrill pipes gave forth.

> "I rode on the sky,
> Quite ondestified I,
> And the moon it was under my feet!"

Near these last, stood a delicate woman in that hysterical

condition in which the nerves are incontrollable, and which is vulgarly—and almost blasphemously—termed the "holy laugh." A hideous grin distorted her mouth, and was accompanied with a maniac's chuckle; while every muscle and nerve of her face twitched and jerked in horrible spasms.[1]

Amid all this confusion and excitement Suggs stood unmoved. He viewed the whole affair as a grand deception —a sort of "opposition line" running against his own, and looked on with a sort of professional jealousy. Sometimes he would mutter running comments upon what passed before him.

"Well now," said he, as he observed the full-faced brother who was "officiating" among the women, "that ere feller takes *my* eye!—thar he's been this half-hour, a-figurin amongst them galls, and's never said the fust word to nobody else. Wonder what's the reason these here preachers never hugs up the old ugly women? Never seed one do it in my life—the sperrit never moves 'em that way! It's nater tho'; and the women, *they* never flocks round one o' the old dried-up breethring—bet two to one old splinter-legs thar,"—nodding at one of the ministers—"won't git a chance to say turkey to a good-lookin gall to-day! Well! who blames 'em? Nater will be nater, all the world over; and I judge ef I was a preacher, I should save the purtiest souls fust, myself!"

While the Captain was in the middle of this conversation with himself, he caught the attention of the preacher in the pulpit, who inferring from an indescribable some-

---

[1] The reader is requested to bear in mind, that the scenes described in this story are not *now* to be witnessed. Eight or ten years ago, all classes of population of the Creek country were very different from what they now are. Of course no disrespect is intended to any denomination of Christians. We believe that camp meetings are not peculiar to any church, though most usual in the Methodist—a denomination whose respectability in Alabama is attested by the fact, that *very many* of its worthy clergymen and lay members, hold honourable and profitable offices in the gift of the state legislature; of which, indeed, almost a controlling portion are themselves Methodists.

thing about his appearance that he was a person of some consequence, immediately determined to add him at once to the church if it could be done; and to that end began a vigorous, direct personal attack.

"Breethring," he exclaimed, "I see yonder a man that's a sinner; I *know* he's a sinner! Thar he stands," pointing at Simon, "a missubble old crittur, with his head a-blos-somin for the grave! A few more short years, and d-o-w-n he'll go to perdition, lessen the Lord have mer-cy on him! Come up here, you old hoary-headed sinner, a-n-d git down upon your knees, a-n-d put up your cry for the Lord to snatch you from the bottomless pit! You're ripe for the devil—you're b-o-u-n-d for hell, and the Lord only knows what'll become on you!"

"D—n it," thought Suggs, "ef I only had you down in the krick swamp for a minit or so, *I'd* show you who's *old!* *I'd* alter your tune *mighty* sudden, you sassy, 'saitful old rascal!" But he judiciously held his tongue and gave no ut-terance to the thought.

The attention of many having been directed to the Cap-tain by the preacher's remarks, he was soon surrounded by numerous well-meaning, and doubtless very pious persons, each one of whom seemed bent on the application of his own particular recipe for the salvation of souls. For a long time the Captain stood silent, or answered the incessant stream of exhortations only with a sneer; but at length, his countenance began to give token of inward emotion. First his eye-lids twitched—then his upper lip quivered—next a transparent drop formed on one of his eye-lashes, and a similar one on the tip of his nose—and, at last, a sudden bursting of air from nose and mouth, told that Captain Suggs was overpowered by his emotions. At the moment of the explosion, he made a feint as if to rush from the crowd, but he was in experienced hands, who well knew that the battle was more than half won.

"Hold to him!" said one—"it's a-workin in him as strong as a Dick horse!"

"Pour it into him," said another, "it'll all come right directly!"

"That's the way I love to see 'em do," observed a third; "when you begin to draw the water from their eyes, taint gwine to be long afore you'll have 'em on their knees!"

And so they clung to the Captain manfully, and half dragged, half led him to the mourner's bench; by which he threw himself down, altogether unmanned, and bathed in tears. Great was the rejoicing of the brethren, as they sang, shouted, and prayed around him—for by this time it had come to be generally known that the "convicted" old man was Captain Simon Suggs, the very "chief of sinners" in all that region.

The Captain remained grovelling in the dust during the usual time, and gave vent to even more than the requisite number of sobs, and groans, and heart-piercing cries. At length, when the proper time had arrived, he bounced up, and with a face radiant with joy, commenced a series of vaultings and tumblings, which "laid in the shade" all previous performances of the sort at that camp-meeting. The brethren were in ecstasies at this demonstrative evidence of completion of the work; and whenever Suggs shouted "Gloree!" at the top of his lungs, every one of them shouted it back, until the woods rang with echoes.

The effervescence having partially subsided, Suggs was put upon his pins to relate his experience, which he did somewhat in this style—first brushing the tear-drops from his eyes, and giving the end of his nose a preparatory wring with his fingers, to free it of the superabundant moisture:

"Friends," he said, "it don't take long to curry a short horse, accordin' to the old sayin', and I'll give you the per-ticklers of the way I was 'brought to a knowledge'"—here the Captain wiped his eyes, brushed the tip of his nose and snuffled a little—"in less'n no time."

"Praise the Lord!" ejaculated a bystander.

"You see I come here full o' romancin' and devilment, and jist to make game of all the purceedins. Well, sure enough, I done so for some time, and was a-thinkin how I should play some trick——"

"Dear soul alive! *don't* he talk sweet!" cried an old lady in black silk—"Whar's John Dobbs? You Sukey!" screaming at a negro woman on the other side of the square—"ef you don't hunt up your mass John in a minute, and have him here to listen to this 'sperience, I'll tuck you up when I git home and give you a hundred and fifty lashes, madam!—see ef I don't! Blessed Lord!"—referring again to the Captain's relation—"ain't it a *precious* 'scource!"

"I was jist a-thinkin' how I should play some trick to turn it all into redecule, when they began to come round me and talk. Long at fust I didn't mind it, but arter a little that brother"—pointing to the reverend gentleman who had so successfully carried the unbeliever through the Old and New Testament, and who Simon was convinced was the "big dog of the tanyard"—"that brother spoke a word that struck me kleen to the heart, and run all over me, like fire in dry grass——"

"*I-I-I* can bring 'em!" cried the preacher alluded to, in a tone of exultation—"Lord thou knows ef thy servant can't stir 'em up, nobody else needn't try—but the glory aint mine! I'm a poor worrum of the dust," he added, with ill-managed affectation.

"And so from that I felt somethin' a-pullin' me inside——"

"Grace! grace! nothin' but grace!" exclaimed one; meaning that "grace" had been operating in the Captain's gastric region.

"And then," continued Suggs, "I wanted to git off, but they hilt me, and bimeby I felt so missuble, I had to go yonder"—pointing to the mourner's seat—"and when I lay down thar it got wuss and wuss, and 'peared like somethin' was a-mashin' down on my back——"

"That was his load o' sin," said one of the brethren—"never mind, it'll tumble off presently, see ef it don't!" and he shook his head professionally and knowingly.

"And it kept a-gittin heavier and heavier, ontwell it looked like it might be a four year old steer, or a big pine log, or somethin' of that sort——"

"Glory to my soul," shouted Mrs. Dobbs, "it's the sweetest talk I *ever* hearn! You Sukey! ain't you got John yit? never mind, my lady, I'll settle wi' you!" Sukey quailed before the finger which her mistress shook at her.

"And arter awhile," Suggs went on, " 'peared like I fell into a trance, like, and I seed——"

"Now we'll git the good on it!" cried one of the sanctified.

"And I seed the biggest, longest, rip-roarenest, blackest, scaliest——" Captain Suggs paused, wiped his brow, and ejaculated, "Ah, L-o-r-d!" so as to give full time for curiosity to become impatience to know what he saw.

"*Sarpent!* warn't it?" asked one of the preachers.

"No, not a sarpent," replied Suggs, blowing his nose.

"Do tell us *what* it war, soul alive!—whar *is* John?" said Mrs. Dobbs.

"Allegator!" said the Captain.

"Alligator!" repeated every woman present, and screamed for very life.

Mrs. Dobbs's nerves were so shaken by the announcement, that after repeating the horrible word, she screamed to Sukey, "You Sukey, I say, you Su-u-ke-e-y! ef you let John come a-nigh this way, whar the dreadful alliga—shaw! what am I thinkin' 'bout? 'Twarn't nothin' but a vishin!'"

"Well," said the Captain in continuation, "the alligator kept a-comin' and a-comin' to'ards me, with his great long jaws a-gapin' open like a ten-foot pair o' tailor's shears——"

"Oh! oh! oh! Lord! gracious above!" cried the women.

"Satan!" was the laconic ejaculation of the oldest preacher present, who thus informed the congregation that it was the devil which had attacked Suggs in the shape of an alligator.

"And then I concluded the jig was up, 'thout I could block his game some way; for I seed his idee was to snap off my head——"

The women screamed again.

"So I fixed myself jist like I was purfectly willin' for him to take my head, and rather he'd do it as not"—here the women shuddered perceptibly—"and so I hilt my head straight out"—the Captain illustrated by elongating his neck —"and when he come up and was a gwine to *shet down* on it, I jist pitched in a big rock which choked him to death, and that minit I felt the weight slide off, and I had the best feelins—sorter like you'll have from *good* sperrits —any body ever had!"

"Didn't I *tell* you so? Didn't I *tell* you so?" asked the brother who had predicted the off-tumbling of the load of sin. "Ha, Lord! fool *who!* I've been *all* along thar!—yes, *all along thar!* and I know every inch of the way jist as good as I do the road home!"—and then he turned round and round, and looked at all, to receive a silent tribute to his superior penetration.

Captain Suggs was now the "lion of the day." Nobody could pray so well, or exhort so movingly, as "brother Suggs." Nor did his natural modesty prevent the proper performance of appropriate exercises. With the reverend Bela Bugg (him to whom, under providence, he ascribed his conversion) he was a most especial favorite. They walked, sang, and prayed together for hours.

"Come, come up; thar's room for all!" cried brother Bugg, in his evening exhortation. "Come to the 'seat,' and ef you won't pray yourselves, let *me* pray for you!"

"Yes!" said Simon, by way of assisting his friend; "it's a game that all can win at! Ante up! ante up, boys—friends I mean—don't back out!"

"Thar aint a sinner here," said Bugg, "no matter ef his soul's black as a nigger, but what thar's room for him!"

"No matter what sort of a hand you've got," added Simon in the fulness of his benevolence; "take stock! Here am *I*, the wickedest and blindest of sinners—has spent my whole life in the service of the devil—has come now in on *narry pair* and won a *pile!*" and the Captain's face beamed with holy pleasure.

"D-o-n-'t be afeard!" cried the preacher; "come along! the meanest won't be turned away! humble yourselves and come!"

"No!" said Simon, still indulging in his favourite style of metaphor; "the bluff game aint played here! No runnin' of a body off! Every body holds four aces, and when you bet, you win!"

And thus the Captain continued, until the services were concluded, to assist in adding to the number at the mourners' seat; and up to the hour of retiring, he exhibited such enthusiasm in the cause, that he was unanimously voted to be the most efficient addition the church had made during that meeting.

The next morning, when the preacher of the day first entered the pulpit, he announced that "brother Simon Suggs," mourning over his past iniquities, and desirous of going to work in the cause as speedily as possible, would take up a collection to found a church in his own neighbourhood, at which he hoped to make himself useful as soon as he could prepare himself for the ministry, which the preacher didn't doubt, would be in a very few weeks, as brother Suggs was "a man of mighty good judg*ment,* and of a great discorse." The funds were to be collected by "brother Suggs," and held in trust by brother Bela Bugg, who was the financial officer of the circuit, until some arrangement could be made to build a suitable house.

"Yes, breethring," said the Captain, rising to his feet; "I want to start a little 'sociation close to me, and I want you all to help. I'm mighty poor myself, as poor as any of you —don't leave, breethring"—observing that several of the well-to-do were about to go off—"don't leave; ef you aint able to afford any thing, jist give your blessin' and it'll be all the same!"

This insinuation did the business, and the sensitive individuals reseated themselves.

"It's mighty little of this world's goods I've got," resumed Suggs, pulling off his hat and holding it before him; "but I'll bury *that* in the cause any how," and he deposited his last five-dollar bill in the hat.

There was a murmur of approbation at the Captain's liberality throughout the assembly.

Suggs now commenced collecting, and very prudently attacked first the gentlemen who had shown a disposition to escape. These, to exculpate themselves from anything like poverty, contributed handsomely.

"Look here, breethring," said the Captain, displaying the bank-notes thus received, "brother Snooks has drapt a five wi' me, and brother Snodgrass a ten! In course 'taint expected that you *that aint as well off as them,* will give *as much;* let every one give *accordin'* to ther means."

This was another chain-shot that raked as it went! "Who

so low" as not to be able to contribute as much as Snooks and Snodgrass?

"Here's all the *small* money I've got about me," said a burly old fellow, ostentatiously handing to Suggs, over the heads of a half dozen, a ten dollar bill.

"That's what I call maganimus!" exclaimed the Captain; "that's the way *every* rich man ought to do!"

These examples were followed, more or less closely, by almost all present, for Simon had excited the pride of purse of the congregation, and a very handsome sum was collected in a very short time.

The reverend Mr. Bugg, as soon as he observed that our hero had obtained all that was to be had at that time, went to him and inquired what amount had been collected. The Captain replied that it was still uncounted, but that it couldn't be much under a hundred.

"Well, brother Suggs, you'd better count it and turn it over to me now. I'm goin' to leave presently."

"No!" said Suggs—"can't do it!"

"Why?—what's the matter?" inquired Bugg.

"It's got to be *prayed over*, fust!" said Simon, a heavenly smile illuminating his whole face.

"Well," replied Bugg, "les go one side and do it!"

"No!" said Simon, solemnly.

Mr. Bugg gave a look of inquiry.

"You see that krick swamp?" asked Suggs—"I'm gwine down in *thar*, and I'm gwine to lay this money down *so*" —showing how he would place it on the ground—"and I'm gwine to git on these here knees"—slapping the right one— "and I'm *n-e-v-e-r* gwine to quit the grit ontwell I feel it's got the blessin'! And nobody aint got to be thar but me!"

Mr. Bugg greatly admired the Captain's fervent piety, and bidding him God-speed, turned off.

Captain Suggs "struck for" the swamp sure enough, where his horse was already hitched. "Ef them fellers aint done to a cracklin," he muttered to himself as he mounted, "I'll never bet on two pair agin! They're peart at the snap game, theyselves; but they're badly lewed this hitch! Well! Live and let live is a good old motter, and it's my sentiments adzactly!" And giving the spur to his horse, off he cantered.

T. B. Thorpe

Like George Washington Harris, the author of *Sut Lovingood*, Thomas Bangs Thorpe was a southerner who was born in the North. After two years at Wesleyan College in Connecticut, he moved to the South for reasons of health. Settling in Louisiana, he had a varied career as a painter, politician, and newspaper editor. A great admirer of Zachary Taylor, Thorpe painted his portrait, accompanied him to the Mexican War, and in 1848 campaigned for Taylor for President. In the 50s Thorpe returned to New York to live, and in 1860 became editor of the *Spirit of the Times*. During the Civil War he chose to remain loyal to the Union and served on General Butler's staff.

Viewed in its entirety, Thorpe's life seems to have been an experiment in national citizenship; certainly in his career as a Whig politician he endeavored to avoid sectional splits and to hold the country together. When the increasing population of the North and South over the slavery issue destroyed the Whig party in the 1850s, Thorpe turned to the American party—the Know-Nothings, so-called—which attempted to unite the country by avoiding the slavery issue and erecting a xenophobic platform of anti-foreignism and anti-Catholicism on which all true Americans could stand together. In 1855 Thorpe allowed his name to be listed as co-author of a book entitled *A Voice to America,* which confidently set forth the American party's solution to the national crisis. Yet even before the book's publication the party was already falling apart; *A Voice to America* expressed the optimism of campaign propaganda, not the despair of Thorpe's true feelings. Those he had set forth the previous year, 1854, in his remarkable novel, *The Master's House.*

The novel tells the story of a temperate southern gentleman named Mildmay, who has been educated in the North and who attempts to steer a middle course between the extremists of the two sections. He defends the North and the egalitarian ideal against the attacks of his dissolute planter friend Moreton, just as he stands up for the South and the slavery system against the criticisms of ill-bred abolitionists. He treats his slaves with the utmost gentleness, but when his overseer, Sylvanus Toadvine, murders one of them, Mildmay saves Toadvine from being lynched because he believes in government by law. For a time Mildmay singlehandedly holds the entire social structure in balance. Then disaster strikes. Toadvine is acquitted by an ignorant jury; Moreton is defeated for office by a piney-woods candidate who cannot even write his name; because of a misunderstanding, Moreton challenges Mildmay to a duel. Stung by Moreton's taunts, Mildmay's vaunted self-control gives way and he kills his friend. At the end a broken, ostracized Mildmay sits in the darkness in a graveyard. The world he had known and upheld has been destroyed.

But this was the Thorpe of the mid-50s. In the early 40s he was not so despairing about the future of American society. "The Big Bear of Arkansas," which first appeared in the *Spirit of the Times* in March of 1841, expresses a more ambivalent vision. Its greatness lies precisely in its subtle mixture of grandiloquent confidence with foreboding of disaster. The scene of the story, a Mississippi steamboat, anticipates Melville's use of the same setting in *The Confidence-Man,* but Melville's bitter comedy, called by Professor Perry Miller in a fine phrase "a long farewell to national greatness," belongs to the same period as *The Mas-*

ter's House. In "The Big Bear" there is still room for hope. The death of the bear has tragic overtones, but Jim Doggett's colossal imagination reaffirms the continuing vitality of the "creation state."

Thorpe had the eye of a painter, which stood him in good stead as a writer. In particular, his descriptions of the bear show a fine sense of its appearance in motion. Like Faulkner, Thorpe was a good hunter and had a genuine love for the woods, an awareness of what Thorpe called its "mysteries." There is mystery in "The Big Bear," and it is that quality in the story to which Faulkner responded when he thought of Thorpe's masterpiece in the process of writing *The Bear.*

However, Faulkner's bear story is very different from Thorpe's; it is a rite of passage for a boy moving from childhood to manhood, a dimension totally absent in "The Big Bear." Possessed, too, of a deeper religious insight than Thorpe, Faulkner knows that the moral issue of the subjection of the Negro is not a question which self-controlled gentlemen like Mildmay could even hope to resolve; indeed, Faulkner would regard the anguish of Mildmay at the end of *The Master's House,* which Mildmay can deal with only by blaming himself, as not a personal lapse, but as the working-out of a more general Fall. Faulkner's hero, Ike McCaslin, comes to realize that the crime of white against black is not to be exorcised by kindness, but only by a total surrender, even of the land itself, a position Thorpe would not have understood.

The Big Bear of Arkansas

A steamboat on the Mississippi frequently, in making her regular trips, carries between places varying from one to two thousand miles apart; and as these boats advertise to land passengers and freight at "all intermediate landings," the heterogeneous character of the passengers of one of these up-country boats can scarcely be imagined by one who has never seen it with his own eyes. Starting from New Orleans in one of these boats, you will find yourself associated with men from every state in the Union, and from every portion of the globe; and a man of observation need not lack for amusement or instruction in such a crowd, if he will take the trouble to read the great book of character so favourably opened before him. Here may be seen jostling together the wealthy Southern planter, and the pedlar of tin-ware from New England—the Northern merchant, and the Southern jockey—a venerable bishop, and a desperate gambler—the land speculator, and the honest farmer—professional men of all creeds and characters—Wolvereens, Suckers, Hoosiers, Buckeyes, and Corn-crackers, beside a "plentiful sprinkling of the half-horse and half-alligator species of men, who are peculiar to "old Mississippi," and who appear to gain a livelihood simply by going up and down the river. In the pursuit of pleasure or business, I have frequently found myself in such a crowd.

On one occasion, when in New Orleans, I had occasion to take a trip of a few miles up the Mississippi, and I hurried on board the well-known "high-pressure-and-beat-every-thing" steamboat *Invincible*, just as the last note of the last bell was sounding; and when the confusion and bustle that is natural to a boat's getting under way had subsided, I discovered that I was associated in as heterogeneous a crowd as was ever got together. As my trip was to be of a few hours' duration only, I made no endeavours to become acquainted with my fellow passengers, most of whom would be together many days. Instead of this, I took out of my pocket the "latest paper," and more critically than usual examined its contents; my fellow passengers at the same time disposed themselves in little groups. While I was thus busily employed in reading, and my companions were more busily employed in discussing such subjects as suited their humours best, we were startled most unexpectedly by a loud Indian whoop, uttered in the "social hall," that part of the cabin fitted off for a bar; then was to be heard a loud crowing, which would not have continued to have interested us—such sounds being quite common in that place of spirits—had not the hero of these windy accomplishments stuck his head into the cabin and hallooed out, "Hurra for the Big Bar of Arkansaw!" and then might be heard a confused hum of voices, unintelligible, save in such broken sentences as "horse," "screamer," "lightning is slow," &c. As might have been expected, this continued interruption attracted the attention of every one in the cabin; all conversation dropped, and in the midst of this surprise the "Big Bar" walked into the cabin, took a chair, put his feet on the stove, and looking back over his shoulder, passed the general and familiar salute of "Strangers, how are you?" He then expressed himself as much at home as if he had been at "the Forks of Cypress," and "perhaps a little more so." Some of the company at this familiarity looked a little angry, and some astonished; but in a moment every face was wreathed in a smile. There was something about the intruder that won the heart on sight. He appeared to be a man enjoying perfect health and contentment: his eyes were as sparkling as diamonds, and good-natured to simplicity. Then his perfect confidence in himself was irresistibly droll. "Perhaps," said he, "gentlemen," running on without a person speaking, "perhaps you have been to New Orleans often; I never made *the first visit before,* and I don't intend to make another in a crow's life. I am thrown away in that ar place, and useless, that ar a fact. Some of the gentlemen thar called me *green*—well, perhaps I am, said I, *but I arn't so at home;* and if I ain't off my trail much, the heads of them perlite chaps themselves weren't much the hardest; for according to my notion, they were real *know-nothings,* green as a pumpkin vine—couldn't, in farming, I'll bet, raise a crop of turnips: and as for shooting, they'd miss a barn if the door was swinging, and that, too, with the best rifle in the country. And then they talked to me 'bout hunting, and laughed at my calling the principal game in Arkansaw poker, and high-low-jack. 'Perhaps,' said I, 'you prefer chickens and rolette'; at this they laughed harder than ever, and asked me if I lived in the woods, and didn't know what *game* was? At this I rather think I laughed. 'Yes,' I roared, and says, 'Strangers, if you'd asked me *how we got our meat* in Arkansaw, I'd a told you at once, and given you a list of varmints that would make a caravan, beginning with the bar, and ending off with the cat; that's *meat* though, not game.' Game, indeed that's what city folks call it; and with them it means chippen-birds and shite-pokes; maybe such trash live in my diggins, but I arn't noticed them yet: a bird any way is too trifling. I never did shoot at but one, and I'd never forgiven myself for that, had it weighed less than forty pounds. I wouldn't draw a rifle on any thing less than that; and when I meet with another wild turkey of the same weight I will drap him."

"A wild turkey weighing forty pounds!" exclaimed twenty voices in the cabin at once.

"Yes, strangers, and wasn't it a whopper? You see, the thing was so fat that it couldn't fly far; and when he fell out of the tree, after I shot him, on striking the ground he bust open behind, and the way the pound gobs of tallow rolled out of the opening was perfectly beautiful."

"Where did all that happen?" asked a cynical-looking Hoosier.

"Happen! happened in Arkansaw: where else could it have happened, but in the creation state, the finishing-up country—a state where the *sile* runs down to the centre of the 'arth, and government gives you a title to every inch of it? Then its airs—just breathe them, and they will make you snort like a horse. It's a state without a fault, it is."

"Excepting mosquitoes," cried the Hoosier.

"Well, stranger, except them; for it ar a fact that they are rather *enormous*, and do push themselves in somewhat troublesome. But, stranger, they never stick twice in the same place; and give them a fair chance for a few months, and you will get as much above noticing them as an alligator. They can't hurt my feelings, for they lay under the skin; and I never knew but one case of injury resulting from them, and that was to a Yankee: and they take worse to foreigners, any how, than they do to natives. But the way they used that fellow up! first they punched him until he swelled up and busted; then he su-per-a-ted, as the doctor called it, until he was as raw as beef; then he took the ager, owing to the warm weather, and finally he took a steamboat and left the country. He was the only man that ever took mosquitoes to heart that I know of. But mosquitoes is natur, and I never find fault with her. If they ar large, Arkansaw is large, her varmints ar large, her trees ar large, her rivers ar large, and a small mosquito would be of no more use in Arkansaw than preaching in a cane-brake."

This knock-down argument in favour of big mosquitoes used the Hoosier up, and the logician started on a new track, to explain how numerous bear were in his "diggins," where he represented them to be "about as plenty as blackberries, and a little plentifuler."

Upon the utterance of this assertion, a timid little man near me inquired if the bear in Arkansaw ever attacked the settlers in numbers.

"No," said our hero, warming with the subject, "no, stranger, for you see it ain't the natur of bar to go in droves; but the way they squander about in pairs and single ones is edifying. And the way I hunt them the old black rascals know the crack of my gun as well as they know a pig's squealing. They grow thin in our parts, it frightens them so, and they do take the noise dreadfully, poor things. That gun of mine is perfect *epidemic among bar;* if not watched closely, it will go off as quick on a warm scent as my dog Bowie-knife will: and then that dog—whew! why the fellow thinks that the world is full of bar, he finds them so easy. It's lucky he don't talk as well as think; for with his natural modesty, if he should suddenly learn how much he is acknowledged to be ahead of all other dogs in the universe, he would be astonished to death in two min-utes. Strangers, the dog knows a bar's way as well as a horse-jockey knows a woman's: he always barks at the right time, bites at the exact place, and whips without getting a scratch. I never could tell whether he was made ex-pressly to hunt bar, or whether bar was made expressly for him to hunt: any way, I believe they were ordained to go together as naturally as Squire Jones says a man and woman is, when he moralizes in marrying a couple. In fact, Jones once said, said he, 'Marriage according to law is a civil contract of divine origin; it's common to all countries as well as Arkansaw, and people take to it as naturally as Jim Doggett's Bowie-knife takes to bar.'"

"What season of the year do your hunts take place?" inquired a gentlemanly foreigner, who, from some peculiarities of his baggage, I suspected to be an Englishman, on some hunting expedition, probably at the foot of the Rocky Mountains.

"The season for bar hunting, stranger," said the man of Arkansaw, "is generally all the year round, and the hunts take place about as regular. I read in history that varmints have their fat season, and their lean season. That is not the case in Arkansaw, feeding as they do upon the *spontenacious* productions of the sile, they have one continued fat season the year round: though in winter things in this way is rather more greasy than in summer, I must admit. For that reason bar with us run in warm weather, but in winter, they only waddle. Fat, fat! it's an enemy to speed; it tames everything that has plenty of it. I have seen wild turkeys, from its influence, as gentle as chickens. Run a bar in this fat condition, and the way it improves the critter for eating is amazing; it sort of mixes the ile up with the meat, until you can't tell t'other from which. I've done this often. I recollect one perty morning in particular, of putting an old fellow on the stretch, and considering the weight he carried, he run well. But the dogs soon tired him down, and when I came up with him wasn't he in a beautiful sweat—I might say fever; and then to see his tongue sticking out of his mouth a feet, and his sides sinking and opening like a bellows, and his cheeks so fat he couldn't look cross. In this fix I blazed at him, and pitch me naked into a briar patch if the steam didn't come out of the bullet-hole ten foot in a straight line. The fellow, I reckon was made on the high-pressure system, and the lead sort of bust his biler."

"That column of steam was rather curious, or else the

bear must have been *warm*," observed the foreigner, with a laugh.

"Stranger, as you observe, that bar was WARM, and the blowing off of the steam show'd it, and also how hard the varmint had been run. I have no doubt if he had kept on two miles farther his insides would have been stewed; and I expect to meet with a varmint yet of extra bottom, who will run himself into a skinfull of bar's grease: it is possible, much onlikelier things have happened."

"Whereabouts are these bears so abundant?" inquired the foreigner, with increasing interest.

"Why, stranger, they inhabit the neighbourhood of my settlement, one of the prettiest places on old Mississippi —a perfect location, and no mistake; a place that had some defects until the river made the 'cut-off' at 'Shirt-tail bend,' and that remedied the evil, as it brought my cabin on the edge of the river—a great advantage in wet weather, I assure you, as you can now roll a barrel of whiskey into my yard in high water from a boat, as easy as falling off a log. It's a great improvement, as toting it by land in a jug, as I used to do, *evaporated* it too fast, and it became expensive. Just stop with me, stranger, a month or two, or a year if you like, and you will appreciate my place. I can give you plenty to eat; for beside hog and hominy, you can have bar-ham, and bar sausages, and a mattrass of bar-skins to sleep on, and a wildcat-skin, pulled off hull, stuffed with corn-shucks, for a pillow. That bed would put you to sleep if you had the rheumatics in every joint in your body. I call that ar bed a *quietus*. Then look at my land—the government ain' got another such a piece to dispose of. Such timber, and such bottom land, why you can't preserve any thing natural you plant in it unless you pick it young, things thar will grow out of shape so quick. I once planted in those diggins a few potatoes and beets: they took a fine start, and after that an ox team couldn't have kept them from growing. About that time I went off to old Kentuck on bisiness, and did not hear from them things in three months, when I accidentally stumbled on a fellow who had stopped at my place, with an idea of buying me out. 'How did you like things?' said I. 'Pretty well,' said he; 'the cabin is convenient, and the timber land is good; but that bottom land ain't worth the first red cent.' 'Why?' said I. ''Cause,' said he. ''Cause what?' said I. ''Cause it's full of cedar stumps and Indian mounds,' said he, *and it can't be cleared.* 'Lord,' said I, 'them ar "cedar stumps" is beets, and them ar "Indian mounds" ar tater hills.' As I expected, the crop was overgrown and useless: the sile is too rich, *and planting in Arkansaw is dangerous.* I had a good-sized sow killed in that same bottom land. The old thief stole an ear of corn, and took it down where she slept at night to eat. Well, she left a grain or two on the ground, and lay down on them: before morning the corn shot up, and the percussion killed her dead. I don't plant any more; natur intended Arkansaw for a hunting ground, and I go according to natur."

The questioner who thus elicited the description of our hero's settlement, seemed to be perfectly satisfied, and said no more; but the "Big Bar of Arkansaw" rambled on from one thing to another with a volubility perfectly astonishing, occasionally disputing with those around him, particularly with a "live Sucker" from Illinois, who had the daring to say that our Arkansaw friend's stories "smelt rather tall."

In this manner the evening was spent; but conscious that my own association with so singular a personage would probably end before morning, I asked him if he would not give me a description of some particular bear hunt; adding that I took great interest in such things, though I was no sportsman. The desire seemed to please him, and he squared himself round towards me, saying, that he could give me an idea of a bar hunt that was never beat in this world, or in any other. His manner was so singular, that half of his story consisted in his excellent way of telling it, the great peculiarity of which was, the happy manner he had of emphasizing the prominent parts of his conversation. As near as I can recollect, I have italicized them, and given the story in his own words.

"Stranger," said he, "in bar hunts *I am numerous*, and which particular one, as you say, I shall tell, puzzles me. There was the old she devil I shot at the Hurricane last fall —then there was the old hog thief I popped over at the

Bloody Crossing, and then—Yes, I have it! I will give you an idea of a hunt, in which the greatest bar was killed that ever lived, *none excepted;* about an old fellow that I hunted, more or less, for two or three years; and if that ain't a particular bar hunt, I ain't got one to tell. But in the first place, stranger, let me say, I am pleased with you, because you ain't ashamed to gain information by asking, and listening, and that's what I say to Countess's pups every day when I'm home; and I have got great hopes of them ar pups, because they are continually *nosing* about; and though they stick it sometimes in the wrong place, they gain experience any how, and may learn something useful to boot. Well, as I was saying about this big bar, you see when I and some more first settled in our region, we were drivin to hunting naturally; we soon liked it, and after that we found it an easy matter to make the thing our business. One old chap who had pioneered 'afore us, gave us to understand that we had settled in the right place. He dwelt upon its merits until it was affecting, and showed us, to prove his assertions, more marks on the sassafras trees than I ever saw on a tavern door 'lection time. 'Who keeps that ar reckoning?' said I. 'The bar,' said he. 'What for?' said I. 'Can't tell,' said he; 'but so it is: the bar bite the bark and wood too, at the highest point from the ground they can reach, and you can tell, by the marks,' said he, 'the length of the bar to an inch.' 'Enough,' said I; 'I've learned something here a'ready, and I'll put it in practice.'

"Well, stranger, just one month from that time I killed a bar, and told its exact length before I measured it, by those very marks; and when I did that, I swelled up considerable—I've been a prouder man ever since. So I went on, larning something every day, until I was reckoned a buster, and allowed to be decidedly the best bar hunter in my district; and that is a reputation as much harder to earn than to be reckoned first man in Congress, as an iron ramrod is harder than a toadstool. Did the varmints grow over-cunning by being fooled with by green-horn hunters, and by this means get troublesome, they send for me as a matter of course; and thus I do my own hunting, and most of my neighbours'. I walk into the varmints though, and it has become about as much the same to me as drinking. It is told in two sentences—a bar is started, and he is killed. The thing is somewhat monotonous now—I know just how much they will run, where they will tire, how much they will growl, and what a thundering time I will have in getting them home. I could give you this history of the chase with all particulars at the commencement, I know the signs so well— *Stranger, I'm certain.* Once I met a match though, and I will tell you about it; for a common hunt would not be worth relating.

"On a fine fall day, long time ago, I was trailing about for bar, and what should I see but fresh marks on the sassafras trees, about eight inches above any in the forests that I knew of. Says I, 'them marks is a hoax, or it indicates the d———t bar that was ever grown.' In fact, stranger, I couldn't believe it was real, and I went on. Again I saw the same marks, at the same height, and *I knew the thing lived.* That conviction came home to my soul like an earthquake. Says I, 'here is something a-purpose for me; that bar is mine, or I give up the hunting business.' The very next morning what should I see but a number of buzzards hovering over my cornfield. 'The rascal has been there,' said I, 'for that sign is certain': and, sure enough, on examining, I found the bones of what had been as beautiful a hog the day before, as was ever raised by a Buckeye. Then I tracked the critter out of the field to the woods, and all the marks he left behind, showed me that he was *the bar.*

"Well, stranger, the first fair chase I ever had with that big critter, I saw him no less than three distinct times at a distance: the dogs run him over eighteen miles and broke down, my horse gave out, and I was as nearly used up as a man can be, made on *my* principle, *which is patent.* Before this adventure, such things were unknown to me as possible; but, strange as it was, that bar got me used to it before I was done with him; for he got so at last, that he would leave me on a long chase *quite easy.* How he did it, I never could understand. That a bar runs at all, is puzzling; but how this one could tire down and bust up a pack of hounds and a horse, that were used to overhauling everything they started after in no time, was past my understanding. Well, stranger, that bar finally got so sassy, that he used to help himself to a hog off my premises whenever he wanted one; the buzzards followed after what he left, and so between the *bar and buzzard*, I rather think I was *out of pork*.

"Well, missing that bar so often took hold of my vitals, and I wasted away. The thing had been carried too far, and it reduced me in flesh faster than an ager. I would see that bar in every thing I did: *he hunted me,* and that, too, like a devil, which I began to think he was. While in this fix, I made preparations to give him a last brush, and be done with it. Having completed every thing to my satisfaction, I started at sunrise, and to my great joy, I discovered from the way the dogs run, that they were near him; finding his trail was nothing, for that had become as plain to the pack as a turnpike road. On we went, and coming to an open country, what should I see but the bar very leisurely ascending a hill, and the dogs close at his heels, either a match for him in speed, or else he did not care to get out of their way—I don't know which. But wasn't he a beauty, though? I loved him like a brother.

"On he went, until he came to a tree, the limbs of which formed a crotch about six feet from the ground. Into this crotch he got and seated himself, the dogs yelling all around it; and there he sat eyeing them as quiet as a pond in low water. A green-horn friend of mine, in company, reached shooting distance before me, and blazed away, hitting the critter in the centre of his forehead. The bar shook his head as the ball struck it, and then walked down from that tree as gently as a lady would from a carriage. 'Twas a beautiful sight to see him do that—he was in such a rage that he seemed to be as little afraid of the dogs as if they had been sucking pigs; and the dogs warn't slow in making a ring around him at a respectful distance, I tell you; even Bowie-knife, himself, stood off. Then the way his eyes flashed—why the fire of them would have singed a cat's hair; in fact that bar was *wrath all over.* Only one pup came near him, and he was brushed out so totally with the bar's left paw, that he entirely disappeared; and that made the old dogs more cautious still. In the mean time, I came up, and taking deliberate aim as a man should do, at his side, just back of his foreleg, *if my gun did not snap*, call me a coward, and I won't take it personal. Yes, stranger, *it snapped*, and I could not find a cap about my person. While in this predicament, I turned round to my fool friend—says I, 'Bill,' says I, 'you're an ass—you're a fool— you might as well have tried to kill that bar by barking the tree under his belly, as to have done it by hitting him in the head. Your shot has made a tiger of him, and blast me, if a dog gets killed or wounded when they come to blows, I will stick my knife into your liver, I will—' my wrath was up. I had lost my caps, my gun had snapped, the fellow with me had fired at the bar's head, and I expected every moment to see him close in with the dogs, and kill a dozen of them at least. In this thing I was mistaken, for the bar leaped over the ring formed by the dogs, and giving a fierce growl, was off—the pack, of course, in full cry after him. The run this time was short, for coming to the edge of a lake the varmint jumped in, and swam to a little island in the lake, which it reached just a moment before the dogs. 'I'll have him now,' said I, for I had found my caps in the *lining of my coat*—so, rolling a log into the lake, I paddled myself across to the island, just as the dogs had cornered the bar in a thicket. I rushed up and fired—at the same time the critter leaped over the dogs and came within three feet of me, running like mad; he jumped into the lake, and tried to mount the log I had just deserted, but every time he got half his body on it, it would roll over and send him under; the dogs, too, got around him, and pulled him about, and finally Bowie-knife clenched with him, and they sunk into the lake together. Stranger, about this time, I was excited, and I stripped off my coat, drew my knife, and intended to have taken a part with Bowie-knife myself, when the bar rose to the surface. But the varmint staid under—Bowie-knife came up alone, more dead than alive, and with the pack came ashore. 'Thank God,' said I, 'the old villain has got his deserts at last.' Determined to have the body, I cut a grape-vine for a rope, and dove down where I could see the bar in the water, fastened my queer rope to his leg, and fished him, with great difficulty, ashore.

Stranger, may I be chawed to death by young alligators, if the thing I looked at wasn't a *she bar, and not the old critter after all*. The way matters got mixed on that island was onaccountably curious, and thinking of it made me more than ever convinced that I was hunting the devil himself. I went home that night and took to my bed—the thing was killing me. The entire team of Arkansaw in bar-hunting, acknowledged himself used up, and the fact sunk into my feelings like a snagged boat will in the Mississippi. I grew as cross as a bar with two cubs and a sore tail. The thing got out 'mong my neighbours, and I was asked how come on that individu-al that never lost a bar when once started? and if that same individu-al didn't wear telescopes when he turned a she bar, of ordinary size, into an old he one, a little larger than a horse? 'Perhaps,' said I, 'friends' —getting wrathy—'perhaps you want to call somebody a liar.' 'Oh, no,' said they, 'we only heard such things as being *rather common* of late, but we don't believe one word of it; oh, no,'—and then they would ride off and laugh like so many hyenas over a dead nigger. It was too much, and I determined to catch that bar, go to Texas, or die,—and I made my preparations accordin'. I had the pack shut up and rested. I took my rifle to pieces and iled it. I put caps in every pocket about my person, *for fear of the lining*. I then told my neighbours, that on Monday morning—naming the day—I would start THAT BAR, and bring him home with me, or they might divide my settlement among them, the owner having disappeared. Well, stranger, on the morning previous to the great day of my hunting expedition, I went into the woods near my house, taking my gun and Bowie-knife along, just *from habit*, and there sitting down also from habit, what should I see, getting over my fence, but *the bar!* Yes, the old varmint was within a hundred yards of me, and the way he walked *over that fence*— stranger, he loomed up like a *black mist*, he seemed so large, and he walked right towards me. I raised myself, took deliberate aim, and fired. Instantly the varmint wheeled, gave a yell, and *walked through the fence* like a falling tree would through a cobweb. I started after, but was tripped up by my inexpressibles, which either from habit, or the excitement of the moment, were about my heels, and before I had really gathered myself up, I heard the old varmint groaning in a thicket near by, like a thousand sinners, and by the time I reached him he was a corpse. Stranger, it took five niggers and myself to put that carcase on a mule's back and old long-ears waddled under the load, as if he was foundered in every leg of his body, and with a common whopper of a bar, he would have trotted off, and enjoyed himself. 'Twould astonish you to know how big he was: I made a *bed-spread of his skin,* and the way it used to cover my bar mattress, and leave several feet on each side to tuck up, would have delighted you. It was in fact a creation bar, and if it had lived in Samson's time, and had met him, in a fair fight, it would have licked him in the twinkling of a dice-box. But, strangers, I never like the way I hunted, and *missed him.* There is something curious about it, I could never understand,—and I never was satisfied at his giving in so easy at last. Perhaps, he had heard of my preparations to hunt him the next day, so he jist come in, like Capt. Scott's coon, to save his wind to grunt with in dying; but that ain't likely. My private opinion is, that that bar was an *unhuntable bar, and died when his time come.*"

When the story was ended, our hero sat some minutes with his auditors in a grave silence; I saw there was a mystery connected with the bear whose death he had just related, that had evidently made a strong impression on his mind. It was also evident that there was some superstitious awe connected with the affair,—a feeling common with all "children of the wood," when they meet with any thing out of their everyday experience. He was the first one, however, to break the silence, and jumping up, he asked all present to "liquor" before going to bed,—a thing which he did, with a number of companions, evidently to his heart's content.

Long before day, I was put ashore at my place of destination, and I can only follow with the reader, in imagination, our Arkansas friend, in his adventures at the "Forks of Cypress" on the Mississippi.

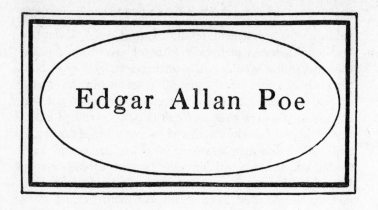

Edgar Allan Poe

Poe's decade of editorial experience and free-lancing—1835 to 1845—was an exhausting period of hard work and little pay, but it gave him without a doubt a professional knowledge of literary commercialism that was unrivaled in the United States. As a writer he developed a tremendous versatility of style, tone, and theme, and seemingly at will could produce the type of story that the magazines were looking for at the moment. As an editor, Poe had increased the circulation of the *Southern Literary Messenger* by seven times and of *Graham's Magazine* by almost as much during his brief tours of duty on these publications, so that he was probably more sensitively aware of the fluctuations on the literary market than any editor to whom he sold his work. When the publisher of the *Southern Literary Messenger* objected to the theme of "Berenice," Poe wrote him a letter which in a paragraph brilliantly analyzed the fictional taste of the day. "The history of all Magazines," he wrote the publisher, "shows plainly that those which have attained celebrity were indebted for it to articles *similar in nature to Berenice*—although, I grant you, far superior in style and execution. I say similar in *nature*. You ask me in what does this nature consist? In the ludicrous heightened into the grotesque; the fearful coloured into the horrible;

the witty exaggerated into the burlesque; the singular wrought out into the strange and mystical."

This excited awareness of what was selling and what wasn't sometimes prompted Poe to write stories which parodied current fads. Early in his career he projected a volume of take-offs on popular fiction called *Tales of the Folio Club*. The book was never published, but Poe nevertheless remained fond of the literary burlesque as a form. In writing burlesque, Poe held nothing sacred; he was just as ready to compose a merciless imitation of a style he approved of as of one he despised. His satire called "Never Bet Your Head" is a take-off on stories which end with a moral, a device Poe thought was characteristic of the Transcendentalists, whom he loathed. But one of his most devastating burlesques, "How to Write a Blackwood Article," while also paying its respects to the Transcendentalists, parodies a style, a manner, a pseudo-erudition, a horror, which seem to come straight out of the stories of Edgar Allan Poe. Set forth in the accents of an absurdly pretentious literary lady (who sounds remarkably like the comic southern females whom Eudora Welty sometimes employs as narrators of her stories), "Blackwood" laughs at as meretricious all the literary qualities of Poe's most notable fiction.

Apart from its considerable merit as a literary burlesque, the story is important because it raises a fundamental question about the nature of Poe's art. Does "Blackwood" mean, as one critic believes it does, that Poe's tales were composed with tongue in cheek, that their terror was not a product, as Poe once said, of his soul, but of his all-encompassing knowledge of what would sell in the literary market place? One is tempted to say yes, if only because this view of Poe is useful as a counterweight to the discredited but persistent notion that his tales are the helpless recordings of an opium addict's dreams. But finally it must be dismissed as false because it basically misunderstands the nature of Poe's humor.

In a paper published in 1928 Freud asserted that the essence of humor is that one spares oneself the affects to which a tragic situation would naturally give rise, and overrides with a joke the possibility of a display of tragic emotion. "By its repudiation of the possibility of suffering," Freud says, humor "takes its place in the great series of methods devised by the mind of man for evading the compulsion to suffer—a series which begins with neuroses and culminates in delusions. . . ." Freud's paper seems to me relevant to all of American humor, but especially so in the particular case of Poe. That Poe should make jokes about terror stories is not a sign that the Gothicism of his own tales was a spurious commodity manufactured for the purpose of crashing the pages of *Blackwood's Magazine,* or of its American imitators; Poe's humor is, rather, a function of his familiarity with psychological suffering, and the best of his hoaxes, burlesques, and comic tales are those which transmute into laughter those very situations that he returns to most obsessively in such masterpieces as "The Masque of the Red Death" and "Ligeia."

One of the ways in which Poe best understood the nature of suffering was through his experience of the social disregard that was the fate of the artist in America, particularly in the South, an experience which emerges again and again in his tales in images of suffocation, in the disappearance of manuscripts and the indecipherability of messages, in the doom of the man of sensibility. In "Blackwood," a fine contempt is expressed for the Gothic fakery pervading the popular magazines, but at the heart of the story there is the despair of an artist living in a culture which regarded all writers as Grub Street hacks, because it recognized no other motive than money for becoming a professional writer, and made no attempt to discriminate between the good and the bad, the real and the fake. The humor of the story triumphantly conceals the despair, but if you would see the despair naked and undisguised, you need only remember Roderick Usher, painting his abstractions and playing his music in the isolated, crumbling house.

How to Write a Blackwood Article

I presume everybody has heard of me. My name is the Signora Psyche Zenobia. This I know to be a fact. Nobody but my enemies ever calls me Suky Snobbs. I have been assured that Suky is but a vulgar corruption of Psyche, which is good Greek, and means "the soul" (that's me, I'm *all* soul), and sometimes "a butterfly," which latter meaning undoubtedly alludes to my appearance in my new crimson satin dress, with the sky-blue Arabian *mantelet*, and the trimmings of green *agraffas*, and the seven flounces of orange-colored *auriculas*. As for Snobbs—any person who should look at me would be instantly aware that my name wasn't Snobbs. Miss Tabitha Turnip propagated that report through sheer envy. Tabitha Turnip indeed! Oh, the little wretch! But what can we expect from a turnip? Wonder if she remembers the old adage about "blood out of a turnip, etc." (Mem.: put her in mind of it the first opportunity.) (Mem. again—pull her nose.) Where was I? Ah! I have been assured that Snobbs is a mere corruption of Zenobia, and that Zenobia was a queen (so am I. Dr. Moneypenny always calls me the Queen of Hearts), and that Zenobia, as well as Psyche, is good Greek, and that my father was "a Greek," and that consequently I have a right to our patronymic, which is Zenobia, and not by any means Snobbs. Nobody but Tabitha Turnip calls me Suky Snobbs. I am the Signora Psyche Zenobia.

As I said before, everybody has heard of me. I am that very Signora Psyche Zenobia so justly celebrated as corresponding secretary to the "Philadelphia, Regular, Exchange, Tea, Total, Young, Belles, Lettres, Universal, Experimental, Bibliographical, Association, To, Civilize, Hu-

manity." Dr. Moneypenny made the title for us, and says
he chose it because it sounded big, like an empty rum-
puncheon. (A vulgar man that sometimes, but he's deep.)
We all sign the initials of the society after our names,
in the fashion of the R.S.A., Royal Society of Arts—the
S.D.U.K., Society for the Diffusion of Useful Knowledge,
etc., etc. Dr. Moneypenny says that S stands for *stale,* and
that D.U.K. spells duck (but it don't), and that S.D.U.K.
stands for Stale Duck, and not for Lord Brougham's Society; but then Dr. Moneypenny is such a queer man that
I am never sure when he is telling me the truth. At any
rate we always add to our names the initials P.R.E.T.T.Y.-
B.L.U.E.B.A.T.C.H.—that is to say, Philadelphia, Regular,
Exchange, Tea, Total, Young, Belles, Lettres, Universal,
Experimental, Bibliographical, Association, To, Civilize,
Humanity—one letter for each word, which is a decided improvement upon Lord Brougham. Dr. Moneypenny will
have it that our initials give our true character, but for my
life I can't see what he means.

Notwithstanding the good offices of the Doctor, and the
strenuous exertions of the Association to get itself into notice, it met with no very great success until I joined it. The
truth is, members indulged in too flippant a tone of discussion. The papers read every Saturday evening were characterized less by depth than buffoonery. They were all
whipped syllabub. There was no investigation of first
causes, first principles. There was no investigation of anything at all. There was no attention paid to that great
point, the "fitness of things." In short, there was no fine
writing like this. It was all low—very! No profundity, no
reading, no metaphysics, nothing which the learned call
spirituality and which the unlearned choose to stigmatize
as cant. (Dr. M. says I ought to spell "cant" with a capital
K—but I know better.)

When I joined the Society it was my endeavor to introduce a better style of thinking and writing, and all the
world knows how well I have succeeded. We get up as
good papers now in the P.R.E.T.T.Y.B.L.U.E.B.A.T.C.H.
as any to be found even in "Blackwood." I say "Blackwood,"

because I have been assured that the finest writing, upon every subject, is to be discovered in the pages of that justly celebrated magazine. We now take it for our model upon all themes, and are getting into rapid notice accordingly. And, after all, it's not so very difficult a matter to compose an article of the genuine "Blackwood" stamp, if one only goes properly about it. Of course I don't speak of the political articles. Everybody knows how *they* are managed, since Dr. Moneypenny explained it. Mr. Blackwood has a pair of tailor's-shears, and three apprentices who stand by him for orders. One hands him the "Times," another the "Examiner," and a third a Gulley's "New Compendium of Slang-Whang." Mr. B—— merely cuts out and intersperses. It is soon done: nothing but "Examiner," "Slang-Whang," and "Times;" then "Times," "Slang-Whang," and "Examiner;" and then "Times," "Examiner," and "Slang-Whang."

But the chief merit of the magazine lies in its miscellaneous articles; and the best of these come under the head of what Dr. Moneypenny calls the *bizarreries* (whatever that may mean) and what everybody else calls the *intensities*. This is a species of writing which I have long known how to appreciate, although it is only since my late visit to Mr. Blackwood (deputed by the Society) that I have been made aware of the exact method of composition. This method is very simple, but not so much so as the politics. Upon my calling at Mr. B——'s, and making known to him the wishes of the Society, he received me with great civility, took me into his study, and gave me a clear explanation of the whole process.

"My dear madam," said he, evidently struck with my majestic appearance, for I had on the crimson satin, with the green *agraffas*, and orange-colored *auriculas*, "my *dear* madam," said he, "sit down. The matter stands thus. In the first place, your writer of intensities must have very black ink, and a very big pen, with a very blunt nib. And, mark me, Miss Psyche Zenobia!" he continued, after a pause, with the most impressive energy and solemnity of manner, "mark me!—*that pen—must—never be mended!* Herein, madam, lies the secret, the soul, of intensity. I assume upon myself to say, that no individual, of however great genius, ever wrote with a good pen—understand me—a good article. You may take it for granted that when manuscript can be read it is never worth reading. This is a leading principle in our faith, to which if you cannot readily assent, our conference is at an end."

He paused. But, of course, as I had no wish to put an end to the conference, I assented to a proposition so very obvious, and one, too, of whose truth I had all along been sufficiently aware. He seemed pleased, and went on with his instructions.

"It may appear invidious in me, Miss Psyche Zenobia, to refer you to any article, or set of articles, in the way of model or study; yet perhaps I may as well call your attention to a few cases. Let me see. There was 'The Dead Alive,' a capital thing! the record of a gentleman's sensations when entombed before the breath was out of his body; full of taste, terror, sentiment, metaphysics, and erudition. You would have sworn that the writer had been born and brought up in a coffin. Then we had the 'Confessions of an Opium-eater'—fine, very fine!—glorious imagination—deep philosophy—acute speculation—plenty of fire and fury, and a good spicing of the decidedly unintelligible. That was a nice bit of flummery, and went down the throats of the people delightfully. They would have it that Coleridge wrote the paper—but not so. It was composed by my pet baboon, Juniper, over a rummer of Hollands and water, 'hot, without sugar.'" (This I could scarcely have believed had it been anybody but Mr. Blackwood, who assured me of it.) "Then there was 'The Involuntary Experimentalist,' all about a gentleman who got baked in an oven, and came out alive and well, although certainly done to a turn. And then there was 'The Diary of a Late Physician,' where the merit lay in a good rant, and indifferent Greek—both of them taking things with the public. And then there was 'The Man in the Bell,' a paper, by the bye, Miss Zenobia, which I cannot sufficiently recommend to your attention. It is the history of a young person who goes to sleep under the clapper of a church bell, and is awakened by its tolling for a funeral. The sound drives him mad, and, accordingly, pulling out his tablets, he gives a record of his sensations. Sensations are the great things, after all. Should you ever be drowned or hung, be sure and make a note of your sensations; they will be worth to you ten guineas a sheet. If you wish to write forcibly, Miss Zenobia, pay minute attention to the sensations."

"That I certainly will, Mr. Blackwood," said I.

"Good!" he replied. "I see you are a pupil after my own heart. But I must put you *au fait* to the details necessary in composing what may be denominated a genuine 'Blackwood' article of the sensation stamp, the kind which you will understand me to say I consider the best for all purposes.

"The first thing requisite is to get yourself into such a scrape as no one ever got into before. The oven, for instance,—that was a good hit. But if you have no oven or big bell at hand, and if you cannot conveniently tumble out of a balloon, or be swallowed up in an earthquake, or get stuck fast in a chimney, you will have to be contented with simply imagining some similar misadventure. I should prefer, however, that you have the actual fact to bear you out. Nothing so well assists the fancy as an experimental knowledge of the matter in hand. 'Truth is strange,' you know, 'stranger than fiction'—besides being more to the purpose."

Here I assured him I had an excellent pair of garters, and would go and hang myself forthwith.

"Good!" he replied, "do so; although hanging is somewhat hackneyed. Perhaps you might do better. Take a dose of Brandreth's pills, and then give us your sensations. However, my instructions will apply equally well to any variety of misadventure, and on your way home you may easily get knocked in the head, or run over by an omnibus, or bitten by a mad dog, or drowned in a gutter. But to proceed.

"Having determined upon your subject, you must next consider the tone, or manner, of your narration. There is the tone didactic, the tone enthusiastic, the tone natural— all commonplace enough. But then there is the tone laconic, or curt, which has lately come much into use. It consists in short sentences. Somehow thus: Can't be too brief. Can't be too snappish. Always a full stop. And never a paragraph.

"Then there is the tone elevated, diffusive, and interjectional. Some of our best novelists patronize this tone. The words must be all in a whirl, like a humming-top, and make a noise very similar, which answers remarkably well instead of meaning. This is the best of all possible styles where the writer is in too great a hurry to think.

"The tone metaphysical is also a good one. If you know any big words this is your chance for them. Talk of the Ionic and Eleatic schools—of Archytas, Gorgias, and Alcmæon. Say something about objectivity and subjectivity. Be sure and abuse a man named Locke. Turn up your nose at things in general, and when you let slip anything a little *too* absurd, you need not be at the trouble of scratching it out, but just add a foot-note, and say that you are indebted for the above profound observation to the *Kritik der reinen Vernunft*, or to the *Metaphysische Anfangsgrunde der Naturwissenschaft*. This will look erudite and—and—and frank.

"There are various other tones of equal celebrity, but I shall mention only two more, the tone transcendental and the tone heterogeneous. In the former the merit consists in seeing into the nature of affairs a very great deal farther than anybody else. This second sight is very efficient when properly managed. A little reading of the 'Dial' will carry you a great way. Eschew, in this case, big words; get them as small as possible, and write them upside down. Look over Channing's poems and quote what he says about a 'fat little man with a delusive show of Can.' Put in something about the Supernal Oneness. Don't say a syllable about the Infernal Twoness. Above all, study innuendo. Hint everything—assert nothing. If you feel inclined to say 'bread and butter,' do not by any means say it outright. You may say anything and everything *approaching* to 'bread and butter.' You may hint at buckwheat cake, or you may even go so far as to insinuate oatmeal porridge, but if bread and butter be your real meaning, be cautious, my *dear* Miss Psyche, not on any account to say 'bread and butter'!"

I assured him that I should never say it again as long as I lived. He kissed me, and continued:

"As for the tone heterogeneous, it is merely a judicious mixture, in equal proportions, of all the other tones in the world, and is consequently made up of everything deep, great, odd, piquant, pertinent, and pretty.

"Let us suppose now you have determined upon your incidents and tone. The most important portion—in fact, the soul of the whole business, is yet to be attended to; I allude to *the filling up*. It is not to be supposed that a lady, or gentleman either, has been leading the life of a bookworm. And yet above all things it is necessary that your article have an air of erudition, or at least afford evidence of extensive general reading. Now I'll put you in the way of accomplishing this point. See here!" (pulling down some three or four ordinary-looking volumes, and opening them at random). "By casting your eye down almost any page of any book in the world, you will be able to perceive at once a host of little scraps of either learning or *bel-esprit-ism,* which are the very thing for the spicing of a 'Blackwood' article. You might as well note down a few while I read them to you. I shall make two divisions: first, *Piquant Facts for the Manufacture of Similes;* and second, *Piquant Expressions to be introduced as occasion may require.* Write now!"—and I wrote as he dictated.

"PIQUANT FACTS FOR SIMILES. 'There were originally but three Muses—Melete, Mneme, Aœde—meditation, memory, and singing.' You may make a great deal of that little fact if properly worked. You see it is not generally known, and looks *recherché.* You must be careful and give the thing with a downright improviso air.

"Again. 'The river Alpheus passed beneath the sea, and emerged without injury to the purity of its waters.' Rather stale that, to be sure, but, if properly dressed and dished up, will look quite as fresh as ever.

"Here is something better. 'The Persian Iris appears to some persons to possess a sweet and very powerful perfume,

while to others it is perfectly scentless.' Fine that, and very
delicate! Turn it about a little, and it will do wonders. We'll
have something else in the botanical line. There's nothing
goes down so well, especially with the help of a little Latin.
Write!

"'*The Epidendrum Flos Aeris*, of Java, bears a very
beautiful flower, and will live when pulled up by the roots.
The natives suspend it by a cord from the ceiling, and enjoy its fragrance for years.' That's capital! That will do for
the Similes. Now for the Piquant Expressions.

"PIQUANT EXPRESSIONS. '*The venerable Chinese novel
Ju-Kiao-Li.*' Good! By introducing these few words with
dexterity you will evince your intimate acquaintance with
the language and literature of the Chinese. With the aid of
this you may possibly get along without either Arabic, or
Sanskrit, or Chickasaw. There is no passing muster, however, without Spanish, Italian, German, Latin, and Greek.
I must look you out a little specimen of each. Any scrap
will answer, because you must depend upon your own ingenuity to make it fit into your article. Now write!

"'*Aussi tendre que Zaïre*'—as tender as Zaïre—French. Alludes to the frequent repetition of the phrase, *la tendre
Zaïre*, in the French tragedy of that name. Properly introduced, will show not only your knowledge of the language,
but your general reading and wit. You can say, for instance, that the chicken you were eating (write an article
about being choked to death by a chicken-bone) was not
altogether *aussi tendre que Zaïre*. Write!

> '*Ven muerts tan ascondida,*
> *Que no te sienta venir,*
> *Porque el plazer del morir*
> *No me torne à dar la vida.*'

That's Spanish, from Miguel de Cervantes. 'Come quickly,
O death! but be sure and don't let me see you coming, lest
the pleasure I shall feel at your appearance should unfortu-
nately bring me back again to life.' This you may slip in
quite *à propos* when you are struggling in the last agonies
with the chicken-bone. Write!

> '*Il pover' huomo che non sen' era accorto,*
> *Andava combattendo, ed era morto.*'

That's Italian, you perceive—from Ariosto. It means that a great hero, in the heat of combat, not perceiving that he had been fairly killed, continued to fight valiantly, dead as he was. The application of this to your own case is obvious; for I trust, Miss Psyche, that you will not neglect to kick for at least an hour and a half after you have been choked to death by that chicken-bone. Please to write!

> '*Und sterb' ich doch, so sterb' ich denn*
> *Durch sie—durch sie!*'

That's German—from Schiller. 'And if I die, at least I die —for thee—for thee!' Here it is clear that you are apostrophizing the *cause* of your disaster, the chicken. Indeed, what gentleman (or lady either) of sense, *wouldn't* die, I should like to know. for a well-fattened capon of the right Molucca breed, stuffed with capers and mushrooms, and served up in a salad-bowl, with orange-jellies *en mosaïques*. Write! (You can get them that way at Tortoni's.)—Write, if you please!

"Here is a nice little Latin phrase, and rare too (one can't be too *recherché* or brief in one's Latin, it's getting so common)—*ignoratio elenchi*. He has committed an *ignoratio elenchi;* that is to say, he has understood the words of your proposition, but not the idea. The man was a *fool*, you see. Some poor fellow whom you addressed while choking with that chicken-bone, and who therefore didn't precisely understand what you were talking about. Throw the *ignoratio elenchi* in his teeth, and at once you have him annihilated. If he dare to reply, you can tell him from Lucan (here it is) that speeches are mere *anemonœ verborum*, anemone words. The anemone, with great brilliancy, has no smell. Or, if he begin to bluster, you may be down upon him with *insomnia Jovis*, reveries of Jupiter—a phrase which Silius Italicus (see here!) applies to thoughts pompous and inflated. This will be sure and cut him to the heart. He can do nothing but roll over and die. Will you be kind enough to write?

"In Greek we must have something pretty—from Demosthenes, for example. Ἀνὴρ ὁ φεύγων καὶ πάλιν μαχήσεται. (Aner o pheugon kai palin makesetai.) There is a tolerably good translation of it in 'Hudibras'—

> 'For he that flies may fight again,
> Which he can never do that's slain.'

In a 'Blackwood' article nothing makes so fine a show as your Greek. The very letters have an air of profundity about them. Only observe, madam, the astute look of that Epsilon! That Phi ought certainly to be a bishop! Was ever there a smarter fellow than that Omicron? Just twig that Tau! In short, there is nothing like Greek for a genuine sensation-paper. In the present case your application is the most obvious thing in the world. Rap out the sentence, with a huge oath, and by way of ultimatum at the good-for-nothing dunder-headed villain who couldn't understand your plain English in relation to the chicken-bone. He'll take the hint and be off, you may depend upon it."

These were all the instructions Mr. B—— could afford me upon the topic in question, but I felt they would be entirely sufficient. I was, at length, able to write a genuine "Blackwood" article, and determined to do it forthwith. In taking leave of me, Mr. B—— made a proposition for the purchase of the paper when written; but, as he could offer me only fifty guineas a sheet, I thought it better to let our society have it than sacrifice it for so paltry a sum. Notwithstanding this niggardly spirit, however, the gentleman showed his consideration for me in all other respects, and indeed treated me with the greatest civility. His parting words made a deep impression upon my heart, and I hope I shall always remember them with gratitude.

"My dear Miss Zenobia," he said, while the tears stood in his eyes, "is there *any*thing else I can do to promote the success of your laudable undertaking? Let me reflect! It is just possible that you may not be able, so soon as convenient, to—to—get yourself drowned, or—choked with a

chicken-bone, or—or hung,—or—bitten by a—but stay! Now
I think me of it, there are a couple of very excellent bull-
dogs in the yard—fine fellows, I assure you—savage, and all
that—indeed just the thing for your money—they'll have you
eaten up, *auriculas* and all, in less than five minutes (here's
my watch!)—and then only think of the sensations! Here!
I say—Tom!—Peter!—Dick, you villain!—let out those"—but
as I was really in a great hurry, and had not another moment to spare, I was reluctantly forced to expedite my departure, and accordingly took leave *at once*—somewhat
more abruptly, I admit, than strict courtesy would have
otherwise allowed. . . .

"Diddling," like "Blackwood," makes a joke out of Poe's
hatred of the materialism of American society. The late
F. O. Matthiessen has compared this story to Melville's *The
Confidence-Man*, and the comparison is an apt one, for the
bitterness of both writers is so terribly and unrelievedly intense as to produce a somewhat strained "dark comedy."
The story contains no character as memorable as Johnson J.
Hooper's incarnation of the con man (nor does Melville's
novel), but the last of the diddlers to appear deserves a
place, however modest, in that great galaxy of American
Tartuffes which includes such star performers as Simon
Suggs, the King and the Duke, and an assortment of comic
characterizations by W. C. Fields.

Diddling Considered as One of the Exact Sciences

Hey, diddle diddle,
The cat and the fiddle.
Mother Goose

Since the world began there have been two Jeremys. The one wrote a Jeremiad about usury, and was called Jeremy Bentham. He has been much admired by Mr. John Neal, and was a great man in a small way. The other gave name to the most important of the Exact Sciences, and was a great man in a great way; I may say, indeed, in the very greatest of ways.

Diddling, or the abstract idea conveyed by the verb to diddle, is sufficiently well understood. Yet the fact, the deed, the thing, *diddling*, is somewhat difficult to define. We may get, however, at a tolerably distinct conception of the matter in hand, by defining—not the thing, diddling, in itself—but man, as an animal that diddles. Had Plato but hit upon this, he would have been spared the affront of the picked chicken.

Very pertinently it was demanded of Plato why a picked chicken, which was clearly a "biped without feathers," was not, according to his own definition, a man? But I am not to be bothered by any similar query. Man is an animal that diddles, and there is no animal that diddles *but* man. It will take an entire hen-coop of picked chickens to get over that.

What constitutes the essence, the nare, the principle of diddling is, in fact, peculiar to the class of creatures that wear coats and pantaloons. A crow thieves; a fox cheats; a weasel outwits; a man diddles. To diddle is his destiny. "Man was made to mourn," says the poet. But not so:—he was made to diddle. This is his aim—his object—his *end*. And for this reason when a man's diddled we say he's *done*.

Diddling, rightly considered, is a compound, of which the

ingredients are minuteness, interest, perseverance, ingenuity, audacity, nonchalance, originality, impertinence, and *grin*.

Minuteness:—Your diddler is minute. His operations are upon a small scale. His business is retail, for cash or approved paper at sight. Should he ever be tempted into magnificent speculation, he then at once loses his distinctive features, and becomes what we term "financier." This latter word conveys the diddling idea in every respect except that of magnitude. A diddler may thus be regarded as a banker *in petto;* a "financial operation," as a diddle at Brobdingnag. The one is to the other as Homer to "Flaccus," as a mastodon to a mouse, as the tail of a comet to that of a pig.

Interest:—Your diddler is guided by self-interest. He scorns to diddle for the mere *sake* of the diddle. He has an object in view—his pocket—and yours. He regards always the main chance. He looks to Number One. You are Number Two, and must look to yourself.

Perseverance:—Your diddler perseveres. He is not readily discouraged. Should even the banks break he cares nothing about it. He steadily pursues his end, and

"Ut canis a corio nunquam absterrebitur uncto,"

so he never lets go of his game.

Ingenuity:—Your diddler is ingenious. He has constructiveness large. He understands plot. He invents and circumvents. Were he not Alexander, he would be Diogenes. Were he not a diddler, he would be a maker of patent rattraps or an angler for trout.

Audacity:—Your diddler is audacious. He is a bold man. He carries the war into Africa. He conquers all by assault. He would not fear the daggers of the Frey Herren. With a little more prudence Dick Turpin would have made a good diddler; with a little less blarney, Daniel O'Connell; with a pound or two more brains, Charles the Twelfth.

Nonchalance:—Your diddler is nonchalant. He is not at all nervous. He never *had* any nerves. He is never seduced into a flurry. He is never put out—unless put out of doors.

He is cool—cool as a cucumber. He is calm—"calm as a smile from Lady Bury." He is easy—easy as an old glove, or the damsels of ancient Baiæ.

Originality:—Your diddler is original—conscientiously so. His thoughts are his own. He would scorn to employ those of another. A stale trick is his aversion. He would return a purse, I am sure, upon discovering that he had obtained it by an unoriginal diddle.

Impertinence:—Your diddler is impertinent. He swaggers. He sets his arms akimbo. He thrusts his hands in his trousers' pockets. He sneers in your face. He treads on your corns. He eats your dinner, he drinks your wine, he borrows your money, he pulls your nose, he kicks your poodle, and he kisses your wife.

Grin:—Your *true* diddler winds up all with a grin. But this nobody sees but himself. He grins when his daily work is done—when his allotted labors are accomplished—at night in his own closet, and altogether for his own private entertainment. He goes home. He locks his door. He divests himself of his clothes. He puts out his candle. He gets into bed. He places his head upon the pillow. All this done, and your diddler *grins.* This is no hypothesis. It is a matter of course. I reason *a priori,* and a diddle would be *no* diddle without a grin.

The origin of the diddle is referable to the infancy of the Human Race. Perhaps the first diddler was Adam. At all events, we can trace the science back to a very remote period of antiquity. The moderns, however, have brought it to a perfection never dreamed of by our thick-headed progenitors. Without pausing to speak of the "old saws," therefore, I shall content myself with a compendious account of some of the more "modern instances."

A very good diddle is this. A housekeeper in want of a sofa, for instance, is seen to go in and out of several cabinet warehouses. At length she arrives at one offering an excellent variety. She is accosted, and invited to enter, by a polite and voluble individual at the door. She finds a sofa well adapted to her views, and, upon inquiring the price, is surprised and delighted to hear a sum named at least twenty per cent. lower than her expectations. She hastens to make the purchase, gets a bill and receipt, leaves her address, with a request that the article be sent home as speedily as possible, and retires amid a profusion of bows from the shop-keeper. The night arrives, and no sofa. The next day passes, and still none. A servant is sent to make inquiry about the delay. The whole transaction is denied. No sofa has been sold—no money received—except by the diddler, who played shop-keeper for the nonce.

Our cabinet warehouses are left entirely unattended, and thus afford every facility for a trick of this kind. Visitors enter, look at furniture, and depart unheeded and unseen. Should any one wish to purchase, or to inquire the price of an article, a bell is at hand, and this is considered amply sufficient.

Again, quite a respectable diddle is this. A well-dressed individual enters a shop; makes a purchase to the value of a dollar; finds, much to his vexation, that he has left his pocket-book in another coat pocket; and so says to the shop-keeper—

"My dear sir, never mind!—just oblige me, will you, by sending the bundle home? But stay! I really believe that I have nothing less than a five-dollar bill, even there. However, you can send four dollars in change with the bundle, you know."

"Very good, sir," replies the shop-keeper, who entertains at once a lofty opinion of the high-mindedness of his customer. "I know fellows," he says to himself, "who would just have put the goods under their arm, and walked off with a promise to call and pay the dollar as they came by in the afternoon."

A boy is sent with the parcel and change. On the route, quite accidentally, he is met by the purchaser, who exclaims:—

"Ah! this is my bundle, I see—I thought you had been home with it, long ago. Well, go on! My wife, Mrs. Trotter, will give you the five dollars—I left instructions with her to that effect. The change you might as well give to *me*—I shall want some silver for the Post Office. Very good! One, two, is this a good quarter?—three, four—quite right! Say to Mrs. Trotter that you met me, and be sure now and do not loiter on the way."

The boy doesn't loiter at all; but he is a very long time in getting back from his errand, for no lady of the precise name of Mrs. Trotter is to be discovered. He consoles himself, however, that he has not been such a fool as to leave the goods without the money, and, reëntering his shop with a self-satisfied air, feels sensibly hurt and indignant when his master asks him what has become of the change.

A very simple diddle, indeed, is this. The captain of a ship, which is about to sail, is presented by an official looking person with an unusually moderate bill of city charges. Glad to get off so easily, and confused by a hundred duties pressing upon him all at once, he discharges the claim forthwith. In about fifteen minutes, another and less reasonable bill is handed him by one who soon makes it evident that the first collector was a diddler, and the original collection a diddle.

And here, too, is a somewhat similar thing. A steamboat is casting loose from a wharf. A traveller, portmanteau in hand, is discovered, running towards the wharf at full speed. Suddenly, he makes a dead halt, stoops, and picks up something from the ground in a very agitated manner. It is a pocket-book, and—"Has any gentleman lost a pocket-book?" he cries. No one can say that he has exactly lost a pocket-book; but a great excitement ensues, when the treasure trove is found to be of value. The boat, however, must not be detained.

"Time and tide wait for no man," says the captain.

"For God's sake, stay only a few minutes," says the finder of the book—"the true claimant will presently appear."

"Can't wait!" replies the man in authority; "cast off there, d'ye hear?"

"What *am* I to do?" asks the finder, in great tribulation. "I am about to leave the country for some years, and I cannot conscientiously retain this large amount in my possession. I beg your pardon, sir" (here he addresses a gentleman on shore), "but you have the air of an honest man. *Will* you confer upon me the favor of taking charge of this pocket-book—I *know* I can trust you—and of advertising it? The notes, you see, amount to a very considerable sum. The owner will, no doubt, insist upon rewarding you for your trouble——"

"*Me!*—no, *you!*—it was *you* who found the book."

"Well, if you *must* have it so—*I* will take a small reward —just to satisfy your scruples. Let me see—why, these notes are all hundreds—bless my soul! a hundred is too much to take—fifty would be quite enough, I am sure——"

"Cast off there!" says the captain.

"But then I have no change for a hundred, and upon the whole *you* had better——"

"Cast off there!" says the captain.

"Never mind!" cries the gentleman on shore, who has been examining his own pocket-book for the last minute or so—"never mind! *I* can fix it—here is a fifty on the Bank of North America—throw me the book."

And the over-conscientious finder takes the fifty with marked reluctance, and throws the gentleman the book, as desired, while the steamboat fumes and fizzes on her way. In about half an hour after her departure the "large amount" is seen to be a "counterfeit presentment," and the whole thing a capital diddle.

A bold diddle is this. A camp-meeting, or something similar, is to be held at a certain spot which is accessible only by means of a free bridge. A diddler stations himself upon this bridge, respectfully informs all passers-by of the new county law, which establishes a toll of one cent for foot passengers, two for horses and donkeys, and so forth, and so forth. Some grumble, but all submit, and the diddler goes home a wealthier man by some fifty or sixty dollars well earned. This taking a toll from a great crowd of people is an excessively troublesome thing.

A neat diddle is this. A friend holds one of the diddler's promises to pay, filled up and signed in due form upon the ordinary blanks printed in red ink. The diddler purchases one or two dozen of these blanks, and every day dips one

of them in his soup, makes his dog jump for it, and finally
gives it to him as a *bonne bouche*. The note arriving at
maturity, the diddler, with the diddler's dog, calls upon the
friend, and the promise to pay is made the topic of discussion. The friend produces it from his *éscritoire*, and is in
the act of reaching it to the diddler, when up jumps the
diddler's dog and devours it forthwith. The diddler is not
only surprised but vexed and incensed at the absurd be-
havior of his dog, and expresses his entire readiness to can-
cel the obligation at any moment when the evidence of the
obligation shall be forthcoming.

A very minute diddle is this. A lady is insulted in the
street by a diddler's accomplice. The diddler himself flies
to her assistance, and, giving his friend a comfortable
thrashing, insists upon attending the lady to her own door.
He bows, with his hand upon his heart, and most respectfully bids her adieu. She entreats him, as her deliverer, to
walk in and be introduced to her big brother and her papa.
With a sigh, he declines to do so. "Is there no way, then,
sir," she murmurs, "in which I may be permitted to testify
my gratitude?"

"Why, yes, madam, there is. Will you be kind enough to
lend me a couple of shillings?"

In the first excitement of the moment the lady decides
upon fainting outright. Upon second thought, however, she
opens her purse-strings and delivers the species. Now this,
I say, is a diddle minute—for one entire moiety of the sum
borrowed has to be paid to the gentleman who had the
trouble of performing the insult, and who had then to stand
still and be thrashed for performing it.

Rather a small, but still a scientific diddle is this. The
diddler approaches the bar of a tavern, and demands a
couple of twists of tobacco. These are handed to him,
when, having slightly examined them, he says:—

"I don't much like this tobacco. Here, take it back, and
give me a glass of brandy and water in its place."

The brandy and water is furnished and imbibed, and
the diddler makes his way to the door. But the voice of the
tavern-keeper arrests him.

"I believe, sir, you have forgotten to pay for your brandy and water."

"Pay for my brandy and water!—didn't I give you the tobacco for the brandy and water? What more would you have?"

"But, sir, if you please, I don't remember that you paid for the tobacco."

"What do you mean by that, you scoundrel?—Didn't I give you back your tobacco? Isn't *that* your tobacco lying *there*? Do you expect me to pay for what I did not take?"

"But, sir," says the publican, now rather at a loss what to say, "but, sir——"

"But me no buts, sir," interrupts the diddler, apparently in very high dudgeon, and slamming the door after him, as he makes his escape.—"But me no buts, sir, and none of your tricks upon travellers."

Here again is a very clever diddle, of which the simplicity is not its least recommendation. A purse, or pocket-book, being really lost, the loser inserts in *one* of the daily papers of a large city a fully descriptive advertisement.

Whereupon our diddler copies the *facts* of this advertisement, with a change of heading, of general phraseology, and *address*. The original, for instance, is long and verbose, is headed "A Pocket-Book Lost!" and requires the treasure when found, to be left at No. 1 Tom Street. The copy is brief and, being headed with "Lost" only, indicates No. 2 Dick, or No. 3 Harry Street, as the locality at which the owner may be seen. Moreover, it is inserted in at least five or six of the daily papers of the day, while in point of time it makes its appearance only a few hours after the original. Should it be read by the loser of the purse, he would hardly suspect it to have any reference to his own misfortune. But, of course, the chances are five or six to one that the finder will repair to the address given by the diddler, rather than to that pointed out by the rightful proprietor. The former pays the reward, pockets the treasure, and decamps.

Quite an analogous diddle is this. A lady of *ton* has dropped, somewhere in the street, a diamond ring of very unusual value. For its recovery, she offers some forty or

fifty dollars' reward—giving in her advertisement a very
minute description of the gem, and of its settings, and declaring that, upon its restoration to No. So and So, in such
and such Avenue; the reward will be paid *instanter*, without a single question being asked. During the lady's absence
from home, a day or two afterwards, a ring is heard at the
door of No. So and So, in such and such Avenue; a servant
appears; the lady of the house is asked for and is declared
to be out, at which astounding information the visitor expresses the most poignant regret. His business is of importance and concerns the lady herself. In fact, he had the
good fortune to find her diamond ring. But perhaps it
would be as well that he should call again. "By no means!"
says the servant; and "By no means!" say the lady's sister
and the lady's sister-in-law, who are summoned forthwith.
The ring is clamorously identified, the reward is paid, and
the finder nearly thrust out of doors. The lady returns, and
expresses some little dissatisfaction with her sister and
sister-in-law, because they happen to have paid forty or
fifty dollars for a fac-simile of her diamond ring—a fac-
simile made out of real pinchbeck and unquestionable
paste.

But, as there is really no end to diddling, so there would
be none to this essay, were I even to hint at half the variations, or inflections, of which this science is susceptible. I
must bring this paper, perforce, to a conclusion, and this
I cannot do better than by a summary notice of a very
decent but rather elaborate diddle, of which our own city
was made the theatre, not very long ago, and which was
subsequently repeated with success in other still more verdant localities of the Union. A middle-aged gentleman arrives in town from parts unknown. He is remarkably precise, cautious, staid, and deliberate in his demeanor. His
dress is scrupulously neat, but plain, unostentatious. He
wears a white cravat, an ample waistcoat, made with an
eye to comfort alone; thick-soled cosey-looking shoes, and
pantaloons without straps. He has the whole air, in fact,
of your well-to-do, sober-sided, exact, and respectable
"man of business," *par excellence*—one of the stern and out-
wardly hard, internally soft, sort of people that we see in

the crack high comedies; fellows whose words are so many bonds, and who are noted for giving away guineas, in charity, with the one hand, while in the way of mere bargain, they exact the uttermost fraction of a farthing with the other.

He makes much ado before he can get suited with a boarding-house. He dislikes children. He has been accustomed to quiet. His habits are methodical—and then he would prefer getting into a private and respectable small family, piously inclined. Terms, however, are no object; only he must insist upon settling his bill on the first of every month (it is now the second), and begs his landlady, when he finally obtains one to his mind, *not* on any account to forget his instructions upon this point—but to send in a bill, *and* receipt, precisely at ten o'clock on the *first* day of every month, and under no circumstances to put it off to the second.

These arrangements made, our man of business rents an office in a reputable rather than in a fashionable quarter of the town. There is nothing he more despises than pretence. "Where there is much show," he says, "there is seldom anything very solid behind;" an observation which so profoundly impresses his landlady's fancy that she makes a pencil memorandum of it forthwith, in her great family Bible, on the broad margin of the Proverbs of Solomon.

The next step is to advertise, after some such fashion as this, in the principal business sixpennies of this city—the pennies are eschewed as not "respectable" and as demanding payment for all advertisements in advance. Our man of business holds it as a point of his faith that work should never be paid for until done.

"WANTED.—The advertisers, being about to commence extensive business operations in this city, will require the services of three or four intelligent and competent clerks, to whom a liberal salary will be paid. The very best recommendations, not so much for capacity, as for integrity, will be expected. Indeed, as the duties to be performed involve high responsibilities, and large amounts of money must necessarily pass through the hands of those engaged, it is deemed advisable to demand a deposit of fifty dollars from each clerk employed. No person need apply, therefore, who is not prepared to leave this sum in the possession of the advertisers, and who cannot furnish the most satisfactory testimonials of morality. Young gentlemen piously inclined will be preferred. Application should be made between the hours of ten and eleven, A.M., and four and five, P.M., of Messrs.

> "Bogs, Hogs, Logs, Frogs, & Co.
> "No. 110 Dog Street"

By the thirty-first day of the month, this advertisement has brought to the office of Messrs. Bogs, Hogs, Logs, Frogs, and Company, some fifteen or twenty young gentlemen piously inclined. But our man of business is in no hurry to conclude a contract with any—no man of business is *ever* precipitate—and it is not until the most rigid catechism, in respect to the piety of each young gentleman's inclination, that his services are engaged and his fifty dollars receipted for, *just* by way of proper precaution, on the part of the respectable firm of Bogs, Hogs, Logs, Frogs, and Company. On the morning of the first day of the next month, the landlady does *not* present her bill, according to promise; a piece of neglect for which the comfortable head of the house ending in *ogs* would no doubt have chided her severely, could he have been prevailed upon to remain in town a day or two for that purpose.

As it is, the constables have had a sad time of it, running hither and thither, and all they can do is to declare the man of business most emphatically a "hen knee high"—by which some persons imagine them to imply that, in fact he is n. e. i.—by which again the very classical phrase *non est inventus* is supposed to be understood. In the mean time the young gentlemen, one and all, are somewhat less piously inclined than before, while the landlady purchases a shilling's worth of the best Indian rubber, and very carefully obliterates the pencil memorandum that some fool has made in her great family Bible, on the broad margin of the Proverbs of Solomon.

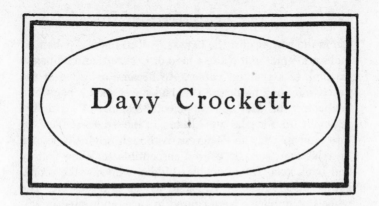

Davy Crockett

The patriotic exuberance which led Melville to envisage Shakespeares being born on the banks of the Ohio prompted him, in *Moby Dick*, to describe Hercules as an antique Crockett. The Tennessee bear hunter had been dead for only a quarter of a century when Melville wrote his story of a whale hunt, but in that time Crockett had become such a colossal figure in the American imagination that the greatest writer of the age could compare him to a hero of Greek mythology and mean it not only as a joke, but as a serious statement about democratic heroism.

The story of the legendary Crockett begins with the birth of the historical Davy in the mountains of east Tennessee in 1786. His boyhood was a classic story of frontier hardship and brutality. Bound out as an apprentice at twelve, he escaped in a snowstorm. He was next sent to school, but after a fight with another student, in which Crockett "scratched his face all to a flitter jig," he was afraid to go back, for fear of the brutal master. When Crockett's father, a hard-drinking, powerful man, heard of his son's truancy, he swore he would give him the beating of his life, and so Crockett, like Huck Finn fleeing the drunken wrath of his Pap, ran away. He was then thirteen years old.

A dozen years later he appeared as a soldier under Jackson in the war against the Creeks. Just as the war enhanced Jackson's fame, so it made a hero of Crockett, and he began to think of a political career. He became a justice of the peace, although he boasted he had never read a page of a lawbook in his life, and was elected colonel of his militia regiment. In 1821 he was elected to the Tennessee legislature, and in 1827 to Congress. Although originally known as a Jackson man, he proved susceptible to Whig flattery and bank loans from Nicholas Biddle, who saw the propaganda possibilities of Crockett as an anti-Jackson. The wheels of publicity were caused to turn, and anti-administration newspapers soon were full of apocryphal stories about a lovable, unpolished diamond from the Tennessee canebrake. The process of converting a rough, violent-tempered product of a brutal upbringing into simply another version of pastoral was fully launched. Matthew St. Clair Clark, a friend of Biddle's, next wrote a biography of Crockett for the campaign of 1833, which proved tremendously popular, particularly in the West, and other books, including an autobiography, quickly followed. In 1834 the Whigs sent him on a tour of the North and East, where he was paraded, applauded for his wit—although his speeches were written by others—and heralded as the next President of the United States, an idea which Crockett seemed to take seriously. He told cheering throngs that he "was no man's follower," but by this time he was no more than the kept clown of the Whigs.

In 1835 came disaster. Jackson's fury had been aroused by the gibes of what he called "Crockett and Co.," and he was determined to defeat him in the next election. Aided by the fact that Crockett had not mended his political fences in Tennessee, a Jackson man crushed him at the polls. Crockett's response was, "You may all go to hell and I will go to Texas." His martyrdom a few months later was the final requisite for myth, just as it would be for Lincoln. With the Alamo, Crockett passed fully into legend.

The Crockett almanacs, published between the mid-1830s and the mid-1850s in more than fifty different versions, were one of the most important factors in the perpetuation of the Crockett myth. In their pages the tall tales of the frontier were retold, with Crockett as their hero. Combining savage cruelty with a surprising strain of sadness, the almanac stories strove to express an intense but uncertain emotion. If, however, their meaning was often obscure, the stories brilliantly rendered the vernacular language of the western boatman, hunter, and squatter. At their best, the writers of the Crockett almanacs transcended the outrageous neologisms and hyperbolic absurdities which were their stock in trade, and achieved what Professor Howard Mumford Jones has called a "lawless lyricism"; in such pieces as "Death of Crockett" and "Crockett's Morning Hunt," they anticipated Whitman's prophecy that "Americans are going to be the most fluent and melodious-voiced people in the world—and the most perfect users of words. The new times, the new people, the new vistas need a new tongue according—yes, and what is more, they will have such a new tongue."

Death of Crockett

Thar's a great rejoicin' among the bears of Kaintuck, and the alligators of the Mississippi rolls up thar shining ribs to the sun, and has grown so fat and lazy that they will hardly move out of the way for a steamboat. The rattlesnakes come up out of thar holes and frolic within ten foot of the clearings, and the foxes goes to sleep in the goose-pens. It is bekase the rifle of Crockett is silent forever, and the print of his moccasins is found no more in our woods. His old fox-skin cap hangs up in the cabin, and every hunter, whether he are a Puke, a Wolverine, or a Sucker, never looks at it without turnin' away his head and droppin' a salt tear.

Luke Wing entered the cabin the other day and took down old Killdevil to look at it. The muzzle was half stopped up with rust, and a great green spider run out of it and made his escape in the cracks of the wall. The varmints of the forest will fear it no more. His last act to defend it, war when the poor gallant Kurnill drew a bead on a pesky Mexican and brought him down. Crockett went to put "Big Butcher" into another, and the feller on the ground turned half over, and stuck a knife into him. Another come up behind and run his bayonet into Crockett's back, for the cretur would as soon have faced a hindred live mammoths as to have faced Crockett at any time.

Down fell the Kurnill like a lion struck by thunder and lightning. He never spoke again. It war a great loss to the country, and the world, and to ole Kaintuck in particklar. Thar were never known such a member of Congress as Crockett, and never will be agin. The painters and bears will miss him, for he never missed them.

He died like a member o' Congress ought to die. While he war about to do his country some sarvice, and raise her name as high as her mountains, he war cut down in the prime o' life, and at a time when he war most wanted. His screams and yells are heard no more, and the whole country are clouded with a darkness for the gallant Kurnill. He war an ornament to the forest, and war never known to refuse his whiskey to a stranger. When he war alive, it war most beautiful to hear his scream coming through the forest; it would turn and twist itself into some of the most splendifferous knots, and then untie itself and keep on till it got clar into nowhere.

But he are a dead man now, and if you want to see old Kaintuck's tears, go thar, and speak o' her gallant Kurnill, and thar's not a human but what will turn away and go behind some tree and dry up thar tears. He are dead now, and may he rest forever and a day arter.

Crockett's Morning Hunt

One January morning it was so all-screwen-up cold that the forest trees war so stiff that they couldn't shake, and the very day-break froze fast as it war tryin' to dawn. The tinder-box in my cabin would no more ketch fire than a sunk raft at the bottom o' the sea. Seein' that daylight war so far behind time, I thought creation war in a fair way for freezin' fast.

"So," thinks I, "I must strike a leetle fire from my fingers, light my pipe, travel out a few leagues, and see about it."

Then I brought my knuckles together like two thunder clouds, but the sparks froze up afore I could begin to collect 'em—so out I walked, and endeavored to keep myself unfriz by goin' at a hop, step, and jump gait, and whistlin' the tune of "fire in the mountains!" as I went along in three double quick time. Well, arter I had walked about twenty-five miles up the peak o' Daybreak Hill, I soon discovered what war the matter. The airth had actually friz fast in her axis, and couldn't turn round; the sun had got jammed between two cakes o' ice under the wheels, an' thar he had bin shinin' and workin' to get loose, till he friz fast in his cold sweat.

"C-r-e-a-t-i-o-n!" thought I, "this are the toughest sort o' suspension, and it mustn't be endured—somethin' must be done, or human creation is done for."

It war then so antedeluvian and premature cold that my upper and lower teeth an' tongue war all collapsed together as tight as a friz oyster. I took a fresh twenty pound bear off o' my back that I'd picked up on the road, an' beat the animal agin the ice till the hot ile began to walk out on him at all sides. I then took an' held him over the airth's axes, an' squeezed him till I thaw'd 'em loose, poured about a ton on it over the sun's face, give the airth's cog-wheel one kick backward, till I got the sun loose—whistled "Push along, keep movin'!" an' in about fifteen seconds the airth gin a grunt, and begun movin'—the sun walked up beautiful, salutin' me with sich a wind o' gratitude that it made me sneeze. I lit my pipe by the blaze o' his top-knot, shouldered my bear, an' walked home, introducin' the people to fresh daylight with a piece of sunrise in my pocket, with which I cooked my bear steaks, an' enjoyed one o' the best breakfasts I had tasted for some time. If I didn't, jist wake some mornin' and go with me to the office o' sunrise!

James Kirke Paulding

The Lion of the West, by Irving's friend and onetime collaborator, James Kirke Paulding, was the first American comedy to focus on the western frontiersman. In a letter to James H. Hackett, a well-known actor of the day who had undertaken to play the leading role, Paulding insisted that the hero, Nimrod Wildfire, was not typical of Kentucky gentlemen, or of Kentuckians generally, but "of a peculiar class, originally Mississippi Boatmen, one of whom by a rare chance rises to a higher station in society than might be expected from his early situation," details which make it sound as if Wildfire were based on some such river demigod as Mike Fink. He was in fact, however, entirely inspired by Colonel Davy Crockett, the bear hunter and congressman from east Tennessee.

For such is the fluidity of myth that many of the stories being told about Crockett had a Mississippi River locale, and he was often depicted as a keelboatman. Furthermore, the references in the play to an impending congressional election, and the fact that Wildfire is a colonel, could have had only one meaning to an audience in the early 1830s: Wildfire was Crockett. Before the play was produced the author wrote a letter to Crockett denying his intention of portraying Crockett, and Crockett responded at once, saying that "the frankness of your letter induces me to say that you were incapable of wounding the feelings of a stranger and unlettered man who had never injured you." But all of this was deliberately designed to promote a play on the one hand and a politican on the other. In his *Reminiscences of Sixty Years in the National Metropolis,* Benjamin Perley Poore relates that at Crockett's request Hackett presented the play in Washington. Crockett had a front-row seat, and when he entered the theater the audience burst into cheers. When Hackett came on stage as Wildfire he bowed first to the audience and then to Crockett. Crockett scrambled to his feet again, bowed to the spectators and then to Hackett, while the theater went wild.

Like the Whig version of Crockett, Nimrod Wildfire talks like a wild man, but is basically a domesticated house pet. The spectacle of a half horse, half alligator who scared away pretentious Englishmen without actually resorting to violence proved enormously reassuring to eastern audiences, and *The Lion of the West* remained a part of Hackett's repertoire for many years.

From *The Lion of the West*

ACT II, SCENE 2

Room in a boarding house. Enter Percival with a newspaper.

PERCIVAL. (*reads*) "February 5th died suddenly at the Hermitage near Swansea the right Honorable Lord George Grandby—" Can this be possible? My rival an imposter? Can he dare so great an insult to his country? When I consider his conduct my doubts rise to conviction. How shall I proceed? To denounce him on so slight a proof might look like envy, yet to hazard the happiness of her whom I love above all breathing beings is impossible. I will enclose this paper to her father. (*Sits and writes.*)

Wildfire heard without

WILDFIRE. Upstairs, is he? Never mind, I'll find him.

PERCIVAL. Ah, my Kentucky friend; like most uncultivated plants, a sound core with all his roughness of exterior.

Enter Wildfire

WILDFIRE. Ah, Percival my boy, how goes it? What, so I discovered last night that you are clinched in a love match with my cousin Carry. Well, she's a peeler, ain't she? But, I say, Percy, you must mind—hunt close upon the trail.

PERCIVAL. Ah, Colonel, I'm afraid I shall never run down the game.

WILDFIRE. What, why the little cretur hasn't dodged you? As we hunters say, won't she squat?

PERCIVAL. Why, to confess the truth, circumstances have recently transpired which involve me in some difficulty.

WILDFIRE. What! not out of ammunition—don't want money? If you do, I'm your man for five hundred or a thousand dollars. Draw upon *me;* I'll answer your drafts —draw like a horse.

PERCIVAL. I'm obliged to your generosity, but you mistake me. My difficulties are not pecuniary. To be candid with you, I am not a favorite with your aunt. You must have observed last night the preference she displayed towards my noble countryman.

WILDFIRE. Last night: No, I didn't see much of anything— I put too much brandy in my water. I was pretty particularly sprung.

PERCIVAL. Briefly, then—his Lordship is a suitor for your cousin's hand.

WILDFIRE. Oh, it's nothing but her vanity makes her listen to that Lord, and "Vanity, thy name is woman." So says Shakspeare, and warn't he a screamer?

PERCIVAL. But what adds to my uneasiness is my strong suspicion that he is not what he pretends to be.

WILDFIRE. What? Why, you don't think he is cheating, do you—as we say in Kaintuck, "playing possum"?

PERCIVAL. I must confess I have had cause.

WILDFIRE. Well, look here, Percival—I like an honest man

let him come from what land he may and *perhaps* I like
John Bull the best because we all come from one mother
hen, tho' our brood was hatched this side of the water,
but I hate a cheating possum, and if you are sure this
Lord is a possum—

PERCIVAL. I have no proof upon the point. My doubts arise
from a few words in a paper which I confess I can't understand.

WILDFIRE. Well, that's not my case. He has sent me a paper that I do (*Gives one to Percival*). It's a beautiful
piece of furniture—read it.

PERCIVAL. (*Reads*) "Sir—Your presumptuous familiarity
with me last night and your subsequent display of Kentucky civility towards a lady who has claimed my protection warrant me in demanding from you the satisfaction
of a gentleman. You will let me know before tomorrow
where a friend can wait upon you. Grandby." Why,
Colonel, this certainly does look very like a challenge, but
do you mean to fight him?

WILDFIRE. Distinctly. He'll find there's no mistake in me. I
always go primed for such fun!

PERCIVAL. But, Colonel, you'll not be too hasty in this
business.

WILDFIRE. Hasty? I'm always as cool as an Ingen, but if
he wants to pick a quarrel with *me*, he'll stand a mighty
sudden chance of being *used up*.

PERCIVAL. You, of course, allude to the treatment of a gentleman.

WILDFIRE. A gentleman? Oh, I'll put it to him *like* a *gentleman*, but if this had happened about ten years ago—
when I was chock full of fun and fight—I wouldn't have
minded going it in Old Mississippi style.

PERCIVAL. Some mode once peculiar to the wildness of the
region?

WILDFIRE. Why, I'll tell you how it was. I was riding along
the Mississippi one day when I came across a fellow
floating down the stream sitting cock'd up in the starn of
his boat fast asleep. Well, I hadn't had a fight for as
much as ten days—felt as though I must kiver myself up

in a salt bin to keep—"so wolfy" about the head and shoulders. So, says I, hullo, stranger, if you don't take keer your boat will run away wi' you. So he looked up at me "slantindickular," and I looked down on him "slanchwise." He took out a chaw of tobacco from his mouth and, says he, I don't value you tantamount to that, and then he flopp'd his wings and crowed like a cock. I ris up, shook my mane, crooked my neck, and neighed like a horse. Well, he run his boat foremost ashore. I stopped my waggon and set my triggers. Mister, says he, I'm the best man—if I ain't, I wish I may be tetotaciously exflunctified! I can whip my weight in wild cats and ride strait through a crab apple orchard on a flash of lightning—clear meat axe disposition! And what's more, I once backed a bull off a bridge. Poh, says I, what do I keer for that? I can tote a steam boat up the Mississippi and over the Alleghany mountains. My father can whip the best man in old Kaintuck, and I can whip my father. When I'm good natured I weigh about a hundred and seventy, but when I'm mad, I weigh about a *ton*. With that I fetched him the regular Ingen war-whoop. Out he jumped from his boat, and down I tumbled from my waggon—and, I say, we came together like two steam boats going sixty mile an hour. He was a pretty severe colt, but no part of a priming to such a feller as me. I put it to him mighty droll—tickled the varmint till he squealed like a young colt, bellowed "enough" and swore I was a "rip staver." Says I, *ain't* I a horse? Says he, stranger, you're a *beauty* anyhow, and if you'd stand for Congress I'd vote for you next *lection*. Says I, would you? My name's Nimrod Wildfire. Why, I'm the yaller flower of the forest. I'm all *brimstone but the head*, and that's *aky fortis*.

PERCIVAL. A renowned achievement. Well, Colonel, I feel it my duty before I leave New York to disclose the rumor I have heard to your uncle. Proceed in this affair as you think best, but remember, if you do meet his Lordship, it must be with the weapons of a gentleman. (*Exit*)

WILDFIRE. A gentleman's weapons? Oh, of course, he

means rifles. May be that Lord has heard of mine. She's a noisy varmint made of Powder house lightning-rod steel and twisted like our Kentucky widow. She's got but one peeper, but if she blinks that at him, his head will hum like a hornet's nest—he'll see the stars dance in the day time. He'll come off as badly as a feller I once hit a sledge hammer lick over the head—a rale "sogdolloger." He disappeared altogether; all they could ever find of him was a little grease spot in one corner. (*Exit*)

James Russell Lowell

In the First Series of *The Biglow Papers*, most of which were first published in the *National Anti-Slavery Standard*, Lowell combined the nasal twang, the iron-willed self-righteousness, and the macabre humor of his Yankee heritage into a political weapon of considerable power. When collected between covers, the First Series sold an amazing fifteen hundred copies in one week. As Lowell himself later wrote, "The success of my experiment soon began not only to astonish me, but to make me feel the responsibility of knowing that I held in my hand a weapon instead of the mere fencing-stick I had supposed."

Speaking through the mask of the cracker-barrel philosopher, Hosea Biglow, Lowell ridiculed the Mexican War, the southern slavocracy and a variety of politicans, most of them Democrats. In Number Three, for example, Biglow satirically commented on a Massachusetts gubernatorial race, throwing his weight behind the Whig governor, Briggs, while denouncing the Democratic candidate, Caleb Cushing, who had been made a general during the Mexican War, and his last-minute supporter, John P. Robinson. Birdofredum Sawin was also one of Lowell's masks, although this grotesque creature, who incarnates all the headlong recklessness of the American character, can hardly be said to have represented Lowell's point of view. Given Lowell's conception of the slavocracy as a violent, intemperate society, it is significant that Sawin intends to settle in the South after the Mexican War is over.

In the Second Series of the *Papers,* published after the close of the Civil War, Lowell was more interested in exploring the possibilities of an American national literature than he was in political commentary. He felt that by "turning into one of our narrow New England lanes" and listening to the "ordinary talk of unlettered men among us" American authors could find the way to greatness. "The Courtin'" is one of his best-known efforts to use American speech as a vehicle for comedy. Edward Eggleston, Mark Twain, and Joel Chandler Harris, themselves masters of local idiom, greatly admired Lowell's sensitive representation of New England dialect.

What Mr. Robinson Thinks

Guvener B. is a sensible man;
   He stays to his home an' looks arter his folks;
He draws his furrer ez straight ez he can,
   An' into nobody's tater-patch pokes;
        But John B.
        Robinson he
    Sez he wunt vote fer Guvener B.

My! aint it terrible! Wut shall we du?
   We can't never choose him o'course,—thet's flat;
Guess we shall hev to come round, (don't you?)
   An' go in fer thunder an' guns, an' all that;
        Fer John B.
        Robinson he
    Sez he wunt vote fer Guvener B.

Gineral C. is a dreffle smart man:
   He's ben on all sides thet give places or pelf;
But consistency still wuz a part of his plan,—
   He's ben true to *one* party—an' thet is himself;—
         So John P.
         Robinson he
   Sez he shall vote fer Gineral C.

Gineral C. he goes in fer the war;
   He don't vally principle more 'n an old cud;
Wut did God make us raytional creeturs fer,
   But glory an' gunpowder, plunder an' blood?
         So John P.
         Robinson he
   Sez he shall vote for Gineral C.

We were gittin' on nicely up here to our village,
   With good old idees o' wut's right an' wut aint,
We kind o'thought Christ went agin war an' pillage,
   An' thet eppyletts worn't the best mark of a saint;
         But John P.
         Robinson he
   Sez this kind o' thing's an exploded idee.

The side of our country must ollers be took,
   An' President Polk, you know, *he* is our country.
An' the angel thet writes all our sins in a book
   Puts the *debit* to him, an' to us the *per contry;*
         An' John P.
         Robinson he
   Sez this is his view o' the thing to a T.

Parson Wilbur he calls all these argimunts lies;
   Sez they're nothin' on airth but jest *fee, faw, fum:*
An' thet all this big talk of our destinies
   Is half on it ign'ance, an' t'other half rum;
         But John P.
         Robinson he
   Sez it aint no sech thing; an' of course, so must we.

Parson Wilbur sez *he* never heerd in his life
    Thet th' Apostles rigged out in their swaller-tail coats,
An' marched round in front of a drum an' a fife,
    To git some on 'em office, an' some on 'em votes;
             But John P.
             Robinson he
    Sez they didn't know everythin' down in Judee.

Wal, it's a marcy we've gut folks to tell us
    The rights an' the wrongs o' these matters, I vow,—
God sends country lawyers, an' other wise fellers,
    To start the world's team wen it gits in a slough;
             Fer John P.
             Robinson he
    Sez the world'll go right, ef he hollers out Gee!

A Second Letter from B. Sawin, Esq.

I spose you wonder ware I be; I can't tell, fer the soul o'
    me,
Exactly ware I be myself,—meanin' by thet the holl o' me.
Wen I left hum, I hed two legs, an' they worn't bad ones
    neither,
(The scaliest trick they ever played wuz bringin' on me
    hither,)
Now one on 'em's I dunno ware;—they thought I wuz
    adyin',
An' sawed it off because they said 't wuz kin' o' mortifyin';
I'm willin' to believe it wuz, an' yit I don't see, nuther,
Wy one shoud take to feelin' cheap a minnit sooner 'n t'
    other,
Sence both wuz equilly to blame; but things is ez they be;
It took on so they took it off, an' thet's enough fer me:
There's one good thing, though, to be said about my
    wooden new one,—

The liquor can't get into it ez 't used to in the true one;
So it saves drink; an' then, besides, a feller could n't beg
A gretter blessin' then to hev one ollers sober peg;
It's true a chap's in want o' two fer follerin' a drum,
But all the march I'm up to now is jest to Kingdom Come.

I've lost one eye, but thet's a loss it's easy to supply
Out o' the glory that I've gut, fer thet is all my eye;
An' one is big enough, I guess, by diligently usin' it,
To see all I shall ever git by way o' pay fer losin' it;
Off'cers I notice, who git paid fer all our thumps an' kickins,
Du wal by keepin' single eyes arter the fattest pickins;
So, ez the eye's put fairly out, I'll larn to go without it,
An' not allow *myself* to be no gret put out about it.
Now, le' me see, thet is n't all; I used, 'fore leavin Jaalam,
To count things on my finger-eends, but sutthin' seems to
    ail 'em:
Ware's my left hand? O, darn it, yes, I recollect wut 's come
    on 't;
I haint no left arm but my right, an' thet 's gut jest a thumb
    on 't;
It aint so hendy ez it wuz to cal'late a sum on 't.
I've hed some ribs broke,—six (I b'lieve),—I haint kep' no
    account on 'em;
Wen pensions git to be the talk, I'll settle the amount on
    'em.
An' now I'm speakin' about ribs, it kin' o' brings to mind
One thet I could n't never break,—the one I lef' behind;
Ef you should see her, jest clear out the spout o' your in-
    vention
An' pour the longest sweetnin' in about an annooal pension,
An' kin' o' hint (in case, you know, the critter should refuse
    to be
Consoled) I aint so 'xpensive now to keep ez wut I used
    to be;
There's one arm less, ditto one eye, an' then the leg thet's
    wooden
Can be took off an' sot away wenever ther 's a puddin'.

I spose you think I'm comin' back ez opperlunt ez thunder,
With shiploads o' gold images an' varus sorts o' plunder;
Wal, 'fore I vullinteered, I thought this country wuz a
sort o'
Canaan, a reg'lar Promised Land flowin' with rum an'
water,
Ware propaty growed up like time, without no cultivation,
An' gold wuz dug ez taters be among our Yankee nation,
Ware nateral advantages were pufficly amazin',
Ware every rock there wuz about with precious stuns wuz
blazin',
Ware mill-sites filled the country up ez thick ez you could
cram 'em
An' desput rivers run about a beggin' folks to dam 'em;
Then there were meetinhouses, tu, chockful o' gold an'
silver
Thet you could take, an' no one could n't hand ye in no
bill fer;—
Thet's wut I thought afore I went, thet's wut them fellers
told us
Thet stayed to hum an' speechified an' to the buzzards sold
us;
I thought thet gold-mines could be gut cheaper than Chiny
asters,
An' see myself acomin' back sixty Jacob Astors;
But sech idees soon melted down an' did n't leave a grease-
spot;
I vow my holl sheer o' the spiles would n't come nigh a V
spot;
Although, most anywares we 've ben, you need n't break
no locks,
Nor run no kin' o' risks, to fill your pocket full o' rocks.
I 'xpect I mentioned in my last some o' the nateral feeturs
O' this all-fiered buggy hole in th' way o' awfle creeturs,
But I fergut to name (new things to speak on so abounded)
How one day you'll most die o' thust, an' 'fore the next git
drownded.
The clymit seems to me jest like a teapot made o' pewter

Our Prudence hed, thet would n't pour (all she could du)
    to suit her;
Fust place the leaves 'ould choke the spout, so 's not a drop
    'ould dreen out,
Then Prude 'ould tip an' tip an' tip, till the holl kit bust
    clean out,
The kiver-hinge-pin bein' lost, tea-leaves an' tea an' kiver
'ould all come down *kerswosh!* ez though the dam bust in
    a river.
Jest so 't is here; holl months there aint a day o' rainy
    weather,
An' jest ez th' officers 'ould be a layin' heads together
Ez t' how they'd mix their drink at sech a milingtary
    deepot,—
'T would pour ez though the lid wuz off the everlastin' tea-
    pot.
The cons'quence is, thet I shall take, wen I'm allowed to
    leave here,
One piece o' propaty along, an' thet 's the shakin' fever;
It's reggilar employment, though, an' thet aint thought to
    harm one,
Nor 't aint so tiresome ez it wuz with t' other leg an' arm on;
An' it 's a consolation, tu, although it doos n't pay,
To hev it said you're some gret shakes in any kin' o' way.
'T worn't very long, I tell ye wut, I thought o' fortin-
    makin',—
One day a reg'lar shiver-de-freeze, an' next ez good ez
    bakin',—
One day abrilin' in the sand, then smoth'rin' in the mashes,—
Git up all sound, be put to bed a mess o' hacks an' smashes.
But then, thinks I, at any rate there's glory to be hed,—
Thet's an investment, arter all, thet may n't turn out so bad;
But somehow, wen we'd fit an' licked, I ollers found the
    thanks
Gut kin' o' lodged afore they come ez low down ez the
    ranks;
The Gin'rals gut the biggest sheer, the Cunnles next, an'
    so on,—
We never gut a blasted mite o' glory ez I know on;

An' spose we hed, I wonder how you're goin' to contrive its
Division so 's to give a piece to twenty thousand privits;
Ef you should multiply by ten the portion o' the brav'st one,
You would n't git more 'n half enough to speak of on a
     grave-stun;
We git the licks,—we're jest the grist thet 's put into War's
     hoppers;
Leftenants is the lowest grade thet helps picks up the
     coppers.
It may suit folks thet go agin a body with a soul in 't,
An' aint contented with a hide without a bagnet hole in 't;
But glory is a kin' o' thing I sha' n't pursue no furder,
Coz thet 's the off'cers parquisite,—yourn 's on'y jest the
     murder.

Wal, arter I gin glory up, thinks I at least there 's one
Thing in the bills we aint hed yit, an' thet 's the GLORI-
     OUS FUN;
Ef once we git to Mexico, we fairly may persume we
All day an' night shall revel in the halls o' Montezumy.
I'll tell ye wut *my* revels wuz, an' see how you would like
     'em;
We never gut inside the hall: the nighest ever *I* come
Wuz stan'in sentry in the sun ('an', fact, it *seemed* a
     cent'ry)
A ketchin' smells o' biled an' roast thet come out thru the
     entry,
An' hearin' ez I sweltered thru my passes an' repasses,
A rat-tat-too o' knives an' forks, a clinkty-clink o' glasses:
I can't tell off the bill o' fare the Ginrals hed inside;
All I know is, thet out o' doors a pair o' soles wuz fried,
An' not a hundred miles away frum ware this child was
     posted,
A Massachusetts citizen wuz baked an' biled an' roasted;
The on'y thing like revellin' thet ever come to me
Wuz bein' routed out o' sleep by thet darned revelee.

They say the quarrel 's settled now; fer my part I 've some
     doubt on 't;

't 'll take more fish-skin than folks think to take the rile
    clean out on 't;
At any rate I 'm so used up I can't do no more fightin',
The on'y chance thet 's left to me is politics or writin';
Now, ez the people's gut to hev a milingtary man,
An' I aint nothin' else jest now, I've hit upon a plan;
The can'idatin' line, you know, 'ould suit me to a T,
An' ef I lose, 't wunt hurt my ears to lodge another flea;
So I 'll set up ez can'idate fer any kin' o' office.
(I mean fer any thet includes good easy-cheers an' soffies;
Fer ez tu runnin' fer a place ware work 's the time o' day,
You know thet 's wut I never did,—except the other way;)
Ef it 's the Presidential cheer fer wich I 'd better run,
Wut two legs anywares about could keep up with my one?
There aint no kin' o' quality in can'idates, it 's said,
So useful ez a wooden leg,—except a wooden head;
There's nothin' aint so poppylar—(wy, it 's a parfect sin
To think wut Mexico hez paid fer Santy Anny's pin;)—
Then I haint gut no princerples, an', sence I wuz knee-high,
I never *did* hev any gret, ez you can testify;
I 'm a decided peace-man, tu, an' go agin the war,—
Fer now the holl on 't 's gone an' past, wut is there to go
    for?
Ef, wile you 're 'lectioneerin' round, some curus chaps
    should beg
To know my views o' state affairs, jest answer WOODEN
    LEG!
Ef they aint settisfied with thet, an' kin' o' pry an' doubt
An' az fer sutthin' deffynit, jest say ONE EYE PUT OUT!
Thet kin' o' talk I guess you 'll find 'll answer to a charm,
An' wen you 're druv tu nigh the wall, hol' up my missin'
    arm;
Ef they should nose round fer a pledge, put on a vartoous
    look
An' tell 'em thet's percisely wut I never gin nor—took!

Then you can call me "Timbertoes,"—thet 's wut the people
    likes;
Sutthin' combinin' morril truth with phrases sech ez strikes;

Some say the people 's fond o' this, or thet, or wut you
　　please,—
I tell ye wut the people want is jest correct idees;
"Old Timbertoes," you see, 's a creed it 's safe to be quite
　　bold on,
It's a good tangible idee, a sutthin' to embody
Thet valooable class o' men who look thru brandy-toddy;
It gives a Party Platform, tu, jest level with the mind
Of all right-thinkin', honest folks thet mean to go it blind;
Then there air other good hooraws to dror on ez you need
　　'em,
Sech ez the ONE-EYED SLARTERER, the BLOODY BIRDO-
　　FREDUM:
Them 's wut takes hold o' folks thet think, ez well ez o' the
　　masses,
An' makes you sartin o' the aid o' good men of all classes.

There 's one thing I 'm in doubt about; in order to be
　　Presidunt,
It's absolutely ne'ssary to be a Southern residunt;
The Constitution settles thet, an' also thet a feller
Must own a nigger o' some sort, jet black, or brown, or
　　yeller.
Now I haint no objections agin particklar climes,
Nor agin ownin' anythin' (except the truth sometimes),
But, ez I haint no capital, up there among ye, maybe,
You might raise funds enough fer me to buy a low-priced
　　baby,
An' then to suit the No'thern folks, who feel obleeged to say
They hate an' cuss the very thing they vote fer every day,
Say you're assured I go full butt fer Libbaty's diffusion
An' made the purchis on'y jest to spite the Institootion;—
But, golly! there 's the currier's hoss upon the pavement
　　pawin'!
I 'll be more 'xplicit in my next.

Yourn,
BIRDOFREDUM SAWIN

The Courtin'

God makes sech nights, all white an' still
    Fur 'z you can look or listen,
Moonshine an' snow on field an' hill,
    All silence an' all glisten.

Zekle crep' up quite unbeknown
    An' peeked in thru' the winder,
An' there sot Huldy all alone,
    'ith no one nigh to hender.

A fireplace filled the room's one side
    With half a cord o' wood in—
There warn't no stoves (tell comfort died)
    To bake ye to a puddin'.

The wa'nut logs shot sparkles out
    Towards the pootiest, bless her,
An' leetle flames danced all about
    The chiny on the dresser.

Agin the chimbley crook-necks hung,
    An' in amongst 'em rusted
The ole queen's-arm thet gran'ther Young
    Fetched back f'om Concord busted.

The very room, coz she was in,
    Seemed warm f'om floor to ceilin',
An' she looked full ez rosy agin
    Ez the apples she was peelin'.

'Twas kin' o' kingdom-come to look
    On sech a blessed cretur,
A dogrose blushin' to a brook
    Ain't modester nor sweeter.

He was six foot o' man, A-1,
    Clear grit an' human natur';
None couldn't quicker pitch a ton
    Nor dror a furrer straighter.

He'd sparked it with full twenty gals,
    He'd squired 'em, danced 'em, druv 'em,
Fust this one, an' then thet, by spells—
    All is, he couldn't love 'em.

But long o' her his veins 'ould run
    All crinkly like curled maple,
The side she breshed felt full o' sun
    Ez a south slope in Ap'il.

She thought no v'ice hed sech a swing
    Ez hisn in the choir;
My! when he made Ole Hunderd ring,
    She *knowed* the Lord was nigher.

An' she'd blush scarlit, right in prayer,
    When her new meetin'-bunnet
Felt somehow thru' its crown a pair
    O' blue eyes sot upon it.

Thet night, I tell ye, she looked *some!*
    She seemed to've gut a new soul,
For she felt sartin-sure he'd come,
    Down to her very shoe-sole.

She heered a foot, an' knowed it tu,
    A-raspin' on the scraper,—
All ways to once her feelin's flew
    Like sparks in burnt-up paper.

He kin' o' l'itered on the mat
    Some doubtfle o' the sekle,
His heart kep' goin' pity-pat
    But hern went pity Zekle.

An' yet she gin her cheer a jerk
    Ez though she wished him furder,
An' on her apples kep' to work,
    Parin' away like murder.

"You want to see my Pa, I s'pose?"
 "Wal . . . no . . . I come dasaignin'"—
"To see my Ma? She's sprinklin' clo'es
 Agin to-morrer's i'nin'."

To say why gals acts so or so,
 Or don't, 'ould be presumin';
Mebby to mean *yes* an' say *no*
 Comes nateral to women.

He stood a spell on one foot fust,
 Then stood a spell on t'other,
An' on which one he felt the wust
 He couldn't ha' told ye nuther.

Says he, "I'd better call agin";
 Says she, "Think likely, Mister":
Thet last word pricked him like a pin,
 An' . . . Wal, he up an' kist her.

When Ma bimeby upon 'em slips,
 Huldy sot pale ez ashes,
All kin' o' smily roun' the lips
 An' teary roun' the lashes.

For she was jes' the quiet kind
 Whose naturs never vary,
Like streams that keep a summer mind
 Snowhid in Jenooary.

The blood clost roun' her heart felt glued
 Too tight for all expressin',
Tell mother see how metters stood,
 An' gin 'em both her blessin'.

Then her red come back like the tide
 Down to the Bay o' Fundy,
An' all I know is they was cried
 In meetin' come nex' Sunday.

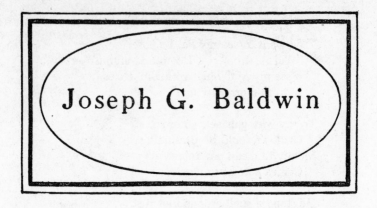

Joseph G. Baldwin

In *The Seventeenth Century Background,* Professor Basil Willey states that recognition of the discrepancy between the ideal and the norm of human conduct is the necessary condition for satire. The personal history of Joseph G. Baldwin made him peculiarly aware of the gulf separating the ideal of the Declaration of Independence from the reality of life in the American Southwest; out of that awareness came *The Flush Times of Alabama and Mississippi.*

Baldwin was a Virginia gentleman, brought up in the climate of Jeffersonian rationalism. The nature of the faith in which he was raised can be seen in the Jefferson chapter of his book on *Party Leaders,* in which Baldwin pays tribute to the great vision of the founding fathers. In the year 1836, however, young Baldwin, embarrassingly short of funds, left Virginia for the southwestern frontier, the world he would later describe in *Flush Times.*

It was a world at the furthest possible remove from the Jeffersonian ideal. The state of the law profession, to which Baldwin belonged, was characterized by chicanery, fraud, bribery, corruption of judges and juries, the fixing of evidence, perjury of witnesses, and wholesale intimidation. The ministry was shot through with hypocrites, and medicine with quacks and fakes. The representative man of this new society, as Baldwin saw it, was Simon Suggs, Jr., who was even more of a scoundrel than Johnson J. Hooper's rogue, for whom he was named. Specifically, Junior was a sadist, a cheater at cards, a forger, a seducer, and a jail breaker.

Flush Times satirizes this social chaos in an attempt to impose a coherence upon it, to accommodate raw, wide-open Mississippi to the social structure and the cultural traditions of the Old Dominion. Written in a vocabulary of considerable elegance and in a highly finished style, the book effectively marks off the author from his material, thereby defining his superiority to the shady, courthouse operators with whom, as an ambitious lawyer—and later as a well-known judge—he was forced to associate. But the main point of Baldwin's satire is that Simon Suggs, Jr., is not to be taken seriously. With resolute amusement Baldwin regards all the confidence men who populate his book as simply rather colorful, Dickensian characters. This attitude enables him to project the future of the new society with optimism, to think of it even as potentially superior to Virginia. Yet the essential fact about the fluid, wide-open world of *Flush Times* is that the future is not predictable, because anything might happen. That ruthless Suggses and not well-bred Baldwins might eventually take the reins of power is a fear that renders Baldwin's gentlemanly laughter slightly hollow.

Simon Suggs, Jr., Esq., of Rackinsack—Arkansaw

This distinguished lawyer, unlike the majority of those favored subjects of the biographical muse, whom a patriotic ambition to add to the moral treasures of the country, has prevailed on, over the instincts of a native and professional modesty, to supply subjects for the pens and pencils of their friends, was not quite, either in a literal or metaphorical sense, a self-made man. He had ancestors. They were, moreover, men of distinction; and, on the father's

side, in the first and second degrees of ascent known to
fame. The father of this distinguished barrister was, and,
happily, is Capt. Simon Suggs, of the Tallapoosa volunteers, and celebrated not less for his financial skill and abil-
ities, than for his martial exploits. His grandfather, the Rev.
Jedediah Suggs, was a noted divine of the Anti-Missionary
or Hardshell Baptist persuasion in Georgia. For further information respecting these celebrities, the ignorant reader—
the well-informed already know them—is referred to the
work of Johnson Hooper, Esq., one of the most authentic
of modern biographers.

The question of the propagability of moral and intellectual qualities is a somewhat mooted point, into the metaphysics of which we do not propose to enter; but that there
are instances of moral and intellectual as well as physical
likenesses in families, is an undisputed fact, of which the
subject of this memoir is a new and striking illustration.

In the month of July, Anno Domini, 1810, on the ever
memorable fourth day of the month, in the county of Car-
roll, and State of Georgia, Simon Suggs, Jr., first saw the
light, mingling the first noise he made in the world with
the patriotic explosions and rejoicings going on in honor of
the day. We have endeavored in vain to ascertain, whether
the auspicious period of the birth of young Simon was a
matter of accident, or of human calculation, and sharp foresight, for which his immediate ancestor on the paternal side
was so eminently distinguished; but, beyond a knowing
wink, and a characteristic laudation of his ability to accomplish wonderful things, and to keep the run of the cards,
on the part of the veteran captain, we have obtained no
reliable information on this interesting subject. It is something, however, to be remarked upon, that the natal day of
his country and of Simon were the same.

Very early in life, our hero—for Peace hath her victories,
and, of course, her heroes, as well as war—gave a promise
of the hereditary genius of the Suggs's; but as the incidents
in proof of this rest on the authority, merely, of family tradition, we shall not violate the sanctity of the domestic fire-

side, by relating them. In the ninth year of his age he was sent to the public school in the neighborhood. Here he displayed that rare vivacity and enterprise, and that shrewdness and invention, which subsequently distinguished his riper age. Like his father, his study was less of books than of men. Indeed, it required a considerable expenditure of birch, and much wear and tear of patience, to overcome his constitutional aversion to letters sufficiently to enable him to master the alphabet. Not that he was too lazy to learn; on the contrary, it was his extreme industry in other more congenial pursuits that stood in the way of the sedentary business of instruction. It was not difficult to see that the mantle of the Captain had fallen upon his favorite son; at any rate, the breeches in which young Simon's lower proportions were encased, bore a wonderful resemblance to the old cloak that the Captain had sported on so many occasions.

Simon's course at school was marked by many of the traits which distinguished him in after life; so true is the aphorism which the great Englishman enounced, that the boy is father to the man. His genius was eminently commercial, and he was by no means deficient in practical arithmetic. This peculiar turn of mind displayed itself in his barterings for the small wares of schoolboy merchandise—tops, apples, and marbles, sometimes rising to the dignity of a pen-knife. In these exercises of infantile enterprise, it was observable that Simon always got the advantage in the trade; and in that sense of charity which conceals defects, he may be said to have always displayed that virtue to a considerable degree. The same love of enterprise early led him into games of hazard, such as push-pin, marbles, chuck-a-luck, heads and tails, and other like boyish pastimes, in which his ingenuity was rewarded by marked success. The vivacious and eager spirit of this gifted urchin sometimes evolved and put in practice, even in the presence of the master, expedients of such sort as served to enliven the proverbial monotony of scholastic confinement and study: such, for example, were the traps set for the unwary and heedless scholar, made by thrusting a string through

the eye of a needle and passing it through holes in the
school bench—one end of the string being attached to the
machinist's leg, and so fixed, that by pulling the string, the
needle would protrude through the further hole and into
the person of the urchin sitting over it, to the great diver-
tisement of the spectators of this innocent pastime. The
holes being filled with soft putty, the needle was easily replaced, and the point concealed, so that when the outcry
of the victim was heard, Simon was diligently perusing his
book, and the only consequence was a dismissal of the complaint, and the amercement of the complainant by the
master, *pro falso clamore*. Beginning to be a little more
boldly enterprising, the usual fortune of those who "con-
quer or excel mankind" befell our hero, and he was made
the scape-goat of the school; all vagrant offences that could
not be proved against any one else being visited upon him;
a summary procedure, which, as Simon remarked, brought
down genius to the level of blundering mediocrity, and
made of no avail the most ingenious arts of deception and
concealment. The master of the old field school was one of
the regular faculty, who had great faith in the old medicine
for the eradication of moral diseases—the cutaneous tonic,
as he called it—and repelled, with great scorn, the modern
quackeries of kind encouragement and moral suasion. Accordingly, the flagellations and cuffings which Simon received, were such and so many as to give him a high opinion of the powers of endurance, the recuperative energies,
and the immense vitality of the human system. Simon tried,
on one occasion, the experiment of fits; but Dominie Dobbs
was inexorable; and as the fainting posture only exposed to
the Dominie new and fresher points of attack, Simon was
fain to unroll his eyes, draw up again his lower jaw, and
come to. Simon, remarking in his moralizing way upon the
virtue of perseverance, has been heard to declare that he
"lost that game" by being unable to keep from scratching
during a space of three minutes and a half; which he would
have accomplished, but for the Dominie's touching him on
the raw, caused by riding a race bare-backed the Sunday
before. "Upon what slender threads hang the greatest

events!" Doubtless these experiences of young Suggs were not without effect upon so observing and sagacious an intellect. To them we may trace that strong republican bias and those fervid expressions in favor of Democratic principles, which, all through life, and in the ranks of whatever party he might be found, he ever exhibited and made; and probably to the unfeeling, and sometimes unjust inflictions of Dominie Dobbs, was he indebted for his devotion to that principle of criminal justice he so pertinaciously upheld, which requires full proof of guilt before it awards punishment.

We must pass over a few years in the life of Simon, who continued at school, growing in size and wisdom; and not more instructed by what he learned there, than by the valuable information which his reverend father gave him in the shape of sage counsels and sharp experiences of the world and its ways and wiles. An event occurred in Simon's fifteenth year, which dissolved the tie that bound him to his rustic *Alma Mater*, the only institution of letters which can boast of his connection with it. Dominie Dobbs, one Friday evening, shortly after the close of the labors of the scholastic week, was quietly taking from a handkerchief in which he had placed it, a flask of powder; as he pressed the knot of the handkerchief, *it* pressed up on the slide of the flask, which as it revolved, bore upon a lucifer match that ignited the powder; the explosion tore the handkerchief to pieces, and also one ear and three fingers of the Dominie's right hand—those fingers that had wielded the birch upon young Simon with such effect. Suspicion fell on Simon, notwithstanding he was the first boy to leave the school that evening. This suspicion derived some corroboration from other facts; but the evidence was wholly circumstantial. No positive proof whatever connected Simon with this remarkable accident; but the characteristic prudence of the elder Suggs suggested the expediency of Simon's leaving for a time a part of the country where character was held in so little esteem. Accordingly the influence of his father procured for Simon a situation in the neighboring county of Randolph, in the State of Alabama, near the gold mines, as clerk or assistant in a store for retailing spirituous liquors, which the owner, one Dixon Tripes, had set up for refreshment of the public, without troubling the County Court for a license. Here Simon was early initiated into a knowledge of men, in such situations as to present their characters nearly naked to the eye. The neighbors were in the habit of assembling at the grocery, almost every day, in considerable numbers, urged thereto by the attractions of the society, and the beverage there abounding; and games of various sorts added to the charms of conversation and social intercourse. It was the general rendezvous of the fast young gentlemen for ten miles around; and horse-racing, shooting-matches, quoit-pitching, cock-fighting, and card-playing filled up the vacant hours between drinks.

In such choice society it may well be supposed that so sprightly a temper and so inquisitive a mind as Simon's found congenial and delightful employment; and it was not long before his acquirements ranked him among the fore-most in that select and spirited community. Although good at all the games mentioned, card-playing constituted his favorite amusement, not less for the excitement it afforded him, than for the rare opportunity it gave him of studying the human character.

The skill he attained in measuring distances, was equal to that displayed in his youth, by his venerated father, in-somuch that in any disputed question in pitching or shoot-ing, to allow him to measure was to give him the match; while his proficiency "in arranging the papers"—vulgarly called stocking a pack—was nearly equal to sleight of hand. Having been appointed judge of a quarter race on one oc-casion, he decided in favor of one of the parties by three inches and a half; and such was the sense of the winner of Simon's judicial expertness and impartiality, that imme-diately after the decision was made, he took Simon behind the grocery and divided the purse with him. By means of the accumulation of his wonderful industry, Simon went forth with a somewhat heterogeneous assortment of plun-der, to set up a traffic on his own account: naturally desir-ing a wider theatre, which he found in the city of Columbus in his native State. He returned to the paternal roof with an increased store of goods and experience from his sojourn in Alabama. Among other property, he brought with him a small race mare, which excited the acquisitiveness of his father, who, desiring an easier mode of acquisition than by purchase, proposed to stake a horse he had (the same he had swapped for, on the road to Montgomery, with the land speculator), against Simon's mare, upon the issue of a game of *seven up*. Since the game of chess between Mr. Jefferson and the French Minister, which lasted three years, perhaps there never has been a more closely contested match than that between these keen, sagacious and practised sportsmen. It was played with all advantages; all the lights of science were shed upon that game. The old gentleman had the advantage of experience—the young of genius: it was the old fogy against young America. For a long time the result was dubious; as if Dame Fortune was unable or unwilling to decide between her favorites. The game stood *six and six*, and young Simon had the deal. Just as the deal commenced, after one of the most brilliant shuffles the senior had ever made, Simon carelessly laid down his tortoise-shell snuff-box on the table; and the father, affecting *nonchalance*, and inclining his head towards the box, in order to peep under as the cards were being dealt, took a pinch of snuff; the titillating restorative was strongly adulterated with cayenne pepper; the old fogy was compelled to sneeze; and just as he recovered from the concussion, the first object that met his eye was a Jack turning in Simon's hand. A struggle seemed to be going on in the old man's breast between a feeling of pride in his son and a sense of his individual loss. It soon ceased, however. The father congratulated his son upon his success, and swore that he was wasting his genius in a retail business of "shykeenry" when nature had designed him for the bar.

To follow Simon through the eventful and checkered scenes of his nascent manhood, would be to enlarge this sketch to a volume. We must be content to state briefly, that such was the proficiency he made in the polite accomplishments of the day, and such the reputation he acquired in all those arts which win success in legal practice, when thereto energetically applied, that many sagacious men predicted that *the law would yet elevate Simon to a prominent place in the public view*. In his twenty-first year, Simon, starting out with a single mare to trade in horses in the adjoining State of Alabama, returned, such was his success, with a drove of six horses and a mule, and among them the very mare he started with. These, with the exception of the mare, he converted into money; he had found her invincible in all trials of speed, and determined to keep her. Trying his fortune once more in Alabama, where he had been so eminently successful, Simon went to the city of Wetumpka, where he found the races about coming off. As his mare had too much reputation to get bets upon her, an ingenious idea struck Simon—it was to take bets, through an agent, *against* her, in favor of a long-legged horse, entered for the races. It was very plain to see that Simon's mare was bound to win if he let her; and his agent was fortunate enough to pick up a green-looking Georgia sucker, who bet with him the full amount left of Simon's "pile." The stakes were deposited in due form to the amount of some two thousand dollars. Simon was to ride his own mare—wild Kate, as he called her—and he had determined to hold her back, so that the other horse should win. But the Georgian, having by accident overheard the conversation between Simon and his agent, before the race, cut the reins of Simon's bridle nearly through, but in so ingenious a manner that the incision did not appear. The race came off as it had been arranged; and as Simon was carefully holding back his emulous filly, at the same time giving her whip and spur, as though he would have her do her best, the bridle broke under the strain; and the mare released from check, flew to and past the goal like the wind, some three hundred yards ahead of the horse, upon the success of which Simon had "piled" up so largely.

A shout of laughter like that which pursued Mazeppa, arose from the crowd (to whom the Georgian had communicated the facts), as Simon swept by, the involuntary winner of the race; and in that laugh, Simon heard the announcement of the discovery of his ingenious contrivance. He did not return.

Old Simon, when he heard of this counter-mine, fell into paroxysms of grief, which could not find consolation in less than a quart of red-eye. Heart-stricken, the old patriarch exclaimed—"Oh! Simon! my son Simon! to be overcome in that way!—a Suggs to be humbugged! His own Jack to be taken outen his hand and turned on him! Oh! that I should ha' lived to see this day!"

Proceeding to Montgomery, Simon found an opening on the thither side of a faro table; and having disposed of the race mare for three hundred dollars, banked on this capital, but with small success. Mr. Suggs' opinion of the people of Montgomery was not high; they were fashioned on a very diminutive scale, he used to say, and degraded the national amusement, by wagers, which an enterprising boy would scorn to hazard at push-pin. One Sam Boggs, a young lawyer "of that ilk," having been cleaned out of his entire stake of ten dollars, wished to continue the game on credit, and Simon gratified him, taking his law license in pawn for two dollars and a half; which pawn the aforesaid Samuel failed to redeem. Our prudent and careful adventurer filed away the sheepskin, thinking that sometime or other, he might be able to put it to good use.

The losses Simon had met with, and the unpromising prospects of gentlemen who lived on their wits, now that the hard times had set in, produced an awakening influence upon his conscience. He determined to abandon the nomadic life he had led, and to settle himself down to some regular business. He had long felt a call to the law, and he now resolved to "locate," and apply himself to the duties of that learned profession. Simon was not long in deciding upon a location. The spirited manner in which the State of Arkansas had repudiated a public debt of some five hundred thousand dollars gave him a favorable opinion of that people as a community of litigants, while the accounts which came teeming from that bright land, of murders and felonies innumerable, suggested the value of the criminal practice. He wended his way into that State, nor did he tarry until he reached the neighborhood of Fort Smith, a promising border town in the very *Ultima Thule of civilization,* such as it was, just on the confines of the Choctaw nation. It was in this region, in the village of Rackensack, that he put up his sign, and offered himself for practice. I shall not attempt to describe the population. It is indescribable. I shall only say that the Indians and half-breeds across the border complained of it mightily.

The motive for Simon's seeking so remote a location was that he might get in advance of his reputation—being laudably ambitious to acquire forensic distinction, he wished his fame as a lawyer to be independent of all extraneous and adventitious assistance. His first act in the practice was under the statute of *Jeo Fails.* It consisted of an amendment of the license he had got from Boggs, as before related; which amendment, was ingeniously effected by a careful erasure of the name of that gentleman, and the insertion of his own in the place of it. Having accomplished this feat, he presented it to the court, then in session, and was duly admitted an attorney and counsellor at law and solicitor in chancery.

There is a tone and spirit of morality attaching to the profession of the law so elevating and pervasive in its influence, as to work an almost instantaneous reformation in the character and habits of its disciples. If this be not so, it was certainly a most singular coincidence that, just at the time of his adoption of this vocation, Simon abandoned the favorite pastimes of his youth, and the irregularities of his earlier years. Indeed, he has been heard to declare that any lawyer, fulfilling conscientiously the duties of his profession, will find enough to employ all his resources of art, strategem and dexterity, without resorting to other and more equivocal methods for their exercise.

It was not long before Simon's genius began to find occasions and opportunities of exhibition. When he first came to the bar, there were but seven suits on the docket, two of those being appeals from the justice's court. In the course of six months, so indefatigable was he in instructing clients, as to their rights, the number of suits grew to forty. Simon

—or as he is now called—*Colonel* Suggs, determined on winning reputation in a most effective branch of practice—one that he shrewdly perceived was too much neglected by the profession—the branch of preparing cases *out of court* for trial. While other lawyers were busy in getting up the law of their cases, the Colonel was no less busy in getting up the facts of his.

One of the most successful of Col. Suggs' efforts, was in behalf of his landlady, in whom he felt a warm and decided interest. She had been living for many years in ignorant contentedness, with an indolent, easy natured man, her husband, who was not managing her separate estate, consisting of a plantation and about twenty negroes, and some town property, with much thrift. The lady was buxom and gay, and the union of the couple was unblessed with children. By the most insinuating manners, Col. Suggs at length succeeded in opening the lady's eyes to a true sense of her hapless condition, and the danger in which her property was placed, from the improvident habits of her spouse; and, having ingeniously deceived the unsuspecting husband into some suspicious appearances, which were duly observed by a witness or two provided for the purpose, he soon prevailed upon his fair hostess to file a bill of divorce; which she readily procured under the Colonel's auspices. Under the pretence of protecting her property from the claims of her husband's creditors, the Colonel was kind enough to take a conveyance of it to himself; and shortly afterwards, the fair libellant; by which means he secured himself from those distracting cares which beset the young legal practitioner, who stands in immediate need of the wherewithal.

Col. Suggs' prospects now greatly improved, and he saw before him an extended field of usefulness. The whole community felt the effects of his activity. Long dormant claims came to light; and rights, of the very existence of which, suitors were not before aware, were brought into practical assertion. From restlessness and inactivity, the population became excited, inquisitive and intelligent, as to the laws of their country; and the ruinous effects of servile acquiescence in wrong and oppression, were averted.

The fault of lawyers in preparing their cases was too generally a dilatoriness of movement, which sometimes deferred until it was too late, the creating of the proper impression upon the minds of the jury. This was not the fault of Col. Suggs; he always took time by the forelock. Instead of waiting to create prejudices in the minds of the jury, until they were in the box, or deferring until then the arts of persuasion, he waited upon them before they were empanelled; and he always succeeded better at that time, as they had not then received an improper bias from the testimony. In a case of any importance, he always managed to have his friends in the court room, so that when any of the jurors were challenged, he might have their places filled by good men and true; and, although this increased his expenses considerably, by a large annual bill at the grocery, he never regretted any expense, either of time, labor or money, necessary to success in his business. Such was his zeal for his clients!

He was in the habit, too, of free correspondence with the opposite party, which enabled him at once to conduct his case with better advantage, and to supply any omissions or chasms in the proof: and so far did he carry the habit of testifying in his own cases, that his clients were always assured that in employing him, they were procuring counsel and witness at the same time, and by the same retainer. By a very easy process, he secured a large debt barred by the statute of limitations, and completely circumvented a fraudulent defendant who was about to avail himself of that mendacious defence. He ante-dated the writ, and thus brought the case clear of the statute.

One of the most harassing annoyances that were inflicted upon the emigrant community around him, was the revival of old claims contracted in the State from which they came, and which the Shylocks holding them, although they well knew that the pretended debtors had, expressly in consideration of getting rid of them, put themselves to the pains of exile and to the losses and discomforts of leaving their old homes and settling in a new country, in fraudulent violation of this object, were ruinously seeking to enforce, even to the deprivation of the property of the citizen. In one instance, a cashier of a Bank in Alabama brought on claims against some of the best citizens of the country, to a large amount, and instituted suits on them. Col. Suggs was retained to defend them. The cashier, a venerable-looking old gentleman, who had extorted promises of payment, or at least had heard from the debtors promises of payment, which their necessitous circumstances had extorted, but to which he well knew they did not attach much importance, was waiting to become a witness against them. Col. Suggs so concerted operations, as to have some half-dozen of the most worthless of the population follow the old gentleman about whenever he went out of doors, and to be seen with him on various occasions; and busying himself in circulating through the community, divers reports disparaging the reputation of the witness, got the cases ready for trial. It was agreed that *one* verdict should settle all the cases. The defendant pleaded the statute of limitations; and to do away with the effect of it, the plaintiff offered the cashier as a witness. Not a single question was asked on cross-examination; but a smile of derision, which was accompanied by a foreordained titter behind the bar, was visible on the faces of Simon and his client, as he testified. The defendant then offered a dozen or more witnesses, who, much to the surprise of the venerable cashier, discredited him; and the jury, without leaving the box, found a verdict for the defendant. The cashier was about moving for a new trial, when, it being intimated to him that a warrant was about to be issued for his apprehension on a charge of perjury, he concluded not to see the result of such a process, and indignantly left the country.

The criminal practice, especially, fascinated the regards and engaged the attention of Col. Suggs, as a department of his profession and energies. He soon became acquainted with all the arts and contrivances by which public justice is circumvented. Indictments that could not be quashed, were sometimes mysteriously out of the way; and the clerk had occasion to reproach his carelessness in not filing them in the proper places, when, some days after cases had been dismissed for the want of them, they were discovered by him in some old file, or among the executions. He was requested, or rather he volunteered in one capital case, to draw a recognizance for a committing magistrate, as he (Suggs) was idly looking on, not being concerned in the trial, and so felicitously did he happen to introduce the negative particle in the condition of the bond, that he bound the defendant, under a heavy penalty, "*not*" to appear at court and answer to the charge; which appearance, doubtless, much against his will, and merely to save his sureties, the defendant proceeded faithfully not to make.

Col. Suggs also extricated a client and his sureties from a forfeited recognizance, by having the defaulting defendant's obituary notice somewhat prematurely inserted in the newspapers; the solicitor, seeing which, discontinued proceedings; for which service, the deceased, immediately after the adjournment of court, returned to the officer his personal acknowledgements: "not that," as he expressed it, "it mattered any thing to him personally, but because it *would have aggravated the feelings* of his friends he had left behind him, to of let the thing rip arter he was defunck."

The most difficult case Col. Suggs ever had to manage, was to extricate a client from jail, after sentence of death had been passed upon him. But difficulties, so far from discouraging him, only had the effect of stimulating his energies. He procured the aid of a young physician in the premises—the prisoner was suddenly taken ill—the physician pronounced the disease small pox. The wife of the prisoner, with true womanly devotion, attended on him. The prisoner, after a few days, was reported dead, and the doctor gave out that it would be dangerous to approach the corpse. A coffin was brought into the jail, and the wife was put into it by the physician—she being enveloped in her husband's clothes. The coffin was put in a cart and driven off—the husband, habited in the woman's apparel, following after, mourning piteously, until, getting out of the village, he disappeared in the thicket, where he found a horse prepared for him. The wife obstinately refused to be buried in the husband's place when she got to the grave; but the mistake was discovered too late for the recapture of the prisoner.

The tact and address of Col. Suggs opposed such obstacles to the enforcement of the criminal law in that part of the country, that, following the example of the English government, when Irish patriotism begins to create annoyances, the State naturally felt anxious to engage his services in its behalf. Accordingly, at the meeting of the Arkansas legislature, at its session of 184–, so soon as the matter of the killing a member on the floor of the house, by the speaker, with a Bowie knife, was disposed of by a resolution of mild censure, for imprudent precipitancy, Simon Suggs, Jr., Esquire, was elected solicitor for the Rackensack district. Col. Suggs brought to the discharge of the duties of his office energies as unimpaired and vigorous as in the days of his first practice; and entered upon it with a mind free from the vexations of domestic cares, having procured a divorce from his wife on the ground of infidelity, but magnanimously giving her one of the negroes, and a horse, saddle and bridle.

The business of the State now flourished beyond all precedent. Indictments multiplied: and though many of them were not tried—the solicitor discovering, after the finding of them, as he honestly confessed to the court, that the evidence would not support them: yet, the Colonel could well say, with an eminent English barrister, that if he tried fewer cases in court, he settled more cases out of court than any other counsel.

The marriage of Col. Suggs, some three years after his appointment of solicitor, with the lovely and accomplished Che-wee-na-tubbe, daughter of a distinguished prophet and warrior, and head-man of the neighboring territory of the Choctaw Indians, induced his removal into that beautiful and improving country. His talents and connections at once raised him to the councils of that interesting people; and he received the appointment of agent for the settlement of claims on the part of that tribe, and particular individuals of it, upon the treasury of the United States. This responsible and lucrative office now engages the time and talents of Col. Suggs, who may be seen every winter at Washington, faithfully and laboriously engaged with members of Congress and in the departments, urging the matters of his mission upon the dull sense of the Janitors of the Federal Treasury.

May his shadow never grow less; and may the Indians live to get their dividends of the arrears paid to their agent.

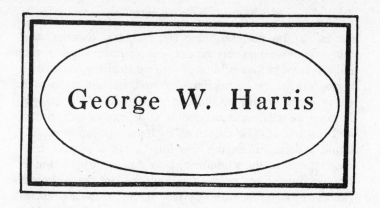

George W. Harris

Asked who are his favorite characters in literature, Faulkner has asserted that he is fond of Falstaff, Don Quixote, Huck Finn, Mrs. Gamp, and Bottom, among others. "And then," Faulkner says, "I like Sut Lovingood. . . . He had no illusions about himself, did the best he could; at certain times he was a coward and knew it and wasn't ashamed; he never blamed his misfortunes on anyone and never cursed God for them." In praising Sut, Faulkner adds his name to a long list of admirers. Professor Walter Blair has said that "in *Sut Lovingood*, the antebellum humor of the South reaches its highest level of achievement before Mark Twain," a statement which reminds us that Twain, too, was fond of Sut. The late F. O. Matthiessen thought that Sut's creator, George Washington Harris, brought "us closer than any other writer to the indigenous and undiluted resources of the American language," and certainly if Mencken's description of the qualities of the American language is correct (a "bold and somewhat grotesque imagination . . . contempt for dignified authority . . . lack of aesthetic sensitiveness . . . extravagant humor"), then *Sut Lovingood* must be regarded as one of its principal avatars.

The book has also alarmed certain critics, for Sut's humor consists largely of inflicting pain on those whom he dislikes—and the list of his aversions is very long. He hates his father; he despises ministers, teachers, dandies, and temperance workers; he has only contempt for himself. His mildest form of joke is to pour the foul-smelling contents of a slop bucket on his victim; the most forceful expression of his sense of fun is, simply, manslaughter. He regards Negroes as animals, and animals as objects to be tortured and laughed at. The sadism of his humor has shocked Edmund Wilson into saying that Sut "is not a pioneer contending against the wilderness; he is a peasant squatting in his own filth." Even more alarming is the fact that although Harris uses the "frame" device of enclosing his stories within the language and point of view of a coolly detached gentleman (named "George"), there is a much closer identification between Harris and the sadistic Sut than can be seen in the work of any other humorist of the Southwest. When Hooper was referred to as "Simon Suggs," he cringed in embarrassment, but in and around Knoxville, Tennessee, where he lived for a number of years, Harris was glad to be known as "Sut." Joking, Freud tells us, can be a means of aggression, and for Harris, a violently pro-slavery and eventually secessionist Democrat living in Unionist east Tennessee, Sut Lovingood and his cruel jokes were a way of venting his spleen against a society which he despised.

Yet what saves Harris's stories from dissolving into a sickening welter of pain is that Sut is in many ways a sympathetic character. He is a lost and rather lonely boy; if his parents are still alive, he is nevertheless estranged from them to the point where Sut must be considered as belonging to the illustrious company of orphans and castaways who are so often the heroes of American literature. In a world full of adult hypocrites the boy is honest, particularly about himself, which is why Faulkner is so fond of him. Sometimes, it is true, you lose sympathetic contact with Sut and see him from "George's" point of view as just another backwoods grotesque. At other times Harris violates Sut's character and puts into his mouth cogent opinions about life, in particular politics, which are nothing more than the comments of a southern gentleman transposed into the vernacular. But at his best, Harris shows us the world through Sut's eyes. As in *Huckleberry Finn,* the humor and the freshness of *Sut Lovingood* derive in large part from the naïveté of the boy narrator. There is a kind of awe, a child-like awe, about Sut's exact notation of Parson Bullen's movement as he tries to shake the lizards off his body that leads directly to Huck's descriptions of the King and the Duke. Both Harris and Twain expose the ludicrousness of the adult world by reporting it from a boy's point of view.

But Sut is also different from Huck. Huck is scared, but fear is not his only emotion, as fundamentally it is Sut's. The psychology of *Sut Lovingood* is therefore perhaps closer to Poe than it is to Twain. The haunted minds of Poe's gentlemen heroes resemble, for all their sophistication and learning, the terrified imagination of squalid Sut. An even better comparison than to Poe's tales is to his novel, *Arthur Gordon Pym,* for the hero of the book is a boy, and his adventures lead him into a dreamworld of terror and death. The same boy psychology operates in *Sut* as in *Pym,* a psychology of adolescent fear, in which language and plot situation are constantly pushing us beyond the bounds of familiar, reassuring reality into fantasies of panic and pain.

Powerless and alone, the boy Sut saves himself the way Br'er Rabbit does in the Negro fantasies—by playing pranks. What keeps Sut's mind from disintegrating is the relief that jokes afford him. After he has finished telling one of his stories Sut achieves a momentary peace; the terror of being so alienated from other people is discharged through laughter.

Parson John Bullen's Lizards

'TENSHUN BELEVERS AND KONSTABLES!
KETCH 'IM! KETCH 'IM!

This kash wil be pade in korn, ur uther projuce, tu be kolected at ur about nex camp-meetin, *ur thararter,* by eny wun what ketches him, fur the karkus ove a sartin wun SUT LOVINGOOD, dead ur alive, ur ailin, an' safely giv over to the purtectin care ove Parson John Bullin, ur lef' well tied, at Squire Mackjunkins, fur the raisin ove the devil pussonely, an' permiskusly discumfurtin the wimen very powerful, an' skeerin ove folks generly a heap, an' bustin up a promisin, big warm meetin, an' a makin the wickid larf, an' wus, an' wus, insultin ove the passun orful.

Test,   JEHU WETHERO.
Sined by me,
JOHN BULLEN, the passun.

I found written copies of the above highly intelligible and vindictive proclamation, stuck up on every blacksmith shop, doggery, and store door, in the Frog Mountain Range. Its bloodthirsty spirit, its style, and above all, its chirography, interested me to the extent of taking one down from a tree for preservation.

In a few days I found Sut in a good crowd in front of Capehart's Doggery, and as he seemed to be about in good tune, I read it to him.

"Yas, George, that ar dockymint am in dead yearnist sartin. Them hard shells over thar dus want me the wus kine, powerful bad. *But,* I spect ait dullers won't fetch me, nither wud ait hundred, bekase thar's nun ove 'em fas' enuf tu ketch me, nither is thar hosses by the livin jingo! Say,

George, much talk 'bout this fuss up whar yu're been?" For the sake of a joke I said yes, a great deal.

"Jis' es I 'spected, durn 'em, all git drunk, an' skeer thar fool sefs ni ontu deth, an' then lay hit ontu me, a poor innersent youf, an' es soun' a belever as they is. Lite, lite, ole feller an' let that roan ove yourn blow a littil, an' I'll 'splain this cussed misfortnit affar: hit hes ruinated my karacter es a pius pusson in the s'ciety roun' yere, an' is a spreadin faster nur meazils. When ever yu hear eny on 'em a spreadin hit, gin hit the dam lie squar, will yu? I haint dun nuffin tu one ove 'em. Hits true, I did sorter frustrate a few lizzards a littil, but they haint members, es I knows on.

"You see, las' year I went tu the big meetin at Rattilsnaik Springs, an' wer a sittin in a nice shady place convarsin wif a frien' ove mine, intu the huckilberry thickit, jis' duin nuffin tu nobody an' makin no fuss, when, the fust thing I remembers, I woke up frum a trance what I hed been knocked inter by a four-year old hickory-stick, hilt in the paw ove ole Passun Bullin, durn his alligator hide; an' he wer standin a striddil ove me, a foamin at the mouf, a-chompin his teeth—gesterin wif the hickory club—an' a-preachin tu me so you cud a hearn him a mile, about a sartin sin gineraly, an' my wickedness pussonely, an' mensunin the name ove my frien' loud enuf tu be hearn tu the meetin 'ous. My poor innersent frien' were dun gone an' I wer glad ove hit, fur I tho't he ment tu kill me rite whar I lay, an' I didn't want her tu see me die."

"Who was she, the friend you speak of Sut?" Sut opened his eyes wide.

"Hu the devil, an' durnashun tole *yu* that hit wer a she?"

"Why, you did, Sut"——

"I *didn't*, durn ef I did. Ole Bullin dun hit, an' I'll hev tu kill him yet, the cussed, infernel ole tale-barer!"——

"Well, well, Sut, who was she?"

"Nun ove y-u-r-e b-i-s-n-i-s-s, durn yure littil ankshus picter! I *sees yu* a lickin ove yure lips. I *will* tell you one thing, George; that night, a neighbor gal got a all fired, overhandid stroppin frum her mam, wif a stirrup leather, an' ole Passun Bullin, hed et supper thar, an' what's wus nur all, that poor innersent, skeer'd gal hed dun her levil bes' a cookin hit fur 'im. She begged him, a trimblin, an' a-cryin not tu tell on her. He et her cookin, he promised her he'd keep dark—an' then went strait an' tole her mam. Warnt that rale low down, wolf mean? The durnd infunel, hiper-kritikal, pot-bellied, scaley-hided, whisky-wastin, stinkin ole groun'-hog. He'd a heap better a stole sum *man's* hoss; I'd a tho't more ove 'im. But I paid him plum up fur hit, an' I means tu keep a payin him, ontil one ur tuther ove our toes pints up tu the roots ove the grass.

"Well, yere's the way I lifted that note ove han'. At the nex big meetin at Rattilsnaik—las' week hit wer—I wer on han' es solemn es a ole hat kivver on collection day. I hed my face draw'd out intu the shape an' perporshun ove a tayler's sleeve-board, pint down. I hed put on the convicted sinner so pufeckly that an' ole obsarvin she pillar ove the church sed tu a ole he pillar, es I walked up tu my bainch:

"'Law sakes alive, ef thar ain't that *orful* sinner, Sut Lovingood, pearced plum thru; hu's nex?'

"Yu see, by golly, George, I *hed* tu promis the ole tub ove soap-greas tu cum an' hev myself convarted, jis' tu keep him frum killin me. An' es I know'd hit wudn't interfare wif the relashun I bore tu the still housis roun' thar, I didn't keer a durn. I jis' wanted tu git *ni* ole Bullin, onst onsus-pected, an' this wer the bes' way tu du hit. I tuk a seat on the side steps ove the pulpit, an' kivvered es much ove my straitch'd face es I could wif my han's, tu prove I wer in yearnis. Hit tuck powerful—fur I hearn a sorter thankful kine ove buzzin all over the congregashun. Ole Bullin his-sef looked down at me, over his ole copper specks, an' hit sed jis' es plain es a look cud say hit: 'Yu am thar, ar yu —durn yu, hits well fur yu that yu cum.' I tho't sorter dif-frent frum that. I tho't hit wud a been well fur *yu*, ef I hadent a-cum, but I didn't say hit jis then. Thar wer a monstrus crowd in that grove, fur the weather wer fine, an' b'levers wer plenty roun' about Rattilsnaik Springs. Ole Bullin gin out, an' they sung that hyme, yu know:

"Thar will be mournin, mournin yere, an' mournin thar,
On that dredful day tu cum."

"Thinks I, ole hoss, kin hit be possibil enybody hes tole yu what's a gwine tu happin; an' then I tho't that nobody know'd hit but me, and I wer cumforted. He nex tuck hissef a tex pow'fly mixed wif brimstone, an' trim'd wif blue flames, an' then he open'd. He cummenced ontu the sinners; he threaten'd 'em orful, tried tu skeer 'em wif all the wust varmints he cud think ove, an' arter a while he got ontu the idear ove Hell-sarpints, an' he dwelt on it sum. He tole 'em how the ole Hell-sarpints wud sarve 'em if they didn't repent; how cold they'd crawl over thar nakid bodys, an' how like untu pitch they'd stick tu 'em es they crawled; how they'd rap thar tails roun' thar naiks chokin clost, poke thar tungs up thar noses, an' hiss intu thar years. This wer the way they wer tu sarve men folks. Then he turned ontu the wimen: tole 'em how they'd quile intu thar buzzims, an' how they *wud* crawl down onder thar frock-strings, no odds how tite they tied 'em, an' how sum ove the oldes' an' wus ones wud crawl up thar laigs, an' travil *onder* thar garters, no odds how tight they tied *them,* an' when the two armys ove Hell-sarpints met, then—— That las' remark *fotch 'em.* Ove all the screamin, an' hollerin, an' loud cryin, I ever hearn, begun all at onst, all over the hole groun' jis' es he hollered out that word 'then.' He kep on a bellerin, but I got so buisy jis' then, that I didn't listen tu him much, fur I saw that my time fur ackshun hed cum. Now yu see, George, I'd cotch seven ur eight big pot-bellied lizzards, an' hed 'em in a littil narrer bag, what I had made a-purpus. Thar tails at the bottim, an' so crowdid fur room that they cudent turn roun'. So when he wer a-ravin ontu his tiptoes, an' a-poundin the pulpit wif his fis'—onbenowenst tu enybody, I ontied my bag ove reptiles, put the mouf ove hit onder the bottim ove his britches-laig, an' sot intu pinchin thar tails. Quick es gunpowder they all tuck up his bar laig, makin a nise like squirrils a-climbin a shell-bark hickory. He stop't preachin rite in the middil ove the word 'damnation,' an' looked fur a moment like he wer a listenin fur sumthin—sorter like a ole sow dus, when she hears yu a-whistlin fur the dorgs. The tarifick shape ove his feeters stop't the shoutin an' screamin; instuntly yu cud hearn a cricket chirp, I gin a long groan, an' hilt my head a-twixt my knees. He gin hisself sum orful open-handed slaps wif fust one han' an' then tuther, about the place whar yu cut the bes' steak outen a beef. Then he'd fetch a vigrus ruff rub whar a hosses tail sprouts; then he'd stomp one foot, then tuther, then bof at onst. Then he run his han' atween his waisbun an' his shut an' reach'd way down, an' roun' wif hit; then he spread his big laigs, an' gin his back a good rattlin rub agin the pulpit, like a hog scratches hissef agin a stump, leanin tu hit pow'ful, an' twitchin, an' squirmin all over, es ef he'd slept in a dorg bed, ur ontu a pisant hill. About this time, one ove my lizzards scared an' hurt by all this poundin' an' feelin, an' scratchin, popp'd out his head frum the passun's shut collar, an' his ole brown naik, an' wer a-surveyin the crowd, when ole Bullin struck at 'im, jis' too late, fur he'd dodged back agin. The hell desarvin ole raskil's speech now cum tu 'im, an' sez he, 'Pray fur me brethren an' sisteren, fur I is a-rastilin wif the great inimy rite now! an' his voice wer the mos' pitiful, trimblin thing I ever hearn. Sum ove the wimen fotch a painter yell, an' a young docter, wif ramrod laigs, lean'd toward me monstrus knowin like, an' sez he, 'Clar case ove Delishus Tremenjus.' I nodded my head an' sez I, 'Yas, spechuly the tremenjus part, an' Ise feard hit haint at hits worst. Ole Bullin's eyes wer a-stickin out like ontu two buckeyes flung agin a mud wall, an' he wer a-cuttin up more shines nor a cockroach in a hot skillet. Off went the clamhammer coat, an' he flung hit ahine 'im like he wer a-gwine intu a fight; he hed no jackid tu take off, so he unbuttoned his galluses, an' vigrusly flung the ainds back over his head. He fotch his shut over-handed a durnd site faster nor I got outen my pasted one, an' then flung hit strait up in the air, like he jis' wanted hit tu keep on up furever; but hit lodged ontu a black-jack, an' I sed one ove my lizzards wif his tail up, a-racin about all over the ole dirty shut, skared too bad tu jump. Then he gin a sorter shake, an' a stompin kine ove twis', an' he cum outer his britches. He tuck 'em by the bottim ove the laigs, an' swung 'em roun' his head a time ur two, an' then fotch 'em down cherall-up over the frunt ove the pulpit. You cud a hearn the smash a quarter

ove a mile! Ni ontu fifteen shorten'd biskits, a boiled
chicken, wif hits laigs crossed, a big dubbil-bladed knife,
a hunk ove terbacker, a cob-pipe, sum copper ore, lots ove
broken glass, a cork, a sprinkil ove whisky, a squirt, an'
three lizzards flew permiskusly all over that meetin-groun',
outen the upper aind ove them big flax britches. One ove
the smartes' ove my lizzards lit head-fust intu the buzzim
ove a fat 'oman, es big es a skin'd hoss, an' ni ontu es ugly,
who sot thuty yards a fannin hersef wif a tucky-tail. Smart
tu the las', by golly, he imejuntly commenced runnin down
the centre ove her breas'-bone, an' kep on, I speck. She wer
jis' boun' tu faint; an' she did hit fust rate—flung the tucky-
tail up in the air, grabbed the lap ove her gown, gin hit a
big histin an' fallin shake, rolled down the hill, tangled her
laigs an' garters in the top ove a huckilberry bush, wif her
head in the branch an' jis' lay still. She wer interestin, she
wer, ontil a serious-lookin, pale-faced 'oman hung a nan-
keen ridin skirt over the huckilberry bush. That wer all that
wer dun to'ards bringin her too, that I seed. Now ole Bullin
hed nuffin left ontu 'im but a par ove heavy, low quarter'd
shoes, short woolen socks, an' eel-skin garters tu keep off
the cramp. His skeer hed druv him plum crazy, fur he felt
roun' in the air, abuv his head, like he wer huntin sumthin
in the dark, an' he beller'd out, 'Brethren, brethren, take
keer ove yerselves, the Hell-sarpints *hes got me!*' When
this cum out, yu cud a-hearn the screams tu Halifax. He
jis' spit in his han's, an' loped over the frunt ove the pulpit
kerdiff! He lit on top ove, an' rite amung the mos' pius part
ove the congregashun. Ole Misses Chaneyberry sot wif her
back tu the pulpit, sorter stoopin forrid. He lit astradil ove
her long naik, a shuttin her up wif a snap, her head atwix
her knees, like shuttin up a jack-knife, an' he sot intu gittin away his levil durndest; he went in a heavy lumberin
gallop, like a ole fat waggon hoss, skared at a locomotive.
When he jumpt a bainch he shook the yeath. The bonnets,
an' fans clar'd the way an' jerked most ove the children
wif em, an' the rest he scrunched. He open'd a purfeckly
clar track tu the woods, ove every livin thing. He
weighed ni ontu three hundred, hed a black stripe down

his back, like ontu a ole bridil rein, an' his belly wer 'bout the size an' color ove a beef paunch, an' hit a-swingin out frum side tu side; he leand back frum hit, like a littil feller a-totin a big drum, at a muster, an' I hearn hit plum tu whar I wer. Thar wer cramp-knots on his laigs es big es walnuts, an' mottled splotches on his shins; an' takin him all over, he minded ove a durnd crazy ole elephant, pussessed ove the devil, rared up on hits hind aind, an' jis' *gittin* frum sum imijut danger ur tribulashun. He did the loudest, an' skariest, an' fussiest runnin I ever seed, tu be no faster nur hit wer, since dad tried tu outrun the ho'nets.

"Well, he disapear'd in the thicket jis' bustin—an' ove all the noises yu ever hearn, wer made thar on that camp groun': sum wimen screamin—they wer the skeery ones; sum larfin—they wer the wicked ones; sum cryin—they wer the fool ones, (sorter my stripe yu know;) sum tryin tu git away wif thar faces red—they wer the modest ones; sum lookin arter ole Bullin—they wer the curious ones; sum hangin clost tu thar sweethearts—they wer the sweet ones; sum on thar knees wif thar eyes shot, but facin the way the old mud turtil wer a-runnin—they wer the 'saitful ones; sum duin nuthin—they wer the waitin ones; an' the mos' dangerus ove all ove em by a durnd long site.

"I tuck a big skeer mysef arter a few rocks, an' sich like fruit, spattered ontu the pulpit ni ontu my head; an' es the Lovingoods, durn em! knows nuffin but tu run, when they gits skeerd, I jis' put out fur the swamp on the krick. As I started, a black bottil ove bald-face smashed agin a tree furninst me, arter missin the top ove my head 'bout a inch. Sum durn'd fool professor dun this, who hed more zeal or sence; fur I say that eny man who wud waste a quart ove even mean sperrits, fur the chance ove knockin a poor ornary devil like me down wif the bottil, is a bigger fool nur ole Squire Mackmullen, an' he tried tu shoot hissef wif a onloaded hoe-handle."

"Did they catch you, Sut?"

"Ketch thunder! *No sir!* jis' look at these yere laigs! Skeer me, hoss, jis' skeer me, an' then watch me while I stay in site, an' yu'll never ax that fool question agin. Why, durn it, man, that's what the ait dullers am fur.

"Ole Barbelly Bullin, es they calls 'im now, never preached ontil yesterday, an' he hadn't the fust durn'd 'oman tu hear 'im, *they hev seed too much ove 'im.* Passuns ginerly hev a pow'ful strong holt on wimen; but, hoss, I tell yu thar ain't meny ove em kin run stark nakid over an' thru a crowd ove three hundred wimen an' not injure thar karacters *sum.* Enyhow, hits a kind ove show they'd ruther see one at a time, an' pick the passun at that. His tex' wer, 'Nakid I cum intu the world, an' nakid I'm gwine outen hit, ef I'm spard ontil then.' He sed nakidness warnt much ove a sin, purtickerly ove dark nights. That he wer a weak, frail wum ove the dus', an' a heap more sich truck. Then he totch ontu me; sed I wer a livin proof ove the hell-desarvin nater ove man, an' that thar warnt grace enuf in the whole 'sociation tu saften my outside rind; that I wer 'a lost ball' forty years afore I wer born'd, an' the bes' thing they cud du fur the church, wer tu turn out, an' still hunt fur me ontil I wer shot. An' he never said Hell-sarpints onst in the hole preach. I b'leve, George, the durnd fools am at hit.

"Now, I wants yu tu tell ole Barbelly this fur me, ef he'll let me an' Sall alone, I'll let him alone—a-while; an' ef he don't, ef I don't lizzard him agin, I jis' wish I may be dod durnd! *Skeer him if yu ken.*

"Let's go tu the spring an' take a ho'n.

"Say George, didn't that ar Hell-sarpint sermon ove his'n, hev sumthin like a Hell-sarpint aplicashun? Hit looks sorter so to me."

Mrs. Yardley's Quilting

"Thar's one durn'd nasty muddy job, an' I is jis' glad enuf tu take a ho'n ur two, on the straingth ove hit."

"What have you been doing, Sut?"

"Helpin tu salt ole Missis Yardley down."

"What do you mean by that?"

"Fixin her fur rotten cumfurtably, kiverin her up wif sile, tu keep the buzzards frum cheatin the wurms."

"Oh, you have been helping to bury a woman."

"That's hit, by golly! Now why the devil can't I 'splain mysef like yu? I ladles out my words at random, like a calf kickin at yaller-jackids; yu jis' rolls em out tu the pint, like a feller a-layin bricks—every one fits. How is it that bricks fits so clost enyhow? Rocks won't ni du hit."

"Becaze they'se all ove a size," ventured a man with a wen over his eye.

"The devil yu say, ho'ney-head! haint reapin-mersheens ove a size? I'd like tu see two ove em fit clost. Yu wait ontil yu sprouts tuther ho'n, afore yu venters tu 'splain mix'd questions. George, did yu know ole Missis Yardley?"

"No."

"Well, she wer a curious 'oman in her way, an' she wore shiney specks. Now jis' listen: Whenever yu see a ole 'oman ahine a par ove *shiney* specks, yu keep yer eye skinn'd; they am dang'rus in the extreme. Thar is jis' no knowin what they ken du. I hed one a-stradil ove me onst, fur kissin her gal. She went fur my har, an' she went fur my skin, ontil I tho't she ment tu kill me, an' wud a-dun hit, ef my hollerin hadent fotch ole Dave Jordan, a *bacheler*, tu my aid. He, like a durn'd fool, cotch her by the laig, an' drug her back'ards ofen me. She jis' kivered him, an' I run, by golly! The nex time I seed him he wer bald headed, an' his face looked like he'd been a-fitin wild cats.

"Ole Missis Yardley wer a great noticer ove littil things, that nobody else ever seed. She'd say right in the middil ove sumbody's serious talk: 'Law sakes! thar goes that yaller slut ove a hen, a-flingin straws over her shoulder; she's arter settin now, an' haint laid but seven aigs. I'll disapint *her*, see ef I don't; I'll put a punkin in her nes', an' a feather in her nose. An' bless my soul! jis' look at that cow wif the wilted ho'n, a-flingin up dirt an' a-smellin the place where hit cum frum, wif the rale ginuine still-wurim twis' in her tail, too; what upon the face ove the yeath kin she be arter

now, the ole fool? watch her, Sally. An' sakes alive, jis' look
at that ole sow; she's a-gwine in a fas' trot, wif her empty
bag a-floppin agin her sides. Thar, she hes stop't, an's
a-listenin! massy on us! what a long yearnis grunt she gin;
hit cum frum way back ove her kidneys. Thar she goes
agin; she's arter no good, sich kerryin on means no good.'

"An' so she wud gabble, no odds who wer a-listenin. She
looked like she mout been made at fust 'bout four foot long,
an' the common thickness ove wimen when they's at thar-
sefs, an' then had her har tied tu a stump, a par ove steers
hitched to her heels, an' then straiched out a-mos' two foot
more—mos' ove the straichin cumin outen her laigs an' naik.
Her stockins, a-hangin on the clothesline tu dry, looked like
a par ove sabre scabbards, an' her naik looked like a dry
beef shank smoked, an' mout been ni ontu es tough. I never
felt hit mysef, I didn't, I jis' jedges by looks. Her darter Sal
wer bilt at fust 'bout the laingth ove her mam, but wer
never straiched eny by a par ove steers, an' she wer fat
enuf tu kill; she wer taller lyin down than she wer a-standin
up. Hit wer her who gin me the 'hump shoulder.' Jis' look
at me; haint I'se got a tech ove the dromedary back thar
bad? haint I humpy? Well, a-stoopin tu kiss that squatty
lard-stan ove a gal is what dun hit tu me. She wer the
fairest-lookin gal I ever seed. She allers wore thick woolin
stockins 'bout six inches too long fur her laig; they rolled
down over her garters, lookin like a par ove life-presarvers
up thar. I tell yu she wer a tarin gal enyhow. Luved kissin,
wrastlin, an' biled cabbige, an' hated tite clothes, hot
weather, an' suckit-riders. B'leved strong in married folk's
ways, cradles, an' the remishun ove sins, an' didn't b'leve
in corsets, fleas, peaners, nur the fashun plates."

"What caused the death of Mrs. Yardley, Sut?"

"Nuffin, only her heart stop't beatin 'bout losin a nine
dimunt quilt. True, she got a skeer'd hoss tu run over her,
but she'd a-got over that ef a quilt hadn't been mix'd up
in the catastrophy. Yu see quilts wer wun ove her speshul
gifts; she run strong on the bed-kiver question. Irish chain,
star ove Texas, sun-flower, nine dimunt, saw teeth, checker-
board, an' shell quilts; blue, an' white, an' yaller an' black

coverlids, an' callickercumfurts reigned triumphan' 'bout her hous'. They wer packed in drawers, layin in shelfs full, wer hung four dubbil on lines in the lof, packed in chists, piled on cheers, an' wer everywhar, even ontu the beds, an' wer changed every bed-makin. She told everybody she cud git tu listen tu hit that she ment tu give every durn'd one ove them tu Sal when she got married. Oh, lordy! what es fat a gal es Sal Yardley cud ever du wif half ove em, an' sleepin wif a husbun at that, is more nor I ever cud see through. Jis' think ove her onder twenty layer ove quilts in July, an' yu in thar too. Gewhillikins! George, look how I is sweatin' now, an' this is December. I'd 'bout es lief be shet up in a steam biler wif a three hundred pound bag ove lard, es tu make a bisiness ove sleepin wif that gal— 'twould kill a glass-blower.

"Well, tu cum tu the serious part ove this conversashun, that is how the old quilt-mersheen an' coverlid-loom cum tu stop operashuns on this yeath. She hed narrated hit thru the neighborhood that nex Saterday she'd gin a quiltin—three quilts an' one cumfurt tu tie. 'Goblers, fiddils, gals, an' whisky,' wer the words she sent tu the men-folk, an' more tetchin ur wakenin words never drap't ofen an 'oman's tongue. She sed tu the gals, 'Sweet toddy, huggin, dancin, an' huggers in 'bundance.' Them words struck the gals rite in the pit ove the stumick, an' spread a ticklin sensashun bof ways, ontil they scratched thar heads wif one han, an' thar heels wif tuther.

"Everybody, he an' she, what wer baptized b'levers in the righteousnes ove quiltins wer thar, an' hit jis' so happen'd that everybody in them parts, frum fifteen summers tu fifty winters, wer unannamus b'levers. Strange, warn't hit? Hit wer the bigges' quiltin ever Missis Yardley hilt, an' she hed hilt hundreds; everybody wer thar, 'scept the constibil an' suckit-rider, two dam easily-spared pussons; the numbers ni ontu even too; jis' a few more boys nur gals; that made hit more exhitin, fur hit gin the gals a chance tu kick an' squeal a littil, wifout eny risk ove not gittin kissed at all, an' hit gin reasonabil grouns fur a few scrimmages amung the he's. Now es kissin an' fitin am the pepper

an' salt ove all soshul getherins, so hit wer more espishully
wif this ove ours. Es I swung my eyes over the crowd,
George, I thought quiltins, managed in a morril an' sensibil
way, truly good things—good fur free drinkin, good fur free
eatin, good fur free huggin, good fur free dancin, good fur
free fitin, an' goodest ove all fur poperlatin a country fas'.

"Thar am a fur-seein wisdum in quiltins, ef they hes
proper trimmins: 'vittils, fiddils, an' sperrits in 'bundance.'
One holesum quiltin am wuf three old pray'r meetins on
the poperlashun pint, purtickerly ef hits hilt in the dark ove
the moon, an' runs intu the night a few hours, an' April ur
May am the time chosen. The moon don't suit quiltins whar
everybody is well acquainted an' already fur along in
courtin. She dus help pow'ful tu begin a courtin match
onder, but when hit draws ni ontu a head, nobody wants
a moon but the ole mammys.

"The mornin cum, still, saft, sunshiney; cocks crowin,
hens singin, birds chirpin, tuckeys gobblin—jis' the day tu
sun quilts, kick, kiss, squeal, an' make love.

"All the plow-lines an' clothes-lines wer straiched tu every post an' tree. Quilts purvailed. Durn my gizzard ef
two acres roun that ar house warn't jis' one solid quilt, all
out a-sunnin, an' tu be seed. They dazzled the eyes,
skeered the hosses, gin the wimen the heart-burn, an' per-
dominated.

"To'ards sundown the he's begun tu drap in. Yearnis'
needil-drivin cummenced tu lose groun; threads broke
ofen, thimbils got los', an' quilts needed anuther roll. Gig-
glin, winkin, whisperin, smoofin ove har, an' gals a-ticklin
one anuther, wer a-gainin every inch ove groun what the
needils los'. Did yu ever notis, George, at all soshul getherins, when the he's begin tu gather, that the young she's
begin tu tickil one anuther an' the ole maids swell thar
tails, roach up thar backs, an' sharpen thar nails ontu the
bed-posts an' door jams, an' spit an' groan sorter like cats
a-courtin? Dus hit mean *rale* rath, ur is hit a dare tu the
he's, sorter kivered up wif the outside signs ove danger?
I honestly b'leve that the young shes' ticklin means, 'Cum
an' take this job ofen our hans.' But that swellin I jis' don't

onderstan; dus yu? Hit looks skeery, an' I never tetch one ove em when they am in the swellin way. I may be mistaken'd 'bout the ticklin bisiness too; hit may be dun like a feller chaws poplar bark when he haint got eny terbacker, a-sorter better nur nun make-shif. I dus know one thing tu a certainty: that is, when the he's take hold the ticklin quits, an' ef yu gits one ove the ole maids out tu herself, then she subsides an' is the smoofes, saft thing yu ever seed, an' dam ef yu can't hear her purr, jis' es plain!

"But then, George, gals an' ole maids haint the things tu fool time away on. Hits widders, by golly, what am the rale sensibil, steady-goin, never-skeerin, never-kickin, willin, sperrited, smoof pacers. They cum clost up tu the hoss-block, standin still wif that purty silky years playin, an' the naik-veins a-throbbin, an' waits fur the word, which ove course yu gives, arter yu finds yer feet well in the stirrup, an' away they moves like a cradil on cushioned rockers, ur a spring buggy runnin in damp san'. A tetch ove the bridil, an' they knows yu wants em tu turn, an' they dus hit es willin es ef the idear wer thar own. I be dod rabbited ef a man can't 'propriate happiness by the skinful ef he is in contack wif sumbody's widder, an' is smart. Gin me a willin widder, the yeath over: what they don't know, haint worth larnin. They hes all been tu Jamakey an' larnt how sugar's made, an' knows how tu sweeten wif hit; an' by golly, they is always ready tu use hit. All yu hes tu du is tu find the spoon, an' then drink cumfort till yer blind. Nex tu good sperrits an' my laigs, I likes a twenty-five year ole widder, wif roun ankils, an' bright eyes, honestly an' squarly lookin intu yurn, an' sayin es plainly es a partrige sez 'Bob White,' 'Don't be afraid ove me; I hes been thar; yu know hit ef yu hes eny sense, an' thar's no use in eny humbug, ole feller—cum ahead!'

"Ef yu onderstans widder nater, they ken save yu a power ove troubil, onsartinty, an' time, an' ef yu is interprisin yu gits mons'rous well paid fur hit. The very soun ove thar littil shoe-heels speak full trainin, an' hes a knowin click as they tap the floor; an' the rustil ove thar dress sez, 'I dar yu tu ax me.'

"When yu hes made up yer mind tu court one, jis' go at hit like hit wer a job ove rail-maulin. Ware yer workin close, use yer common, every-day moshuns an' words, an' abuv all, fling away yer cinamint ile vial an' burn all yer love songs. No use in tryin tu fool em, fur they sees plum thru yu, a durn'd sight plainer than they dus thru thar veils. No use in a pasted shut; she's been thar. No use in borrowin a cavortin fat hoss; she's been thar. No use in har-dye; she's been thar. No use in cloves, tu kill whisky breff; she's been thar. No use in buyin clost curtains fur yer bed, fur she has been thar. Widders am a speshul means, George, fur ripenin green men, killin off weak ones, an' makin 'ternally happy the soun ones.

"Well, es I sed afore, I flew the track an' got ontu the widders. The fellers begun tu ride up an' walk up, sorter slow, like they warn't in a hurry, the durn'd 'saitful raskils, hitchin thar critters tu enything they cud find. One red-comb'd, long-spurr'd, dominecker feller, frum town, in a red an' white gridiron jackid an' patent leather gaiters, hitched his hoss, a wild, skeery, wall-eyed devil, inside the yard palins, tu a cherry tree lim'. Thinks I, that hoss hes a skeer intu him big enuf tu run intu town, an' perhaps beyant hit, ef I kin only tetch hit off; so I sot intu thinkin.

"One aind ove a long clothes-line, wif nine dimunt quilts ontu hit, wer tied tu the same cherry tree that the hoss wer. I tuck my knife and socked hit thru every quilt, 'bout the middil, an' jis' below the rope, an' tied them thar wif bark, so they cudent slip. Then I went tu the back aind, an' ontied hit frum the pos', knottin in a hoe-handil, by the middil, tu keep the quilts frum slippin off ef my bark strings failed, an' laid hit on the groun. Then I went tu the tuther aind: thar wer 'bout ten foot tu spar, a-lyin on the groun arter tyin tu the tree. I tuck hit atwix Wall-eye's hine laigs, an' tied hit fas' tu bof stirrups, an' then cut the cherry tree lim' betwix his bridil an' the tree, almos' off. Now, mine yu thar wer two ur three uther ropes full ove quilts atween me an' the hous', so I wer purty well hid frum thar. I jis' tore off a palin frum the fence, an' tuck hit in bof hans, an' arter raisin hit 'way up yander, I fotch hit down, es hard es I cud, flatsided to'ards the groun, an' hit acksidentally happen'd tu hit Wall-eye, 'bout nine inches ahead ove the root ove his tail. Hit landed so hard that hit made my hans tingle, an' then busted intu splinters. The first thing I did wer tu feel ove mysef, on the same spot whar hit hed hit the hoss. I cudent help duin hit tu save my life, an' I swar I felt sum ove Wall-eye's sensashun, jis' es plain. The fust thing he did, wer tu tare down the lim' wif a twenty foot jump, his head to'ards the hous'. Thinks I, now yu hev dun hit, yu durn'd wall-eyed fool! tarin down that lim' wer the beginin ove all the troubil, an' the hoss did hit hissef; my conshuns felt clar es a mountin spring, an' I wer in a frame ove mine tu obsarve things es they happen'd, an' they soon begun tu happen purty clost arter one anuther rite then, an' thar, an' tharabouts, clean ontu town, thru hit, an' still wer a-happenin, in the woods beyant thar ni ontu eleven mile frum ole man Yardley's gate, an' four beyant town.

"The fust line ove quilts he tried tu jump, but broke hit down; the nex one he ran onder; the rope cotch ontu the ho'n ove the saddil, broke at bof ainds, an' went along wif the hoss, the cherry tree lim' an' the fust line ove quilts, what I hed proverdensally tied fas' tu the rope. That's what I calls foresight, George. Right furnint the frunt door he cum in contack wif ole Missis Yardley hersef, an' anuther ole 'oman; they wer a-holdin a nine dimunt quilt spread out, a-'zaminin hit, an' a-praisin hits purfeckshuns. The durn'd onmanerly, wall-eyed fool run plum over Missis Yardley, frum ahine, stompt one hine foot through the quilt, takin hit along, a-kickin ontil he made hits corners snap like a whip. The gals screamed, the men hollered wo! an' the ole 'oman wer toted intu the hous' limber es a wet string, an' every word she sed wer, 'Oh, my preshus nine dimunt quilt!'

"Wall-eye busted thru the palins, an' Dominicker sed 'im, made a mortal rush fur his bitts, wer too late fur them, but in good time fur the strings ove flyin quilts, got tangled among em, an' the gridiron jackid patren wer los' tu my sight amung star an' Irish chain quilts; he went frum that

quiltin at the rate ove thuty miles tu the hour. Nuffin lef
on the lot ove the hole consarn, but a nine biler hat, a par
ove gloves, an' the jack ove hearts.

"What a onmanerly, suddin way ove leavin places sum
folks hev got, enyhow.

"Thinks I, well, that fool hoss, tarin down that cherry
tree lim', hes dun sum good, enyhow; hit hes put the ole
'oman outen the way fur the balance ove the quiltin, an'
tuck Dominicker outen the way an' outen danger, fur that
gridiron jackid wud a-bred a scab on his nose afore mid-
nite; hit wer morrily boun tu du hit.

"Two months arterwards, I tracked the route that hoss
tuck in his kalamatus skeer, by quilt rags, tufts ove cotton,
bunches ove har, (human an' hoss,) an' scraps ove a gridiron jackid stickin ontu the bushes, an' plum at the aind ove
hit, whar all signs gin out, I foun a piece ove watch chain
an' a hosses head. The places what know'd Dominicker,
know'd 'im no more.

"Well, arter they'd tuck the ole 'oman up stairs an' cam-
fired her tu sleep, things begun tu work agin. The widders
broke the ice, an' arter a littil gigilin, goblin, an' gabblin,
the kissin begun. *Smack!*—'Thar, now,' a widder sed that.
Pop!—'Oh, don't!' *Pfip!*—'Oh, yu quit!' *Plosh!*—'Go *way* yu
awkerd critter, yu kissed me in the eye!' anuther widder
sed that. *Bop!*—'Now yu ar satisfied, I recon, big mouf!' *Vip!*
—'That haint fair!' *Spat!*—'Oh, lordy! May, cum pull Bill
away; he's a-tanglin my har.' *Thut!*—'I jis' d-a-r-e yu tu du
that agin!' a widder sed that, too. Hit sounded all 'roun
that room like poppin co'n in a hot skillet, an' wer pow'ful
sujestif.

"Hit kep on ontil I be durn'd ef *my* bristils didn't begin
tu rise, an' sumthin like a cold buckshot wud run down the
marrow in my back-bone 'bout every ten secons, an' then
run up agin, tolerabil hot. I kep a swallerin wif nuthin tu
swaller, an' my face felt swell'd; an' yet I wer fear'd tu
make a bulge. Thinks I, I'll ketch one out tu hersef torreckly,
an' then I guess we'll rastil. Purty soon Sal Yardley started
fur the smoke-'ous, so I jis' gin my head a few short shakes,
let down one ove my wings a-trailin, an' sirkiled roun her

wif a side twis' in my naik, steppin sidewise, an' a-fetchin up my hinmos' foot wif a sorter jerkin slide at every step. Sez I, 'Too coo-took a-too.' She onderstood hit, an stopt, sorter spreadin her shoulders. An' jis' es I hed pouch'd out my mouf, an' wer a-reachin forrid wif hit, fur the article hitsef, sumthin interfared wif me, hit did. George, wer yu ever ontu yer hans an' knees, an' let a hell-tarin big, mad ram, wif a ten-yard run, but yu yearnis'ly, jis' onst, right squar ontu the pint ove yer back-bone?"

"No, you fool; why do you ask?"

"Kaze I wanted tu know ef yu cud hev a realizin' noshun ove my shock. Hits scarcely worth while tu try tu make yu onderstan the case by words only, onless yu hev been tetched in that way. Gr-eat golly! the fust thing I felt, I tuck hit tu be a back-ackshun yeathquake; an' the fust thing I seed wer my chaw'r terbacker a-flyin over Sal's head like a skeer'd bat. My mouf wer pouch'd out, ready fur the article hitsef, yu know, an' hit went outen the roun hole like the wad outen a pop-gun—thug! an' the fust thing I know'd, I wer a-flyin over Sal's head too, an' a-gainin on the chaw'r terbacker fast. I wer straitened out strait, toes hinemos', middil fingernails foremos', an' the fust thing I hearn wer, 'Yu dam Shanghi!' Great Jerus-a-lam! I lit ontu my all fours jis' in time tu but the yard gate ofen hits hinges, an' skeer loose sum more hosses—kep on in a four-footed gallop, clean acrost the lane afore I cud straiten up, an' yere I cotch up wif my chaw'r terbacker, stickin flat agin a fence-rail. I hed got so good a start that I thot hit a pity tu spile hit, so I jis' jump'd the fence an' tuck thru the orchurd. I tell yu I dusted these yere close, fur I tho't hit were arter me.

"Arter runnin a spell, I ventered tu feel roun back thar, fur sum signs ove what hed happened tu me. George, arter two pow'ful hardtugs, I pull'd out the vamp an' sole ove one ove ole man Yardley's big brogans, what he hed los' amung my coat-tails. Dre'ful! dre'ful! Arter I got hit away frum thar, my flesh went fas' asleep, frum abuv my kidneys tu my knees; about now, fur the fust time, the idear struck me, what hit wer that hed interfar'd wif me, an' los' me the kiss. Hit wer ole Yardley hed kicked me. I walked fur a month like I wer straddlin a thorn hedge. Sich a shock, at sich a time, an' on sich a place—jis' think ove hit! hit am tremenjus, haint hit? The place feels num, right now."

"Well, Sut, how did the quilting come out?"

"How the hell du yu 'speck me tu know? I warn't thar eny more."

Nathaniel
Hawthorne

On rainy days in the early 1840s Hawthorne was wont to read volumes of Puritan theology, a collection of which he had found in the attic of the Old Manse in Concord. His opinion, finally, was that Puritanism was a "stupendous impertinence"; he was glad its day was done.

But if after two hundred years the religion of his New England ancestors had "cooled down even to the freezing point," there nevertheless loomed in Hawthorne's imagination vital, unforgettable images of Puritan forebears. Of William Hathorne, his great-great-great-grandfather, Hawthorne wrote in his introduction to *The Scarlet Letter*, "The figure of that first ancestor still haunts me. . . . He was a soldier, legislator, judge; he was a ruler in the Church; he had all the Puritanic traits, both good and evil. He was likewise a bitter persecutor. . . . His son, too, inherited the persecuting spirit, and made himself so conspicuous in the martyrdom of the witches, that their blood may fairly be said to have left a stain upon him." Grand, awful men, who, whatever their sins, may also fairly be said to have lived, and it was to their vitality which Hawthorne responded above all else. If Puritanism was now cold, it had once been blood-hot. About such a people one could write great tragedy.

The emotional temperature of the modern age, however, was tepid, as Hawthorne read the thermometer. Like Herman Melville, Henry Thoreau and Ralph Waldo Emerson, Hawthorne had been raised in shabby-genteel circumstances, which gave him a special view of the blandly complacent leaders of American society. His family was an old one in Salem, but its fortunes had declined; walking past the great houses on Chestnut Street, young Nathaniel Hawthorne was an outsider looking in. What he saw was shallowness, complacency, and moral blindness. About such people one could only write satire.

Hawthorne's satires are not hate-filled or vengeful; neither are they gay. Just as he occasionally ridicules the importance of the sinners' suffering in *The Scarlet Letter* to the point where tragedy verges, as Anthony Trollope noted, on burlesque, so his humor is sometimes melancholy, sometimes tragic, sometimes terrifying. Mrs. James T. Fields, the wife of his Boston publisher, said that Hawthorne was witty, but not joyful; and Hawthorne said of himself that "the merriest man can hardly contrive to laugh at his broadest humor." While that latter statement is to be understood as self-mockery, the very fact that it is furnishes a clue to the basic nature of Hawthorne's joking: first and last, his humor mocks mankind's pretensions to significance.

Hawthorne's sister Elizabeth reported that he had read *Pilgrim's Progress* at age six; at eight or nine he dipped into the book again between fishing trips on Sebago Lake; judging from the number of references to Bunyan's work in his novels and tales, there was no other author whom Hawthorne knew so well. In "The Celestial Railroad," he turns Bunyan on his head and mockingly records the progress of ultra-respectable modern Christians toward hell.

The Celestial Railroad

Not a great while ago, passing through the gate of
dreams, I visited that region of the earth in which lies the
famous City of Destruction. It interested me much to learn
that by the public spirit of some of the inhabitants a railroad has recently been established between this populous
and flourishing town and the Celestial City. Having a little
time upon my hands, I resolved to gratify a liberal curiosity
by making a trip thither. Accordingly, one fine morning
after paying my bill at the hotel, and directing the porter
to stow my luggage behind a coach, I took my seat in the
vehicle and set out for the station-house. It was my good
fortune to enjoy the company of a gentleman—one Mr.
Smooth-it-away—who, though he had never actually visited
the Celestial City, yet seemed as well acquainted with its
laws, customs, policy, and statistics, as with those of the
City of Destruction, of which he was a native townsman.
Being, moreover, a director of the railroad corporation and
one of its largest stockholders, he had it in his power to give
me all desirable information respecting that praiseworthy
enterprise.

Our coach rattled out of the city, and at a short distance
from its outskirts passed over a bridge of elegant construction, but somewhat too slight, as I imagined, to sustain any
considerable weight. On both sides lay an extensive quag-
mire, which could not have been more disagreeable, either
to sight or smell, had all the kennels of the earth emptied
their pollution there.

"This," remarked Mr. Smooth-it-away, "is the famous
Slough of Despond—a disgrace to all the neighborhood; and
the greater that it might so easily be converted into firm
ground."

"I have understood," said I, "that efforts have been
made for that purpose from time immemorial. Bunyan

mentions that above twenty thousand cartloads of wholesome instructions had been thrown in here without effect."

"Very probably! And what effect could be anticipated from such unsubstantial stuff?" cried Mr. Smooth-it-away. "You observe this convenient bridge. We obtained a sufficient foundation for it by throwing into the slough some editions of books of morality; volumes of French philosophy and German rationalism; tracts, sermons, and essays of modern clergymen; extracts from Plato, Confucius, and various Hindoo sages, together with a few ingenious commentaries upon texts of Scripture,—all of which by some scientific process, have been converted into a mass like granite. The whole bog might be filled up with similar matter."

It really seemed to me, however, that the bridge vibrated and heaved up and down in a very formidable manner; and, in spite of Mr. Smooth-it-away's testimony to the solidity of its foundation, I should be loath to cross it in a crowded omnibus, especially if each passenger were encumbered with as heavy luggage as that gentleman and myself. Nevertheless we got over without accident, and soon found ourselves at the station-house. This very neat and spacious edifice is erected on the site of the little wicket gate, which formerly, as all old pilgrims will recollect, stood directly across the highway, and, by its inconvenient narrowness, was a great obstruction to the traveller of liberal mind and expansive stomach. The reader of John Bunyan will be glad to know that Christian's old friend Evangelist, who was accustomed to supply each pilgrim with a mystic roll, now presides at the ticket office. Some malicious persons it is true deny the identity of this reputable character with the Evangelist of old times, and even pretend to bring competent evidence of an imposture. Without involving myself in a dispute I shall merely observe that, so far as my experience goes, the square pieces of pasteboard now delivered to passengers are much more convenient and useful along the road than the antique roll of parchment. Whether they will be as readily received at the gate of the Celestial City I decline giving an opinion.

A large number of passengers were already at the station-house awaiting the departure of the cars. By the aspect and demeanor of these persons it was easy to judge that the feelings of the community had undergone a very favorable change in reference to the celestial pilgrimage. It would have done Bunyan's heart good to see it. Instead of a lonely and ragged man with a huge burden on his back, plodding along sorrowfully on foot while the whole city hooted after him, here were parties of the first gentry and most respectable people in the neighborhood setting forth towards the Celestial City as cheerfully as if the pilgrimage were merely a summer tour. Among the gentlemen were characters of deserved eminence—magistrates, politicians, and men of wealth, by whose example religion could not but be greatly recommended to their meaner brethren. In the ladies' apartment, too, I rejoiced to distinguish some of those flowers of fashionable society who are so well fitted to adorn the most elevated circles of the Celestial City. There was much pleasant conversation about the news of the day, topics of business and politics, or the lighter matters of amusement; while religion, though indubitably the main thing at heart, was thrown tastefully into the background. Even an infidel would have heard little or nothing to shock his sensibility.

One great convenience of the new method of going on pilgrimage I must not forget to mention. Our enormous burdens, instead of being carried on our shoulders as had been the custom of old, were all snugly deposited in the baggage car, and, as I was assured, would be delivered to their respective owners at the journey's end. Another thing, likewise, the benevolent reader will be delighted to understand. It may be remembered that there was an ancient feud between Prince Beelzebub and the keeper of the wicket gate, and that the adherents of the former distinguished personage were accustomed to shoot deadly arrows at honest pilgrims while knocking at the door. This dispute, much to the credit as well of the illustrious potentate above mentioned as of the worthy and enlightened directors of the railroad, has been pacifically arranged on the principle of mutual compromise. The prince's subjects are now pretty numerously employed about the station-house, some in taking care of the baggage, others in collecting fuel, feeding engines, and such congenial occupations; and I can conscientiously affirm that persons more attentive to their business, more willing to accommodate, or more generally agreeable to the passengers, are not to be found on any railroad. Every good heart must surely exult at so satisfactory an arrangement of an immemorial difficulty.

"Where is Mr. Greatheart?" inquired I. "Beyond a doubt the directors have engaged that famous old champion to be chief conductor on the railroad?"

"Why, no," said Mr. Smooth-it-away, with a dry cough. "He was offered the situation of brakeman; but to tell you the truth, our friend Greatheart has grown preposterously stiff and narrow in his old age. He has so often guided pilgrims over the road on foot that he considers it a sin to travel in any other fashion. Besides, the old fellow had entered so heartily into the ancient feud with Prince Beelzebub that he would have been perpetually at blows or ill language with some of the prince's subjects, and thus have embroiled us anew. So, in the whole, we were not sorry when honest Greatheart went off to the Celestial City in a huff and left us at liberty to choose a more suitable and accommodating man. Yonder comes the engineer of the train. You will probably recognize him at once."

The engine at this moment took its station in advance of the cars, looking, I must confess, much more like a sort of mechanical demon that would hurry us to the infernal regions than a laudable contrivance for smoothing our way to the Celestial City. On its top sat a personage almost enveloped in smoke and flame, which, not to startle the reader, appeared to gush from his own mouth and stomach as well as from the engine's brazen abdomen.

"Do my eyes deceive me?" cried I. "What on earth is this! A living creature? If so, he is own brother to the engine he rides upon!"

"Poh, poh, you are obtuse!" said Mr. Smooth-it-away, with a hearty laugh. "Don't you know Apollyon, Christian's old enemy, with whom he fought so fierce a battle in the Valley of Humiliation? He was the very fellow to manage the engine; and so we have reconciled him to the custom of going on pilgrimage, and engaged him as chief engineer."

"Bravo, bravo!" exclaimed I, with irrepressible enthusiasm; "this shows the liberality of the age; this proves, if anything can, that all musty prejudices are in a fair way to be obliterated. And how will Christian rejoice to hear of this happy transformation of his old antagonist! I promise myself great pleasure in informing him of it when we reach the Celestial City."

The passengers being all comfortably seated, we now rattled away merrily, accomplishing a greater distance in ten minutes than Christian probably trudged over in a day. It was laughable, while we glanced along, as it were, at the tail of a thunderbolt, to observe two dusty foot travellers in the old pilgrim guise, with cockle shell and staff, their mystic rolls of parchment in their hands and their intolerable burdens on their backs. The preposterous obstinacy of these honest people in persisting to groan and stumble along the difficult pathway rather than take advantage of modern improvements, excited great mirth among our wiser brotherhood. We greeted the two pilgrims with many pleasant gibes and a roar of laughter; whereupon they gazed at us with such woful and absurdly compassionate visages that our merriment grew tenfold more obstreperous. Apollyon also entered heartily into the fun, and contrived to flirt the smoke and flame of the engine, or of his own breath, into their faces and envelop them in an atmosphere of scalding steam. These little practical jokes amused us mightily, and doubtless afforded the pilgrims the gratification of considering themselves martyrs.

At some distance from the railroad Mr. Smooth-it-away pointed to a large, antique edifice, which he observed, was a tavern of long standing, and had formerly been a noted stopping-place for pilgrims. In Bunyan's road-book it is mentioned as the Interpreter's House.

"I have long had a curiosity to visit that old mansion," remarked I.

"It is not one of our stations, as you perceive," said my companion. "The keeper was violently opposed to the railroad; and well he might be, as the track left his house of entertainment on one side, and thus was pretty certain to deprive him of all his reputable customers. But the footpath still passes his door, and the old gentleman now and then receives a call from some simple traveller, and entertains him with fare as old-fashioned as himself."

Before our talk on this subject came to a conclusion we were rushing by the place where Christian's burden fell from his shoulders at the sight of the Cross. This served as a theme for Mr. Smooth-it-away, Mr. Live-for-the-world, Mr. Hide-sin-in-the-heart, Mr. Scaly-conscience, and a knot of gentlemen from the town of Shun-repentance, to descant upon the inestimable advantages resulting from the safety of our baggage. Myself, and all the passengers indeed, joined with great unanimity in this view of the matter; for our burdens were rich in many things esteemed precious throughout the world; and, especially, we each of us possessed a great variety of favorite Habits, which we trusted would not be out of fashion even in the polite circles of the Celestial City. It would have been a sad spectacle to see such an assortment of valuable articles tumbling into the sepulchre. Thus pleasantly conversing on the favorable circumstances of our position as compared with those past pilgrims and of narrow-minded ones at the present day, we soon found ourselves at the foot of the Hill Difficulty. Through the very heart of this rocky mountain a tunnel has been constructed of most admirable architecture, with a lofty arch and a spacious double track; so that, unless the earth and rocks should chance to crumble down, it will remain an eternal monument of the builder's skill and enterprise. It is a great though incidental advantage that the materials from the heart of the Hill Difficulty have been employed in filling up the Valley of Humiliation, thus obviating the necessity of descending into that disagreeable and unwholesome hollow.

"This is a wonderful improvement, indeed," said I. "Yet I should have been glad of an opportunity to visit the

Palace Beautiful and be introduced to the charming young ladies—Miss Prudence, Miss Piety, Miss Charity, and the rest—who have the kindness to entertain pilgrims there."

"Young ladies!" cried Mr. Smooth-it-away, as soon as he could speak for laughing. "And charming young ladies! Why, my dear fellow, they are old maids, every soul of them—prim, starched, dry, and angular; and not one of them, I will venture to say, has altered so much as the fashion of her gown since the days of Christian's pilgrimage."

"Ah, well," said I, much comforted, "then I can very dispense with their acquaintance."

The respectable Apollyon was now putting on the steam at a prodigious rate, anxious, perhaps, to get rid of the unpleasant reminiscences connected with the spot where he had so disastrously encountered Christian. Consulting Mr. Bunyan's road-book, I perceived that we must now be within a few miles of the Valley of the Shadow of Death, into which doleful region, at our present speed, we should plunge much sooner than seemed at all desirable. In truth, I expected nothing better than to find myself in the ditch on one side or the quag on the other; but on communicating my apprehensions to Mr. Smooth-it-away, he assured me that the difficulties of passage, even in its worst condition, had been vastly exaggerated, and that, in its present state of improvement, I might consider myself as safe as on any railroad in Christendom.

Even while we were speaking the train shot into the entrance of this dreaded Valley. Though I plead guilty to some foolish palpitations of the heart during our headlong rush over the causeway here constructed, yet it were unjust to withhold the highest encomiums on the boldness of its original conception and the ingenuity of those who executed it. It was gratifying, likewise, to observe how much care had been taken to dispel the everlasting gloom and supply the defect of cheerful sunshine, not a ray of which has ever penetrated among these awful shadows. For this purpose, the inflammable gas which exudes plentifully from the soil is collected by means of pipes, and thence communicated to a quadruple row of lamps along the whole extent of the passage. Thus a radiance has been created even out of the fiery and sulphurous curse that rests forever upon the valley—a radiance hurtful, however, to the eyes, and somewhat bewildering, as I discovered by the changes which it wrought in the visages of my companions. In this respect, as compared with natural daylight, there is the same difference as between truth and falsehood; but if the reader have ever travelled through the dark Valley, he will have learned to be thankful for any light that he could get—if not from the sky above, then from the blasted soil beneath. Such was the red brilliancy of these lamps that they appeared to build walls of fire on both sides of the track, between which we held our course at lightning speed, while a reverberating thunder filled the Valley with its echoes. Had the engine run off the track,—a catastrophe, it is whispered, by no means unprecedented,—the bottomless pit, if there be any such place, would undoubtedly have received us. Just as some dismal fooleries of this nature had made my heart quake there came a tremendous shriek, careering along the valley as if a thousand devils had burst their lungs to utter it, but which proved to be merely the whistle of the engine on arriving at a stopping-place.

The spot where we had now paused is the same that our friend Bunyan—a truthful man, but infected with many fantastic notions—has designated, in terms plainer than I like to repeat, as the mouth of the infernal region. This, however, must be a mistake, inasmuch as Mr. Smooth-it-away, while we remained in the smoky and lurid cavern, took occasion to prove that Tophet has not even a metaphorical existence. The place, he assured us, is no other than the crater of a half-extinct volcano, in which the directors had caused forges to be set up for the manufacture of railroad iron. Hence, also, is obtained a plentiful supply of fuel for the use of the engines. Whoever had gazed into the dismal obscurity of the broad cavern mouth, whence ever and anon darted huge tongues of dusky flame, and had seen the strange, half-shaped monsters, and visions of faces horribly grotesque, into which the smoke seemed to wreathe itself, and had heard the awful murmurs, and shrieks, and deep, shuddering whispers of the blast, sometimes forming themselves into words almost articulate, would have seized upon Mr. Smooth-it-away's comfortable explanation as greedily as we did. The inhabitants of the cavern, moreover, were unlovely personages, dark, smoke-begrimed, generally deformed, with misshapen feet, and a glow of dusky redness in their eyes as if their hearts had caught fire and were blazing out of the upper windows. It struck me as a peculiarity that the laborers at the forge and those who brought fuel to the engine, when they began to draw short breath, positively emitted smoke from their mouth and nostrils.

Among the idlers about the train, most of whom were puffing cigars which they had lighted at the flame of the crater, I was perplexed to notice several who, to my certain knowledge, had heretofore set forth by railroad for the Celestial City. They looked dark, wild, and smoky, with a singular resemblance, indeed, to the native inhabitants, like whom, also, they had a disagreeable propensity to ill-natured gibes and sneers, the habit of which had wrought a settled contortion of their visages. Having been on speaking terms with one of these persons,—an indolent, good-for-nothing fellow, who went by the name of Take-it-easy,—I called him, and inquired what was his business there.

"Did you not start," said I, "for the Celestial City?"

"That's a fact," said Mr. Take-it-easy, carelessly puffing some smoke into my eyes. "But I heard such bad accounts that I never took pains to climb the hill on which the city stands. No business doing, no fun going on, nothing to drink, and no smoking allowed, and a thrumming of church music from morning till night. I would not stay in such a place if they offered me house room and living free."

"But, my good Mr. Take-it-easy," cried I, "why take up your residence here, of all places in the world?"

"Oh," said the loafer, with a grin, "it is very warm hereabouts, and I meet with plenty of old acquaintances, and altogether the place suits me. I hope to see you back again some day soon. A pleasant journey to you."

While he was speaking the bell of the engine rang, and we dashed away after dropping a few passengers, but receiving no new ones. Rattling onward through the Valley, we were dazzled with the fiercely gleaming gas lamps, as before. But sometimes, in the dark of intense brightness, grim faces, that bore the aspect and expression of individual sins, or evil passions, seemed to thrust themselves through the veil of light, glaring upon us, and stretching forth a great, dusky hand, as if to impede our progress. I almost thought that they were my own sins that appalled me there. These were freaks of imagination—nothing more, certainly—mere delusions, which I ought to be heartily ashamed of; but all through the Dark Valley I was tormented, and pestered, and dolefully bewildered with the same kind of waking dreams. The mephitic gases of that region intoxicate the brain. As the light of natural day, however, began to struggle with the glow of the lanterns, these vain imaginations lost their vividness, and finally vanished with the first ray of sunshine that greeted our escape from the Valley of the Shadow of Death. Ere we had gone a mile beyond it I could well nigh have taken my oath that this whole gloomy passage was a dream.

At the end of the valley, as John Bunyan mentions, is a cavern, where, in his days, dwelt two cruel giants, Pope and Pagan, who had strown the ground about their residence with the bones of slaughtered pilgrims. These vile old troglodytes are no longer there; but into their deserted cave another terrible giant has thrust himself, and makes it his business to seize upon honest travellers and fatten them for his table with plentiful meals of smoke, mist, moonshine, raw potatoes, and sawdust. He is a German by birth, and is called Giant Transcendentalist; but as to his form, his features, his substance, and his nature generally, it is the chief peculiarity of this huge miscreant that neither he for himself, nor anybody for him has ever been able to describe them. As we rushed by the cavern's mouth we caught a hasty glimpse of him, looking somewhat like an ill-proportioned figure, but considerably more like a heap of fog and duskiness. He shouted after us, but in so strange a phraseology that we knew not what he meant, nor whether to be encouraged or affrighted.

It was late in the day when the train thundered into the ancient city of Vanity, where Vanity Fair is still at the height of prosperity, and exhibits an epitome of whatever is brilliant, gay, fascinating beneath the sun. As I purposed to make a considerable stay here, it gratified me to learn that there is no longer the want of harmony between the town's-people and pilgrims, which impelled the former to such lamentably mistaken measures as the persecution of Christian and the fiery martyrdom of Faithful. On the contrary, as the new railroad brings with it great trade and a constant influx of strangers, the lord of Vanity Fair is its chief patron, and the capitalists of the city are among the largest stockholders. Many passengers stop to take their pleasure or make their profit in the Fair, instead of going onward to the Celestial City. Indeed, such are the charms of the place that people often affirm it to be the true and only heaven; stoutly contending that there is no other, that those who seek further are mere dreamers, and that, if the fabled brightness of the Celestial City lay but a bare mile beyond the gates of Vanity, they would not be fools enough to go thither. Without subscribing to these perhaps exaggerated encomiums, I can truly say that my abode in the city was mainly agreeable, and my intercourse with the inhabitants productive of much amusement and instruction.

Being naturally of a serious turn, my attention was directed to the solid advantages derivable from a residence here, rather than to the effervescent pleasures which are the grand object with too many visitants. The Christian reader, if he have had no accounts of the city later than Bunyan's time, will be surprised to hear that almost every street has its church, and that the reverend clergy are nowhere held in higher respect than at Vanity Fair. And well do they deserve such honorable estimation; for the maxims of wisdom and virtue which fall from their lips come from as deep a spiritual source, and tend to as lofty a religious aim, as those of the sagest philosophers of old. In justification of this high praise I need only mention the names of the Rev. Mr. Shallow-deep, the Rev. Mr. Stumble-at-truth, that fine old clerical character the Rev. Mr. This-to-day, who expects shortly to resign his pulpit to the Rev. Mr. That-to-morrow; together with the Rev. Mr. Bewilderment, the Rev. Mr. Clog-the-spirit, and the last and greatest, the Rev. Dr. Wind-of-doctrine. The labors of these eminent divines are aided by those innumerable lecturers, who diffuse such a various profundity, in all subjects of human or celestial science, that any man may acquire an omnigenous erudition without the trouble of even learning to read. Thus literature is etherealized by assuming for its medium the human voice; and knowledge, depositing all its heavier particles, except, doubtless, its gold, becomes exhaled into a sound, which forthwith steals into the ever-open ear of the community. These ingenious methods constitute a sort of machinery, by which thought and study are done to every person's hand without his putting himself to the slightest inconvenience in the matter. There is another species of machine for the wholesale manufacture of individual morality. This excellent result is effected by societies for all manner of virtuous purposes, with which a man has merely to connect himself, throwing, as it were, his quota of virtue into the common stock, and the president and directors will take care that the aggregate amount be well applied. All these, and other wonderful improvements in ethics, religion, and literature, being made plain to my comprehension by the ingenious Mr. Smooth-it-away, inspired me with a vast admiration of Vanity Fair.

It would fill a volume, in an age of pamphlets, were I to record all my observations in this great capital of human business and pleasure. There was an unlimited range of society—the powerful, the wise, the witty, and the famous in every walk of life; princes, presidents, poets, generals, artists, actors, and philanthropists,—all making their own market at the fair, and deeming no price too exorbitant for such commodities as hit their fancy. It was well worth one's while, even if he had no idea of buying or selling, to loiter through the bazaars and observe the various sorts of traffic that were going forward.

Some of the purchasers, I thought, made very foolish bargains. For instance, a young man having inherited a splendid fortune, laid out a considerable portion of it in the purchase of diseases, and finally spent all the rest for a heavy lot of repentance and a suit of rags. A very pretty girl bartered a heart as clear as crystal, and which seemed her most valuable possession, for another jewel of the same kind, but so worn and defaced as to be utterly worthless. In one shop there were a great many crowns of laurel and myrtle, which soldiers, authors, statesmen, and various other people pressed eagerly to buy; some purchased these paltry wreaths with their lives, others by a toilsome servitude of years, and many sacrificed whatever was most valuable, yet finally slunk away without the crown. There was a sort of stock or scrip, called Conscience, which seemed to be in great demand, and would purchase almost anything. Indeed, few rich commodities were to be obtained without paying a heavy sum in this particular stock, and a man's business was seldom very lucrative unless he knew precisely when and how to throw his hoard of conscience into the market. Yet as this stock was the only thing of permanent value, whoever parted with it was sure to find himself a loser in the long run. Several of the speculations were of a questionable character. Occasionally a member of Congress recruited his pocket by the sale of his constituents; and I was assured that public officers have often sold their country at very moderate prices. Thousands sold their happiness for a whim. Gilded chains were in great demand, and purchased with almost any sacrifice. In truth, those who desired, according to the old adage, to sell anything valuable for a song, might find customers all over the Fair; and there were innumerable messes of pottage, piping hot, for such as chose to buy them with their birthrights. A few articles, however, could not be found genuine at Vanity Fair. If a customer wished to renew his stock of youth the dealers offered him a set of false teeth and an auburn wig; if he demanded peace of mind, they recommended opium or a brandy bottle.

Tracts of land and golden mansions, situate in the Celestial City, were often exchanged, at very disadvantageous rates, for a few years' lease of small, dismal, inconvenient tenements in Vanity Fair. Prince Beelzebub himself took great interest in this sort of traffic, and sometimes condescended to meddle with smaller matters. I once had the pleasure to see him bargaining with a miser for his soul, which, after much ingenious skirmishing on both sides, his highness succeeded in obtaining at about the value of sixpence. The prince remarked with a smile, that he was a loser by the transaction.

Day after day, as I walked the streets of Vanity, my manners and deportment became more and more like those of the inhabitants. The place began to seem like home; the idea of pursuing my travels to the Celestial City was almost obliterated from my mind. I was reminded of it, however, by the sight of the same pair of simple pilgrims at whom we had laughed so heartily when Apollyon puffed smoke and steam into their faces at the commencement of our journey. There they stood amidst the densest bustle of Vanity; the dealers offering them their purple and fine linen and jewels, the men of wit and humor gibing at them, a pair of buxom ladies ogling them askance, while the benevolent Mr. Smooth-it-away whispered some of his wisdom at their elbows, and pointed to a newly-erected temple; but there were these worthy simpletons, making the scene look wild and monstrous, merely by their sturdy repudiation of all part in its business or pleasures.

One of them—his name was Stick-to-the-right—perceived in my face, I suppose, a species of sympathy and almost admiration, which, to my own great surprise, I could not help feeling for this pragmatic couple. It prompted him to address me.

"Sir," inquired he, with a sad, yet mild and kindly voice, "do you call yourself a pilgrim?"

"Yes," I replied, "my right to that appellation is indubitable. I am merely a sojourner here in Vanity Fair, being bound to the Celestial City by the new railroad."

"Alas, friend," rejoined Mr. Stick-to-the-right, "I do assure you, and beseech you to receive the truth of my words, that that whole concern is a bubble. You may travel on it all your lifetime, were you to live thousands of years, and yet never get beyond the limits of Vanity Fair. Yea, though you should deem yourself entering the gates of the blessed city, it will be nothing but a miserable delusion."

"The Lord of the Celestial City," began the other pilgrim, whose name was Mr. Foot-it-to-heaven, "has refused, and will ever refuse, to grant an act of incorporation for this railroad; and unless that be obtained, no passenger can ever hope to enter his dominions. Wherefore every man who buys a ticket must lay his account with losing the purchase money, which is the value of his own soul."

"Poh, nonsense!" said Mr. Smooth-it-away, taking my arm and leading me off, "these fellows ought to be indicted for a libel. If the law stood as it once did in Vanity Fair we should see them grinning through the iron bars of the prison window."

This incident made a considerable impression on my mind, and contributed with other circumstances to indispose me to a permanent residence in the city of Vanity; although, of course, I was not simple enough to give up my original plan of gliding along easily and commodiously by railroad. Still, I grew anxious to be gone. There was one strange thing that troubled me. Amid the occupations or amusements of the Fair, nothing was more common than for a person—whether at feast, theatre, or church, or trafficking for wealth and honors, or whatever he might be doing, and however unseasonable the interruption—suddenly to vanish like a soap bubble, and be never more seen of his fellows; and so accustomed were the latter to such little accidents that they went on with their business as quietly as if nothing had happened. But it was otherwise with me.

Finally, after a pretty long residence at the Fair, I resumed my journey towards the Celestial City, still with Mr. Smooth-it-away at my side. At a short distance beyond the suburbs of Vanity we passed the ancient silver mine, of which Demas was the first discoverer, and which is now wrought to great advantage, supplying nearly all the coined currency of the world. A little further onward was the spot where Lot's wife had stood forever under the semblance of a pillar of salt. Curious travellers have long since carried it away piecemeal. Had all regrets been punished as rigorously as this poor dame's were, my yearning for the relinquished delights of Vanity Fair might have produced a similar change in my own corporeal substance, and left me a warning to future pilgrims.

The next remarkable object was a large edifice, constructed of mossgrown stone, but in a modern and airy style of architecture. The engine came to a pause in its vicinity, with the usual tremendous shriek.

"This was formerly the castle of the redoubted giant Despair," observed Mr. Smooth-it-away; "but since his death Mr. Flimsy-faith has repaired it, and keeps an excellent house of entertainment here. It is one of our stopping-places."

"It seems but slightly put together," remarked I, looking at the frail yet ponderous walls. "I do not envy Mr. Flimsy-faith his habitation. Some day it will thunder down upon the heads of the occupants."

"We shall escape at all events," said Mr. Smooth-it-away, "for Apollyon is putting on the steam again."

The road now plunged into a gorge of the Delectable Mountains, and traversed the field where in former ages the blind men wandered and stumbled among the tombs. One of these ancient tombstones had been thrust across the track by some malicious person, and gave the train of cars a terrible jolt. Far up the rugged side of a mountain I perceived a rusty iron door, half overgrown with bushes and creeping plants, but with smoke issuing from its crevices.

"Is that," inquired I, "the very door in the hill-side which the shepherds assured Christian was a by-way to hell?"

"That was a joke on the part of the shepherds," said Mr. Smooth-it-away, with a smile. "It is neither more nor less than the door of a cavern which they use as a smoke-house for the preparation of mutton hams."

My recollections of the journey are now, for a little space, dim and confused, inasmuch as a singular drowsiness here overcame me, owing to the fact that we were passing over the enchanted ground, the air of which encourages a disposition to sleep. I awoke, however, as soon as we crossed the borders of the pleasant land of Beulah. All the passengers were rubbing their eyes, comparing watches, and congratulating one another on the prospect of arriving so seasonably at the journey's end. The sweet breezes of this happy clime came refreshingly to our nostrils; we beheld the glimmering gush of silver fountains, overhung by trees of beautiful foliage and delicious fruit, which were propagated by grafts from the celestial gardens. Once, as we dashed onward like a hurricane, there was a flutter of wings and the bright appearance of an angel in the air, speeding forth on some heavenly mission. The engine now announced the close vicinity of the final station-house by one last and horrible scream, in which there seemed to be distinguishable every kind of wailing and woe, and bitter fierceness of wrath, all mixed up with the wild laughter of a devil or a madman. Throughout our journey, at every stopping-place, Apollyon had exercised his ingenuity in screwing the most abominable sounds out of the whistle of the steam-engine; but in this closing effort he outdid himself and created an infernal uproar, which, besides disturbing the peaceful inhabitants of Beulah, must have sent its discord even through the celestial gates.

While the horrid clamor was still ringing in our ears we heard an exulting strain, as if a thousand instruments of music, with height and depth and sweetness in their tones, at once tender and triumphant, were struck in unison, to greet the approach of some illustrious hero, who had fought the good fight and won a glorious victory, and was come to lay aside his battered arms forever. Looking to ascertain what might be the occasion of this glad harmony, I perceived, on alighting from the cars, that a multitude of shining ones had assembled on the other side of the river, to welcome two poor pilgrims, who were just emerging from its depth. They were the same whom Apollyon and ourselves had persecuted with taunts, and gibes, and scalding steam, at the commencement of our journey—the same whose unworldly aspect and impressive words had stirred my conscience amid the wild revellers of Vanity Fair.

"How amazingly well those men have got on," cried I to

Mr. Smooth-it-away. "I wish we were secure of as good a reception."

"Never fear, never fear!" answered my friend. "Come, make haste; the ferry boat will be off directly, and in three minutes you will be on the other side of the river. No doubt you will find coaches to carry you up to the city gates."

A steam ferry boat, the last improvement on this important route, lay at the river side, puffing, snorting, and emitting all those other disagreeable utterances which betoken the departure to be immediate. I hurried on board with the rest of the passengers, most of whom were in great perturbation: some bawling out for their baggage; some tearing their hair and exclaiming that the boat would explode or sink; some already pale with the heaving of the stream; some gazing affrighted at the ugly aspect of the steersman; and some still dizzy with the slumberous influences of the Enchanted Ground. Looking back to the shore, I was amazed to discern Mr. Smooth-it-away waving his hand in token of farewell.

"Don't you go over to the Celestial City?" exclaimed I.

"Oh, no!" answered he with a queer smile, and that same disagreeable contortion of visage which I had remarked in the inhabitants of the Dark Valley. "Oh, no! I have come thus far only for the sake of your pleasant company. Good-by! We shall meet again."

And then did my excellent friend Mr. Smooth-it-away laugh outright, in the midst of which cachinnation a smoke-wreath issued from his mouth and nostrils, while a twinkle of lurid flame darted out of either eye, proving indubitably that his heart was all of a red blaze. The impudent fiend! To deny the existence of Tophet, when he felt its fiery tortures raging within his breast. I rushed to the side of the boat, intending to fling myself on shore; but the wheels, as they began their revolutions, threw a dash of spray over me so cold—so deadly cold, with the chill that will never leave those waters until Death be drowned in his own river —that with a shiver and a heartquake I awoke. Thank heaven it was a Dream!

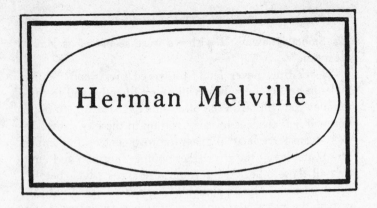

Herman Melville

"Oh, Ahab!" Melville exclaimed in *Moby Dick,* "what shall be grand in thee, it must needs be plucked at from the skies, and dived for in the deep, and featured in the unbodied air!" One of the ways in which Melville sought to pluck Ahab's grandness from the skies was by associating him with the most recurrent of all American symbols of pride, defiance, and unlimited assertion of the self, the gamecock of the wilderness. The clearest instance of the association occurs in what is in many ways the richest chapter in *Moby Dick,* the chapter called "The Doubloon." On the face of the golden coin that has been nailed to the mainmast are the likenesses of three summits in the Andes. Above one summit rises a flame; a tower tops the second; perched on the third is a crowing cock. Addressing the coin, Ahab says: "There's something ever egotistical in mountaintops and towers, and all other grand and lofty things; look here,—three peaks as proud as Lucifer. The firm tower, that is Ahab; the volcano, that is Ahab; the courageous, the undaunted and victorious fowl, that, too, is Ahab."

Davy Crockett had also boasted that he was such a bird, as had Mike Fink, the broadhorn tough, and Captain Sam Brady, the Pennsylvania Regulator. When the bee hunter Paul Hover in Cooper's *The Prairie* succeeds in storming a rocky redoubt, his first act is "to sound the note of victory,

after the quaint and ludicrous manner that is so often practised among the borderers of the West. Flapping his sides
with his hands, as the conquering gamecock is wont to do
with his wings, he raised a loud and laughable imitation
of the exultation of this bird." In Robert Montgomery Bird's
Nick of the Woods, the captain of horse thieves screams,
"'I'm a gentleman and my name's Fight! Foot and hand,
tooth and nail, claw and mud-scraper, knife, gun, and tomahawk, or any other way you choose to take me, I'm your
man! Cock-a-doodle-doo!' And with that the gentleman
jumped into the air, and flapped his wings." Thoreau's tone
is very different from that of Bird's horse thief, but in the
epigraph to *Walden*, Thoreau nevertheless asserts his ruthless self-reliance by proposing to brag as lustily as chanticleer in the morning, and goes on in the book to satirize
Poor Richard by proclaiming that the way to become un-
speakably healthy, wealthy, and wise is to get up early and
listen to the wild cocks of the woods.

For Melville the problem of pride was central, and early
and late, proud birds soar and scream in his work to embody his meanings. In *Typee* there is the rooster who
stands, as Ahab would, on one leg; in *Mardi* the scream of
the Roman eagle is echoed by "the vauntful cries" of the
American hawk, "his red comb yet reeking with slaughter";
when, in *Moby Dick*, Queequeg defies death to do its worst
by demanding that he be measured for a coffin, mad Pip
cries, "Oh for a game cock now to sit upon his head and
crow!"; brooding on Ahab's mad woefulness, Ishmael thinks
of the "Catskill eagle in some souls that alike dive down
into the blackest gorges, and soar out of them again and
become invisible in the sunny spaces," an image which pre-
pares us for the final great moment when, after the white
whale has destroyed the *Pequod* and the ship is sinking,
the savage Tashtego, in the act of nailing the flag fast to
the top of the subsiding spar, feels a sky hawk intercept
its wing between his hammer and the wood—and "feeling
that etherial thrill, the submerged savage beneath, in his
death-gasp, kept his hammer frozen there; and so the bird
of heaven, with archangelic shrieks, and his imperial beak

thrust upwards, and his whole captive form folded in the flag of Ahab, went down with his ship."

In 1853, having published *Moby Dick* in 1851 and *Pierre* in 1852, even Herman Melville should have been totally exhausted, yet—incredibly—there was enough of his titanic energy left for two stories. One of them was "Bartleby the Scrivener"; the other was "Cock-A-Doodle-Doo!" While not the masterpiece that "Bartleby" is, the latter story is nevertheless extremely interesting. First of all, it shows Melville using the gamecock symbol for the purposes of writing not a tragedy of pride, but a comic satire on self-reliance. The story furthermore gives evidence that in creating the literary vehicle that could carry the tremendous weight of the story of Ahab and the whale, Melville had drawn not only on Shakespeare, as F. O. Matthiessen and other critics have shown, and on epic poetry, as Professor Newton Arvin has suggested, but on opera as well.

The name which the narrator of "Cock-A-Doodle-Doo!" bestows on the inspiring rooster of the story is Beneventano, because, he says, "the preceding autumn I had been to the city and had chanced to be present at a performance of the Italian Opera. In that opera figured in some royal character a certain Signor Beneventano—a man of a tall, imposing person, and . . . a most remarkable, majestic, scornful stride. . . . For all the world, the proud pace of the cock seemed the very stage-pace of the Signor Beneventano." The narrator's statement mirrors a moment in Melville's own experience, for in the winter of 1847–48, when Melville was living in New York City and beginning to experiment in *Mardi* with the possibilities of magnifying prose expression to meet the requirements of his vision, he occasionally went to hear Italian opera. On Christmas Eve, 1847, for example, he went to the new Astor Place Opera House to hear Donizetti's *Lucia di Lammermoor*, with the role of Lord Henry Ashton being sung by a gentleman with the resounding name of Ferdinando Beneventano.

Like Whitman, who haunted the opera houses of New York in the same period, Melville may have found that Italian opera could serve as one of the bases for a new American art. Melville's reading of Shakespeare enriched his language and deepened his whole view of life, but the alternation of recitative and aria in Italian opera was in some ways a better structural model for *Moby Dick* than the drama. For the "action" of the *Pequod's* final cruise is not so much a dramatic development as it is a sequence of spaced crises, almost all of which involve Ahab—a sequence of recitatives, one might say, which are punctuated by Ahab's arias. Ahab's great speeches are pure, sheeted flames of emotion; occasionally startlingly close to the soliloquies of Shakespearean drama, they are more often like the crowing of a haughty cock, or the singing of a Beneventano; they have the operatic intensity of Lucia's mad song. The solitary human voice is the purest medium for the assertion of man's awareness of his essential tragedy, and while Lear on the heath and Antigone on the Theban plain are dramatic examples of that voice's defiance of the cosmos, Melville attempted to drive expression to some final reach of emotion which can be attained only when the voice is lifted to an operatic pitch—or shrieks with the archangelic fury of an imperial bird.

Cock-A-Doodle-Doo! or the Crowing of the Noble Cock Beneventano

---

In all parts of the world many high-spirited revolts from rascally despotisms had of late been knocked on the head; many dreadful casualties, by locomotive and steamer, had likewise knocked hundreds of high-spirited travelers on the head (I lost a dear friend in one of them); my own private affairs were also full of despotisms, casualties, and knockings on the head, when early one morning in spring, being too full of hypoes to sleep, I sallied out to walk on my hillside pasture.

It was a cool and misty, damp, disagreeable air. The country looked underdone, its raw juices squirting out all round. I buttoned out this squitchy air as well as I could with my lean, double-breasted dress-coat—my overcoat being so long-skirted I only used it in my wagon—and spitefully thrusting my crab-stick into the oozy sod, bent my blue form to the steep ascent of the hill. This toiling posture brought my head pretty well earthward, as if I were in the act of butting it against the world. I marked the fact, but only grinned at it with a ghastly grin.

All round me were tokens of a divided empire. The old grass and the new grass were striving together. In the low wet swales the verdure peeped out in vivid green; beyond, on the mountains, lay light patches of snow, strangely relieved against their russet sides; all the humped hills looked like brindled kine in the shivers. The woods were strewn with dry dead boughs, snapped off by the riotous winds of March, while the young trees skirting the woods were just beginning to show the first yellowish tinge of the nascent spray.

I sat down for a moment on a great rotting log nigh the top of the hill, my back to a heavy grove, my face presented toward a wide sweeping circuit of mountains enclosing a rolling, diversified country. Along the base of one long range of heights ran a lagging, fever-and-agueish river, over which was a duplicate stream of dripping mist, exactly corresponding in every meander with its parent water below. Low down, here and there, shreds of vapor listlessly wandered in the air, like abandoned or helmless nations or ships—or very soaky towels hung on criss-cross clothes-lines to dry. Afar, over a distant village lying in a bay of the plain formed by the mountains, there rested a great flat canopy of haze, like a pall. It was the condensed smoke of the chimneys, with the condensed, exhaled breath of the villagers, prevented from dispersion by the imprisoning hills. It was too heavy and lifeless to mount of itself; so there it lay, between the village and the sky, doubtless hiding many a man with the mumps, and many a queasy child.

My eye ranged over the capacious rolling country, and over the mountains, and over the village, and over a farm-house here and there, and over woods, groves, streams, rocks, fells—and I thought to myself, what a slight mark, after all, does man make on this huge great earth. Yet the earth makes a mark on him. What a horrid accident was that on the Ohio, where my good friend and thirty other good fellows were sloped into eternity at the bidding of a thick-headed engineer, who knew not a valve from a flue. And that crash on the railroad just over yon mountains there, where two infatuate trains ran pell-mell into each other, and climbed and clawed each other's backs; and one locomotive was found fairly shelled like a chick, inside of a passenger car in the antagonist train; and near a score of noble hearts, a bride and her groom, and an innocent little infant, were all disembarked into the grim hulk of Charon, who ferried them over, all baggageless, to some clinkered iron-foundry country or other. Yet what's the use of complaining? What justice of the peace will right the matter? Yea, what's the use of bothering the very heavens about it? Don't the heavens themselves ordain these things—else they could not happen?

A miserable world! Who would take the trouble to make a fortune in it, when he knows not how long he can keep it, for the thousand villains and asses who have the management of railroads and steamboats, and innumerable other vital things in the world. If they would make me Dictator in North America awhile I'd string them up! and hang, draw, and quarter; fry, roast and boil; stew, grill, and devil them like so many turkey-legs—the rascally numskulls of stokers; I'd set them to stokering in Tartarus—I would!

Great improvements of the age! What! to call the facilitation of death and murder an improvement! Who wants to travel so fast? My grandfather did not, and he was no fool. Hark! here comes that old dragon again—that gigantic gadfly of a Moloch—snort! puff! scream!—here he comes straight-bent through these vernal woods, like the Asiatic cholera cantering on a camel. Stand aside! Here he comes, the chartered murderer! the death monopolizer! judge, jury, and hangman all together, whose victims die always without benefit of clergy. For two hundred and fifty miles that iron fiend goes yelling through the land, crying "More!

more! more!" Would fifty conspiring mountains would fall atop of him! and, while they were about it, would they would also fall atop of that smaller dunning fiend, my creditor, who frightens the life out of me more than any locomotive—a lantern-jawed rascal, who seems to run on a railroad track too, and duns me even on Sunday, all the way to church and back, and comes and sits in the same pew with me, and pretending to be polite and hand me the prayerbook opened at the proper place, pokes his pesky bill under my nose in the very midst of my devotions, and so shoves himself between me and salvation; for how can one keep his temper on such occasions?

I can't pay this horrid man, and yet they say money was never so plentiful—a drug on the market; but blame me if I can get any of the drug, though there never was a sick man more in need of that particular sort of medicine. It's a lie; money ain't plenty—feel of my pocket. Ha! here's a powder I was going to send to the sick baby in yonder hovel, where the Irish ditcher lives. That baby has the scarlet fever. They say the measles are rife in the country too, and the varioloid, and the chicken-pox, and it's bad for teething children. And after all, I suppose many of the poor little ones, after going through all this trouble snap off short; and so they had the measles, mumps, croup, scarlet fever, chicken-pox, cholera-morbus, summer-complaint, and all else, in vain! Ah! there's that twinge of the rheumatics in my right shoulder. I got it one night on the North River, when, in a crowded boat, I gave up my berth to a sick lady, and staid on deck till morning in drizzling weather. There's the thanks one gets for charity! Twinge! Shoot away, ye rheumatics! Ye couldn't lay on worse if I were some villain who had murdered the lady instead of befriending her. Dyspepsia too—I am troubled with that.

Hallo! here come the calves, the two-year-olds, just turned out of the barn into the pasture, after six months of cold victuals. What a miserable-looking set, to be sure! A breaking up of a hard winter, that's certain; sharp bones sticking out like elbows; all quilted with a strange stuff dried on their flanks like layers of pancakes. Hair worn quite off too, here and there; and where it ain't pancaked, or worn off, looks like the rubbed sides of mangy old hair-trunks. In fact, they are not six two-year-olds, but six abominable old hair-trunks wandering about here in this pasture.

Hark! By Jove, what's that? See! the very hair-trunks prick their ears at it, and stand and gaze away down into the rolling country yonder. Hark again! How clear! how musical! how prolonged! What a triumphant thanksgiving of a cock-crow! *"Glory be to God in the highest!"* It says those very words as plain as ever cock did in this world. Why, why, I began to feel a little in sorts again. It ain't so very misty, after all. The sun yonder is beginning to show himself; I feel warmer.

Hark! there again! Did ever such a blessed cock-crow so ring out over the earth before! Clear, shrill, full of pluck, full of fire, full of fun, full of glee. It plainly says—*"Never say die!"* My friends, it is extraordinary, is it not?

Unwittingly, I found that I had been addressing the two-year-olds—the calves—in my enthusiasm; which shows how one's true nature will betray itself at times in the most unconscious way. For what a very two-year-old, and calf, I had been to fall into the sulks, on a hill-top too, when a cock down in the lowlands there, without discourse of reason, and quite penniless in the world, and with death hanging over him at any moment from his hungry master, sends up a cry like a very laureate celebrating the glorious victory of New Orleans.

Hark! there it goes again! My friends, that must be a Shanghai; no domestic-born cock could crow in such prodigious exulting strains. Plainly, my friends, a Shanghai of the Emperor of China's breed.

But my friends the hair-trunks, fairly alarmed at last by such clamorously-victorious tones, were now scampering off, with their tails flirting in the air, and capering with their legs in clumsy enough sort of style, sufficiently evincing that they had not freely flourished them for the six months last past.

Hark! there again! Whose cock is that? Who in this region can afford to buy such an extraordinary Shanghai?

Bless me—it makes my blood bound—I feel wild. What? jumping on this rotten old log here, to flap my elbows and crow too? And just now in the doleful dumps. And all this from the simple crow of a cock. Marvelous cock! But soft— this fellow now crows most lustily; but it's only morning; let's see how he'll crow about noon, and towards nightfall. Come to think of it, cocks crow most lustily in the beginning of the day. Their pluck ain't lasting, after all. Yes, yes; even cocks have to succumb to the universal spell of tribulation: jubilant in the beginning, but down in the mouth at the end.

. . . Of fine mornings,
We fine lusty cocks begin our crows in gladness;
But when the eve does come we don't crow quite so much,
For then cometh despondency and madness.

The poet had this very Shanghai in mind when he wrote that. But stop. There he rings out again, ten times richer, fuller, longer, more obstreperously exulting than before! In fact, that bell ought to be taken down, and this Shanghai put in its place. Such a crow would jollify all London, from Mile-End (which is no end) to Primrose Hill (where there ain't any primroses), and scatter the fog.

Well, I have an appetite for my breakfast this morning, if I have not had it for a week before. I meant to have only tea and toast; but I'll have coffee and eggs—no, brown stout and a beefsteak. I want something hearty. Ah, here comes the down-train: white cars, flashing through the trees like a vein of silver. How cheerfully the steam-pipe chirps! Gay are the passengers. There waves a handker-chief—going down to the city to eat oysters, and see their friends, and drop in at the circus. Look at the mist yonder; what soft curls and undulations round the hills, and the sun weaving his rays among them. See the azure smoke of the village, like the azure tester over a bridal-bed. How bright the country looks there where the river overflowed the meadows. The old grass has to knock under to the new. Well, I feel the better for this walk. Home now, and walk into that steak and crack that bottle of brown stout; and by the time that's drank—a quart of stout—by that time, I shall feel about as stout as Samson. Come to think of it, that dun may call, though. I'll just visit the woods and cut a club. I'll club him, by Jove, if he duns me this day.

Hark! there goes Shanghai again. Shanghai says, "Bravo!" Shanghai says, "Club him!"

Oh, brave cock!

I felt in rare spirits the whole morning. The dun called about eleven. I had the boy Jake send the dun up. I was reading *Tristram Shandy,* and could not go down under the circumstances. The lean rascal (a lean farmer, too—think of that!) entered, and found me seated in an arm-chair, with my feet on the table, and the second bottle of brown stout handy, and the book under eye.

"Sit down," said I, "I'll finish this chapter, and then attend to you. Fine morning. Ha! ha!—this is a fine joke about my Uncle Toby and the Widow Wadman! Ha! ha! ha! let me read this to you."

"I have no time; I've got my noon *chores* to do."

"To the deuce with your *chores!*" said I. "Don't drop your old tobacco about here, or I'll turn you out."

"Sir!"

"Let me read you this about the Widow Wadman. Said the Widow Wadman——"

"There's my bill, sir."

"Very good. Just twist it up, will you—it's about my smoking-time; and hand a coal, will you, from the hearth yonder!"

"My bill, sir!" said the rascal, turning pale with rage and amazement at my unwonted air (formerly I had always dodged him with a pale face), but too prudent as yet to betray the extremity of his astonishment. "My bill, sir"—and he stiffly poked it at me.

"My friend," said I, "what a charming morning! How sweet the country looks! Pray, did you hear that extraordinary cock-crow this morning? Take a glass of my stout!"

"*Yours?* First pay your debts before you offer folks *your* stout!"

"You think, then, that, properly speaking, I have no

stout," said I, deliberately rising. "I'll undeceive you. I'll show you stout of a superior brand to Barclay and Perkins."

Without more ado, I seized that insolent dun by the slack of his coat—(and, being a lean, shad-bellied wretch, there was plenty of slack to it)—I seized him that way, tied him with a sailor-knot, and, thrusting his bill between his teeth, introduced him to the open country lying round about my place of abode.

"Jake," said I, "you'll find a sack of blue-nosed potatoes lying under the shed. Drag it here, and pelt this pauper away; he's been begging pence of me, and I know he can work, but he's lazy. Pelt him away, Jake!"

Bless my stars, what a crow! Shanghai sent up such a perfect pæan and *laudamus*—such a trumpet blast of triumph, that my soul fairly snorted in me. Duns!—I could have fought an army of them! Plainly, Shanghai was of the opinion that duns only came into the world to be kicked, hanged, bruised, battered, choked, walloped, hammered, drowned, clubbed!

Returning indoors, when the exultation of my victory over the dun had a little subsided, I fell to musing over the mysterious Shanghai. I had no idea I would hear him so nigh my house. I wondered from what rich gentleman's yard he crowed. Nor had he cut short his crows so easily as I had supposed he would. This Shanghai crowed till midday, at least. Would he keep a-crowing all day? I resolved to learn. Again I ascended the hill. The whole country was now bathed in a rejoicing sunlight. The warm verdure was bursting all round me. Teams were a-field. Birds, newly arrived from the South, were blithely singing in the air. Even the crows cawed with a certain unction, and seemed a shade or two less black than usual.

Hark! there goes the cock! How shall I describe the crow of the Shanghai at noontide! His sunrise crow was a whisper to it. It was the loudest, longest and most strangely musical crow that ever amazed mortal man. I had heard plenty of cock-crows before, and many fine ones;—but this one! so smooth, and flutelike in its very clamor—so self-possessed in its very rapture of exultation—so vast, mounting, swelling, soaring, as if spurted out from a golden throat, thrown far back. Nor did it sound like the foolish, vain-glorious crow of some young sophomorean cock, who knew not the world, and was beginning life in audacious gay spirits, because in wretched ignorance of what might be to come. It was the crow of a cock who crowed not without advice; the crow of a cock who knew a thing or two; the crow of a cock who had fought the world and got the better of it and was resolved to crow, though the earth should heave and the heavens should fall. It was a wise crow; an invincible crow; a philosophic crow; a crow of all crows.

I returned home once more full of reinvigorated spirits, with a dauntless sort of feeling. I thought over my debts and other troubles, and over the unlucky risings of the poor oppressed peoples abroad, and over the railroad and steamboat accidents, and even over the loss of my dear friend, with a calm, good-natured rapture of defiance, which astounded myself. I felt as though I could meet Death, and invite him to dinner, and toast the Catacombs with him, in pure overflow of self-reliance and a sense of universal security.

Toward evening I went up to the hill once more to find whether, indeed, the glorious cock would prove game even from the rising of the sun unto the going down thereof. Talk of Vespers or Curfew!—the evening crow of the cock went out of his mighty throat all over the land and inhabited it, like Xerxes from the East with his double-winged host. It was miraculous. Bless me, what a crow! The cock went game to roost that night, depend upon it, victorious over the entire day, and bequeathing the echoes of his thousand crows to night.

After an unwontedly sound, refreshing sleep I rose early, feeling like a carriage-spring—light—elliptical—airy—buoyant as sturgeon-nose—and, like a foot-ball, bounded up the hill. Hark! Shanghai was up before me. The early bird that caught the worm—crowing like a bugle worked by an engine—lusty, loud, all jubilation. From the scattered farmhouses a multitude of other cocks were crowing, and replying to each other's crows. But they were as flageolets to a trombone. Shanghai would suddenly break in, and overwhelm all their crows with his one domineering blast. He seemed to have nothing to do with any other concern. He replied to no other crow, but crowed solely by himself, on his own account, in solitary scorn and independence.

Oh, brave cock!—oh, noble Shanghai!—oh, bird rightly offered up by the invincible Socrates, in testimony of his final victory over life.

As I live, thought I, this blessed day, will I go and seek out the Shanghai, and buy him, if I have to clap another mortgage on my land.

I listened attentively now, striving to mark from what direction the crow came. But it so charged and replenished, and made bountiful and overflowing all the air, that it was impossible to say from what precise point the exultation came. All that I could decide upon was this: the crow came from out of the east, and not from out of the west. I then considered with myself how far a cock-crow might be heard. In this still country, shut in, too, by mountains, sounds were audible at great distances. Besides, the undulations of the land, the abuttings of the mountains into the rolling hill and valley below, produced strange echoes, and reverberations, and multiplications, and accumulations of resonance, very remarkable to hear, and very puzzling to think of. Where lurked this valiant Shanghai—this bird of cheerful Socrates—the game-fowl Greek who died unappalled? Where lurked he? Oh, noble cock, where are you? Crow once more, my Bantam! my princely, my imperial Shanghai! my bird of the Emperor of China! Brother of the sun! Cousin of great Jove! where are you?—one crow more, and tell me your number!

Hark! like a full orchestra of the cocks of all nations, forth burst the crow. But where from? There it is; but where? There was no telling, further than it came from out of the east.

After breakfast I took my stick and sallied down the road. There were many gentlemen's seats dotting the neighboring country, and I made no doubt that some of these opulent gentlemen had invested a hundred dollar bill in some royal Shanghai recently imported in the ship *Trade Wind,* or the ship *White Squall,* or the ship *Sovereign of the Seas;* for it must needs have been a brave ship with a brave name which bore the fortunes of so brave a cock. I resolved to walk the entire country, and find this noble foreigner out; but thought it would not be amiss to inquire on the way at the humblest homesteads, whether, peradventure, they had heard of a lately-imported Shanghai belonging to any gentlemen settlers from the city; for it was plain that no poor farmer, no poor man of any sort, could own such an Oriental trophy—such a Great Bell of St. Paul's swung in a cock's throat.

I met an old man, plowing, in a field nigh the road-side fence.

"My friend, have you heard an extraordinary cock-crow of late?"

"Well, well," he drawled, "I don't know—the Widow Crowfoot has a cock—and Squire Squaretoes has a cock—and I have a cock, and they all crow. But I don't know of any on 'em with 'straordinary crows."

"Good-morning to you," said I, shortly; "it's plain that you have not heard the crow of the Emperor of China's chanticleer."

Presently I met another old man mending a tumble-down old rail-fence. The rails were rotten, and at every move of the old man's hand they crumbled into yellow ochre. He had much better let the fence alone, or else get him new rails. And here I must say, that one cause of the sad fact why idiocy more prevails among farmers than any other class of people, is owing to their undertaking the mending of rotten rail-fences in warm, relaxing spring weather. The enterprise is a hopeless one. It is a laborious one; it is a bootless one. It is an enterprise to make the heart break. Vast pains squandered upon a vanity. For how can one make rotten rail-fences stand up on their rotten pins? By what magic put pitch into sticks which have lain freezing and baking through sixty consecutive winters and summers? This it is, this wretched endeavor to mend rotten rail-fences with their own rotten rails, which drives many farmers into the asylum.

On the face of the old man in question incipient idiocy was plainly marked. For, about sixty rods before him extended one of the most unhappy and desponding brokenhearted Virginia rail-fences I ever saw in my life. While in a field behind, were a set of young steers, possessed as by devils, continually butting at this forlorn old fence, and breaking through it here and there, causing the old man to drop his work and chase them with a piece of rail huge as Goliath's beam, but as light as cork. At the first flourish, it crumbled into powder.

"My friend," said I, addressing this woeful mortal, "have you heard an extraordinary cock-crow of late?"

I might as well as have asked him if he had heard the death-tick. He stared at me with a long, bewildered, doleful, and unutterable stare, and without reply resumed his unhappy labors.

What a fool, thought I, to have asked such an uncheerful and uncheerable creature about a cheerful cock!

I walked on. I had now descended the high land where my house stood, and being in a low tract could not hear the crow of the Shanghai, which doubtless overshot me there. Besides, the Shanghai might be at lunch of corn and oats, or taking a nap, and so interrupted his jubilations for a while.

At length, I encountered riding along the road, a portly gentleman—nay, a *pursy* one—of great wealth, who had recently purchased him some noble acres, and built him a noble mansion, with a goodly fowl-house attached, the fame whereof spread through all the country. Thought I, Here now is the owner of the Shanghai.

"Sir," said I, "excuse me, but I am a countryman of yours, and would ask, if so be you own any Shanghais?"

"Oh, yes; I have ten Shanghais."

"Ten!" exclaimed I, in wonder; "and do they all crow?"

"Most lustily; every soul of them; I wouldn't own a cock that wouldn't crow."

"Will you turn back, and show me those Shanghais?"

"With pleasure: I am proud of them. They cost me, in the lump, six hundred dollars."

As I walked by the side of his horse, I was thinking to myself whether possibly I had not mistaken the harmoniously combined crowing of ten Shanghais in a squad, for the supernatural crow of a single Shanghai by himself.

"Sir," said I, "is there one of your Shanghais which far exceeds all the others in the lustiness, musicalness, and inspiring effects of his crow?"

"They crow pretty much alike, I believe," he courteously replied. "I really don't know that I could tell their crow apart."

I began to think that after all my noble chanticleer might not be in the possession of this wealthy gentleman. However, we went into his fowl-yard, and saw his Shanghais. Let me say that hitherto I had never clapped eye on this species of imported fowl. I had heard what enormous prices were paid for them, and also that they were of an enormous size, and had somehow fancied they must be of a beauty and brilliancy proportioned both to size and price. What was my surprise, then, to see ten carrot-colored monsters, without the smallest pretension to effulgence of plumage. Immediately, I determined that my royal cock was neither among these, nor could possibly be a Shanghai at all; if these gigantic gallows-bird fowl were fair specimens of the true Shanghai.

I walked all day, dining and resting at a farmhouse, inspecting various fowl-yards, interrogating various owners of fowls, hearkening to various crows, but discovered not the mysterious chanticleer. Indeed, I had wandered so far and deviously, that I could not hear his crow. I began to suspect that this cock was a mere visitor in the country, who had taken his departure by the eleven o'clock train for the South, and was now crowing and jubilating somewhere on the verdant banks of Long Island Sound.

But next morning, again I heard the inspiring blast, again felt my blood bound in me, again felt superior to all the ills of life, again felt like turning my dun out of doors. But displeased with the reception given him at his last visit, the dun stayed away, doubtless being in a huff. Silly fellow that he was to take a harmless joke in earnest.

Several days passed, during which I made sundry excursions in the regions roundabout, but in vain sought the cock. Still, I heard him from the hill, and sometimes from the house, and sometimes in the stillness of the night. If at times I would relapse into my doleful dumps straightway at the sound of the exultant and defiant crow, my soul, too, would turn chanticleer, and clap her wings, and throw back her throat, and breathe forth a cheerful challenge to all the world of woes.

At last, after some weeks I was necessitated to clap another mortgage on my estate, in order to pay certain debts, and among others the one I owed the dun, who of late had commenced a civil-process against me. The way the process was served was a most insulting one. In a private room I had been enjoying myself in the village tavern over a bottle of Philadelphia porter, and some Herkimer cheese, and a roll, and having apprised the landlord who was a friend of mine, that I would settle with him when I received my next remittances, stepped to the peg where I had hung my hat in the bar-room, to get a choice cigar I had left in the hall, when lo! I found the civil-process enveloping the cigar. When I unrolled the cigar, I unrolled the civil-process, and the constable standing by rolled out, with a thick tongue, "Take notice!" and added, in a whisper, "Put that in your pipe and smoke it!"

I turned short round upon the gentlemen then and there present in that bar-room. Said I, "Gentlemen, is this an honorable—nay, is this a lawful way of serving a civil-process? Behold!"

One and all they were of opinion, that it was a highly inelegant act in the constable to take advantage of a gentleman's lunching on cheese and porter, to be so uncivil as to slip a civil-process into his hat. It was ungenerous; it was cruel; for the sudden shock of the thing coming instanter upon the lunch, would impair the proper digestion of the cheese, which is proverbially not so easy of digestion as *blanc-mange*.

Arrived at home I read the process, and felt a twinge of melancholy. Hard world! hard world! Here I am, as good a fellow as ever lived—hospitable—open-hearted—generous to a fault; and the Fates forbid that I should possess the fortune to bless the country with my bounteousness. Nay, while many a stingy curmudgeon rolls in idle gold, I, heart of nobleness as I am, I have civil-processes served on me! I bowed my head, and felt forlorn—unjustly used—abused —unappreciated—in short, miserable.

Hark! like a clarion! yea, like a bolt of thunder with bells to it—came the all-glorious and defiant crow! Ye gods, how it set me up again! Right on my pins! Yes, verily on stilts!

Oh, noble cock!

Plain as cock could speak, it said, "Let the world and all aboard of it go to pot. Do you be jolly, and never say die! What's the world compared to you? What is it, anyhow, but a lump of loam? Do you be jolly!"

Oh, noble cock!

"But my dear and glorious cock," mused I, upon second thought, "one can't so easily send this world to pot; one can't so easily be jolly with civil-processes in his hat or hand."

Hark! the crow again. Plain as cock could speak, it said: "Hang the process, and hang the fellow that sent it! If you have not land or cash, go and thrash the fellow, and tell him you never mean to pay him. Be jolly!"

Now this was the way—through the imperative intimations of the cock—that I came to clap the added mortgage on my estate; paid all my debts by fusing them into this one added bond and mortgage. Thus made at ease again, I renewed my search for the noble cock. But in vain, though I heard him every day. I began to think there was some sort of deception in this mysterious thing: some wonderful ventriloquist prowled around my barns, or in my cellar, or on my roof, and was minded to be gayly mischievous. But no—what ventriloquist could so crow with such an heroic and celestial crow?

At last, one morning there came to me a certain singular man, who had sawed and split my wood in March—some

five-and-thirty cords of it—and now he came for his pay.
He was a singular man, I say. He was tall and spare, with
a long saddish face, yet somehow a latently joyous eye,
which offered the strangest contrast. His air seemed staid,
but undepressed. He wore a long, gray, shabby coat, and
a big battered hat. This man had sawed my wood at so
much a cord. He would stand and saw all day in a driving
snow-storm, and never wink at it. He never spoke unless
spoken to. He only sawed. Saw, saw, saw—snow, snow,
snow. The saw and the snow went together like two natural
things. The first day this man came, he brought his dinner
with him, and volunteered to eat it sitting on his buck in
the snow-storm. From my window, where I was reading
Burton's *Anatomy of Melancholy*, I saw him in the act. I
burst out of doors bareheaded. "Good heavens!" cried I;
"what are you doing? Come in. *This* your dinner!"

He had a hunk of stale bread and another hunk of salt
beef, wrapped in a wet newspaper, and washed his morsels
down by melting a handful of fresh snow in his mouth. I
took this rash man indoors, planted him by the fire, gave
him a dish of hot pork and beans, and a mug of cider.

"Now," said I, "don't you bring any of your damp dinners
here. You work by the job, to be sure, but I'll dine you for
all that."

He expressed his acknowledgements in a calm, proud,
but not ungrateful way, and dispatched his meal with satisfaction to himself, and me also. It afforded me pleasure to
perceive that he quaffed down his mug of cider like a man.
I honored him. When I addressed him in the way of business at his buck, I did so in a guardedly respectful and
deferential manner. Interested in his singular aspect, struck
by his wondrous intensity of application at his saw—a most
wearisome and disgustful occupation to most people—I
often sought to gather from him who he was, what sort of
a life he led, where he was born, and so on. But he was
mum. He came to saw my wood, and eat my dinners—if
I chose to offer them—but not to gabble. At first, I somewhat resented his sullen silence under the circumstances.
But better considering it, I honored him the more. I in-

creased the respectfulness and deferentialness of my address toward him. I concluded within myself that this man
had experienced hard times; that he had had many sore
rubs in the world; that he was of a solemn disposition; that
he was of the mind of Solomon; that he lived calmly, decorously, temperately; and though a very poor man, was,
nevertheless, a highly respectable one. At times I imagined
that he might even be an elder or deacon of some small
country church. I thought it would not be a bad plan to
run this excellent man for President of the United States.
He would prove a great reformer of abuses.

His name was Merrymusk. I had often thought how jolly
a name for so unjolly a wight. I inquired of people whether
they knew Merrymusk. But it was some time before I
learned much about him. He was by birth a Marylander,
it appeared, who had long lived in the country round
about; a wandering man; until within some ten years ago,
a thriftless man, though perfectly innocent of crime; a man
who would work hard a month with surprising soberness,
and then spend all his wages in one riotous night. In youth
he had been a sailor, and run away from his ship at Batavia,
where he caught the fever, and came nigh dying. But he
rallied, reshipped, landed home, found all his friends dead,
and struck for the Northern interior, where he had since
tarried. Nine years back he had married a wife, and now
had four children. His wife was become a perfect invalid;
one child had the white-swelling and the rest were rickety.
He and his family lived in a shanty on a lonely barren patch
nigh the railroad track, where it passed close to the base of
the mountain. He had bought a fine cow to have plenty of
wholesome milk for his children; but the cow died during
an accouchement, and he could not afford to buy another.
Still, his family never suffered for lack of food. He worked
hard and brought it to them. Now, as I said before, having
long previously sawed my wood, this Merrymusk came for
his pay.

"My friend," said I, "do you know of any gentleman
hereabouts who owns an extraordinary cock?"

The twinkle glittered quite plain in the wood sawyer's eye.

"I know of no *gentleman*," he replied, "who has what might well be called an extraordinary cock."

Oh, thought I, this Merrymusk is not the man to enlighten me. I am afraid I shall never discover this extraordinary cock.

Not having the full change to pay Merrymusk, I gave him his due, as nigh as I could make it, and told him that in a day or two I would take a walk and visit his place, and hand him the remainder. Accordingly one fine morning I sallied forth upon the errand. I had much ado finding the best road to the shanty. No one seemed to know where it was exactly. It lay in a very lonely part of the country, a densely-wooded mountain on one side (which I call October Mountain, on account of its bannered aspect in that month), and a thicketed swamp on the other, the railroad cutting the swamp. Straight as a die the railroad cut it; many times a day tantalizing the wretched shanty with the sight of all the beauty, rank, fashion, health, trunks, silver and gold, dry-goods and groceries, brides and grooms, happy wives and husbands, flying by the lonely door—no time to stop—flash! here they are—and there they go! out of sight at both ends—as if that part of the world were only made to fly over, and not to settle upon. And this was about all the shanty saw of what people call life.

Though puzzled somewhat, yet I knew the general direction where the shanty lay, and on I trudged. As I advanced, I was surprised to hear the mysterious cock crow with more and more distinctness. Is it possible, thought I, that any gentleman owning a Shanghai can dwell in such a lonesome, dreary region? Louder and louder, nigher and nigher, sounded the glorious and defiant clarion. Though somehow I may be out of the track to my wood-sawyer's, I said to myself, yet, thank heaven, I seem to be on the way toward that extraordinary cock. I was delighted with this auspicious accident. On I journeyed; while at intervals the crow sounded most invitingly, and jocundly, and superbly; and the last crow was ever nigher than the former one. At last, emerging from a thicket of elders, straight before me I saw the most resplendent creature that ever blessed the sight of man.

A cock, more like a golden eagle than a cock. A cock, more like a field marshal than a cock. A cock, more like Lord Nelson with all his glittering arms on, standing on the *Vanguard's* quarter-deck going into battle, than a cock. A cock, more like the Emperor Charlemagne in his robes at Aix le Chapelle, than a cock.

Such a cock!

He was of a haughty size, stood haughtily on his haughty legs. His colors were red, gold, and white. The red was on his crest, along which was a mighty and symmetric crest, like unto Hector's helmet, as delineated on antique shields. His plumage was snowy, traced with gold. He walked in front of the shanty, like a peer of the realm; his crest lifted, his chest heaved out, his embroidered trappings flashing in the light. His pace was wonderful. He looked like some Oriental king in some magnificent Italian opera.

Merrymusk advanced from the door.

"Pray is not that the Signor Beneventano?"

"Sir!"

"That's the cock," said I, a little embarrassed. The truth was, my enthusiasm had betrayed me into a rather silly inadvertence. I had made a somewhat learned sort of allusion in the presence of an unlearned man. Consequently, upon discovering it by this honest stare, I felt foolish; but carried it off by declaring that *this was the cock*.

Now, during the preceding autumn I had been to the city, and had chanced to be present at a performance of the Italian Opera. In that opera figured in some royal character, a certain Signor Beneventano—a man of a tall, imposing person, clad in rich raiment, like to plumage, and with a most remarkable, majestic, scornful stride. The Signor Beneventano seemed on the point of tumbling over backward with exceeding haughtiness. And for all the world, the proud pace of the cock seemed the very stage-pace of the Signor Beneventano.

Hark! suddenly the cock paused, lifted his head still

higher, ruffled his plumes, seemed inspired, and sent forth a lusty crow. October Mountain echoed it; other mountains sent it back; still others rebounded it; it overran the country round. Now I plainly perceived how it was I had chanced to hear the gladdening sound on my distant hill.

"Good heavens! do you own the cock? Is that cock yours?"

"Is it my cock!" said Merrymusk, looking slyly gleeful out of the corner of his long solemn face.

"Where did you get it?"

"It chipped the shell here. I raised it."

"You?"

Hark? Another crow. It might have raised the ghosts of all the pines and hemlocks ever cut down in that country. Marvelous cock! Having crowed, he strode on again, surrounded by a bevy of admiring hens.

"What will you take for Signor Beneventano?"

"Sir?"

"That magic cock—what will you take for him?"

"I won't sell him."

"I will give you fifty dollars."

"Pooh!"

"One hundred!"

"Pish!"

"Five hundred!"

"Bah!"

"And you a poor man."

"No; don't I own that cock, and haven't I refused five hundred dollars for him?"

"True," said I, in profound thought; "that's a fact. You won't sell him, then?"

"No."

"Will you give him?"

"No."

"Will you *keep* him, then!" I shouted, in a rage.

"Yes."

I stood awhile admiring the cock, and wondering at the man. At last I felt a redoubled admiration of the one, and a redoubled deference for the other.

"Won't you step in?" said Merrymusk.

"But won't the cock be prevailed upon to join us?" said I.

"Yes. Trumpet! hither, boy! hither!"

The cock turned round, and strode up to Merrymusk.

"Come!"

The cock followed us into the shanty.

"Crow!"

The roof jarred.

Oh, noble cock!

I turned in silence upon my entertainer. There he sat on an old battered chest, in his old battered gray coat, with patches at his knees and elbows, and a deplorably bunged hat. I glanced round the room. Bare rafters overhead, but solid junks of jerked beef hanging from them. Earth floor, but a heap of potatoes in one corner, and a sack of Indian meal in another. A blanket was strung across the apartment at the further end, from which came a woman's ailing voice and the voices of ailing children. But somehow in the ailing of these voices there seemed no complaint.

"Mrs. Merrymusk and children?"

"Yes."

I looked at the cock. There he stood majestically in the middle of the room. He looked like a Spanish grandee caught in a shower, and standing under some peasant's shed. There was a strange supernatural look of contrast about him. He irradiated the shanty; he glorified its meanness. He glorified the battered chest, and tattered gray coat, and the bunged hat. He glorified the very voices which came in ailing tones from behind the screen.

"Oh, father," cried a little sickly voice, "let Trumpet sound again."

"Crow," cried Merrymusk.

The cock threw himself into a posture. The roof jarred.

"Does not this disturb Mrs. Merrymusk and the sick children?"

"Crow again, Trumpet."

The roof jarred.

"It does not disturb them, then?"

"Didn't you hear 'em *ask* for it?"

"How is it, that your sick family like this crowing?" said I. "The cock is a glorious cock, with a glorious voice, but not exactly the sort of thing for a sick chamber, one would suppose. Do they really like it?"

"Don't *you* like it? Don't it do *you* good? Ain't it inspiring? Don't it impart pluck? give stuff against despair?"

"All true," said I, removing my hat with profound humility before the brave spirit disguised in the base coat.

"But then," said I, still with some misgivings, "so loud, so wonderfully clamorous a crow, methinks might be amiss to invalids, and retard their convalescence."

"Crow your best now, Trumpet!"

I leaped from my chair. The cock frightened me, like some overpowering angel in the Apocalypse. He seemed crowing over the fall of wicked Babylon, or crowing over the triumph of righteous Joshua in the vale of Askelon. When I regained my composure somewhat, an inquisitive thought occurred to me. I resolved to gratify it.

"Merrymusk, will you present me to your wife and children?"

"Yes. Wife, the gentleman wants to step in."

"He is very welcome," replied a weak voice.

Going behind the curtain, there lay a wasted, but strangely cheerful human face; and that was pretty much all; the body, hid by the counterpane and an old coat, seemed too shrunken to reveal itself through such impediments. At the bedside sat a pale girl, ministering. In another bed lay three children, side by side; three more pale faces.

"Oh, father, we don't mislike the gentleman, but let us see Trumpet too."

At a word, the cock strode behind the screen, and perched himself on the children's bed. All their wasted eyes gazed at him with a wild and spiritual delight. They seemed to sun themselves in the radiant plumage of the cock.

"Better than a 'pothecary, eh," said Merrymusk. "This is Dr. Cock himself."

We retired from the sick ones, and I reseated myself again, lost in thought, over this strange household.

"You seem a glorious independent fellow," said I.

"And I don't think you a fool, and never did. Sir, you are a trump."

"Is there any hope of your wife's recovery?" said I, modestly seeking to turn the conversation.

"Not the least."

"The children?"

"Very little."

"It must be a doleful life, then, for all concerned. This lonely solitude—this shanty—hard work—hard times."

"Haven't I Trumpet? He's the cheerer. He crows through all; crows at the darkest: Glory to God in the highest! Continually he crows it."

"Just the import I first ascribed to his crow, Merrymusk, when first I heard it from my hill. I thought some rich nabob owned some costly Shanghai; little weening any such poor man as you owned this lusty cock of a domestic breed."

"*Poor* man like *me*? Why call *me* poor? Don't the cock *I* own glorify this otherwise inglorious, lean, lantern-jawed land? Didn't *my* cock encourage *you*? And *I* give you all this glorification away gratis. I am a great philanthropist. I am a rich man—a very rich man, and a very happy one. Crow, Trumpet."

The roof jarred.

I returned home in a deep mood. I was not wholly at rest concerning the soundness of Merrymusk's view of things, though full of admiration for him. I was thinking on the matter before my door, when I heard the cock crow again. Enough. Merrymusk is right.

Oh, noble cock! oh, noble man!

I did not see Merrymusk for some weeks after this; but hearing the glorious and rejoicing crow, I supposed that all went as usual with him. My own frame of mind remained a rejoicing one. The cock still inspired me. I saw another mortgage piled on my plantation; but only bought another dozen of stout in preference to porter, stout being of the darker color. I heard the cock crow the instant I received the unwelcome tidings.

"Your health in this stout, oh, noble cock!"

I thought I would call on Merrymusk again, not having seen or heard of him for some time now. Approaching the place, there were no signs of motion about the shanty. I felt a strange misgiving. But the cock crew from within doors, and the boding vanished. I knocked at the door. A feeble voice bade me enter. The curtain was no longer drawn; the whole house was a hospital now. Merrymusk lay on a heap of old clothes; wife and children were all in their beds. The cock was perched on an old hogshead hoop, swung from the ridge-pole in the middle of the shanty.

"You are sick, Merrymusk," said I mournfully.

"No, I am well," he feebly answered.

"Crow, Trumpet."

I shrunk. The strong soul in the feeble body appalled me. But the cock crew.

The roof jarred.

"How is Mrs. Merrymusk?"

"Well."

"And the children?"

"Well. All well."

The last two words he shouted forth in a kind of wild ecstasy of triumph over ill. It was too much. His head fell back. A white napkin seemed dropped upon his face. Merrymusk was dead.

An awful fear seized me.

But the cock crew.

The cock shook his plumage as if each feather were a banner. The cock hung from the shanty roof as erewhile the trophied flags from the dome of St. Paul's. The cock terrified me with exceeding wonder.

I drew nigh the bedsides of the woman and children. They marked my look of strange affright; they knew what had happened.

"My good man is just dead," breathed the woman lowly. "Tell me true?"

"Dead," said I.

The cock crew.

She fell back, without a sigh, and through long-loving sympathy was dead.

The cock crew.

The cock shook sparkles from his golden plumage. The cock seemed in a rapture of benevolent delight. Leaping from the hoop, he strode up majestically to the pile of old clothes, where the wood-sawyer lay, and planted himself, like an armorial supporter, at his side. Then raised one long, musical, triumphant, and final sort of a crow, with throat heaved far back, as if he meant the blast to waft the wood-sawyer's soul sheer up to the seventh heavens. Then he strode, king-like, to the woman's bed. Another upturned and exultant crow, mated to the former.

The pallor of the children was changed to radiance. Their faces shone celestially through grime and dirt. They seemed children of emperors and kings, disguised. The cock sprang upon their bed, shook himself, and crowed, and crowed again, and still and still again. He seemed bent upon crowing the souls of the children out of their wasted bodies. He seemed bent upon rejoining instanter this whole family in the upper air. The children seemed to second his endeavors. Far, deep, intense longings for release transfigured them into spirits before my eyes. I saw angels where they lay.

They were dead.

The cock shook his plumage over them. The cock crew. It was now like a Bravo! like a Hurrah! like a Three-times-three! hip! hip! He strode out of the shanty. I followed. He flew upon the apex of the dwelling, spread wide his wings, sounded one supernatural note, and dropped at my feet.

The cock was dead.

If now you visit that hilly region, you will see, nigh the railroad track, just beneath October Mountain, on the other side of the swamp—there you will see a gravestone, not with skull and cross-bones, but with a lusty cock in act of crowing, chiseled on it, with the words beneath:

O death, where is thy sting?
O grave, where is thy victory?

The wood-sawyer and his family, with the Signor Beneventano, lie in that spot; and I buried them, and planted
the stone, which was a stone made to order; and never
since then have I felt the doleful dumps, but under all circumstances crow late and early with a continual crow.

Cock-A-Doodle-Doo!—oo!—oo!—oo!—oo!

One of the important unwritten histories of the American imagination is a study of the image of Benjamin Franklin as it has changed and developed over the past two
hundred years. To Melville, certainly, Franklin was a chal-
lenging and complex figure. Looked at one way, Franklin
symbolized the cunning boldness of the Yankee, which had
made New England whalemen imperial lords of the sea;
as Melville wrote in *Moby Dick*, "the grandmother of Benjamin Franklin was . . . one of the old settlers of Nan-
tucket, and the ancestress to a long line of . . . harpooneers
—all kith and kin to noble Benjamin—this day darting the
barbed iron from one side of the world to the other." But
if Franklin embodied the democratic grandeur of Nan-
tucket harpooneers, he also incarnated the mean, calculating traits of the Yankee, which in *Moby Dick* Melville
superbly portrayed in the character of Captain Bildad. In
Israel Potter, Franklin is seen as the skillful author of a di-
plomacy that would eventually result in the glorious victory of the *Bonhomme Richard*, the flagship named in
his honor, but Chapter IX of the novel makes Poor Richard's prudential creator the object of a sharply observed
satire.

From *Israel Potter*

Chapter IX

Israel Is Initiated into the Mysteries of Lodging-Houses in the Latin Quarter

Closing the door upon himself, Israel advanced to the middle of the chamber, and looked curiously round him.

A dark tessellated floor, but without a rug; two mahogany chairs, with embroidered seats, rather the worse for wear; one mahogany bed, with a gay but tarnished counterpane; a marble wash-stand, cracked, with a china vessel of water, minus the handle. The apartment was very large; this part of the house, which was a very extensive one, embracing the four sides of a quadrangle, having, in a former age, been the hotel of a nobleman. The magnitude of the chamber made its stinted furniture look meagre enough.

But in Israel's eyes, the marble mantel (a comparatively recent addition) and its appurtenances, not only redeemed the rest, but looked quite magnificent and hospitable in the extreme. Because, in the first place, the mantel was graced with an enormous old-fashioned square mirror, of heavy plate glass, set fast, like a tablet, into the wall. And in this mirror was genially reflected the following delicate articles: —first, two bouquets of flowers inserted in pretty vases of porcelain; second, one cake of white soap; third, one cake of rose-coloured soap (both cakes very fragrant); fourth, one wax candle; fifth, one china tinder-box; sixth, one bottle of eau-de-Cologne; seventh, one paper of loaf sugar, nicely broken into sugar-bowl size; eighth, one silver teaspoon; ninth, one glass tumbler; tenth, one glass decanter of cool pure water; eleventh, one sealed bottle containing a richly hued liquid, and marked 'Otard.'

'I wonder now what O-t-a-r-d is?' soliloquised Israel, slowly spelling the word. 'I have a good mind to step in and ask Doctor Franklin. He knows everything. Let me smell it. No, it's sealed; smell is locked in. Those are pretty flowers. Let's smell them: no smell again. Ah, I see—sort of flowers in women's bonnets—sort of calico flowers. Beautiful soap. This smells, anyhow—regular soap-roses—a white rose and a red one. That long-necked bottle there looks like a crane. I wonder what's in that? Hallo! E-a-u—d-e—C-o-l-o-g-n-e. I wonder if Doctor Franklin understands that? It looks like his white wine. This is nice sugar. Let's taste. Yes, this is very nice sugar, sweet as—yes, it's sweet as sugar; better than maple sugar, such as they make at home. But I'm crunching it too loud, the doctor will hear me. But here's a teaspoon. What's this for? There's no tea, nor tea-cup; but here's a tumbler, and here's drinking water. Let me see. Seems to me, putting this and that and the other thing together, it's a sort of alphabet that spells something. Spoon, tumbler, water, sugar,—brandy—that's it. O-t-a-r-d is brandy. Who put these things here? What does it all mean? Don't put sugar here for show, don't put a spoon here for ornament, nor a jug of water. There is only one meaning to it, and that is a very polite invitation from some invisible person to help myself, if I like, to a glass of brandy and sugar, and if I don't like, let it alone. That's my reading. I have a good mind to ask Doctor Franklin about it, though, for there's just a chance I may be mistaken, and these things here be some other person's private property, not at all meant for me to help myself from. Cologne, what's that?—never mind. Soap: soap's to wash with. I want to use soap, anyway. Let me see—no, there's no soap on the wash-stand. I see, soap is not given gratis here in Paris, to boarders. But if you want it, take it from the marble, and it will be charged in the bill. If you don't want it let it alone, and no charge. Well, that's fair, anyway. But then to a man who could not afford to use soap, such beautiful cakes as these lying before his eyes all the time, would be a strong temptation. And now that I think of it, the O-t-a-r-d looks rather tempting too. But if I don't like it now, I can let it alone. I've a good mind to try it. But it's sealed. I wonder now if I am right in my understanding of this alphabet? Who knows? I'll venture one little sip, anyhow. Come, cork. Hark!'

There was a rapid knock at the door.

Clapping down the bottle, Israel said, 'Come in.'

It was the man of wisdom.

'My honest friend,' said the doctor, stepping with venerable briskness into the room, 'I was so busy during your visit to the Pont Neuf, that I did not have time to see that your room was all right. I merely gave the order, and heard that it had been fulfilled. But it just occurred to me, that as the landladies of Paris have some curious customs which might puzzle an entire stranger, my presence here for a moment might explain any little obscurity. Yes, it is as I thought,' glancing toward the mantel.

'Oh, doctor, that reminds me; what is O-t-a-r-d, pray?'

'Otard is poison.'

'Shocking.'

'Yes, and I think I had best remove it from the room forthwith,' replied the sage, in a business-like manner putting the bottle under his arm; 'I hope you never use Cologne, do you?'

'What—what is that, doctor?'

'I see. You never heard of the senseless luxury—a wise ignorance. You smelt flowers upon your mountains. You won't want this either'; and the Cologne bottle was put under the other arm. 'Candle—you'll want that. Soap—you want soap. Use the white cake.'

'Is that cheaper, doctor?'

'Yes, but just as good as the other. You don't ever munch sugar, do you? It's bad for the teeth. I'll take the sugar.' So the paper of sugar was likewise dropped into one of the capacious coat pockets.

'Oh, you better take the whole furniture, Doctor Franklin. Here, I'll help you drag out the bedstead.'

'My honest friend,' said the wise man, pausing solemnly, with the two bottles, like swimmer's bladders, under his arm-pits; 'my honest friend, the bedstead you will want; what I propose to remove you will not want.'

'Oh, I was only joking, doctor.'

'I knew that. It's a bad habit, except at the proper time, and with the proper person. The things left on the mantel were there placed by the landlady to be used if wanted; if not, to be left untouched. To-morrow morning, upon the chambermaid's coming in to make your bed, all such articles as remained obviously untouched would have been removed, the rest would have been charged in the bill, whether you used them up completely or not.'

'Just as I thought. Then why not let the bottles stay, doctor, and save yourself all this trouble?'

'Ah! why indeed. My honest friend, are you not my guest? It were unhandsome in me to permit a third person superfluously to entertain you under what, for the time being, is my own roof.'

These words came from the wise man in the most graciously bland and flowing tones. As he ended, he made a sort of conciliatory half-bow toward Israel.

Charmed with his condescending affability, Israel, without another word, suffered him to march from the room, bottles and all. Not till the first impression of the venerable envoy's suavity had left him, did Israel begin to surmise the mild superiority of successful strategy which lurked beneath this highly ingratiating air.

'Ah,' pondered Israel, sitting gloomily before the rifled mantel, with the empty tumbler and teaspoon in his hand, 'it's sad business to have a Doctor Franklin lodging in the next room. I wonder if he sees to all the boarders this way. How the O-t-a-r-d merchants must hate him, and the pastry-cooks too. I wish I had a good pie to pass the time. I wonder if they ever make pumpkin pies in Paris. So I've got to stay in this room one way or another. Never mind, I'm an ambassador, that's satisfaction. Hark! the doctor again.—Come in.'

No venerable doctor, but in tripped a young French lass, bloom on her cheek, pink ribbons in her cap, liveliness in all her air, grace in the very tips of her elbows. The most bewitching little chambermaid in Paris. All art, but the picture of artlessness.

'Monsieur! pardon!'

'Oh, I pardong ye freely,' said Israel. 'Come to call on the ambassador?'

'Monsieur, is de—de——' but, breaking down at the very threshold in her English, she poured out a long ribbon of sparkling French, the purpose of which was to convey a profusion of fine compliments to the stranger, with many tender inquiries as to whether there might not be something, however trifling, wanting to his complete accommodation. But Israel understood nothing, at the time, but the exceeding grace, and trim, bewitching figure of the girl.

She stood eyeing him for a few moments more, with a look of theatrical despair, and, after vaguely lingering a while, with another show of incomprehensible compliments and apologies, tripped like a fairy from the chamber. Directly she was gone Israel pondered upon a singular glance of the girl. It seemed to him that he had, by his reception, in some way, unaccountably disappointed his beautiful visitor. It struck him very strangely that she had entered all sweetness and friendliness, but had retired as if slighted, with a sort of disdainful and sarcastic levity, all the more stinging from its apparent politeness.

Not long had she disappeared, when a noise in the passage apprised him that, in her hurried retreat, the girl must have stumbled against something. The next moment he heard a chair scraping in the adjacent apartment, and there was another knock at the door.

It was the man of wisdom this time.

'My honest friend, did you not have a visitor just now?'

'Yes, doctor, a very pretty girl called upon me.'

'Well, I just stepped in to tell you of another strange custom of Paris. That girl is the chambermaid, but she does not confine herself altogether to one vocation. You must beware of the chambermaids of Paris, my honest friend. Shall I tell the girl, from you, that unwilling to give her the fatigue of going up and down so many flights of stairs, you will for the future waive her visits of ceremony?'

'Why, Doctor Franklin, she is a very sweet little girl.'

'I know it, my honest friend; the sweeter the more dangerous. Arsenic is sweeter than sugar. I know you are a very sensible young man, not to be taken in by an artful Ammonite, and so I think I had better convey your message to the girl forthwith.'

So saying, the sage withdrew, leaving Israel once more gloomily seated before the rifled mantel, whose mirror was not again to reflect the form of the charming chambermaid.

'Every time he comes in he robs me,' soliloquised Israel dolefully; 'with an air all the time, too, as if he were making me presents. If he thinks me such a very sensible young man, why not let me take care of myself?'

It was growing dusk, and Israel, lighting the wax candle, proceeded to read his guide-book.

'This is poor sight-seeing,' muttered he at last, 'sitting here all by myself, with no company but an empty tumbler, reading about the fine things in Paris, and I myself a prisoner in Paris. I wish something extraordinary would turn up now; for instance, a man come in and give me ten thousand pounds. But here's "Poor Richard"; I am a poor fellow myself; so let's see what comfort he has for a comrade.'

Opening the little pamphlet, at random, Israel's eyes fell on the following passages: he read them aloud:—

' "So what signifies waiting and hoping for better times? We may make these times better, if we bestir ourselves. Industry need not wish, and he that lives upon hope will die fasting, as Poor Richard says. There are no gains, without pains. Then help hands, for I have no lands, as Poor Richard says." Oh, confound all this wisdom! It's a sort of insulting to talk wisdom to a man like me. It's wisdom that's cheap, and it's fortune that's dear. That ain't in "Poor Richard"; but it ought to be,' concluded Israel, suddenly slamming down the pamphlet.

He walked across the room, looked at the artificial flowers, and the rose-coloured soap, and again went to the table and took up the two books.

'So here is the Way to Wealth, and here is the Guide to Paris. Wonder now whether Paris lies on the Way to Wealth? if so, I am on the road. More likely, though, it's a parting-of-the-ways. I shouldn't be surprised if the doctor meant something sly by putting these two books in my hand. Somehow, the old gentleman has an amazing sly look —a sort of wild slyness—about him, seems to me. His wisdom seems a sort of sly, too. But all in honour, though. I rather think he's one of those old gentlemen who say a vast deal of sense, but hint a world more. Depend upon it, he's sly, sly, sly. Ah, what's this Poor Richard says: "God helps them that help themselves." Let's consider that. Poor Richard ain't a Dunker, that's certain, though he has lived in Pennsylvania. "God helps them that help themselves." I'll just mark that saw, and leave the pamphlet open to refer to it again—Ah!'

At this point the doctor knocked, summoning Israel to his own apartment. Here, after a cup of weak tea, and a little toast, the two had a long, familiar talk together; during which, Israel was delighted with the unpretending talkativeness, serene insight, and benign amiability of the sage. But, for all this, he could hardly forgive him for the Cologne and Otard depredations.

Discovering that, in early life, Israel had been employed on a farm, the man of wisdom at length turned the conversation in that direction; among other things, mentioning to his guest a plan of his (the doctor's) for yoking oxen, with a yoke to go by a spring instead of a bolt; thus greatly facilitating the operation of hitching on the team to the cart. Israel was very much struck with the improvement; and thought that, if he were home, upon his mountains, he would immediately introduce it among the farmers.

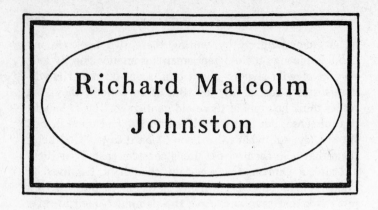

Richard Malcolm Johnston

In the history of southern humor Johnston is a transition figure, standing midway between the generation of Judge Longstreet and the generation of Mark Twain. His first story, "A Georgia School in the Old Times" (retitled "The Goosepond School" in later collections of Johnston's work), was published in the *Spirit of the Times* in 1857. Seven years later his first book of fiction appeared. Its title, *Georgia Sketches,* reflects Johnston's literary indebtedness to Longstreet's *Georgia Scenes,* while one of the most successful stories in the collection—"The Expensive Treat of Colonel Moses Grice"—resembles a circus story by Longstreet's Georgia contemporary, William Tappan Thompson.

The resemblances between Johnston's stories and those of his Georgia predecessors are, however, of less significance than their differences. Johnston, after all, began to write stories not in the expansive 1830s but in the tragic, closing years of the 1850s, when to many Americans the world seemed on the verge of splitting into chaos. A mild Unionist, Johnston was deeply distressed by the extremism of the secessionists and outspokenly opposed them, a position which ultimately made it necessary for him to resign his professorship at the University of Georgia. He was further disturbed by the decline of religious amity, as Protestantism in the South, beset by denominational strife, splintered into intolerant, mutually suspicious sects. Although the son of a Baptist minister, Johnston was eventually converted to Catholicism, which offered him a universal church.

During and after the Civil War, Johnston conducted various private schools, where he put into effect his theory that education should inculcate self-discipline and self-control. In part, his educational views were a reaction to the vicious treatment of rural schoolmasters to which he had been subjected as a boy. From one master, he recalled in later life, "I must have gotten an average of at least a whipping a day, though I was less than seven years old." But in part, too, Johnston's theory that self-control could be taught was surely a response to his well-known fear of his own temper. Challenges to duel, angry disputes with friends over card games, unreasonable outbursts of anger at his students, constituted a recurrent pattern in Johnston's life, which no amount of firm resolution could obliterate. Johnston feared the disastrous hotheadedness, the propensity for violence, of southern society, and he was well aware that it was that society which had formed him.

Beneath the cool, urbane surfaces of Longstreet's *Georgia Scenes* there are glimpses of dark abysses of chaos; in Johnston's stories (primarily his early stories, for by the mid-1880s his fiction had softened into sweetly sentimental recollections of some vanished golden day and self-conscious searchings out of the quaint) the fact of social disintegration is much more overt. Longstreet's man of the cloth, whose cool superiority to the antics of backwoods ruffians seems a warranty of social control, has metamorphosed into a sadistic schoolmaster, whose rule is finally overthrown by the children (shades of the "Examination Evening" in *Tom Sawyer!*). In "The Expensive Treat of Colonel Moses Grice," which probably inspired the circus chapter in *Huckleberry Finn*, the practical joke that the well-to-do militia colonel plays on the naïve rustic becomes a joke on the colonel himself when he loses his temper.

The Expensive Treat of Colonel Moses Grice

Besides an incipient ventriloquist who had included it in a limited provincial tour which he was making in some hope of larger development of his artistic powers, the only show that had visited Dukesborough thus far was the wax figures. The recollection of that had ever remained unsatisfactory. I can just remember that one of the figures was William Pitt, and another the Sleeping Beauty; that the former was the saddest and the yellowest great statesman that I had had opportunity, thus far, to look upon, and the latter—well, it is not pleasant, even now, to recall how dead, how long time dead, she appeared. When Aggy, my nurse, seeing me appalled at the sight, repeatedly asseverated, "De lady is jes' a-tired and a-takin' of a nap," I cried the louder, and plucked so at Aggy that she had to take me away. Though not thus demonstrative, yet even elderly country people acknowledged to disappointment, and there was a general complaint that if what had been was the best that could be done by Dukesborough in the way of public entertainment, it might as well take itself away from the great highway of human travel, suspend its school, sell out its two stores at cost, abolish its tavern and post-office, tear down its blacksmith- and shoe-shops, and, leaving only its meeting-house, resolve itself into the elements from which it had been aggregated. Not that these were the very words; but surely their full equivalents were employed when William Pitt, the Sleeping Beauty, and their pale associates had silently left the town.

As for a circus, such an institution was not known, except by hearsay, even to Colonel Moses Grice, of the Fourteenth Regiment Georgia Militia, though he was a man thirty-five years old, over six feet high, of proportional weight, owned a good plantation and at least twenty negroes, and had seen the theatre as many as three times in the city of Augusta. The ideas the colonel had received there were such, he said, as would last him to the end of his days—a period believed to be remote, barring, of course, all contingencies of future wars. To this theatrical experience he had been desirous, for some time, to add that of the circus, assured in his mind that, from what he had heard, it was a good thing. It happened once, while on a visit to Augusta, whither he had accompanied a wagonload of his cotton, partly on that business, but mainly to see the great world there, that he met at Collier's tavern, where he sojourned, a circus forerunner, who was going the rounds with his advertisements. Getting soon upon terms of intimacy with one who seemed to him the most agreeable, entertaining, and intelligent gentleman that he had ever met, Colonel Grice imparted to him such information about Dukesborough that, although that village was not upon the list of appointments—Dukesborough, in point of fact (to his shame the agent confessed it), not having been even heard of—yet a day was set for the appearance there of the Great World-renowned Circus, which claimed for its native homes London, Paris, and New York.

It would be entertaining to a survivor of that period to make even small boys, from families of most limited means in this generation, comprehend the interest excited by those advertisements, in huge black and red letters, that were tacked upon the wall of Spouter's tavern. From across Beaver Dam, Rocky Creek, the Ogeechee, from even the head-waters of streams leading to the Oconee, they came to read over and spell over the mighty words. Colonel Grice, who had been found, upon his own frank admission, to be the main mover, was forced to answer all inquiries concerning its magnitude, its possible influences upon the future of Dukesborough, and kindred subjects. There would have been a slight drawback to the general eager expectation on grounds moral and religious; but the World-renowned had anticipated and provided against that, as will hereafter appear. Then Colonel Grice had signified his intention of meeting the impending institution on the occasion of at least two of its exhibitions before its arrival, and should take it upon himself to warn it of the kind of people it was coming among.

The colonel resided five miles south of the village. He had a wife, but no child (a point on which he was, perhaps, a little sore), was not in debt, was hospitable, an encourager, especially in words, of public and private enterprises, and enthusiastically devoted, though without experience in wars, to the military profession, which—if he might use the expression—he would call his second wife. Off the muster-field he habitually practised that affability which is pleasant because so rare to see in the warrior class. When in full uniform and at the head of the regiment, with girt sword and pistol-holster, he did indeed look like a man not to be fooled with; and the sound of his voice in utterance of military orders was such as to show that he intended those orders to be heard and obeyed. When the regiment was disbanded, the sternness would depart from his mien, and, though yet unstripped of weapons and regalia, he would smile blandly, as if to reassure spectators that, for the present, the danger was over, and friends might approach without apprehension.

The colonel met the circus even farther away than he at first had intended. He had determined to study it, he said, and he travelled some seventy miles on horseback, attending daily and nightly exhibitions. Several times during this travel and afterwards, on the forenoon of the great day in Dukesborough, he was heard to say that, if he were limited to one word with which to describe what he had seen, that word would be—*grandeur*. "As for what sort of a people them circus people are," he said, "in a moral and in a religious sense, now—ahem! you know, gentlemen and ladies, especially ladies—ah, ha! I'm not a member, but I'm as great a respecter of religion as can be found in the whole State of Georgia. Bein' raised to that, I pride myself on that. Now, these circus people, they ain't what I should call a highly moral, that is, they ain't a strictly *religious* people. You see, gentlemen, that ain't, not religion ain't, so to speak, their business. They ain't goin' about preachin', and havin' camp-meetin' revivals, and givin' singin'-school lessons. They are—I wish I could explain myself about these circus people. These circus people are a-tryin'—you know, gentlemen, different people makes their livin' in different ways; and these circus people are jes a-tryin' to do exactly the same thing in jes exactly the same way. Well, gentlemen, *grandeur* is the word I should say about their performances. I should not confine myself to the word *religion.* Strictly speakin', that word do not embrace all the warious warieties, so to speak, of a circus. *My* word would be GRANDEUR; and I think that's the word you all will use when that tent is up, that door is open, and you are rushin' into its—its—I don't know whether to use the word *jaws* or *departments.* But, for the sake of decency, I'll say—*departments.* As for moral and religious, gentlemen—*and* 'specially, ladies—I tell you, it ain't neither a camp-meetin', a'sociation, a quarterly meetin', nor a singin'-school. I'm not a member, but I'm a respecter; and as to all that, and all them, Dukesborough may go farther and fare worse. That's all I got to say."

On the day before, Colonel Grice, by this time grown intimate with the manager, and as fond of him as if he had been his own brother (some said even fonder), in the fulness of his heart had invited the whole force to breakfast with him on the way to Dukesborough, and the invitation had been accepted. What was consumed was enormous; but he could afford it, and his wife, especially with distinguished visitors, was as hospitable and open-hearted as himself.

Other persons besides boys believed in their hearts that they might not have been able to endure another day's delay of the show. For a brief period the anxiety of school-children amounted to anguish when the master expressed doubts as to a holiday; for holidays then were infrequent, and schoolmasters had to be overpersuaded. But the present incumbent yielded early with becoming reluctance, to what seemed to be the general desire. The eagerly expected morning came at last. Many who knew that the circus was lingering at Colonel Grice's went forth to meet it, some on foot, some on horseback. Some started even in gigs and other carriages, but, being warned by old people, turned, unhooked their horses, and hitched them to swinging limbs in the very farthest part of the graveyard grove, and then set out on foot. The great show had put foremost its best wagon, but nobody had any sort of idea what things those were which the military gentlemen who rode in it carried in their hands. One person, known generally to carry a cool head, said that one of these things looked to him like a drum, though of a size comparatively enormous, but the idea was generally scorned.

"Where you goin' there, Polly Ann?" said Mrs. Watts to her little daughter, who was opening the gate. "My Lord!" exclaimed the mother instantly afterwards, as the band struck up. Then she rushed out herself and ran over Polly Ann, knocking her down. Polly Ann got up again and followed. "Stay behind there, you, Jack, and you, Susan! You want to git eat up by them camels and varmints? I never see sich children for cur'osity. They've got as much cur'osity as—as——"

"As we have," said Mrs. Thompson, laughing, as she attempted in vain to drive back her own little brood.

The effect of the music in the long, covered wagon, drawn by six gray horses slowly before the long procession, no words can describe. It put all, the aged and the young, into a tremor. Old Mr. Leadbetter, one of the deacons, who had been very "jubous," as he said, about the whole thing, was trying to read a chapter somewhere in Romans, when, at the very first blast, his spectacles jumped off his nose, and he told a few of the brethren afterwards, confidentially, that he never could recollect, afterwards, where he had left off. As for Mrs. Bland, she actually danced in her piazza for, probably, as many as a dozen bars, and, when "had up" about it, pleaded in abatement that she did it entirely unbeknownst to herself, and that she couldn't have holp it if it had been to have saved her life. It might have gone hard with the defendant had not some of her triers been known to march in time to the band, and, besides, they had stayed after the close of the animal show, contrary to the special inhibition against the circus. For the World-renowned had provided against the scruples of the straitest sects by attaching to itself a small menagerie of animals, whose exhibition had been appointed for the opening. There were a camel, a lion, a zebra, a hyena, two leopards, a porcupine, six monkeys, a bald eagle, and some parrots. By some means, never fully known, the most scrupulous of the spectators had gotten (late during this first act) to the very loftiest and remotest seats in the amphitheatre, and when the animals were shut from view, these persons, though anxious, were unable to retire without stepping over the shoulders of those beneath—a thing that no decent person could be expected to do. So Mrs. Bland got off with a mild rebuke.

As the cavalcade proceeded, it was a sight to see those who came in late in vehicles hastily turning in, apprehensive of the effect upon their horses of the music and the smell of the wild animals. For the first and only time in the history of Dukesborough, there was momentary danger of a blockade of wheels in its one street.

"A leetle more," said old Tony to the other negroes at home that night—he was the driver of the Booker carriage —"a leetle more, and I'd a driv' right into the camel's mouth."

For some reason, possibly its vast size and the peculiar dip of its under-lip in the pictures, the camel seemed to be regarded as the most carnivorous of the wild beasts, and especially fond of human flesh.

The place selected for the tent was the area west of Sweep's shoe-shop, at the foot of the hill on which the Basil mansion stood. When the door was opened at last, the crowd surged in. Colonel Grice waited long, in order to see that no one of any condition was excluded for want of the entrance-fee. For at last this was regarded by him rather as a treat of his own to his neighbors, and he wanted it to be complete. Then he walked in with the deliberateness of an owner of the establishment, and contemplated everything with benignant complaisance. Those ladies and gentlemen who were within the sound of his voice, as he went the rounds of the boxes containing the animals, were fortunate.

"Be keerful there, boys—be keerful," he said kindly but
seriously to some little fellows who were leaning against the
rope and studying the porcupine. "Be keerful. That's the
cilibrated pockapine. You see them sharp things on him?
Well, them's his quills, and which, when he's mad, he shoots
'em like a bow-'narrow, and they goes clean through
people."

The boys backed, although the little creature looked as
if his quiver had been well-nigh exhausted in previous wars.

"That's the hyner," said the colonel, moving on, "and
they say he's the most rhinocerous varmint of 'em all. Of
all victuals he loves folks the best, though he some rather
that somebody or something else would kill 'em, and then
him come on about a week or sich a matter afterwards.
They scratches up graveyards, and in the countries where
they raise, people has to bury their kin-folks in stone
coffins."

"Oh, goodness gracious, colonel! Let's go on!"

This exclamation was made by Miss Angeline Spouter,
the thinnest of the party, who was locked arm in arm with
Miss Georgiana Pea, the thickest.

"No danger, Miss Angeline—no danger at all," answered
the colonel, briskly raising his arm aloft that all might see
what was between them and the beast, at which he looked
as if it were his own pet hyena and would not think of
leaving its lair without his order. "No danger whatsomever.
Even if he could git out, he'd have to ride over me, and,
besides, it's mostly corpses that he'd be arfter, and—ah—I
don't think, anyway, that *you'd* be in the slightest danger."

As he said this, the colonel looked rather argumentatively,
and at Miss Pea more than Miss Spouter.

"Oh," said Miss Pea, gayly, "if the creetur could git out,
and then took a notion for live folks, I'd be the one he'd
make for, certain sure."

The hyena, though ugly and ferocious, did not look at
his spectators once, but continued pacing up and down in
his narrow cage, at either end of which, when reaching it,

he thrust his snout against the roof, as if his thoughts were tending upwards rather than downwards. I have never forgotten how unhappy seemed that poor beast. To all the other animals there was some relief of captivity in their various degrees of domestication and affiliation with man. The lion evidently loved his keeper; even the leopards seemed rather fond of him. But the hyena, more narrowly caged than all, conquered, not subdued, wholly untamed, constantly rolling his fiery gray eyes, appeared to have his thoughts ever upon revenge and escape to his native wilds. I, a young child, could not but pity him; and it occurred to me then that if ever he should become free, and then be tempted, at least, to an appetizer of living human flesh before reaching the graveyard, he most likely would fasten upon the manager of the Great World-renowned.

Just as the party was about to pass on, the wretched beast, stopping for a moment, his snout pressed to the roof, uttered several short, loud, hoarse, terrific howls. Miss Spouter screamed, Miss Pea laughed hysterically, and Colonel Grice, before he knew it, was on the outside of his knot of followers. Recovering himself—for he was without his sword and pistol-holster—he stepped quickly back to the front, looked threateningly, and afterwards disdainfully, at the hyena, who had resumed his walks, and said,

"You rhinocerous varmint, you! Thinkin' of them graveyards you've robbed, and hungry for some more of 'em, ah! These is live folks, my boy; and they ain't quite ready for you yit, nor won't be for some time, I hope." Then he led on to the monkeys.

"Hello, Bill! I knowed you'd be here; got your boys with you, too, I see."

The person addressed by Colonel Grice was a tall, stout young farmer. Over his other clothes he wore a loosely fitting round jacket, of thick, home-made stuff, with capacious pockets. In each of these were one foot and a considerable portion of a leg of a child about two years old. Their other feet rested easily in the man's hands, which were tucked up for that purpose, while one arm of each was around his neck. The children were exactly alike, except a shade's difference in the color of their eyes. This was Mr. Bill Williams, who, three years before, had been married to Miss Caroline Thigpen. At this double birth, Mr. Williams was proud and even exultant. Out of the many names suggested for the twins, he early selected those of the renowned offspring of Mars and Rhea Sylvia. Modifying them, however, somewhat for his own reasons, he called and so wrote them in his Bible, "Romerlus" and "Remerlus."

"*Remus*, Mr. Bill," urged the friend who had suggested the names. "Remus, not Remulus: Romulus and Remus are the names."

"No, Philip," he answered; "it's Romerlus and Remerlus. One's jest as old as t'other, or nigh and about; and he's as big, and he's as good-lookin', and his brother's name shan't be no bigger'n his'n."

As soon as they were able to stand without harm, he accustomed them to this mode of travel, and he was never so contented as when he and they went out thus together.

"I knowed you'd be here, Bill, and your boys."

"Yes, kurnel, I thought comin' to see the beastesses and varmints might sort o' be a start to 'em in jography. You, Rom—you Reme, you needn't squeeze me so tight. They ain't no danger in *them* things."

The children, plucky for their age, and with considerable experience in travel, had gone easily enough thus far; but when they looked upon these creatures, so like, yet so unlike, mankind, they shrank from the view, and clung closely to their father. Colonel Grice, recovered from the embarrassment occasioned by the hyena, was pleased at the apprehension of the twins.

"Natchel, Bill, perfec'ly natchel. You know some folks says monkeys is kin to us, and the boys, mebbe, don't like the looks of their relations."

"They ain't no kin o' mine, kurnel, nor theirn," answered Mr. Bill. "Ef you think they're humans, supposin' you—as you hain't no children of your own—supposin' you adopt one of 'em?"

Mr. Bill suspected that the colonel might be alluding to the fabled she-wolf. The colonel, however, had never heard of the distinguished originals of Roman story. His remark was a mere *jeu d'esprit,* springing naturally from the numerous sources of satisfaction of the occasion.

The wild beasts were finally hidden from view, and all repaired to their seats. Colonel Grice sat high, and near the entrance of the rear tent from which the circus performers were to emerge. Mr. Williams sat on the lowest tier, near the main entrance. He had taken his boys out of his pockets and held them on his knees. The colonel, when he could get an opportunity, quietly, and in a very pleasant way, called the ringmaster's attention to him, who smiled and nodded. Then the curtain was pushed aside from the rear tent, the band struck up, and the piebald horses came marching in with their silent riders, who, at first, looked as if they had just come from the bath, and had had time for only a limited toilet. Old Miss Sally Cash, cousin and close neighbor of Colonel Grice, exclaimed,

"Lor'-a-mercy, Mose! Them ain't folks, is they? Them's wax figgers, ain't they?"

"I assure you, cousin Sally, that they're folks," answered the colonel, with marked candor. He had great respect for his cousin Sally, and some awe.

"I thought they was wax figgers, sot on springs. They ain't like no folks that I've ever saw, and I've saw a good many people in my time, both here and in Agusty." It was one of Miss Cash's boasts, which few countrywomen of that generation could make, that she had once been to that famous city. After a short interval, she added: "I b'lieve yit they're wax figgers."

At that moment the clown, all spotted and streaked, bringing up the rear, shouted,

"Here we all are, my masters."

"My Lord-a'mighty!" exclaimed Miss Cash and some three hundred other females. Only Colonel Grice, and a very few others, who had been at yesterday's exhibition, could preserve any amount of coolness. The rest abandoned themselves to unlimited wonder.

"I'm sixty-nine year old," said Mr. Pate, "and I never see sich as that before, and I never 'spected to see sich as that."

As they made their involutions and evolutions, destined, apparently, to be endless in number and variety, the old man looked on as if in his age he was vouchsafed the witness of the very last and highest achievement of human endeavor.

"Do you think that's decent, Mose?" asked Miss Cash. The performers were then in the act of the "ground and lofty tumbling," turning somersaults forward, backward, over one another, lying on their backs, throwing up their legs, and springing to their feet, etc., until they were panting and blue in the face. Miss Cash was not disposed that her cousin Mose should know how much she was interested in this performance.

"I shouldn't say it was *on*decent, cousin Sally."

"I don't say it is," said Miss Cash.

"You know," said the colonel, winking slyly to his wife, and other friends of both sexes, "nobody is obleeged to stay and see the show. Anybody can go that wants to. They ain't no law agin goin', if anybody's desires is to git away."

"No," answered Miss Cash, downright. "I've paid my half a dollar, and they sha'n't cheat me out of it, nor nary part of it."

The next scene was one which Colonel Grice had eagerly anticipated. A steed rushed into the ring. He was as wild, apparently, as Mazeppa's, and the clown, when the ringmaster inquired for the rider, answered, in a pitiful tone, that he was sick, and none other of the *troupe* would dare to take his place. Then followed the usual fun of the master ordering the clown to ride the horse, and the clown, after vain remonstrance, trying to catch the horse, and the horse refusing to be caught; and, finally, the giving up the chase, and the master lashing the recusant beast around the ring, and wishing in vain for a rider to set him off properly. In the midst of this, an extremely drunken young man, homely clad, came through the main entrance, after a dispute and a scuffle with the door-keeper, and, staggering to where Mr. Bill Williams sat, looked down upon him.

"Two babies. One (*hic*) yours, s'pose."

"Yes," said Mr. Bill.

"And (*hic*) t'other——"

"My wife's; but that ain't nobody's business but ourn. You pass on."

The stranger declined, and fixing his muddled attention on what was going on in the ring, said:

"I can (*hic*) ride that horse——"

The words were no sooner uttered than the man stumbled upon the track, just after the horse had dashed past. The whole audience, except Colonel Grice and the select few, rose and cried out in horror.

"Take him out, Bill! Take him out!" cried Colonel Grice. Indeed, Mr. Bill had already slid his babies into his wife's lap, and was dragging the man out of the ring. He insisted upon returning.

"Look a-here, my friend," said Mr. Bill, "I don't know you, nor nobody else don't seem to know you; but if I didn't have Rom and Reme——"

The fellow made another rush. Mr. Bill took hold of him, but, receiving a trip, he fell flat, and the stranger fell into the ring, rolling out of the track in lucky time. The ringmaster seemed much embarrassed.

"Oh, give him a little ride, captain!" cried out Colonel Grice. "If he falls, he's too drunk to git badly hurt."

"It's a shame, Mose!" remonstrated Miss Cash. "I didn't come here and pay my money to see people killed. Notwithstandin' and never o'-the-less the poor creeter's drunk, and not hardly fitten to live, he ought by good rights to have some time to prepar' for the awful change that——"

But by this time Mazeppa was mounted and dashing away; and, but that Miss Cash had made up her mind not to be cheated out of any portion of her money, she would have shut her eyes, or veiled her face, as the maddened animal sped along, while the infatuated inebriate clung to his mane. An anxious time it was. Kindhearted people were sorry they had come. In the struggle between life and death, the stranger seemed to be beginning to sober. Sooner than could have been expected, he raised himself from the horse's neck (Miss Cash twisting her mouth and screwing her neck as he reeled back and forth from side to side), gathered up the reins, shook from his feet the thick shoes he was clad with, flung aside his old hat, brushed up his curly hair, and, before Miss Cash could utter a word, was on his feet. Then began that prolonged metamorphosis which old Mr. Pate was never satisfied with recounting, whether to those who saw it or those who saw it not.

"Coat arfter coat, breeches arfter breeches, gallis arfter gallis, shirt arfter shirt, ontwell he shucked hisself nigh as clean as a ear o' corn."

When everybody saw that the stranger was one of the showmen, the fun rose to a height that delayed for full five minutes the next scene. As for Colonel Grice, his handkerchief was positively wet with the tears he shed. Even Mr. Bill forgot his own discomfiture in the universal glee.

"It's a shame, Mose," said Miss Cash, "to put such a trick on Bill Williams, and that right where his wife is. It would be a good thing if he could put it back on you."

Even at this late day, a survivor of that period can scarcely recall without some exaltation of feeling that young girl of eleven (who had been advertised as "Mademoiselle Louise, the Most Celebrated Equestrienne in the World"), as she ran out with the daintiest of frocks, the pinkest of stockings, the goldenest of flounces, the bluest of belts, the curliest of hair, the peachiest of cheeks, kissed her hand, and flew into the saddle. As she went around, dancing upon that horse in full gallop, hopping over her whip and jumping through rings, and, when seated, smoothed down her skirt and waved her sleeveless arms—well, there was one boy (his name was Seaborn Byne) that declared he "would be dinged if it wasn't enough to melt the hearts clean outen a statchit." Other boys cordially endorsed this speech. As for Jack Watts, just turned of his tenth year, with the example before him of his older brother Tommy (dead in love at thirteen and some upwards, with Miss Wilkins the schoolmistress), he ran away from home the next morning, and followed for three miles the circus, begging to be taken into its employ, stipulating for only board and clothes. When caught, brought back, and properly attended to by his mother, the villain was suspected, and almost as good as confessed, that his purpose was to avail himself of an opportunity to seize upon the person of Mademoiselle Louise and her imagined vast treasures, and bear them to some distant foreign shore—on which one in special, in his exigent haste, he had not yet been able fully to determine.

In the interval before the last, named "The Wonderful Tooth-drawing Coffee-pot Firecracker Scene," an incident occurred that was not on the programme—an interlude, as it were, improvised by the exuberant spirits of both spectators and showmen. Colonel Grice, deeply gratified at the success of what, without great stretch, might be called his own treat, was in the mood to receive special attention and compliment from any source. When the pretended inebriate had been lifted upon Mazeppa, the clown took a bottle from his pocket, tasted it when he had gotten behind his master, smacked his lips, set it down by the middle pole, and, being detected in one of his resortings to it, was reproached for not inviting some one to drink with him. They were on the portion of the ring next the main entrance.

"Why don't you invite Colonel Grice?" said Mr. Bill Williams, in a low voice. "He expects it."

The master turned to notice from whom the suggestion proceeded, and, before he could determine, the clown, though with some hesitation, said,

"If Colonel Grice——"

"Stop it!" whispered the master.

But it was too late. The colonel had already risen, and was carefully descending.

"Is you goin' there, Mose, shore enough?" said Miss Cash. "It do look like Mose is completely carried away with them circus people and hisself."

Having gotten safely over the intervening heads and shoulders, the colonel stepped with dignity into the ring, at the same time feeling somewhat of the embarrassment which will sometimes befall the very greatest warrior when, without his weapons, he knows himself to be the object of the attention of a large number of civilians, both male and

female. This embarrassment hindered his observation of the
captain's winks, and the clown's pouring a portion of the
liquor upon the ground. He walked up rapidly and extended
his hand. The clown, with an effort at mirthfulness, the
more eager because he was doubtful of perfect success,
withdrew the bottle from his grasp, spread out his legs,
squatted his body, and applying the thumb of his disen-
gaged hand to his nose, wriggled his fingers at the colonel's
face, winking frantically the while, hoping the latter would
advance the joke by insistence.

In this he miscalculated. Persons who claimed to have
seen Colonel Moses Grice, on previous occasions, what was
called *mad,* said that all these were mere childish fretful-
ness compared with his present condition of mind, when,
after the withdrawal of the bottle, the whole audience,
Miss Cash louder than all, broke into uproarious laughter.
Fortunately the enraged chieftain had no sword, nor pistol,
nor even walking-cane. His only weapon was his tongue.
Stepping back a pace or two, and glaring upon the ludicrous squatter, he shouted,

"You   spotted-backed,   striped-legged,   streaked-faced,
speckled-b-breasted, p'inted-hatted son-of-a-gun!"

With each ejaculation of these successive, uncommon ap-
pellations, the poor clown lifted himself somewhat, and,
by the time their climax was reached, was upright, and,
dressed as he was, seemed most pitiful.

"My dear Colonel Grice——" he began.

"Shet up your old red mouth," broke in the colonel. "I
didn't *want* your whiskey. I got better whiskey at home
than you know anything about. But as you ast me to drink,
like, as I thought, one gentleman would ask another gentleman, I didn't feel like refusin' you. I give the whole of you
your breakfast, your blasted varmints and all; I put at least
twenty into your cussed old show, and arfter that——"

"My dear-est Colonel Grice!"

"Oh, you p'inted-hatted, streaked-fac-ed, speckled-b-
breasted——" beginning, as it were, a back-handed stroke by
reversing the order of his epithets.

At this moment the ring-master, who had not been able

thus far to get in a single word, said in a loud but calm tone:

"Colonel Grice, don't you see that it was a mere jest, and that the suggestion came from one of your neighbors? The bottle contains nothing but water. We beg your pardon if you are offended; but I can but think that the abusive words you have used already are quite enough."

"Come, Mose! come, Mose!" cried Miss Cash, who had just been able to stop her laughter. "Give and take, Mose. You put it on to Bill Williams, and he stood it; and he put it back on to you, and now you can't stand it, eh?" And the old lady again fairly screamed with laughter, while hundreds of others joined.

The colonel stood for a moment, hesitating. Then he suddenly turned, and, remarking that this was no place for a gentleman, walked towards the entrance.

"You goin' to let 'em cheat you out of the balance of your money that way, Mose?" asked Miss Cash. He turned again. Finding himself wholly without support, and unwilling to lose the great scene of the "Tooth-drawing," etc., he halted and stood until it was over. By that time he was considerably mollified, and the manager, approaching, apologized for himself, the clown, and all his *troupe*, and begged that he would join in a glass of the genuine at Spouter's tavern.

How could the colonel refuse? He could not, and he did not.

"Go with us, won't you, sir?" said the manager, addressing Mr. Williams. "We had some little fun at your expense also; but I hope you bear us no malice, as we never intend to hurt feelings."

"Sperrits," answered Mr. Bill, "is a thing I sildom teches —that is, I don't tech it reglar; but I'll try a squirrel-load with you—jes a moderate size squirrel-load."

At Spouter's all was cordially made up. Mr. Bill set Rom and Reme on the counter, and the clown gave them a big lump of white sugar apiece.

"They seem to be nice, peacable little fellows," said he. "Do they ever dispute?"

"Oh, no great deal," answered Mr. Bill.

"Sometimes Rom—that's the bluest-eyed one—he wants to have all his feed before Reme gits any o' his'n, and he claws at the spoon and Reme's nose. But when he does that, I jes set *him* right down, I does, and I makes him wait on-twell Reme's fed. I tends to raise 'em to be peacable, and to give and take, and to be friends as well as brothers, which is mighty fur from bein' always the case in families."

Mr. Bill knew that Colonel Grice and his younger brother Abram had not spoken together for years.

"Right, Bill," said the colonel. "Raise 'em right. Take keer o' them boys, Bill. Two at a time comes right hard on a fellow, though, don't it, Bill? Expensive, eh?" and the colonel winked pleasantly all around.

"Thank ye, kurnel; I'll do the best I can. I shall raise 'em to give and take. No, kurnel, not so very hard. Fact, I wa'n't a-expectin' but one, yit, when Reme come, I thought jest as much o' him as I did o' Rom. No, kurnel, it wouldn't be my desires to be a married man and have nary ar—to leave what little prop'ty I got to. And now, sence I got two instid o' one, and them o' the same size, I feel like I'd be sort o' awk'ard 'ithout both of 'em. You see, kurnel, they balances agin one another in my pockets. No, kurnel, better two than nary one; and in that way you can larn 'em better to give and take. Come, Rom, come Reme—git in; we must be a-travelin'." He backed up to the counter, and the boys, shifting their sugar-lumps to suit, stepped aboard and away they went.

After that day Dukesborough thought she could see no reason why she might not be named among the leading towns of Middle Georgia.

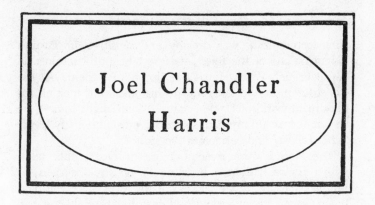

Joel Chandler Harris

"You know," Harris once wrote in a letter, "all of us have two entities, or personalities." In his so-called "daylight" personality, Harris was the chief editorial writer of the Atlanta *Constitution*, by all odds the most articulate and influential voice of the post-Civil War South, a paper which consistently advocated industrial development, as opposed to traditional agrarianism, and an end to the old ways. The *Constitution's* editor, Henry W. Grady, was the most important sectional spokesman of his generation; to the defeated South, he preached not mint-julep reaction but the gospel of progress; his literary inspiration was not Walter Scott but Horatio Alger.

If, however, Harris's editorials matched Grady's enthusiasm for the businessman and his way of life, Harris was nevertheless disturbed by the blatant materialism of the age. In contrast to the railroad barons and mineowners of the New South, who as a class were men "with a narrow range of thought," as one of their eulogists admitted, Harris was a cultivated man. He and his editor also were very different. Grady, always full to the brim with infectious enthusiasm, radiant, eloquent, boyish, was the perennial booster; when he was through work he liked to retire to his "dream farm"—by which he meant his office. Harris, so shy that he refused in horror Mark Twain's proposal of a joint lecture tour, was dreamy and sensitive—in Twain's judgment one of the finest and most beautiful natures he had ever met. When Harris was through for the day at the *Constitution* he did not retire to his office, but took off for the dream world of Uncle Remus. "When night comes," he wrote, "I take up my pen, surrender unconditionally to my 'other fellow,' and out comes the story."

The stories were remembrances of Negro folk tales, which Harris had been listening to—on street corners, at railroad stations, along country roads—ever since the days when, as an impoverished and illegitimate child, he had found solace in the companionship of slaves. In the lore of old black men who had lived close to the earth and the "elements," Harris came upon a dimension of experience which he later felt had been crushed to death in the world of progress and machines. The utilitarian trend in education in the New South, for example, with its exclusive emphasis on facts, had utterly failed, in his opinion, to initiate children into the "mysteries" of life. That children should be so deprived was a tragedy to Harris, because he believed that children, like Negroes, had an affinity for magic and mystical enchantment. To Harris, the Negro and the child seemed to belong together, conjoined in a mysterious communion by the lore of black Africa, with its talking animals, ghosts and witches.

Thus when he came to set down on paper the stories he had heard he framed them in the context of Uncle Remus telling the stories to a white child. With characteristic modesty, Harris felt that the only talent he had as a writer lay in the accuracy of his ear, but Mark Twain wrote him that "in reality the stories are only alligator pears—one eats them merely for the sake of the dressing." To Twain, the heart of the stories was the relationship of the old Negro and the boy. From Uncle Tom and Little Eva, through Huck and Jim, to Lucas Beauchamp and Chick Mallison, the relationship of colored man and white child has been a compelling one to American writers, and the reason for this can be discerned in the relationship of Uncle Remus and the boy: both are alienated from the prosaic world of white adults. In Uncle Remus's cabin there is beauty, mystery, terror, and laughter; in the flickering firelight it is possible to believe in the triumph of the rabbit. As Harris wrote in the preface to his first book, "It needs no scientific investigation to show why [the Negro] selects as his hero the weakest and most harmless of all animals, and brings him out victorious in contest with the bear, the wolf, and the fox." There is no need, either, for scientific investigation to show why the boy is so eager to hear about the triumph of the weak, for the boy is the author himself—who once said that in his "nighttime" personality he was a child. What the child in Harris wished to believe was that the bears and wolves of the adult world, the ruthless competitors so frighteningly praised by Henry Grady, could somehow be outsmarted.

Uncle Remus Initiates the Little Boy

One evening recently, the lady whom Uncle Remus calls "Miss Sally" missed her little seven-year-old. Making search for him through the house and through the yard, she heard the sound of voices in the old man's cabin, and, looking through the window, saw the child sitting by Uncle Remus. His head rested against the old man's arm, and he was gazing with an expression of the most intense interest into the rough, weather-beaten face, that beamed so kindly upon him. This is what "Miss Sally" heard:

"Bimeby, one day, arter Brer Fox bin doin' all dat he could fer ter ketch Brer Rabbit, en Brer Rabbit bin doin' all her could fer ter keep 'im fum it, Brer Fox say to hisse'f dat he'd put up a game on Brer Rabbit, en he ain't mo'n got de wuds out'n his mouf twel Brer Rabbit come a lopin' up de big road, lookin' des ez plump, en ez fat, en ez sassy ez a Moggin hoss in a barley-patch.

" 'Hol' on dar, Brer Rabbit,' sez Brer Fox, sezee.

"'I ain't got time, Brer Fox,' sez Brer Rabbit, sezee, sorter mendin' his licks.

"'I wanter have some confab wid you, Brer Rabbit,' sez Brer Fox, sezee.

"'All right, Brer Fox, but you better holler fum whar you stan'. I'm monstus full er fleas dis mawnin',' sez Brer Rabbit, sezee.

"'I seed Brer B'ar yistiddy,' sez Brer Fox, sezee, 'en he sorter rake me over de coals kaze you en me ain't make frens en live naberly, en I tole 'im dat I'd see you.'

"Den Brer Rabbit scratch one year wid his off hinefoot sorter jub'usly, en den he ups en sez, sezee:

"'All a settin', Brer Fox. Spose'n you drap roun' termorrer en take dinner wid me. We ain't got no great doin's at our house, but I speck de ole 'oman en de chilluns kin sorter scramble roun' en git up sump'n fer ter stay yo' stummuck.'

"'I'm 'gree'ble, Brer Rabbit,' sez Brer Fox, sezee.

"'Den I'll 'pen' on you,' sez Brer Rabbit, sezee.

"Nex' day, Mr. Rabbit an' Miss Rabbit got up soon, 'fo' day, en raided on a gyarden like Miss Sally's out dar, en got some cabbiges, en some roas'n years, en some sparrergrass, en dey fix up a smashin' dinner. Bimeby one er de little Rabbits, playin' out in de back-yard, come runnin' in hollerin', 'Oh, ma! oh, ma! I seed Mr. Fox a comin'!' En den Brer Rabbit he tuck de chilluns by der years en make um set down, en den him en Miss Rabbit sorter dally roun' waitin' for Brer Fox. En dey keep on waitin', but no Brer Fox ain't come. Atter'while Brer Rabbit goes to de do', easy like, en peep out, en dar, stickin' out fum behime de cornder, wuz de tip-een' er Brer Fox tail. Den Brer Rabbit shut de do' en sot down, en put his paws behime his years en begin fer ter sing:

"'De place wharbouts you spill de grease,
    Right dar youer boun' ter slide,
An' whar you fine a bunch er ha'r,
    You'll sholy fine de hide.'

"Nex' day, Brer Fox sont word by Mr. Mink, en skuze hisse'f kaze he wuz too sick fer ter come, en he ax Brer

Rabbit fer ter come en take dinner wid him, en Brer Rabbit say he wuz 'gree'ble.

"Bimeby, w'en de shadders wuz at der shortes', Brer Rabbit he sorter brush up en santer down ter Brer Fox's house, en w'en he got dar, he yer somebody groanin', en he look in de do' en dar he see Brer Fox settin' up in a rockin' cheer all wrop up wid flannil, en he look mighty weak. Brer Rabbit look all 'roun', he did, but he ain't see no dinner. De dishpan wuz settin' on de table, en close by wuz a kyarvin' knife.

"'Look like you gwineter have chicken fer dinner, Brer Fox,' sez Brer Rabbit, sezee.

"'Yes, Brer Rabbit, deyer nice, en fresh, en tender,' sez Brer Fox, sezee.

"Den Brer Rabbit sorter pull his mustarsh, en say: 'You ain't got no calamus root, is you, Brer Fox? I done got so now dat I can't eat no chicken 'ceppin she's seasoned up wid calamus root.' En wid dat Brer Rabbit lipt out er de do' and dodge 'mong de bushes, en sot dar watchin' fer Brer Fox; en he ain't watch long, nudder, kaze Brer Fox flung off de flannil en crope out er de house en got whar he could close in on Brer Rabbit, en bimeby Brer Rabbit holler out: 'Oh, Brer Fox! I'll des put yo' calamus root out yer on dish yer stump. Better come git it while hit's fresh,' and wid dat Brer Rabbit gallop off home. En Brer Fox ain't never kotch 'im yit, en w'at's mo', honey, he ain't gwineter."

Uncle Remus's Wonder Story

Uncle Remus was not a "field hand"; that is to say, he was not required to plough and hoe, and engage in the rough work on the plantation.

It was his business to keep matters and things straight about the house, and to drive the carriage when necessary. He was the confidential family servant, his attitude and his actions showing that he considered himself a partner in the various interests of the plantation. He did no great amount of work, but he was never wholly idle. He tanned leather, he made shoes, he manufactured horse-collars, fish-baskets, foot-mats, scouring-mops and axe-handles for sale; he had his own watermelon and cotton-patches; he fed the hogs, looked after the cows and sheep, and, in short, was the busiest person on the plantation.

He was reasonably vain of his importance, and the other negroes treated him with great consideration. They found it to their advantage to do so, for Uncle Remus was not without influence with his master and mistress. It would be difficult to describe, to the satisfaction of those not familiar with some of the developments of slavery in the South, the peculiar relations existing between Uncle Remus and his mistress, whom he called "Miss Sally." He had taken care of her when she was a child, and he still regarded her as a child.

He was dictatorial, overbearing and quarrelsome. These words do not describe Uncle Remus's attitude, but no other words will do. Though he was dictatorial, overbearing and quarrelsome, he was not even grim. Beneath everything he said there was a current of respect and affection that was thoroughly understood and appreciated. All his quarrels with his mistress were about trifles, and his dictatorial bearing was inconsequential. The old man's disputes with his "Miss Sally" were thoroughly amusing to his master, and the latter, when appealed to, generally gave a decision favorable to Uncle Remus.

Perhaps an illustration of one of Uncle Remus's quarrels will give a better idea than any attempt at description. Sometimes, after tea, Uncle Remus's master would send the house-girl for him, under pretense of giving him orders for the next day, but really for the purpose of hearing him quarrel. The old man would usually enter the house by way of the dining-room, leaving his hat and his cane outside. He would then go to the door of the sitting-room and announce his arrival, whereupon his master would tell him what particular work he wanted done, and then Uncle Remus would say, very humbly,—

"Miss Sally, you ain't got no cold vittles, nor no piece er pie, nor nothin' layin' roun' yer, is you? Dat ar Tildy gal say you all have a mighty nice dinner ter-day."

"No, there's nothing left. I gave the last to Rachel."

"Well, I dunner w'at business dat ar nigger got comin' up yer eatin' Mars John outer house en home. I year tell she larnin' how to cook, en goodness knows, ef eatin' gwine ter make anybody cook good, she de bes' cook on dis hill."

"Well, she earns what she eats, and that's more than I can say for some of the others."

"I lay ef ole miss wuz 'live, she'd sen' 'er dar a-whirlin'. Nigger w'at wrop up 'er ha'r wid a string ain't never seed de day w'en dey kin go on de inside er old miss' kitchen, let 'lone mommuck up de vittles. Now, I boun' you dat!"

"Well, there's nothing here for you, and if there was, you wouldn't get it."

"No'm, dat's so. I done know dat long time ago. All day long, en half de night, hit's 'Remus, come yer,' en 'Remus, go dar,' 'ceppin' w'en it's eatin'-time, en w'en dat time come, dey ain't nobody dast ter name de name er Remus. Dat Rachel nigger new ter de business, yet she mighty quick fer ter larn how ter tote off de vittles, en how ter make all de chillun on de place do her er'n's."

"John," to her husband, "I put some cold potatoes for the children on the sideboard in the dining-room. Please see if they are still there."

"Nummine 'bout gittin' up, Mars John. All de taters is dar. Old Remus ain't never 'grudge w'at dem po' little chillun gits. Let 'lone dat; dey comes down ter my house, en dey looks so puny en lonesome dat I 'vides my own vittles wid um. Goodness knows, I don't 'grudge de po' creeters de little dey gits. Good-night, Mars John! Good-night, Miss Sally!"

"Take the potatoes, Remus," said Mars John.

"I'm mighty much erbleedz ter you," said Uncle Remus, putting the potatoes in his pocket, "en thanky too; but I ain't gwine ter have folks sayin' dat ole Remus tuck 'n' sneaked up yer en tuck de vittles out er deze yer chillun's mouf, dat I ain't."

The tone in which Uncle Remus would carry on his quarrels was inimitable, and he generally succeeded in having his way. He would sometimes quarrel with the little boy to whom he told the stories, but either by dint of coaxing; or by means of complete silence, the youngster usually managed to restore the old man's equanimity.

There was one story that the little boy whom Uncle Remus delighted to entertain asked for with great regularity, perhaps because it has in it an element of witchcraft, and was as marvellous as it was absurd. Sometimes Uncle Remus pretended to resent this continued demand for the story, although he himself, like all the negroes, was very superstitious, and believed more or less in witches and witchcraft.

"Dat same ole tale," he would say. "Well! well! well! W'en is we gwinter year de las' un it? I done tole you dat tale so much dat it makes my flesh crawl, kase I des know dat some er deze yer lonesome nights I'll be a-settin' up yer by de fier atter you done gone. I'll be a-settin' up yer dreamin' 'bout gwine ter bed, en sumpin n'er'll come a-clawin' at de do', en I'll up'n ax, 'Who dat?' En dey'll up'n 'spon', 'Lemme in.' En I'll ondo de do', en dat ole creetur'll walk in, en dat'll be de las' er po' ole Remus. En den w'en dat come ter pass, who gwine take time fer ter tell you tales? Dat w'at I like ter know."

The little boy, although he well knew that there were no witches, would treat this statement with gravity, as the story to him was as fascinating as one of the "Thousand and One Nights."

"Well, Uncle Remus," he would say, "just tell it this time!" Whereupon the old negro, with the usual preliminary flourishes, would begin:

"One time, 'way back yander, w'en de moon wuz lots bigger dan w'at she is now, dey wuz er ole Witch-Wolf livin' off in de swamp, en dish yer ole Witch-Wolf wuz up ter all sorts er contraryiness. Look like she 'uz cross-ways

wid de whole er creation. W'en she wa'n't doin' devilment,
she 'uz studyin' up devilment. She had a mighty way, de
ole Witch-Wolf did, dat w'en she git hungry, she'd change
'erse'f ter be a 'oman. She could des shet 'er eye en' smack
'er mouf, en stiddier bein' a big black wolf, wid long claws
en green eyeballs, she'd 'come ter be de likelies'-lookin' gal
dat you mos' ever seed.

"It seem like she love ter eat folks, but 'fo' she kin eat
um, she hatter marry um; en w'en she take a notion, she
des change 'erse'f ter be a likely-lookin' gal, en sail in en
git married. Den w'en she do dat, she des take en change
'erse'f back ter be a wolf, en eat um up raw. Go whar you
kin, en whar you mought, en yit I don't 'speck you kin fin'
any wuss creetur dan w'at dish yer ole Witch-Wolf wuz.

"Well, sir, at de same time w'en dis ole Witch-Wolf
gwine on dis away, dey wuz a man livin' in de neighborhood w'at she tuck a mighty notion fer ter marry. De man
had lan', but she ain't want de lan'; de man had hosses,
but she ain't want de hosses; de man had cows, but she
ain't want de cows. She des natally want de man hese'f,
kase he mighty fat en nice."

"Did she want to marry him, Uncle Remus?" the little
boy would ask, as though the tale were true, as indeed it
seemed to be while Uncle Remus was telling it and acting
it.

"Tooby sho', honey! Dat 'zactly w'at she want. She want
ter marry 'im, en eat 'im up. Well, den, w'en she git eve'y-
thing good en ready, she des tuck'n back 'er years, en bat
'er eyes, en smack 'er mouf, en dar she wuz, a likely young
gal! She up en go ter de lookin'-glass, she did, en swinge
'er h'ar wid de curl-in'-tongs, en tie ribbins on 'er cloze, en
fix up 'er beau-ketchers. She look nice, fit ter kill, now. Den
she tuck'n pass by de man house, en look back en snicker,
en hol' 'er head on one side, en sorter shake out 'er cloze,
en put 'er han' up fer ter see ef de ha'rpins in der place.
She pass by dis away lots er times, en bimeby de man
kotch a glimp' un 'er; en no sooner is he do dis, dan she
wave her hankcher. De man he watch 'er en watch 'er, en
bimeby, atter she kep' on whippin' by, he come out en hail

'er. En den she tuck'n stop, en nibble at 'er fan en fumble
wid 'er hankcher, en dey tuck'n stan' dar, dey did, en pass
de time er day. Atter dat de sun never rise en set widout
she hol' some confab wid de man; en 'twa'n't long 'fo' de
man tuck a notion dat she de very gal fer a wife, w'at he
bin a-huntin' fer. Wid dat dey des got right down ter ole
fashin' courtin'. Dey'd laugh, dey'd giggle, dey'd 'spute,
dey'd pout. You ain't never see folk a-courtin', is you,
honey?"

The little boy never had, and he said so.

"Well, den," Uncle Remus would continue, "you ain't de
wuss off fer dat, kase dey ain't nothin' in de roun' worl'
dat'll turn yo' stomach quicker. But dar dey wuz, en de
ole Witch-Wolf make sho' she 'uz gwinter git de man; let
'lone dat, de man he make sho' he 'uz gwinter git de gal.
Yit de man he helt back, en ef de Witch-Wolf hadn't er
bin afeard she'd drap de fat in de fier, she'd er des come
right out en pop de question den en dar. But de man he
helt back en helt back, en bimeby he say ter hese'f, he did,
dat he 'speck he better make some inquirements 'bout dish
yer gal. Yit who sh'll he go ter?

"He study en study, en atter w'ile hit come 'cross he min'
dat he better go en ax old Jedge Rabbit 'bout 'er, bein' ez
he bin livin' roun' dar a mighty long time.

"Ole Jedge Rabbit," Uncle Remus would explain, "done
got ole in age en gray in de min'. He done sober up en
settle down, en I let you know dey wa'n't many folks in
dem diggin's but w'at went ter old Jedge Rabbit w'en dey
git in trouble. So de man he went ter Jedge Rabbit house,
en rap at de do'. Jedge Rabbit, he 'low, he did, 'Who dat?'

"Man he up en 'spon, 'Hit's me.'

"Den Jedge Rabbit 'gun ter talk like one er deze yer town
lawyers. He 'low, he did, 'Mighty short name for grown
man. Gimme de full entitlements.'

"Man he gun um ter 'im, en den old Jedge Rabbit open
de do' en let 'im in. Dey sot dar be de fier, dey did, twel
bimeby 'twa'n't long 'fo' de man 'gun to tell 'im 'bout dish
yer great gal w'at he bin courtin' 'long wid. Bimeby Jedge
Rabbit ax 'im, sezee, 'W'at dish yer great gal name?'

"Man he 'low, 'Mizzle-Mazzle.'

"Jedge Rabbit look at de man sorter like he takin' pity on 'im, en den he tuck he cane en make a mark in de ashes. Den he ax de man how ole is dish yer great gal. Man told 'im. Jedge Rabbit make n'er mark in de ashes. Den he ax de man is she got cat eyes. Man sorter study 'bout dis, but he say he 'speck she is. Jedge Rabbit make n'er mark. Den he ax is 'er years peaked at de top. Man 'low he disremember, but he 'speck dey is. Jedge Rabbit make n'er mark in de ashes. Den he ax is she got yaller ha'r. Man say she is. Jedge Rabbit make n'er mark. Den he ax is 'er toofs sharp. Man say dey is. Jedge Rabbit make n'er mark. Atter he done ax all dis, Jedge Rabbit got up, he did, en went 'cross de room ter de lookin'-glass. W'en he see hese'f in dar, he tuck'n shet one eye *s-l-o-w*. Den he sot down en leant back in he cheer, en 'low, sezee,—

" 'I done had de idee in my head dat ole Mizzle-Mazzle done moof out'n de country, en yit yer she is gallopin' roun' des ez natchul ez a dead pig in de sunshine!'

"Man look 'stonish, but he ain't say nothin'. Jedge Rabbit keep on talkin'.

" 'You ain't never bin trouble' wid no trouble yit, but ef you wanter be trouble' wid trouble dat's double and thribble trouble, you des go en marry old Mizzle-Mazzle,' sezee. 'You nee'nter b'lieve me less'n you wanter,' sezee. 'Des go 'long en marry her,' sezee.

"Man he look skeered. He up en 'low, he did, 'W'at de name er goodness I gwine do?'

"Ole Jedge Rabbit look sollumcolly. 'You got any cows?' sezee.

"Man say he got plenty un um.

" 'Well den,' sez ole Jedge Rabbit, sezee, 'ax 'er ef she kin keep house. She'll say yasser. Ax 'er ef she kin cook. She'll say yasser. Ax 'er ef she kin scour. She'll say yasser. Ax 'er ef she kin wash cloze. She'll say yasser. Ax 'er ef she kin milk de red cow. Den see w'at she say.'

"Man, he 'low, he did, dat he mighty much erblije ter ole Jedge Rabbit, en wid dat he make he bow, en tuck he leaf. He went home, he did, en w'en he git dar, sho nuff dar wuz dish nice-lookin' gal a-pommynadin' up en down de road, en shakin' 'er hankcher. Man, he hail 'er, he did, en ax 'er how she come on. She 'low she purty well, en how do he do. Man say he speck he feel po'ly kaze he so powerful lonesome. Den dish yer nice-lookin' gal, she ax 'im w'at make he so powerful lonesome. Man, he say he speck he so powerful lonesome kaze he want ter marry.

"Time de man come out so flat-footed 'bout marryin', de gal, she 'gun ter work wid 'er fan, en chaw at 'er hankcher. Den, atter w'ile, she up en ax 'im who he wanter marry. Man 'low he ain't no ways 'tickerler, kaze he des want somebody fer ter take keer er de house w'en he gone, en fer ter set down by de fire, en keep 'im comp'ny w'en he at home. Den he up'n ax de gal kin she keep house. De gal she 'low, 'Yasser!' Den he ax 'er ef she kin cook. She 'low, 'Yasser!' Den he ax 'er ef she kin scour. She 'low, 'Yasser!' Den he ax 'er ef she kin wash cloze. She 'low 'Yasser!' Den he ax 'er ef she kin milk de red cow. Wid dat she flung up 'er han's, en fetched a squall dat make de man jump.

"'Lawl' se' she, 'does you speck I'm a-gwineter let dat cow hook me?'

"Man, he say de cow des ez gentle ez a dog.

"'Does you speck I'm a-gwineter let dat cow kick me crank-sided?' se' she.

"Man, he 'low, he did, dat de cow won't kick, but dat ar gal, she tuck'n make mo' skuses dan dey is frogs in de spring branch, but bimeby she say she kin try. But she 'low dat fus, 'fo' she try dat, she'll show 'im how she kin keep house. So de nex' mornin' yer she come, en I let you know she sailed in dar, en sot dat house ter rights 'fo' some wimmen folks kin turn 'roun'. Man, he say, he did, dat she do dat mighty nice.

"Nex' day, de gal sot in, en got dinner. Man say, he did, dat dey ain't nobody w'at kin beat dat dinner. Nex' day she sot in en scoured, en she make dat flo' shine same ez a lookin'-glass. Man, he say dey ain't nobody in dat neighborhoods kin beat dat scourin'. Nex' day, she come fer to milk de red cow, en de man, he 'low ter he'self, he did, dat he gwineter see w'at make she don't like ter milk dat cow.

"De gal come, she did, en git de milk-piggin', en scald it out, en den she start for de cow-lot. Man, he crope 'long atter de gal fer ter watch 'er. Gal went on, en w'en she come ter de lot dar wuz de red cow stan'in' in de fence-cornder wallopin' 'er cud. Gal, she sorter shuck de gate, she did, en holler, 'Sook, cow! Sook, cow!' Cow, she pearten up at dat, kaze she know win folks call 'er dat away, she gwineter come in fer a bucket er slops.

"She pearten up, de red cow did, en start todes de gate, but, gentermens! time she smell dat gal, she 'gun a blate like she smell blood, en paw'd de groun' en shuck 'er head des like she fixin' fer ter make fight. Man, he 'low ter hese'f dat dish yer kinder business mighty kuse, en he keep on watchin'. Gal, she open de gate, but stiddier de cow makin' fight, she 'gun ter buck. Gal, she say 'So, cow! so, cow—so!' but de cow she hist her tail in de elements, en run 'roun dat lot like de dogs wuz atter 'er. Gal, she foller on, en hit sorter look like she gwineter git de cow hemmed up in a cornder, but de cow ain't got no notion er dis, en bimeby she whirl en make a splunge at de gal, en ef de gal hadn't er lipt de fence quick es she did, de cow would er got 'er. Es she lipt de fence, de man seed 'er foots, en, lo en beholes, dey wuz wolf foots! Man, he holler out,—

" 'You oughter war shoes w'en you come a-milkin' de red cow!' en wid dat, de ole Witch-Wolf gun a twist, en fetched a yell, en made 'er disappearance in de elements."

Here Uncle Remus would pause awhile. Then he would shake his head, and exclaim,—

" 'Taint no use! Dey may fool folks, but cows knows wil' creeturs by der smell."

This sage remark would bring the story to its close.

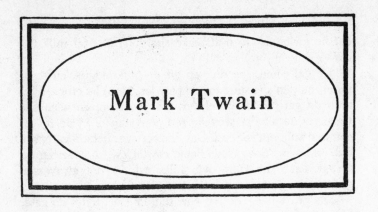

Mark Twain

Intended for publication in *Artemus Ward; His Travels,* the "Jumping Frog" arrived in the East too late to be included in the volume, and so appeared instead in the *Saturday Press* of November 18, 1865. The story was Twain's first great success. James Russell Lowell pronounced it "the finest piece of humorous literature yet produced in America."

In making that statement Lowell was thinking of the "Frog" as the triumphant culmination of thirty-five years of written dialect humor, and certainly the story bears many resemblances to the southwestern humor of Longstreet and Thorpe and G. W. Harris. Like the best of their work, the "Frog" originated as an oral anecdote—years before Twain reached the Far West, it had been a favorite mining-camp joke. In retelling the story for an eastern audience, Twain simulated the speech characteristics of Simon Wheeler with even more care than Thorpe had lavished on Jim Doggett's talk. He further embellished the anecdote with a "frame" which introduced a gentleman narrator, a device much favored by the pre-Civil War humorists.

But if the "Jumping Frog" thus belongs in the great comic tradition of "The Big Bear of Arkansas" and "Parson John Bullen's Lizards," it is also markedly different from its predecessors. The Civil War is the principal watershed in the history of American writing, and nowhere is this more evident than in the comparison of Twain's story to pre-War southwestern humor. The gentleman narrator in the frame of the "Frog" story is no longer an indulgent puppeteer who puts one of his backwoods acquaintances through his paces for our amusement; the tables have been turned, and it is now "Mark Twain," of the genteel language and the eastern friends, who is the butt of the joke, who is "taken in" by the poker-faced slyness of the westerner.

The Celebrated Jumping Frog of Calaveras County

In compliance with the request of a friend of mine, who wrote me from the East, I called on good-natured, garrulous old Simon Wheeler, and inquired after my friend's friend, Leonidas W. Smiley, as requested to do, and I hereunto append the result. I have a lurking suspicion that *Leonidas W.* Smiley is a myth; that my friend never knew such a personage; and that he only conjectured that if I asked old Wheeler about him, it would remind him of his infamous *Jim* Smiley, and he would go to work and bore me to death with some exasperating reminiscence of him as long and as tedious as it should be useless to me. If that was the design, it succeeded.

I found Simon Wheeler dozing comfortably by the barroom stove of the dilapidated tavern in the decayed mining camp of Angel's, and I noticed that he was fat and bald-headed, and had an expression of winning gentleness and simplicity upon his tranquil countenance. He roused up, and gave me good-day. I told him a friend of mine had commissioned me to make some inquiries about a cherished companion of his boyhood named *Leonidas W.* Smiley—*Rev. Leonidas W.* Smiley, a young minister of the Gospel, who he had heard was at one time a resident of Angel's Camp. I added that if Mr. Wheeler could tell me anything about this Rev. Leonidas W. Smiley, I would feel under many obligations to him.

Simon Wheeler backed me into a corner and blockaded me there with his chair, and then sat down and reeled off the monotonous narrative which follows this paragraph. He never smiled, he never frowned, he never changed his voice from the gentle-flowing key to which he tuned his initial sentence, he never betrayed the slightest suspicion of enthusiasm; but all through the interminable narrative there ran a vein of impressive earnestness and sincerity, which showed me plainly that, so far from his imagining that there was anything ridiculous or funny about his story, he regarded it as a really important matter, and admired its two heroes as men of transcendent genius in *finesse*. I let him go on in his own way, and never interrupted him once.

"Rev. Leonidas W. H'm, Reverend Le—well, there was a feller here once by the name of *Jim* Smiley, in the winter of '49—or may be it was the spring of '50—I don't recollect exactly, somehow, though what makes me think it was one or the other is because I remember the big flume warn't finished when he first come to the camp; but any way, he was the curiosest man about always betting on anything that turned up you ever see, if he could get anybody to bet on the other side; and if he couldn't he'd change sides. Any way that suited the other man would suit *him*—any way just so's he got a bet, *he* was satisfied. But still he was lucky, uncommon lucky; he most always come out winner. He was always ready and laying for a chance; there couldn't be no solit'ry thing mentioned but that feller'd offer to bet on it, and take ary side you please, as I was just telling you. If there was a horse-race, you'd find him flush or you'd find him busted at the end of it; if there was a dog-fight, he'd bet on it; if there was a cat-fight, he'd bet on it; if there was a chicken-fight, he'd bet on it; why, if there was two birds setting on a fence, he would bet you which one would fly first; or if there was a camp-meeting, he would be there reg'lar to bet on Parson Walker, which he judged to be the best exhorter about here, and so he was too, and a good man. If he even see a straddle-bug start to go anywheres, he would bet you how long it would take him to get to—to wherever he was going to, and if you took him up, he would foller that straddle-bug to Mexico but what he would find out where he was bound for and how long he was on the road. Lots of the boys here has seen that Smiley, and can tell you about him. Why, it never made no difference to *him*—he'd bet on *any* thing—the dangdest feller. Parson Walker's wife laid very sick once for a good while, and it seemed as if they warn't going to save her; but one morning he come in, and Smiley up and asked him how she was, and he said she was considable better—thank the Lord for his inf'nit mercy—and coming on so smart that with the blessing of Prov'dence she'd get well yet; and Smiley, before he thought says, "Well, I'll resk two-and-a-half she don't anyway."

Thish-yer Smiley had a mare—the boys called her the fifteen-minute nag, but that was only in fun, you know, because of course she was faster than that—and he used to win money on that horse, for all she was so slow and always had the asthma, or the distemper, or the consumption, or something of that kind. They used to give her two or three hundred yards' start, and then pass her under way; but always at the fag-end of the race she'd get excited and desperate-like, and come cavorting and straddling up, and scattering her legs around limber, sometimes in the air, and sometimes out to one side amongst the fences, and kicking up m-o-r-e dust and raisiɔ ˙ m-o-r-e racket with her coughing and sneezing and blowing her nose—and *always* fetch up at the stand just about a neck ahead, as near as you could cipher it down.

And he had a little small bull-pup, that to look at him you'd think he warn't worth a cent but to set around and look ornery and lay for a chance to steal something. But as soon as money was up on him he was a different dog; his under-jaw'd begin to stick out like the fo'castle of a steamboat, and his teeth would uncover and shine like the furnaces. And a dog might tackle him and bully-rag him, and bite him, and throw him over his shoulder two or three times, and Andrew Jackson—which was the name of the pup—Andrew Jackson would never let on but what *he* was satisfied, and hadn't expected nothing else—and the bets being doubled and doubled on the other side all the time, till the money was all up; and then all of a sudden he would grab that other dog jest by the j'int of his hind leg and freeze to it—not chaw, you understand, but only just grip and hang on till they throwed up the sponge, if it was a year. Smiley always come out the winner on that pup, till he harnessed a dog once that didn't have no hind legs, because they'd been sawed off in a circular saw, and when the thing had gone along far enough, and the money was all up, and he come to make a snatch for his pet holt, he see in a minute how he'd been imposed on, and how the other dog had him in the door, so to speak, and he 'peared surprised, and then he looked sorter discouraged-like, and didn't try no more to win the fight, and so he got shucked out bad. He give Smiley a look, as much as to say his heart was broke, and it was *his* fault, for putting up a dog that hadn't no hind legs for him to take holt of, which was his main dependence in a fight, and then he limped off a piece and laid down and died. It was a good pup, was that Andrew Jackson, and would have made a name for hisself if he'd lived, for the stuff was in him and he had genius—I know it, because he hadn't no opportunities to speak of, and it don't stand to reason that a dog could make such a fight as he could under them circumstances if he hadn't no talent. It always makes me feel sorry when I think of that last fight of his'n, and the way it turned out.

Well, thish-yer Smiley had rat-tarriers, and chicken cocks, and tom-cats and all them kind of things, till you couldn't rest, and you couldn't fetch nothing for him to bet on but he'd match you. He ketched a frog one day, and took him home, and said he cal'lated to educate him; and so he never done nothing for three months but set in his back yard and learn that frog to jump. And you bet you he *did* learn him, too. He'd give him a little punch behind, and the next minute, you'd see that frog whirling in the air like a dough-nut—see him turn one summerset, or may be a couple, if he got a good start, and come down flat-footed and all

right, like a cat. He got him up so in the matter of ketch-
ing flies, and kep' him in practice so constant, that he'd nail
a fly every time as fur as he could see him. Smiley said all
a frog wanted was education, and he could do 'most anything—and I believe him. Why, I've seen him set Dan'l
Webster down here on this floor—Dan'l Webster was the
name of the frog—and sing out, "Flies, Dan'l, flies!" and
quicker'n you could wink he'd spring straight up and snake
a fly off'n the counter there, and flop down on the floor
ag'in as solid as a gob of mud, and fall to scratching the
side of his head with his hind foot as indifferent as if he
hadn't no idea he'd been doin' any more'n any frog might
do. You never see a frog so modest and straightfor'ard as
he was, for all he was so gifted. And when it come to fair
and square jumping on a dead level, he could get over more
ground at one straddle than any animal of his breed you
ever see. Jumping on a dead level was his strong suit, you
understand; and when it come to that, Smiley would ante
up money on him as long as he had a red. Smiley was
monstrous proud of his frog, and well he might be, for fellers
that had traveled and been everywhere, all said he laid over
any frog that ever *they* see.

Well, Smiley kep' the beast in a little lattice box, and he
used to fetch him down town sometimes and lay for a bet.
One day a feller—a stranger in the camp, he was—come
acrost him with his box, and says:

"What might it be that you've got in the box?"

And Smiley says, sorter indifferent-like, "It might be a
parrot, or it might be a canary, maybe, but it ain't—it's only
just a frog."

And the feller took it, and looked at it careful, and
turned it round this way and that, and says, "H'm—so 'tis.
Well, what's *he* good for?"

"Well," Smiley says, easy and careless, "he's good enough
for *one* thing. I should judge—he can outjump any frog in
Calaveras county."

The feller took the box again, and took another long,
particular look, and give it back to Smiley, and says, very

deliberate, "Well," he says, "I don't see no p'ints about that frog that's any better'n any other frog."

"Maybe you don't," Smiley says. "Maybe you understand frogs and maybe you don't understand 'em; maybe you've had experience, and maybe you ain't only a amature, as it were. Anyways, I've got *my* opinion and I'll resk forty dollars that he can outjump any frog in Calaveras county."

And the feller studied a minute, and then says, kinder sad like, "Well, I'm only a stranger here, and I ain't got no frog; but if I had a frog, I'd bet you."

And then Smiley says, "That's all right—that's all right— if you'll hold my box a minute, I'll go and get you a frog." And so the feller took the box, and put up his forty dollars along with Smiley's and set down to wait.

So he set there a good while thinking and thinking to his-self, and then he got the frog out and prized his mouth open and took a teaspoon and filled him full of quail shot —filled him pretty near up to his chin—and set him on the floor. Smiley he went to the swamp and slopped around in the mud for a long time, and finally he ketched a frog, and fetched him in, and give him to this feller, and says:

"Now, if you're ready, set him alongside of Dan'l, with his fore-paws just even with Dan'ls, and I'll give the word." Then he says, "One—two—three—*git!*" and him and the feller touched up the frogs from behind, and the new frog hopped off lively, but Dan'l give a heave, and hysted up his shoulders—so—like a Frenchman, but it warn't no use—he couldn't budge; he was planted as solid as a church, and he couldn't no more stir than if he was anchored out. Smiley was a good deal surprised, and he was disgusted too, but he didn't have no idea what the matter was, of course.

The feller took the money and started away; and when he was going out at the door, he sorter jerked his thumb over his shoulder—so—at Dan'l, and says again, very delib-erate, "Well," he says, "*I* don't see no p'ints about that frog that's any better'n any other frog."

Smiley he stood scratching his head and looking down at Dan'l a long time, and at last he says, "I do wonder what in the nation that frog throw'd off for—I wonder if there ain't something the matter with him—he 'pears to look mighty baggy, somehow." And he ketched Dan'l by the nap of the neck, and hefted him, and says, "Why blame my cats if he don't weigh five pound!" and turned him upside down and he belched out a double handful of shot. And then he see how it was, and he was the maddest man —he set the frog down and took out after that feller, but he never ketched him. And——"

(Here Simon Wheeler heard his name called from the front yard, and got up to see what was wanted.) And turning to me as he moved away, he said: "Just set where you are, stranger, and rest easy—I ain't going to be gone a second."

But, by your leave, I did not think that a continuation of the history of the enterprising vagabond *Jim* Smiley would be likely to afford me much information concerning the Rev. *Leonidas W.* Smiley, and so I started away.

At the door I met the sociable Wheeler returning, and he button-holed me and re-commenced:

"Well, thish-yer Smiley had a yaller one-eyed cow that didn't have no tail, only jest a short stump like a bannanner, and——"

However, lacking both time and inclination, I did not wait to hear about the afflicted cow, but took my leave.

On December 17, 1877, a dinner was given at the Brunswick Hotel in Boston by the publishers of the *Atlantic* in commemoration of the poet Whittier's seventieth birthday, as well as of the twentieth anniversary of the magazine. The guests of honor, besides Whittier, were Longfellow, Emerson, and Oliver Wendell Holmes. The Boston *Advertiser* said that "the company was without doubt the most notable that has ever been seen in this country within four walls." Many of those present were called on for speeches, including the famous author of *The Innocents Abroad* and *The Adventures of Tom Sawyer.*

Thirty years later Twain remembered that during his speech the expression on the faces of his audience "turned to a sort of black frost. I wondered what the trouble was. I didn't know. I went on, but with difficulty . . . always hoping—but with a gradually perishing hope—that somebody would laugh, or that somebody would at least smile, but nobody did." Professor Henry Nash Smith has offered evidence that the speech was actually received with considerable merriment, but there is no doubt that subsequently it was criticized by various newspapers as being in poor taste. This so upset Twain that finally he wrote letters to Longfellow, Emerson, and Holmes abjectly apologizing for his performance, saying that he had meant no offense.

Yet to read the "Whittier Dinner Speech" is to be convinced that Twain *did* mean offense, whether consciously or unconsciously. Wearing the mask of a rough miner that makes Twain a kind of California version of D. H. Lawrence's underground man, he smashes the plaster bust of New England culture by exposing the household gods of its literature as pretentious frauds. The card-playing, whiskey-drinking, poetry-quoting bums who invade the miner's cabin are fakers, like the King and the Duke, of whom they are the forerunners, and just as the Shakespeare soliloquy in *Huckleberry Finn* expresses Twain's hatred of Shakespeare as the rhetorical symbol of the phony pomposity of English civilization, so the drunken bellowing of "Mithridates" and "Hiawatha" makes ridiculous a genteel American culture which Twain regarded with contempt. The underground man is in contact with a new vitality and energy, and he mocks the comfortable belief of the diners at the Brunswick that they are the intellectual leaders of the United States. At the end of the story Twain turns his devastating humor against himself as well, with a question which probes at his guilty fear that in following the dictates of his driving ambition, which had led him to become a resident of New England and a speaker at *Atlantic* dinners, he may have become a fraud himself.

The Whittier Dinner Speech

This is an occasion peculiarly meet for the digging up of pleasant reminiscences concerning literary folk; therefore I will drop lightly into history myself. Standing here on the shore of the Atlantic and contemplating certain of its largest literary billows, I am reminded of a thing which happened to me thirteen years ago, when I had just succeeded in stirring up a little Nevadian literary puddle myself, whose spume-flakes were beginning to blow thinly Californiaward. I started an inspection tramp through the southern mines of California. I was callow and conceited, and I resolved to try the virtue of my *nom de guerre*.

I very soon had an opportunity. I knocked at a miner's lonely log cabin in the foot-hills of the Sierras just at nightfall. It was snowing at the time. A jaded, melancholy man of fifty, barefooted, opened the door to me. When he heard my *nom de guerre* he looked more dejected than before. He let me in—pretty reluctantly, I thought—and after the customary bacon and beans, black coffee and hot whiskey, I took a pipe. This sorrowful man had not said three words up to this time. Now he spoke up and said, in the voice of one who is secretly suffering, "You're the fourth—I'm going to move." "The fourth what?" said I. "The fourth literary man that has been here in twenty-four hours—I'm going to move." "You don't tell me!" said I; "who were the others?" "Mr. Longfellow, Mr. Emerson, and Mr. Oliver Wendell Holmes—consound the lot!"

You can easily believe I was interested. I supplicated—three hot whiskies did the rest—and finally the melancholy miner began. Said he:

"They came here just at dark yesterday evening, and I let them in, of course. Said they were going to the Yosemite. They were a rough lot, but that's nothing; everybody looks rough that travels afoot. Mr. Emerson was a seedy little bit of a chap, red-headed. Mr. Holmes was as fat as a balloon; he weighed as much as three hundred, and had double chins all the way down to his stomach. Mr. Longfellow was built like a prize-fighter. His head was cropped and bristly, like as if he had a wig made of hair-brushes. His nose lay straight down his face, like a finger with the end joint tilted up. They had been drinking, I could see that. And what queer talk they used! Mr. Holmes inspected this cabin, then he took me by the buttonhole, and says he:

> " 'Through the deep caves of thought
>   I hear a voice that sings,
> Build thee more stately mansions,
>   O my soul!'

"Says I, 'I can't afford it, Mr. Holmes, and moreover I don't want to.' Blamed if I liked it pretty well, either, coming from a stranger, that way. However, I started to get out my bacon and beans, when Mr. Emerson came and looked on awhile, and then *he* takes me aside by the buttonhole and says:

> " 'Gives me agates for my meat;
> Gives me cantharids to eat;
> From air and ocean bring me foods,
> From all zones and altitudes.'

"Says I, 'Mr. Emerson, if you'll excuse me, this ain't no hotel.' You see it sort of riled me—I warn't used to the ways of littery swells. But I went on a-sweating over my work, and next comes Mr. Longfellow and buttonholes me, and interrupts me. Says he:

> " 'Honor be to Mudjekeewis!
> You shall hear how Pau-Puk-Keewis——'

"But I broke in, and says I, 'Beg your pardon, Mr. Longfellow, if you'll be so kind as to hold your yawp for about five minutes and let me get this grub ready, you'll do me proud.' Well, sir, after they'd filled up I set out the jug. Mr.

Holmes looks at it, and then he fires up all of sudden and yells:

> " 'Flash out a stream of blood-red wine!
> For I would drink to other days.'

"By George, I was getting kind of worked up. I don't deny it, I was getting kind of worked up. I turns to Mr. Holmes, and says I, 'Looky here, my fat friend, I'm a-running this shanty, and if the court knows herself, you'll take whisky straight or you'll go dry.' Them's the very words I said to him. Now I don't want to sass such famous littery people, but you see they kind of forced me. There ain't nothing onreasonable 'bout me; I don't mind a passel of guests a-treadin' on my tail three or four times, but when it comes to *standing* on it it's different, 'and if the court knows herself,' says I, 'you'll take whisky straight or you'll go dry.' Well, between drinks they'd swell around the cabin and strike attitudes and spout; and pretty soon they got out a greasy old deck and went to playing euchre at ten cents a corner—on trust. I began to notice some pretty suspicious things. Mr. Emerson dealt, looked at his hand, shook his head, says:

> " 'I am the doubter and the doubt——'

and ca'mly bunched the hands and went to shuffling for a new layout. Says he:

> " 'They reckon ill who leave me out;
> They know not well the subtle ways I keep
> I pass and deal *again!*'

Hang'd if he didn't go ahead and do it, too! Oh, he was a cool one! Well, in about a minute things were running pretty tight, but all of a sudden I see by Mr. Emerson's eye he judged he had 'em. He had already corralled two tricks, and each of the others one. So now he kind of lifts a little in his chair and says:

> " 'I tire of globes and aces!—
> Too long the game is played!'

—and down he fetched a right bower. Mr. Longfellow smiles as sweet as pie and says:

> " 'Thanks thanks to thee, my worthy friend,
> For the lesson thou hast taught,'

—and blamed if he didn't down with *another* right bower! Emerson claps his hand on his bowie, Longfellow claps his on his revolver, and I went under a bunk. There was going to be trouble; but that monstrous Holmes rose up, wobbling his double chins, and says he, 'Order, gentlemen; the first man that draws, I'll lay down on him and smother him!' All quiet on the Potomac, you bet!

"They were pretty how-come-you-so by now, and they begun to blow. Emerson says, 'The nobbiest thing I ever wrote was "Barbara Frietchie." ' Says Longfellow, 'It don't begin with my "Biglow Papers." ' Says Holmes, 'My "Thanatopsis" lays over 'em both.' They mighty near ended in a fight. Then they wished they had some more company—and Mr. Emerson pointed to me and says:

> " 'Is yonder squalid peasant all
> That this proud nursery could breed?'

He was a-whetting his bowie on his boot—so I let it pass. Well, sir, next they took it into their heads that they would like some music; so they made me stand up and sing "When Johnny Comes Marching Home" till I dropped—at thirteen minutes past four this morning. That's what I've been through, my friend. When I woke at seven, they were leaving, thank goodness, and Mr. Longfellow had my only boots on, and his'n under his arm. Says I, 'Hold on, there, Evangeline, what are you going to do with *them?*' He says, 'Going to make tracks with 'em; because:

> " 'Lives of great men all remind us
> We can make our lives sublime;
> And, departing, leave behind us
> Footprints on the sands of time.'

As I said, Mr. Twain, you are the fourth in twenty-four

hours—and I'm going to move; I ain't suited to a littery atmosphere."

I said to the miner, "Why my dear sir, *these* were not the gracious singers to whom we and the world pay loving reverence and homage; these were imposters.'

The miner investigated me with a calm eye for awhile; then he said, "Ah! imposters, were they? Are *you?*"

I did not pursue the subject, and since then I have not traveled on my *nom de guerre* enough to hurt. Such was the reminiscence I was moved to contribute, Mr. Chairman. In my enthusiasm I may have exaggerated the details a little, but you will easily forgive me that fault, since I believe it is the first time I have ever deflected from the perpendicular fact on an occasion like this.

It is a pity that Twain did not leave "Frescoes from the Past" where it belonged—in *Huckleberry Finn.* For if transposing the chapter enriched *Life on the Mississippi,* it robbed the novel of an episode of great beauty and humor, which sets forth, in the parable about Dick Allbright, the two great themes of Huck's journey down the river: death and rebirth by water, and the search for the father.

From *Life on the Mississippi*

Chapter III
Frescoes from the Past

. . . . By way of illustrating keelboat talk and manners, and that now departed and hardly remembered raft life, I will throw in, in this place, a chapter from a book which I have been working at, by fits and starts, during the past five or six years, and may possibly finish in the course of five or six more. The book is a story which details some passages in the life of an ignorant village boy, Huck Finn, son of the town drunkard of my time out West, there. He has run away from his persecuting father, and from a persecuting good widow who wishes to make a nice, truth-telling, respectable boy of him; and with him a slave of the widow's has also escaped. They have found a fragment of a lumber-raft (it is high water and dead summer-time), and are floating down the river by night, and hiding in the willows by day—bound for Cairo, whence the negro will seek freedom in the heart of the free states. But, in a fog, they pass Cairo without knowing it. By and by they begin to suspect the truth, and Huck Finn is persuaded to end the dismal suspense by swimming down to a huge raft which they have seen in the distance ahead of them, creeping aboard under cover of the darkness, and gathering the needed information by eavesdropping:

But you know a young person can't wait very well when he is impatient to find a thing out. We talked it over, and by and by Jim said it was such a black night, now, that it wouldn't be no risk to swim down to the big raft and crawl aboard and listen—they would talk about Cairo, because they would be calculating to go ashore there for a spree, maybe; or anyway they would send boats ashore to buy whisky or fresh meat or something. Jim had a wonderful level head, for a nigger: he could most always start a good plan when you wanted one.

I stood up and shook my rags off and jumped into the river, and struck out for the raft's light. By and by, when I got down nearly to her, I eased up and went slow and cautious. But everything was all right—nobody at the sweeps. So I swum down along the raft till I was most abreast the camp-fire in the middle, then I crawled aboard and inched along and got in among some bundles of shingles on the weather side of the fire. There was thirteen men there—they was the watch on deck of course. And a mighty rough-looking lot, too. They had a jug, and tin cups, and they kept the jug moving. One man was singing—roaring, you may say; and it wasn't a nice song—for a parlor, anyway. He roared through his nose, and strung out the last word of every line very long. When he was done they all fetched a kind of Injun war-whoop, and then another was sung. It begun:

> "There was a woman in our towdn,
>   In our towdn did dwed'l [dwell],
>   She loved her husband dear-i-lee,
>   But another man twyste as wed'l.

> "Singing too, riloo, riloo, riloo,
>   Ri-too, riloo, rilay—e,
>   She loved her husband dear-i-lee,
>   But another man twyste as wed'l."

And so on—fourteen verses. It was kind of poor, and when he was going to start on the next verse one of them said it was the tune the old cow died on; and another one said: "Oh, give us a rest!" And another one told him to take a walk. They made fun of him till he got mad and jumped up and begun to cuss the crowd, and said he could lam any thief in the lot.

They was all about to make a break for him, but the biggest man there jumped up and says:

"Set whar you are, gentlemen. Leave him to me; he's my meat."

Then he jumped up in the air three times, and cracked his heels together every time. He flung off a buckskin coat that was all hung with fringes, and says, "You lay thar tell the chawin-up's done"; and flung his hat down, which was all over ribbons, and says, "You lay thar tell his sufferin's is over."

Then he jumped in the air and cracked his heels together again, and shouted out:

"Whoo-oop! I'm the old original iron-jawed, brass-mounted, copper-bellied corpse-maker from the wilds of Arkansaw! Look at me! I'm the man they call Sudden Death and General Desolation! Sired by a hurricane, dam'd by an earthquake, half-brother to the cholera, nearly related to the smallpox on the mother's side! Look at me! I take nineteen alligators and a bar'l of whisky for breakfast when I'm in robust health, and a bushel of rattlesnakes and a dead body when I'm ailing. I split the everlasting rocks with my glance, and I squench the thunder when I speak! Whoo-oop! Stand back and give me room according to my strength! Blood's my natural drink, and the wails of the dying is music to my ear. Cast your eye on me, gentlemen! and lay low and hold your breath, for I'm 'bout to turn myself loose!"

All the time he was getting this off, he was shaking his head and looking fierce, and kind of swelling around in a little circle, tucking up his wristbands, and now and then straightening up and beating his breast with his fist, saying, "Look at me, gentlemen!" When he got through, he jumped up and cracked his heels together three times, and let off a roaring "Whoo-oop! I'm the bloodiest son of a wildcat that lives!"

Then the man that had started the row tilted his old slouch hat down over his right eye; then he bent stooping forward, with his back sagged and his south end sticking out far, and his fists a-shoving out and drawing in front of him, and so went around in a little circle about three times, swelling himself up and breathing hard. Then he straightened, and jumped up and cracked his heels together three times before he lit again (that made them cheer), and he began to shout like this:

"Whoo-oop! bow your neck and spread, for the kingdom of sorrow's a-coming! Hold me down to the earth, for I feel my powers a-working! Whoo-oop! I'm a child of sin, *don't* let me get a start! Smoked glass, here for all! Don't attempt to look at me with the naked eye, gentlemen! When I'm playful I use the meridians of longitude and parallels of latitude for a seine and drag the Atlantic Ocean for whales! I scratch my head with the lightning and purr myself to sleep with the thunder! When I'm cold, I bile the Gulf of Mexico and bathe in it; when I'm hot I fan myself with an equinoctial storm; when I'm thirsty I reach up and suck a cloud dry like a sponge; when I range the earth hungry, famine follows in my tracks! Whoo-oop! Bow your neck and spread! I put my hand on the sun's face and make it night in the earth; I bite a piece out of the moon and hurry the seasons; I shake myself and crumble the mountains! Contemplate me through leather—*don't* use the naked eye! I'm the man with a petrified heart and biler-iron bowels! The massacre of isolated communities is the pastime of my idle moments, the destruction of nationalities the serious business of my life! The boundless vastness of the great American desert is my inclosed property, and I bury my dead on my own premises!" He jumped up and cracked his heels together three times before he lit (they cheered him again), and as he come down he shouted out: "Whoo-oop! bow your neck and spread, for the Pet Child of Calamity's a-coming!"

Then the other one went to swelling around and blowing again—the first one—the one they called Bob; next, the Child of Calamity chipped in again, bigger than ever; then they both got at it at the same time, swelling round and round each other and punching their fists most into each other's faces, and whooping and jawing like Injuns; then Bob called the Child names, and the Child called him names back again; next, Bob called him a heap rougher names, and the Child come back at him with the very worst kind of language; next, Bob knocked the Child's hat off, and the Child picked it up and kicked Bob's ribbony hat about six foot; Bob went and got it and said never mind, this warn't going to be the last of this thing, because he was a man that never forgot and never forgive, and so the Child better look out, for there was a time a-coming, just as sure as he was a living man, that he would have to answer to him with the best blood in his body. The Child said no man was willinger than he for that time to come, and he would give Bob fair warning, *now*, never to cross his path again, for he could never rest till he had waded in his blood, for such was his nature, though he was sparing him now on account of his family, if he had one.

Both of them was edging away in different directions, growling and shaking their heads and going on about what

they was going to do; but a little black-whiskered chap
skipped up and says:

"Come back here, you couple of chicken-livered cowards,
and I'll thrash the two of ye!"

And he done it, too. He snatched them, he jerked them
this way and that, he booted them around, he knocked
them sprawling faster than they could get up. Why, it
warn't two minutes till they begged like dogs—and how
the other lot did yell and laugh and clap their hands all the
way through, and shout, "Sail in, Corpse-Maker!" "Hi! at
him again, Child of Calamity!" "Bully for you, little Davy!"
Well, it was a perfect pow-wow for a while. Bob and the
Child had red noses and black eyes when they got through.
Little Davy made them own up that they was sneaks and
cowards and not fit to eat with a dog or drink with a nigger;
then Bob and the Child shook hands with each other, very
solemn, and said they had always respected each other and
was willing to let bygones be bygones. So then they
washed their faces in the river; and just then there was a
loud order to stand by for a crossing, and some of them
went forward to man the sweeps there, and the rest went
aft to handle the after sweeps.

I lay still and waited for fifteen minutes, and had a smoke
out of a pipe that one of them left in reach; then the crossing was finished, and they stumped back and had a drink
around and went to talking and singing again. Next they
got out an old fiddle, and one played, and another patted
juba, and the rest turned themselves loose on a regular old-
fashioned keelboat breakdown. They couldn't keep that up
very long without getting winded, so by and by they settled around the jug again.

They sung "Jolly, Jolly Raftsman's the Life for Me," with
a rousing chorus, and then they got to talking about differences betwixt hogs, and their different kind of habits; and
next about women and their different ways; and next about
the best ways to put out houses that was afire; and next
about what ought to be done with the Injuns; and next
about what a king had to do, and how much he got; and
next about how to make cats fight; and next about what

to do when a man has fits; and next about differences betwixt clear-water rivers and muddy-water ones. The man
they called Ed said the muddy Mississippi water was
wholesomer to drink than the clear water of the Ohio; he
said if you let a pint of this yaller Mississippi water settle,
you have about a half to three-quarters of an inch of mud
in the bottom, according to the stage of the river, and then
it warn't no better than Ohio water—what you wanted to
do was to keep it stirred up—and when the river was low,
keep mud on hand to put in and thicken the water up the
way it ought to be.

The Child of Calamity said that was so; he said there
was nutritiousness in the mud, and a man that drunk Mississippi water could grow corn in his stomach if he wanted
to. He says:

"You look at the graveyards; that tells the tale. Trees
won't grow worth shucks in a Cincinnati graveyard, but in
a Sent Louis graveyard they grow upwards of eight hundred foot high. It's all on account of the water the people
drunk before they laid up. A Cincinnati corpse don't richen
a soil any."

And they talked about how Ohio water didn't like to
mix with Mississippi water. Ed said if you take the Mississippi on a rise when the Ohio is low, you'll find a wide
band of clear water all the way down the east side of the
Mississippi for a hundred mile or more, and the minute you
get out a quarter of a mile from shore and pass the line,
it is all thick and yaller the rest of the way across. Then
they talked about how to keep tobacco from getting moldy,
and from that they went into ghosts and told about a lot
that other folks had seen; but Ed says:

"Why don't you tell something that you've seen yourselves? Now let me have a say. Five years ago I was on a
raft as big as this, and right along here it was a bright
moonshiny night, and I was on watch and boss of the stabboard oar forrard, and one of my pards was a man named
Dick Allbright, and he come along to where I was sitting,
forrard—gaping and stretching, he was—and stooped down
on the edge of the raft and washed his face in the river,

and come and set down by me and got out his pipe, and had just got it filled, when he looks up and says:

"'Why looky-here,' he says, 'ain't that Buck Miller's place, over yander in the bend?'

"'Yes,' says I, 'it is—why?' He laid his pipe down and leaned his head on his hand, and says:

"'I thought we'd be furder down.' I says:

"'I thought it, too, when I went off watch'—we was standing six hours on and six off—'but the boys told me,' I says, 'that the raft didn't seem to hardly move, for the last hour,' says I, 'though she's a-slipping along all right now,' says I. He give a kind of groan, and says:

"'I've seed a raft act so before, along here,' he says, ''pears to me the current has most quit above the head of this bend durin' the last two years,' he says.

"Well, he raised up two or three times, and looked away off and around on the water. That started me at it, too. A body is always doing what he sees somebody else doing, though there mayn't be no sense in it. Pretty soon I see a black something floating on the water away off to stabboard and quartering behind us. I see he was looking at it, too. I says:

"'What's that?' He says, sort of pettish:

"''Tain't nothing but an old empty bar'l.'

"'An empty bar'l!' says I, 'why,' says I, 'a spy-glass is a fool to *your* eyes. How can you tell it's an empty bar'l?' He says:

"'I don't know; I reckon it ain't a bar'l, but I thought it might be,' says he.

"'Yes,' I says, 'so it might be, and it might be anything else, too; a body can't tell nothing about it, such a distance as that,' I says.

"We hadn't nothing else to do, so we kept watching it. By and by I says:

"'Why looky-here, Dick Allbright, that thing's a-gaining on us, I believe.'

"He never said nothing. The thing gained and gained, and I judged it must be a dog that was about tired out. Well, we swung down into the crossing, and the thing floated across the bright streak of the moonshine, and by George, it *was* a bar'l. Says I:

" 'Dick Allbright, what made you think that thing was a bar'l, when it was half a mile off?' says I. Says he:

" 'I don't know.' Says I:

" 'You tell me, Dick Allbright.' Says he:

" 'Well, I knowed it was a bar'l; I've seen it before; lots has seen it; they says it's a ha'nted bar'l.'

"I called the rest of the watch, and they come and stood there, and I told them what Dick said. It floated right along abreast, now, and didn't gain any more. It was about twenty foot off. Some was for having it aboard, but the rest didn't want to. Dick Allbright said rafts that had fooled with it had got bad luck by it. The captain of the watch said he didn't believe in it. He said he reckoned the bar'l gained on us because it was in a little better current than what we was. He said it would leave by and by.

"So then we went to talking about other things, and we had a song, and then a breakdown; and after that the captain of the watch called for another song; but it was clouding up now, and the bar'l stuck right thar in the same place, and the song didn't seem to have much warm-up to it, somehow, and so they didn't finish it, and there warn't any cheers, but it sort of dropped flat, and nobody said anything for a minute. Then everybody tried to talk at once, and one chap got off a joke, but it warn't no use, they didn't laugh, and even the chap that made the joke didn't laugh at it, which ain't usual. We all just settled down glum, and watched the bar'l, and was oneasy and oncomfortable. Well, sir, it shut down black and still, and the wind began to moan around, and next the lightning began to play and the thunder to grumble. And pretty soon there was a regular storm, and in the middle of it a man that was running aft stumbled and fell and sprained his ankle so that he had to lay up. This made the boys shake their heads. And every time the lightning come, there was that bar'l with the blue lights winking around it. We was always on the lookout for it. But by and by, toward dawn, she was gone. When the day come we couldn't see her anywhere, and we warn't sorry, either.

"But the next night about half past nine, when there was songs and high jinks going on, here she comes again, and took her old roost on the stabboard side. There warn't no more high jinks. Everybody got solemn; nobody talked; you couldn't get anybody to do anything but set around moody and look at the bar'l. It begun to cloud up again. When the watch changed, the off watch stayed up, 'stead of turning in. The storm ripped and roared around all night, and in the middle of it another man tripped and sprained his ankle, and had to knock off. The bar'l left toward day, and nobody see it go.

"Everybody was sober and down in the mouth all day. I don't mean the kind of sober that comes of leaving liquor alone—not that. They was quiet, but they all drunk more than usual—not together, but each man sidled off and took it in private, by himself.

"After dark the off watch didn't turn in; nobody sung, nobody talked; the boys didn't scatter around, neither; they sort of huddled together, forrard; and for two hours they set there, perfectly still, looking steady in the one direction, and heaving a sigh once in a while. And then, here comes the bar'l again. She took up her old place. She stayed there all night; nobody turned in. The storm come on again, after midnight. It got awful dark; the rain poured down; hail, too; the thunder boomed and roared and bellowed; the wind blowed like a hurricane; and the lightning spread over everything in big sheets of glare, and showed the whole raft as plain as day; and the river lashed up white as milk as far as you could see for miles, and there was that bar'l jiggering along, same as ever. The captain ordered the watch to man the after sweeps for a crossing, and nobody would go—no more sprained ankles for them, they said. They wouldn't even *walk* aft. Well, then, just then the sky split wide open, with a crash, and the lightning killed two men of the after watch, and crippled two more. Crippled them how, say you? Why, *sprained their ankles!*

"'The bar'l left in the dark betwixt lightnings, toward

dawn. Well, not a body eat a bite at breakfast that morning. After that the men loafed around, in twos and threes, and talked low together. But none of them herded with Dick Allbright. They all give him the cold shake. If he come around where any of the men was, they split up and sidled away. They wouldn't man the sweeps with him. The captain had all the skiffs hauled up on the raft, alongside of his wigwam, and wouldn't let the dead men be took ashore to be planted; he didn't believe a man that got ashore would come back; and he was right.

"After night come, you could see pretty plain that there was going to be trouble if that bar'l come again; there was such a muttering going on. A good many wanted to kill Dick Allbright, because he'd seen the bar'l on other trips, and that had an ugly look. Some wanted to put him ashore. Some said: 'Let's all go ashore in a pile, if the bar'l comes again.'

"This kind of whispers was still going on, the men being bunched together forrard watching for the bar'l, when lo and behold you! here she comes again. Down she comes, slow and steady, and settles into her old tracks. You could 'a' heard a pin drop. Then up comes the captain, and says:

"'Boys, don't be a pack of children and fools; I don't want this bar'l to be dogging us all the way to Orleans, and *you* don't: Well, then, how's the best way to stop it? Burn it up—that's the way. I'm going to fetch it aboard,' he says. And before anybody could say a word, in he went.

"He swum to it, and as he come pushing it to the raft, the men spread to one side. But the old man got it aboard and busted in the head, and there was a baby in it! Yes, sir; a stark-naked baby. It was Dick Allbright's baby; he owned up and said so.

"'Yes,' he says, a-leaning over it, 'yes, it is my own lamented darling, my poor lost Charles William Allbright deceased,' says he—for he could curl his tongue around the bulliest words in the language when he was a mind to, and lay them before you without a jint started anywheres. Yes, he said, he used to live up at the head of this bend, and one night he choked his child, which was crying, not intending to kill it—which was prob'ly a lie—and then he was scared, and buried it in a bar'l, before his wife got home, and off he went, and struck the northern trail and went to rafting; and this was the third year that the bar'l had chased him. He said the bad luck always begun light, and lasted till four men was killed, and then the bar'l didn't come any more after that. He said if the men would stand it one more night—and was a-going on like that—but the men had got enough. They started to get out a boat to take him ashore and lynch him, but he grabbed the little child all of a sudden and jumped overboard with it, hugged up to his breast and shedding tears, and we never seed him again in this life, poor old suffering soul, nor Charles William neither."

"*Who* was shedding tears?" says Bob; "was it Allbright or the baby?"

"Why, Allbright, of course; didn't I tell you the baby was dead? Been dead three years—how could it cry?"

"Well, never mind how it could cry—how could it *keep* all that time?" says Davy. "You answer me that."

"I don't know how it done it," says Ed. "It done it, though—that's all I know about it."

"Say—what did they do with the bar'l?" says the Child of Calamity.

"Why, they hove it overboard, and it sunk like a chunk of lead."

"Edward, did the child look like it was choked?" says one.

"Did it have its hair parted?" says another.

"What was the brand on that bar'l, Eddy?" says a fellow they called Bill.

"Have you got the papers for them statistics, Edmund?" says Jimmy.

"Say, Edwin, was you one of the men that was killed by the lightning?" says Davy.

"Him? Oh, no! he was both of 'em," says Bob. Then they all haw-hawed.

"Say, Edward, don't you reckon you'd better take a pill?

You look bad—don't you feel pale?" says the Child of Calamity.

"Oh, come, now, Eddy," says Jimmy, "show up; you must 'a' kept part of that bar'l to prove the thing by. Show us the bunghole—*do*—and we'll all believe you."

"Say, boys," says Bill, "less divide it up. Thar's thirteen of us. I can swaller a thirteenth of the yarn, if you can worry down the rest."

Ed got up mad and said they could all go to some place which he ripped out pretty savage, and then walked off aft, cussing to himself, and they yelling and jeering at him, and roaring and laughing so you could hear them a mile.

"Boys, we'll split a watermelon on that," says the Child of Calamity; and he came rummaging around in the dark amongst the shingle bundles where I was, and put his hand on me. I was warm and soft and naked; so he says "Ouch!" and jumped back.

"Fetch a lantern or a chunk of fire here, boys—there's a snake here as big as a cow!"

So they run there with a lantern, and crowded up and looked in on me.

"Come out of that, you beggar!" says one.

"Who are you?" says another.

"What are you after here? Speak up prompt, or overboard you go."

"Snake him out, boys. Snatch him out by the heels."

I began to beg, and crept out amongst them trembling. They looked me over, wondering, and the Child of Calamity says:

"A cussed thief! Lend a hand and less heave him overboard!"

"No," says Big Bob, "less get out the paint-pot and paint him a sky-blue all over from head to heel, and *then* heave him over."

"Good! that's it. Go for the paint, Jimmy."

When the paint come, and Bob took the brush and was just going to begin, the others laughing and rubbing their hands, I begun to cry, and that sort of worked on Davy, and he says:

"'Vast there. He's nothing but a cub. I'll paint the man that teches him!"

So I looked around on them, and some of them grumbled and growled, and Bob put down the paint, and the others didn't take it up.

"Come here to the fire, and less see what you're up to here," says Davy. "Now set down there and give an account of yourself. How long have you been aboard here?"

"Not over a quarter of a minute, sir," says I.

"How did you get dry so quick?"

"I don't know, sir. I'm always that way, mostly."

"Oh, you are, are you? What's your name?"

I warn't going to tell my name. I didn't know what to say, so I just says:

"Charles William Allbright, sir."

Then they roared—the whole crowd; and I was mighty glad I said that, because, maybe, laughing would get them in a better humor.

When they got done laughing, Davy says:

"It won't hardly do, Charles William. You couldn't have growed this much in five year, and you was a baby when you come out of the bar'l, you know, and dead at that. Come, now, tell a straight story, and nobody'll hurt you, if you ain't up to anything wrong. What *is* your name?"

"Aleck Hopkins, sir. Aleck James Hopkins."

"Well, Aleck, where did you come from, here?"

"From a trading-scow. She lays up the bend yonder. I was born on her. Pap has traded up and down here all his life; and he told me to swim off here, because when you went by he said he would like to get some of you to speak to a Mr. Jonas Turner, in Cairo, and tell him——"

"Oh, come!"

"Yes, sir, it's as true as the world. Pap he says——"

"Oh, your grandmother!"

They all laughed, and I tried again to talk, but they broke in on me and stopped me.

"Now, looky-here," says Davy; "you're scared, and so you talk wild. Honest, now, do you live in a scow, or is it a lie?"

"Yes, sir, in a trading-scow. She lays up at the head of the bend. But I warn't born in her. It's our first trip."

"Now you're talking! What did you come aboard here for? To steal?"

"No, sir, I didn't. It was only to get a ride on the raft. All boys does that."

"Well, I know that. But what did you hide for?"

"Sometimes they drive the boys off."

"So they do. They might steal. Looky-here; if we let you off this time, will you keep out of these kind of scrapes hereafter?"

" 'Deed I will, boss. You try me."

"All right, then. You ain't but little ways from shore. Overboard with you, and don't you make a fool of yourself another time this way. Blast it, boy, some raftsmen would rawhide you till you were black and blue!"

I didn't wait to kiss good-by, but went overboard and broke for shore. When Jim come along by and by, the big raft was away out of sight around the point. I swum out and got aboard, and was mighty glad to see home again.

The boy did not get the information he was after, but his adventure has furnished the glimpse of the departed raftsman and keelboatman which I desire to offer in this place.

Clearly, Twain was wrong about Cooper—the real Cooper, that is. He never understood the mythological nature of Cooper's art, never appreciated the variety of moods, from serenity to horror, that Cooper could evoke in his descriptions of forest, lake, and prairie. But Cooper to Twain was not so much an author as the symbol of a romantic culture's disastrous blindness to the lurking dangers of the world, a blindness which in Twain's view had produced the tragedy of the Civil War. Written in the early 1890s, at a time when many American writers were publishing their literary credos, "Fenimore Cooper's Literary Offenses" ranks with Howells's *Criticism and Fiction* as one of the two great programmatic statements of post-Civil War American realism.

Fenimore Cooper's Literary Offenses

> *The Pathfinder* and *The Deerslayer* stand at the head of Cooper's novels as artistic creations. There are others of his works which contain parts as perfect as are to be found in these, and scenes even more thrilling. Not one can be compared with either of them as a finished whole.
>
> The defects in both of these tales are comparatively slight. They were pure works of art. *Prof. Lounsbury.*
>
> The five tales reveal an extraordinary fullness of invention.
>
> . . . One of the very greatest characters in fiction, Natty Bumppo. . . .
>
> The craft of the woodsman, the tricks of the trapper, all the delicate art of the forest, were familiar to Cooper from his youth up. *Prof. Brander Matthews.*
>
> Cooper is the greatest artist in the domain of romantic fiction yet produced by America. *Wilkie Collins.*

It seems to me that it was far from right for the Professor of English Literature in Yale, the Professor of English Literature in Columbia, and Wilkie Collins to deliver opinions on Cooper's literature without having read some of it. It would have been much more decorous to keep silent and let persons talk who have read Cooper.

Cooper's art has some defects. In one place in *Deerslayer*, and in the restricted space of two-thirds of a page, Cooper has scored 114 offenses against literary art out of a possible 115. It breaks the record.

There are nineteen rules governing literary art in the domain of romantic fiction—some say twenty-two. In *Deer-*

slayer Cooper violated eighteen of them. These eighteen require:

1. That a tale shall accomplish something and arrive somewhere. But the *Deerslayer* tale accomplishes nothing and arrives in the air.

2. They require that the episodes of a tale shall be necessary parts of the tale, and shall help to develop it. But as the *Deerslayer* tale is not a tale, and accomplishes nothing and arrives nowhere, the episodes have no rightful place in the work, since there was nothing for them to develop.

3. They require that the personages in a tale shall be alive, except in the case of corpses, and that always the reader shall be able to tell the corpses from the others. But this detail has often been overlooked in the *Deerslayer* tale.

4. They require that the personages in a tale, both dead and alive, shall exhibit a sufficient excuse for being there. But this detail also has been overlooked in the *Deerslayer* tale.

5. They require that when the personages of a tale deal in conversation, the talk shall sound like human talk, and be talk such as human beings would be likely to talk in the given circumstances, and have a discoverable meaning, also a discoverable purpose, and a show of relevancy, and remain in the neighborhood of the subject in hand, and be interesting to the reader, and help out the tale, and stop when the people cannot think of anything more to say. But this requirement has been ignored from the beginning of the *Deerslayer* tale to the end of it.

6. They require that when the author describes the character of a personage in his tale, the conduct and conversation of that personage shall justify said description. But this law gets little or no attention in the *Deerslayer* tale, as Natty Bumppo's case will amply prove.

7. They require that when a personage talks like an illustrated, gilt-edged, tree-calf, hand-tooled, seven-dollar Friendship's Offering in the beginning of a paragraph, he shall not talk like a negro minstrel in the end of it. But this rule is flung down and danced upon in the *Deerslayer* tale.

8. They require that crass stupidities shall not be played

upon the reader as "the craft of the woodsman, the delicate art of the forest," by either the author or the people in the tale. But this rule is persistently violated in the *Deerslayer* tale.

9. They require that the personages of a tale shall confine themselves to possibilities and let miracles alone; or, if they venture a miracle, the author must so plausibly set it forth as to make it look possible and reasonable. But these rules are not respected in the *Deerslayer* tale.

10. They require that the author shall make the reader feel a deep interest in the personages of his tale and in their fate; and that he shall make the reader love the good people in the tale and hate the bad ones. But the reader of the *Deerslayer* tale dislikes the good people in it, is indifferent to the others, and wishes they would all get drowned together.

11. They require that the characters in a tale shall be so clearly defined that the reader can tell beforehand what each will do in a given emergency. But in the *Deerslayer* tale this rule is vacated.

In addition to these large rules there are some little ones. These require that the author shall

12. *Say* what he is proposing to say, not merely come near it.

13. Use the right word, not its second cousin.

14. Eschew surplusage.

15. Not omit necessary details.

16. Avoid slovenliness of form.

17. Use good grammar.

18. Employ a simple and straightforward style.

Even these seven are coldly and persistently violated in the *Deerslayer* tale.

Cooper's gift in the way of invention was not a rich endowment; but such as it was he liked to work it, he was pleased with the effects, and indeed he did some quite sweet things with it. In his little box of stage-properties he kept six or eight cunning devices, tricks, artifices for his savages and woodsmen to deceive and circumvent each other with, and he was never so happy as when he was working these innocent things and seeing them go. A favorite one was to make a moccasined person tread in the tracks of the moccasined enemy, and thus hide his own trail. Cooper wore out barrels and barrels of moccasins in working that trick. Another stage-property that he pulled out of his box pretty frequently was his broken twig. He prized his broken twig above all the rest of his effects, and worked it the hardest. It is a restful chapter in any book of his when somebody doesn't step on a dry twig and alarm all the reds and whites for two hundred yards around. Every time a Cooper person is in peril, and absolute silence is worth four dollars a minute, he is sure to step on a dry twig. There may be a hundred handier things to step on, but that wouldn't satisfy Cooper. Cooper requires him to turn out and find a dry twig; and if he can't do it, go and borrow one. In fact, the Leatherstocking Series ought to have been called the Broken Twig Series.

I am sorry there is not room to put in a few dozen instances of the delicate art of the forest, as practised by Natty Bumppo and some of the other Cooperian experts. Perhaps we may venture two or three samples. Cooper was a sailor—a naval officer; yet he gravely tells us how a vessel, driving toward a lee shore in a gale, is steered for a particular spot by her skipper because he knows of an *undertow* there which will hold her back against the gale and save her. For just pure woodcraft, or sailorcraft, or whatever it is, isn't that neat? For several years Cooper was daily in the society of artillery, and he ought to have noticed that when a cannon-ball strikes the ground it either buries itself or skips a hundred feet or so; skips again a hundred feet or so—and so on, till finally it gets tired and rolls. Now in one place he loses some "females"—as he always calls women—in the edge of a wood near a plain at night in a fog, on purpose to give Bumppo a chance to show off the delicate art of the forest before the reader. These mislaid people are hunting for a fort. They hear a cannon-blast, and a cannon-ball presently comes rolling into the wood and stops at their feet. To the females this suggests nothing. The case is very different with the admirable Bumppo.

I wish I may never know peace again if he doesn't strike out promptly and *follow the track* of that cannon-ball across the plain through the dense fog and find the fort. Isn't it a daisy? If Cooper had any real knowledge of Nature's ways of doing things, he had a most delicate art in concealing the fact. For instance: one of his acute Indian experts, Chingachgook (pronounced Chicago, I think), has lost the trail of a person he is tracking through the forest. Apparently that trail is hopelessly lost. Neither you nor I could ever have guessed out the way to find it. It was very different with Chicago. Chicago was not stumped for long. He turned a running stream out of its course, and there, in the slush in its old bed, were that person's moccasin tracks. The current did not wash them away, as it would have done in all other like cases—no, even the eternal laws of Nature have to vacate when Cooper wants to put up a delicate job of woodcraft on the reader.

We must be a little wary when Brander Matthews tells us that Cooper's books "reveal an extraordinary fullness of invention." As a rule, I am quite willing to accept Brander Matthews's literary judgments and applaud his lucid and graceful phrasing of them; but that particular statement needs to be taken with a few tons of salt. Bless your heart, Cooper hadn't any more invention than a horse; and I don't mean a high-class horse, either; I mean a clothes-horse. It would be very difficult to find a really clever "situation" in Cooper's books, and still more difficult to find one of any kind which he has failed to render absurd by his handling of it. Look at the episodes of "the caves"; and at the celebrated scuffle between Magua and those others on the table-land a few days later; and at Hurry Harry's queer water-transit from the castle to the ark; and at Deerslayer's half-hour with his first corpse; and at the quarrel between Hurry Harry and Deerslayer later; and at—but choose for yourself; you can't go amiss.

If Cooper had been an observer his inventive faculty would have worked better; not more interestingly, but more rationally, more plausibly. Cooper's proudest creations in the way of "situations" suffer noticeably from the absence of the observer's protecting gift. Cooper's eye was splendidly inaccurate. Cooper seldom saw anything correctly. He saw nearly all things as through a glass eye, darkly. Of course a man who cannot see the commonest little every-day matters accurately is working at a disadvantage when he is constructing a "situation." In the *Deerslayer* tale Cooper has a stream which is fifty feet wide where it flows out of a lake; it presently narrows to twenty as it meanders along for no given reason, and yet when a stream acts like that it ought to be required to explain itself. Fourteen pages later the width of the brook's outlet from the lake has suddenly shrunk thirty feet, and become "the narrowest part of the stream." This shrinkage is not accounted for. The stream has bends in it, a sure indication that it has alluvial banks and cuts them; yet these bends are only thirty and fifty feet long. If Cooper had been a nice and punctilious observer he would have noticed that the bends were oftener nine hundred feet long than short of it.

Cooper made the exit of that stream fifty feet wide, in the first place, for no particular reason; in the second place, he narrowed it to less than twenty to accommodate some Indians. He bends a "sapling" to the form of an arch over this narrow passage, and conceals six Indians in its foliage. They are "laying" for a settler's scow or ark which is coming up the stream on its way to the lake; it is being hauled against the stiff current by a rope whose stationary end is anchored in the lake; its rate of progress cannot be more than a mile an hour. Cooper describes the ark, but pretty obscurely. In the matter of dimensions "it was little more than a modern canal-boat." Let us guess, then, that it was about one hundred and forty feet long. It was of "greater breadth than common." Let us guess, then, that it was about sixteen feet wide. This leviathan had been prowling down bends which were but a third as long as itself, and scraping between banks where it had only two feet of space to spare on each side. We cannot too much admire this miracle. A low-roofed log dwelling occupies "two-thirds of the ark's length"—a dwelling ninety feet long and sixteen feet wide, let us say—a kind of vestibule train. The dwelling has two rooms—each forty-five feet long and sixteen feet wide, let us guess. One of them is the bedroom of the Hutter girls, Judith and Hetty; the other is the parlor in the daytime, at night it is papa's bedchamber. The ark is arriving at the stream's exit now, whose width has been reduced to less than twenty feet to accommodate the Indians—say to eighteen. There is a foot to spare on each side of the boat. Did the Indians notice that there was going to be a tight squeeze there? Did they notice that they could make money by climbing down out of that arched sapling and just stepping aboard when the ark scraped by? No, other Indians would have noticed these things, but Cooper's Indians never notice anything. Cooper thinks they are marvelous creatures for noticing, but he was almost always in error about his Indians. There was seldom a sane one among them.

The ark is one hundred and forty-feet long; the dwelling is ninety feet long. The idea of the Indians is to drop softly and secretly from the arched sapling to the dwelling as the ark creeps along under it at the rate of a mile an hour, and butcher the family. It will take the ark a minute and a half to pass under. It will take the ninety-foot dwelling a minute to pass under. Now, then, what did the six Indians do? It would take you thirty years to guess, and even then you would have to give it up, I believe. Therefore, I will tell you what the Indians did. Their chief, a person of quite extraordinary intellect for a Cooper Indian, warily watched the canal-boat as it squeezed along under him, and when he had got his calculations fined down to exactly the right shade, as he judged, he let go and dropped. And *missed the house!* That is actually what he did. He missed the house, and landed in the stern of the scow. It was not much of a fall, yet it knocked him silly. He lay there unconscious. If the house had been ninety-seven feet long he would have made the trip. The fault was Cooper's not his. The error lay in the construction of the house. Cooper was no architect.

There still remained in the roost five Indians. The boat has passed under and is now out of their reach. Let me

explain what the five did—you would not be able to reason
it out for yourself. No. 1 jumped for the boat, but fell in
the water astern of it. Then No. 2 jumped for the boat,
but fell in the water still farther astern of it. Then No. 3
jumped for the boat, and fell a good way astern of it. Then
No. 4 jumped for the boat, and fell in the water *away*
astern. Then even No. 5 made a jump for the boat—for he
was a Cooper Indian. In the matter of intellect, the difference between a Cooper Indian and the Indian that stands
in front of a cigar-shop is not spacious. The scow episode
is really a sublime burst of invention; but it does not thrill,
because the inaccuracy of the details throws a sort of air
of factitiousness and general improbability over it. This
comes of Cooper's inadequacy as an observer.

The reader will find some examples of Cooper's high
talent for inaccurate observation in the account of the
shooting-match in *The Pathfinder*.

A common wrought nail was driven lightly into the target, its head having been first touched with paint.

The color of the paint is not stated—an important omission, but Cooper deals freely in important omissions. No,
after all, it was not an important omission; for this nail-head
is a *hundred yards from* the marksmen, and could not be
seen by them at that distance, no matter what its color
might be. How far can the best eyes see a common house-
fly? A hundred yards? It is quite impossible. Very well; eyes
that cannot see a house-fly that is a hundred yards away
cannot see an ordinary nail-head at that distance, for the
size of the two objects is the same. It takes a keen eye to
see a fly or a nail-head at fifty yards—one hundred and fifty
feet. Can the reader do it?

The nail was lightly driven, its head painted, and game
called. Then the Cooper miracles began. The bullet of the
first marksman chipped an edge of the nail-head; the next
man's bullet drove the nail a little way into the target—
and removed all the paint. Haven't the miracles gone far
enough now? Not to suit Cooper; for the purpose of this
whole scheme is to show off his prodigy, Deerslayer-Hawk-

eye-Long-Rifle-Leatherstocking-Pathfinder-Bumppo before the ladies.

"Be all ready to clench it, boys!" cried the Pathfinder, stepping into his friend's tracks the instant they were vacant. "Never mind a new nail; I can see that, though the paint is gone, and what I can see I can hit at a hundred yards, though it were only a mosquito's eye. Be ready to clench!"

The rifle cracked, the bullet sped its way, and the head of the nail was buried in the wood, covered by the piece of flattened lead.

There, you see, is a man who could hunt flies with a rifle, and command a ducal salary in a Wild West show today if we had him back with us.

The recorded feat is certainly surprising just as it stands; but it is not surprising enough for Cooper. Cooper adds a touch. He has made Pathfinder do this miracle with another man's rifle; and not only that, but Pathfinder did not have even the advantage of loading it himself. He had everything against him, and yet he made that impossible shot; and not only made it, but did it with absolute confidence, saying, "Be ready to clench." Now a person like that would have undertaken that same feat with a brickbat, and with Cooper to help he would have achieved it, too.

Pathfinder showed off handsomely that day before the ladies. His very first feat was a thing which no Wild West show can touch. He was standing with the group of marksmen, observing—a hundred yards from the target, mind; one Jasper raised his rifle and drove the center of the bull's-eye. Then the Quartermaster fired. The target exhibited no result this time. There was a laugh. "It's a dead miss," said Major Lundie. Pathfinder waited an impressive moment or two; then said, in that calm, indifferent, know-it-all way of his, "No, Major, he has covered Jasper's bullet, as will be seen if any one will take the trouble to examine the target."

Wasn't it remarkable! How *could* he see that little pellet fly through the air and enter that distant bullet-hole? Yet that is what he did; for nothing is impossible to a Cooper person. Did any of those people have any deep-seated doubts about this thing? No; for that would imply sanity, and these were all Cooper people.

The respect for Pathfinder's skill and for his *quickness and accuracy of sight* [the italics are mine] was so profound and general, that the instant he made this declaration the spectators began to distrust their own opinions, and a dozen rushed to the target in order to ascertain the fact. There, sure enough, it was found that the Quartermaster's bullet had gone through the hole made by Jasper's, and that, too, so accurately as to require a minute examination to be certain of the circumstance, which, however, was soon clearly established by discovering one bullet over the other in the stump against which the target was placed.

They made a "minute" examination; but never mind, how could they know that there were two bullets in that hole without digging the latest one out? for neither probe nor eyesight could prove the presence of any more than one bullet. Did they dig? No; as we shall see. It is the Pathfinder's turn now; he steps out before the ladies, takes aim, and fires.

"If one dared to hint at such a thing," cried Major Duncan, "I should say that the Pathfinder has also missed the target!"

As nobody had missed it yet, the "also" was not necessary; but never mind about that, for the Pathfinder is going to speak.

"No, no, Major," said he, confidently, "that *would* be a risky declaration. I didn't load the piece, and can't say what was in it; but if it was lead, you will find the bullet driving down those of the Quartermaster and Jasper, else is not my name Pathfinder."

A shout from the target announced the truth of this assertion.

Is the miracle sufficient as it stands? Not for Cooper. The

Pathfinder speaks again, as he "now slowly advances toward the stage occupied by the females":

"That's not all, boys, that's not all; if you find the target touched at all, I'll own a miss. The Quartermaster cut the wood, but you'll find no wood cut by that last messenger."

The miracle is at last complete. He knew—doubtless *saw* —at the distance of a hundred yards—that his bullet had passed into the hole *without fraying the edges.* There were now three bullets in that one hole—three bullets embedded processionally in the body of the stump back of the target. Everybody knew this—somehow or other—and yet nobody had dug any of them out to make sure. Cooper is not a close observer, but he is interesting. He is certainly always that, no matter what happens. And he is more interesting when he is not noticing what he is about than when he is. This is a considerable merit.

The conversations in the Cooper books have a curious sound in our modern ears. To believe that such talk really ever came out of people's mouths would be to believe that there was a time when time was of no value to a person who thought he had something to say; when it was the custom to spread a two-minute remark out to ten; when a man's mouth was a rolling-mill, and busied itself all day long in turning four-foot pigs of thought into thirty-foot bars of conversational railroad iron by attenuation; when subjects were seldom faithfully stuck to, but the talk wandered all around and arrived nowhere; when conversations consisted mainly of irrelevancies, with here and there a relevancy, a relevancy with an embarrassed look, as not being able to explain how it got there.

Cooper was certainly not a master in the construction of dialogue. Inaccurate observation defeated him here as it defeated him in so many other enterprises of his. He even failed to notice that the man who talks corrupt English six days in the week must and will talk it on the seventh, and can't help himself. In the *Deerslayer* story he lets Deerslayer talk the showiest kind of book-talk sometimes, and at other times the basest of base dialects. For instance, when some one asks him if he has a sweetheart, and if so, where she abides, this is his majestic answer:

"She's in the forest—hanging from the boughs of the trees, in a soft rain—in the dew on the open grass—the clouds that float about in the blue heavens—the birds that sing in the woods—the sweet springs where I slake my thirst—and in all the other glorious gifts that come from God's Providence!"

And he preceded that, a little before, with this:

"It consarns me as all things that touches a fri'nd consarns a fri'nd."

And this is another of his remarks:

"If I was Injin born, now, I might tell of this, or carry in the scalp and boast of the expl'ite afore the whole tribe; or if my inimy had only been a bear"—[and so on].

We cannot imagine such a thing as a veteran Scotch Commander-in-Chief comporting himself in the field like a windy melodramatic actor, but Cooper could. On one occasion Alice and Cora were being chased by the French through a fog in the neighborhood of their father's fort:

"Point de quartier aux coquins!" cried an eager pursuer, who seemed to direct the operations of the enemy.

"Stand firm and be ready, my gallant 60ths!" suddenly exclaimed a voice above them; "wait to see the enemy; fire low, and sweep the glacis."

"Father! father!" exclaimed a piercing cry from out the mist; "it is I! Alice! thy own Elsie! spare, O! save your daughters!"

"Hold!" shouted the former speaker, in the awful tones of parental agony, the sound reaching even to the woods, and rolling back in solemn echo. " 'Tis she! God has restored me my children! Throw open the sally-port; to the field, 60ths, to the field! pull not a trigger, lest ye kill my lambs! Drive off these dogs of France with your steel!"

Cooper's word-sense was singularly dull. When a person has a poor ear for music he will flat and sharp right along without knowing it. He keeps near the tune, but it is *not* the tune. When a person has a poor ear for words, the result is a literary flatting and sharping; you perceive what he is intending to say, but you also perceive that he doesn't *say* it. This is Cooper. He was not a word-musician. His ear was satisfied with the *approximate* word. I will furnish some circumstantial evidence in support of this charge. My instances are gathered from half a dozen pages of the tale called *Deerslayer*. He uses "verbal" for "oral"; "precision" for "facility"; "phenomena" for "marvels"; "necessary" for "predetermined"; "unsophisticated" for "primitive"; "preparation" for "expectancy"; "rebuked" for "subdued"; "dependent on" for "resulting from"; "fact" for "condition"; "fact" for "conjecture"; "precaution" for "caution"; "explain" for "determine"; "mortified" for "disappointed"; "meretricious" for "factitious"; "materially" for "considerably"; "decreasing" for "deepening"; "increasing" for "disappearing"; "embedded" for "inclosed"; "treacherous" for "hostile"; "stood" for "stooped"; "softened" for "replaced"; "rejoined" for "remarked"; "situation" for "condition"; "different" for "differing"; "insensible" for "unsentient"; "brevity" for "celerity"; "distrusted" for "suspicious"; "mental imbecility" for "imbecility"; "eyes" for "sight"; "counteracting" for "opposing"; "funeral obsequies" for "obsequies."

There have been daring people in the world who claimed that Cooper could write English, but they are all dead now —all dead but Lounsbury. I don't remember that Lounsbury makes the claim in so many words, still he makes it, for he says that *Deerslayer* is a "pure work of art." Pure, in that connection, means faultless—faultless in all details—and language is a detail. If Mr. Lounsbury had only compared Cooper's English with the English which he writes himself —but it is plain that he didn't; and so it is likely that he imagines until this day that Cooper's is as clean and compact as his own. Now I feel sure, deep down in my heart, that Cooper wrote about the poorest English that exists in our language, and that the English of *Deerslayer* is the very worst that even Cooper ever wrote.

I may be mistaken, but it does seem to me that *Deerslayer* is not a work of art in any sense; it does seem to me that it is destitute of every detail that goes to the making of a work of art; in truth, it seems to me that *Deerslayer* is just simply a literary *delirium tremens*.

A work of art? It has no invention; it has no order, system, sequence, or result; it has no life-likeness, no thrill, no stir, no seeming of reality; its characters are confusedly drawn, and by their acts and words they prove that they are not the sort of people the author claims they are; its humor is pathetic; its pathos is funny; its conversations are —oh! indescribable; its love-scenes odious; its English a crime against the language.

Counting these out, what is left is Art. I think we must all admit that.*

A Cooper Indian who has been washed is a poor thing, and commonplace; it is the Cooper Indian in his paint that thrills. Cooper's extra words are Cooper's paint—his paint, his feathers, his tomahawk, his warwhoop.

In the two-thirds of a page elsewhere referred to, wherein Cooper scored 114 literary transgressions out of a possible 115, he appears before us with all his things on. As follows, the italics are mine—they indicate violations of Rule 14:

In a minute he was once more fastened to the tree, *a helpless object of any insult or wrong that might be offered. So eagerly did every one now act, that nothing was said.*

---

* At this point, the original published version of the Cooper essay ends. But the late Bernard De Voto announced in *The New England Quarterly* for September, 1946, that Twain had conceived of the essay as Number I in a series of "Studies in Literary Criticism," supposedly prepared by "Mark Twain, M.A., Professor of Belles Lettres in the Veterinary College of Arizona," and that in publishing it separately he had cut the last seven paragraphs. The second essay in the series, which was never finished, develops some of Twain's most interesting objections to Cooper.

The fire was immediately lighted *in the pile, and the end of all was anxiously expected.*

It was not the intention of the Hurons *absolutely* to destroy *the life of* their victim by *means of* fire. They designed merely to put his *physical fortitude* to the severest proofs it could endure, short of that extremity. In the end, they fully intended to carry his scalp into their village, but it was their wish first to break down his resolution, and to reduce him to *the level of* a complaining sufferer. With this view, the pile of brush *and branches* had been placed at a *proper* distance, *or one* at which it was thought the heat would soon become intolerable, though *it might* not *be* immediately dangerous. *As often happened, however, on these occasions,* this distance had been miscalculated, and the flames *began to wave their forked tongues in a proximity to the face of the victim that* would have proved fatal in another instant had not Hetty rushed through the crowd, armed with a stick, and scattered the blazing pile *in a dozen directions.* More than one hand was raised to strike the *presumptuous* intruder to the earth; but the chiefs prevented the blows by reminding their *irritated* followers of the state of her mind. Hetty, herself, was insensible to the risk she ran; but, *as soon as she had performed this bold act, she* stood looking about her in frowning resentment, as if to rebuke the *crowd of attentive savages for their cruelty.*

'God bless you, dear*est sister,* for that brave and ready act,' murmured Judith, *herself unnerved so much as to be incapable of exertion;* 'Heaven itself has sent you on its holy errand.'

Number of words, 320; necessary ones, 220; words wasted by the generous spendthrift, 100.

In our day those 100 unnecessary words would have to come out. We will take them out presently and make the episode approximate the modern requirement in the matter of compression.

If we may consider each unnecessary word in Cooper's report of that barbecue a separate and individual violation of Rule 14, then that rule is violated 100 times in that report. Other rules are violated in it. Rule 12, two instances;[1] Rule 13, three instances;[2] Rule 15, one instance;[3] Rule 16, two instances;[4] Rule 17, one or two little instances;[5] the Report in its entirety is an offense against Rule 18[6]—also against Rule 16. Total score, about 114 violations of the laws of literary art out of a possible 115.

Let us now bring forward the Report again, with the most of the unnecessary words knocked out. By departing from Cooper's style and manner, all the facts could be put into 150 words, and the effects heightened at the same time —this is manifest, of course—but that would not be desirable. We must stick to Cooper's language as closely as we can:

In a minute he was once more fastened to the tree. The fire was immediately lighted. It was not the intention of the Hurons to destroy Deerslayer's life by fire; they designed merely to put his fortitude to the severest proofs it could endure short of that extremity. In the end, they fully intended to take his life, but it was their wish first to break down his resolution and reduce him to a complaining sufferer. With this view the pile of brush had been placed at a distance at which it was thought the heat would soon become intolerable, without being immediately dangerous. But this distance had been miscalculated; the fire was so close to the victim that he would have been fatally burned in another instant if Hetty had not rushed through the crowd and scattered the brands with a stick. More than one Indian raised his hand to strike her down but the chiefs saved her by reminding them of the state of her mind. Hetty herself was insensible to the risk she ran; she stood looking about her in frowning resentment, as if to rebuke the savages for their cruelty.

[1] Rule 12:   "*Say* what he is proposing to say, not merely come near it."
[2] Rule 13:   "Use the right word, not its second cousin."
[3] Rule 15:   "Not omit necessary details."
[4] Rule 16:   "Avoid slovenliness of form."
[5] Rule 17:   "Use good grammar."
[6] Rule 18:   "Employ a simple and straightforward style."

'God bless you, dear!' cried Judith, 'for that brave and ready act. Heaven itself has sent you on its holy errand, and you shall have a chromo.'

Number of words, 220—and the facts are all in.

II

Young Gentlemen: In studying Cooper you will find it profitable to study him in detail—word by word, sentence by sentence. For every sentence of his is interesting. Interesting because of its make-up; its peculiar make-up, its original make-up. Let us examine a sentence or two, and see. Here is a passage from Chapter XI of *The Last of the Mohicans,* one of the most famous and most admired of Cooper's books:

Notwithstanding the swiftness of their flight, one of the Indians had found an opportunity to strike a straggling fawn with an arrow, and had borne the more preferable fragments of the victim, patiently on his shoulders, to the stopping-place. Without any aid from the science of cookery, he was immediately employed in common with his fellows, in gorging himself with this digestible sustenance. Magua alone sat apart, without participating in the revolting meal, and apparently buried in the deepest thought.

This little paragraph is full of matter for reflection and inquiry. The remark about the swiftness of the flight was unnecessary, as it was merely put in to forestall the possible objection of some over-particular reader that the Indian couldn't have found the needed "opportunity" while fleeing swiftly. The reader would not have made that objection. He would care nothing about having that small matter explained and justified. But that is Cooper's way; frequently he will explain and justify little things that do not need it and then make up for this by as frequently failing to explain important ones that do need it. For instance he allowed that astute and cautious person, Deerslayer-Hawkeye, to throw his rifle heedlessly down and leave it lying on the ground where some hostile Indians would presently be sure to find it—a rifle prized by that person above all things else in the earth—and the reader gets no word of explanation of that strange act. There was a reason, but it wouldn't bear exposure. Cooper meant to get a fine dramatic effect out of the finding of the rifle by the Indians, and he accomplished this at the happy time; but all the same, Hawkeye could have hidden the rifle in a quarter of a minute where the Indians could not have found it. Cooper couldn't think of any way to explain why Hawkeye didn't do that, so he just shirked the difficulty and did not explain at all. In another place Cooper allowed Heyward to shoot at an Indian with a pistol that wasn't loaded—and grants us not a word of explanation to how the man did it.

No, the remark about the swiftness of their flight was not necessary; neither was the one which said that the Indian found an opportunity; neither was the one which said he *struck* the fawn; neither was the one which explained that it was a "straggling" fawn; neither was the one which said the striking was done with an arrow; neither was the one which said the Indian bore the "fragments"; nor the remark that they were preferable fragments; nor the remark that they were *more* preferable fragments; nor the explanation that they were fragments of the "victim"; nor the over-particular explanation that specifies the Indian's "shoulders" as the part of him that supported the fragments; nor the statement that the Indian bore the fragments patiently. None of those details has any value. We don't care what the Indian struck the fawn with; we don't care whether it was a straggling fawn or an unstraggling one; we don't care which fragments the Indian saved; we don't care why he saved the "more" preferable ones when the merely preferable ones would have amounted to just the same thing and couldn't have been told from the more preferable ones by anybody, dead or alive; we don't care whether the Indian carried them on his shoulders or in his handkerchief; and finally, we don't care whether he carried them patiently or struck for higher pay and shorter hours. We are indifferent to that Indian and all his affairs.

There was only one fact in that long sentence that was worth stating, and it could have been squeezed into these few words—and with advantage to the narrative, too:

"During the flight one of the Indians had killed a fawn, and he brought it into camp." You will notice that "During the flight one of the Indians had killed a fawn and he brought it into camp," is more straightforward and business-like, and less mincing and smirky, than it is to say "Notwithstanding the swiftness of their flight, one of the Indians had found an opportunity to strike a straggling fawn with an arrow, and had borne the more preferable fragments of the victim, patiently on his shoulders, to the stopping-place." You will notice that the form "During the flight one of the Indians had killed a fawn and he brought it into camp" holds up its chin and moves to the front with the steady stride of a grenadier, whereas the form "Notwithstanding the swiftness of their flight, one of the Indians had found an opportunity to strike a straggling fawn with an arrow, and had borne the more preferable fragments of the victim, patiently on his shoulders, to the stopping-place," simpers along with an airy, complacent, monkey-with-a-parasol gait which is not suited to the transportation of raw meat.

I beg to remind you that an author's way of setting forth a matter is called his Style, and that an author's style is a main part of his equipment for business. The style of some authors has variety in it, but Cooper's style is remarkable for the absence of this feature. Cooper's style is always grand and stately and noble. Style may be likened to an army, the author to its general, the book to the campaign. Some authors proportion an attacking force to the strength or weakness, the importance or unimportance, of the object to be attacked; but Cooper doesn't. It doesn't make any difference to Cooper whether the object of attack is a hundred thousand men or a cow; he hurls his entire force against it. He comes thundering down with all his battalions at his back, cavalry in the van, artillery on the flanks, infantry massed in the middle, forty bands braying, a thousand banners streaming in the wind; and whether the object be an army or a cow you will see him come marching sublimely in, at the end of the engagement, bearing the more preferable fragments of the victim patiently on his shoulders, to the stopping-place. Cooper's style is grand, awful, beautiful; but it is sacred to Cooper, it is his very own, and no student of the Veterinary College of Arizona will be allowed to filch it from him.

In one of his chapters Cooper throws an ungentle slur at one Gamut because he is not exact enough in his choice of words. But Cooper has that failing himself, as was remarked in our first Lecture. If the Indian had "struck" the fawn with a brick, or with a club, or with his fist, no one could find fault with the word used. And one cannot find much fault when he strikes it with an arrow; still it sounds affected, and it might have been a little better to lean to simplicity and say he shot it with an arrow.

"Fragments" is well enough, perhaps, when one is speaking of the parts of a dismembered deer, yet it hasn't just exactly the right sound—and sound is something; in fact sound is a good deal. It makes the difference between good music and poor music, and it can sometimes make the difference between good literature and indifferent literature. "Fragments" sounds all right when we are talking about the wreckage of a breakable thing that has been smashed; it also sounds all right when applied to cat's-meat; but when we use it to describe large hunks and chunks like the fore- and hind-quarters of a fawn, it grates upon the fastidious ear.

"Without any aid from the science of cookery, he was immediately employed, in common with his fellows, in gorging himself with this digestible sustenance."

This was a mere statistic; just a mere cold, colorless statistic; yet you see Cooper has made a chromo out of it. To use another figure, he has clothed a humble statistic in flowing, voluminous and costly raiment, whereas both good taste and economy suggest that he ought to have saved these splendors for a king, and dressed the humble statistic in a simple breech-clout. Cooper spent twenty-four words here on a thing not really worth more than eight. We will reduce the statistic to its proper proportions and state it in this way:

"He and the others ate the meat raw."

"Digestible sustenance" is a handsome phrase, but it was out of place there, because we do not know these Indians or care for them; and so it cannot interest us to know whether the meat was going to agree with them or not. Details which do not assist a story are better left out.

"Magua alone sat apart, without participating in the revolting meal," is a statement which we understand, but that is our merit, not Cooper's. Cooper is not clear. He does not say who it is that is revolted by the meal. It is really Cooper himself, but there is nothing in the statement to indicate that it isn't Magua. Magua is an Indian and likes raw meat.

The word "alone" could have been left out and space saved. It has no value where it is.

I must come back with some frequency, in the course of these Lectures, to the matter of Cooper's inaccuracy as an Observer. In this way I shall hope to persuade you that it is well to look at a thing carefully before you try to describe it; but I shall rest you between times with other matters and thus try to avoid over-fatiguing you with that detail of our theme. In *The Last of the Mohicans* Cooper gets up a stirring "situation" on an island flanked by great cataracts —a lofty island with steep sides—a sort of tongue which projects downstream from the midst of the divided waterfall. There are caverns in this mass of rock, and a party of Cooper people hide themselves in one of these to get away from some hostile Indians. There is a small exit at each end of this cavern. These exits are closed with blankets and the light excluded. The exploring hostiles back themselves up against the blankets and rave and rage in a blood-curdling way, but they are Cooper Indians and of course fail to discover the blankets; so they presently go away baffled and disappointed. Alice, in her gratitude for this deliverance, flings herself on her knees to return thanks. The darkness in there must have been pretty solid; yet if we may believe Cooper, it was a darkness which could not have been told from daylight; for here are some nice details which were visible in it:

"Both Heyward and the more tempered Cora witnessed the act of involuntary emotion with powerful sympathy, the former secretly believing that piety had never worn a form so lovely as it had now assumed in the youthful person of Alice. Her eyes were radiant with the glow of grateful feelings; the flush of her beauty was again seated on her cheeks, and her whole soul seemed ready and anxious to pour out its thanksgivings, through the medium of her eloquent features. But when her lips moved, the words they should have uttered appeared frozen by some new and sudden chill. Her bloom gave place to the paleness of death; her soft and melting eyes grew hard, and seemed contracting with horror; while those hands which she had raised, clasped in each other, towards heaven, dropped in horizontal lines before her, the fingers pointed forward in convulsed motion."

It is a case of strikingly inexact observation. Heyward and the more tempered Cora could not have seen the half of it in the dark that way.

I must call your attention to certain details of this work of art which invite particular examination. "Involuntary" is surplusage, and violates Rule 14.[1] All emotion is involuntary when genuine, and then the qualifying term is not needed; a qualifying term is needed only when the emotion is pumped-up and ungenuine. "Secretly" is surplusage, too; because Heyward was not believing out loud, but all to himself; and a person cannot believe a thing all to himself without doing it privately. I do not approve of the word "seated," to describe the process of locating a flush. No one can seat a flush. A flush is not a deposit on an exterior surface, it is a something which squashes out from within.

I cannot approve of the word "new." If Alice had had an old chill, formerly, it would be all right to distinguish this one from that one by calling this one the new chill; but she had not had any old chill, this one was the only chill she had had, up till now, and so the tacit reference to an old

[1] Rule 14 "Eschew surplusage."

anterior chill is unwarranted and misleading. And I do not altogether like the phrase "while those hands which she had raised." It seems to imply that she had some other hands—some other ones which she had put on a shelf a minute so as to give her a better chance to raise those ones; but it is not true; she had only the one pair. The phrase is in the last degree misleading. But I like to see her extend these ones in front of her and work the fingers. I think that that is a very good effect. And it would have almost doubled the effect if the more tempered Cora had done it some, too.

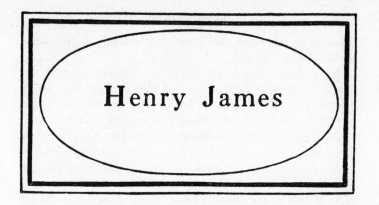

Henry James

Late in the fall of 1881 Henry James returned to the United States after an absence of six years. "I didn't much care for it at first," he wrote to a friend, "but it improves immensely on acquaintance, and after you have got the right point of view and *diapason* it is a wonderfully entertaining and amusing country." Now a well-known author, he was feted wherever he went. He spent a month in Boston and another in New York—"all this was very jolly"—then moved on to Washington for his first glimpse of the nation's capital. Inspired by the city's "enormous spaces . . . charming climate, and the most entertaining society in America," he exuberantly began a short story recording his impressions.

Before he could finish it he received the heaviest blow of his entire life. In January of 1882 his mother died. But he kept the thread of the story through the blackest days, and a few months later, in the "iridescence of a . . . Washington spring" (he had returned to the city for another visit before returning to Europe), he finished it. The story was published in the *Century Magazine* for December of 1882, a month which found James once more returned to America, this time for the funeral of his father, whose health had declined rapidly after his wife's death. In the space of ten months James had lost the two people who, as he admitted, had given him a sense of protection even into middle age.

In writing "The Point of View," James followed the multiple-observer pattern he had already employed in "A Bundle of Letters" because he felt that impressions which mutually conflicted intensified the interest of the experience. The story thus commemorates, as James remarked in his preface to the New York Edition of the story, "its author's perverse and incurable disposition to interest himself less in his own (always so quickly stale) experience . . . than in that of conceivable fellow mortals, which might be mysteriously and refreshingly different."

If, however, the comedy is refreshing, the author's detachment from the experience of his observers is not nearly so complete as he implied. For by employing more than one candid consciousness James was able to project in the story his own unresolved attitudes toward his native land, attitudes which had vastly increased in complexity as a result of his pleasurable rediscovery of America, and of the sorrow which darkened it. What gives the story a bite so sharp as to make it a kind of comic counterpart to Tocqueville's *Democracy in America* is that in essence "The Point of View" is the comic objectification of a dialogue which James had conducted with himself all his adult life. James is both involved with, and yet detached from, at least three of his observers—including the gentleman who deprecates the novels of Henry James—but most of all he is concerned about the young American girl, Aurora Church, who has been trained in Europe and who seems out of place in both the Old World and the New. The theme of being frustrated or rebuffed by America emerges very strongly in James's fiction in these years ("The Siege of London," "Lady Barbarina," etc.), but nowhere more so than in Aurora Church's comically abortive effort to find a husband and settle down in the States. At the end of the story she is gamely headed for the West and another try, but Henry James, having buried both his parents, sailed once again for Europe in the summer of 1883, this time destined not to return for twenty years.

The Point of View

I

From Miss Aurora Church at Sea to Miss Whiteside in Paris

September 1880

. . . My dear child, the bromide of sodium (if that's what you call it) proved perfectly useless. I don't mean that it did me no good, but that I never had occasion to take the bottle out of my bag. It might have done wonders for me if I had needed it; but I didn't, simply because I've been a wonder myself. Will you believe that I've spent the whole voyage on deck, in the most animated conversation and exercise? Twelve times round the deck make a mile, I believe; and by this measurement I've been walking twenty miles a day. And down to every meal, if you please, where I've displayed the appetite of a fish-wife. Of course the weather has been lovely; so there's no great merit. The wicked old Atlantic has been as blue as the sapphire in my only ring—rather a good one—and as smooth as the slippery floor of Madame Galopin's dining-room. We've been for the last three hours in sight of land, and are soon to enter the Bay of New York which is said to be exquisitely beautiful. But of course you recall it, though they say everything changes so fast over here. I find I don't remember anything, for my recollections of our voyage to Europe so many years ago are exceedingly dim; I've only a painful impression that mamma shut me up for an hour every day in the stateroom and made me learn by heart some religious poem. I was only five years old and I believe that as a child I was extremely timid; on the other hand mamma, as you know, had what she called a method with me. She has it to this day; only I've become indifferent; I've been so pinched and pushed—morally speaking, *bien entendu*. It's true, however, that there are children of five on the vessel to-day who have been extremely conspicuous—ranging all over the ship and always under one's feet. Of course they're little compatriots, which means that they're little barbarians. I don't mean to pronounce *all* our compatriots barbarous; they seem to improve somehow after their first communion. I don't know whether it's that ceremony that improves them, especially as so few of them go in for it; but the women are certainly nicer than the little girls; I mean of course in proportion, you know. You warned me not to generalise, and you see I've already begun, before we've arrived. But I suppose there's no harm in it so long as it's favourable.

Isn't it favourable when I say I've had the most lovely time? I've never had so much liberty in my life, and I've been out alone, as you may say, every day of the voyage. If it's a foretaste of what's to come I shall take very kindly to that. When I say I've been out alone I mean we've always been two. But we two were alone, so to speak, and it wasn't like always having mamma or Madame Galopin, or some lady in the pension or the temporary cook. Mamma has been very poorly; she's so very well on land that it's a wonder to see her at all taken down. She says, however, that it isn't the being at sea; it's on the contrary approaching the land. She's not in a hurry to arrive; she keeps well before her that great disillusions await us. I didn't know she *had* any illusions—she has too many opinions, I should think, for that: she discriminates, as she's always saying, from morning till night. Where would the poor illusions find room? She's meanwhile very serious; she sits for hours in perfect silence, her eyes fixed on the horizon. I heard her say yesterday to an English gentleman—a very odd Mr. Antrobus, the only person with whom she converses—that she was afraid she shouldn't like her native land, and that she shouldn't like not liking it. But this is a mistake; she'll like that immensely—I mean the not liking it. If it should prove at all agreeable she'll be furious, for that will go against her system. You know all about mamma's system; I've explained it so often. It goes against her system that

we should come back at all; that was *my* system—I've had
at last to invent one! She consented to come only because
she saw that, having no *dot,* I should never marry in Europe; and I pretended to be immensely pre-occupied with
this idea in order to make her start. In reality *cela m'est
parfaitement égal.* I'm only afraid I shall like it too much—
I don't mean marriage, of course, but the sense of a native
land. Say what you will, it's a charming thing to go out
alone, and I've given notice that I mean to be always *en
course.* When I tell mamma this she looks at me in the same
silence; her eyes dilate and then she slowly closes them. It's
as if the sea were affecting her a little, though it's so beauti-
fully calm. I ask her if she'll try my bromide, which is there
in my bag; but she motions me off and I begin to walk
again, tapping my little boot-soles on the smooth clean
deck. This allusion to my boot-soles, by the way, isn't
prompted by vanity; but it's a fact that at sea one's feet
and one's shoes assume the most extraordinary importance,
so that one should take the precaution to have nice ones.
They're all you seem to see as the people walk about the
deck; you get to know them intimately and to dislike some
of them so much. I'm afraid you'll think that I've already
broken loose; and for aught I know I'm writing as a *dem-
oiselle bien-élevée* shouldn't write. I don't know whether it's
the American air; if it is, all I can say is that the American
air's very charming. It makes me impatient and restless, and
I sit scribbling here because I'm so eager to arrive and the
time passes better if I occupy myself.

I'm in the saloon, where we have our meals, and opposite
me is a big round porthole, wide open to let in the smell
of the land. Every now and then I rise a little and look
through it to see if we're arriving. I mean in the Bay, you
know, for we shall not come up to the city till dark. I don't
want to lose the Bay; it appears it's so wonderful. I don't
exactly understand what it contains except some beautiful
islands; but I suppose you'll know all about that. It's easy
to see that these are the last hours, for all the people about
me are writing letters to put into the post as soon as we
come up to the dock. I believe they're dreadful at the

custom-house, and you'll remember how many new things you persuaded mamma that—with my pre-occupation of marriage—I should take to this country, where even the prettiest girls are expected not to go unadorned. We ruined ourselves in Paris—that's partly accountable for mamma's solemnity—*mais au moins je serai belle!* Moreover I believe that mamma's prepared to say or to do anything that may be necessary for escaping from their odious duties; as she very justly remarks she can't afford to be ruined twice. I don't know how one approaches these terrible *douaniers,* but I mean to invent something very charming. I mean to say, "Voyons, Messieurs, a young girl like me, brought up in the strictest foreign traditions, kept always in the background by a very superior mother—*la voilà;* you can see for yourself!—what is it possible that she should attempt to smuggle in? Nothing but a few simple relics of her convent!" I won't tell them my convent was called the Magasin du Bon Marché. Mamma began to scold me three days ago for insisting on so many trunks, and the truth is that between us we've not fewer than seven. For relics, that's a good many! We're all writing very long letters—or at least we're writing a great number. There's no news of the Bay as yet. Mr. Antrobus, mamma's friend, opposite to me, is beginning on his ninth. He's a Right Honourable and a Member of Parliament; he has written during the voyage about a hundred letters and seems greatly alarmed at the number of stamps he'll have to buy when he arrives. He's full of information, but he hasn't enough, for he asks as many questions as mamma when she goes to hire apartments. He's going to "look into" various things; he speaks as if they had a little hole for the purpose. He walks almost as much as I, and has enormous shoes. He asks questions even of me, and I tell him again and again that I know nothing about America. But it makes no difference; he always begins again, and indeed it's not strange he should find my ignorance incredible. "Now how would it be in one of your Southwestern States?"—that's his favourite way of opening conversation. Fancy me giving an account of one of "my" Southwestern States! I tell him he had better ask mamma—

a little to tease that lady, who knows no more about such places than I. Mr. Antrobus is very big and black; he speaks with a sort of brogue; he has a wife and ten children; he doesn't say—apart from his talking—anything at all to me. But he has lots of letters to people *là-bas*—I forget that we're just arriving—and mamma, who takes an interest in him in spite of his views (which are dreadfully advanced, and not at all like mamma's own), has promised to give him the entrée to the best society. I don't know what she knows about the best society over here today, for we've not kept up our connexions at all, and no one will know—or, I am afraid, care—anything about us. She has an idea we shall be immensely recognised; but really, except the poor little Rucks, who are bankrupt and, I'm told, in no society at all, I don't know on whom we can count. *C'est égal,* mamma has an idea that, whether or no we appreciate America ourselves, we shall at least be universally appreciated. It's true we have begun to be, a little; you would see that from the way Mr. Cockerel and Mr. Louis Leverett are always inviting me to walk. Both of these gentlemen, who are Americans, have asked leave to call on me in New York, and I've said *Mon Dieu oui,* if it's the custom of the country. Of course I've not dared to tell this to mamma, who flatters herself that we've brought with us in our trunks a complete set of customs of our own and that we shall only have to shake them out a little and put them on when we arrive. If only the two gentlemen I just spoke of don't call at the same time I don't think I shall be too much frightened. If they do, on the other hand, I won't answer for it. They've a particular aversion to each other and are ready to fight about poor little me. I'm only the pretext, however; for, as Mr. Leverett says, it's really the opposition of temperaments. I hope they won't cut each other's throats, for I'm not crazy about either of them. They're very well for the deck of a ship, but I shouldn't care about them in a salon; they're not at all distinguished. They think they are, but they're not; at least Mr. Louis Leverett does; Mr. Cockerel doesn't appear to care so much. They're extremely different—with their opposed temperaments—and each very amusing for a while; but I should get dreadfully tired of passing my life with either. Neither has proposed that as yet; but it's evidently what they're coming to. It will be in a great measure to spite each other, for I think that *au fond* they don't quite believe in me. If they don't, it's the only point on which they agree. They hate each other awfully; they take such different views. That is Mr. Cockerel hates Mr. Leverett—he calls him a sickly little ass; he pronounces his opinions half affectation and the other half dyspepsia. Mr. Leverett speaks of Mr. Cockerel as a "strident savage," but he allows he finds him most diverting. He says there's nothing in which we can't find a certain entertainment if we only look at it in the right way, and that we have no business with either hating or loving: we ought only to strive to understand. He "claims"—he's always claiming—that to understand is to forgive. Which is very pretty, but I don't like the suppression of our affections, though I've no desire to fix mine upon Mr. Leverett. He's very artistic and talks like an article in some review. He has lived a great deal in Paris, and Mr. Cockerel, who doesn't believe in Paris, says it's what has made him such an idiot.

That's not complimentary to you, dear Louisa, and still less to your brilliant brother; for Mr. Cockerel explains that he means it (the bad effect of Paris) chiefly of men. In fact he means the bad effect of Europe altogether. This, however, is compromising to mamma; and I'm afraid there's no doubt that, from what I've told him, he thinks mamma also an idiot. (I'm not responsible, you know—I've always wanted to go home.) If mamma knew him, which she doesn't, for she always closes her eyes when I pass on his arm, she would think him disgusting. Mr. Leverett meanwhile assures me he's nothing to what we shall see yet. He's from Philadelphia (Mr. Cockerel); he insists that we shall go and see Philadelphia, but mamma says she saw it in 1855 and it was then *affreux*. Mr. Cockerel says that mamma's evidently not familiar with the rush of improvement in this country; he speaks of 1855 as if it were a hundred years ago. Mamma says she knows it goes only too fast, the rush—it goes so fast that it has time to do nothing well; and then Mr. Cockerel, who, to do him justice, is perfectly good-natured, remarks that she had better wait till she has been ashore and seen the improvements. Mamma retorts that she sees things from here, the awful things, and that they give her a sinking of the heart. (This little exchange of ideas is carried on through me; they've never spoken to each other.) Mr. Cockerel, as I say, is extremely good-natured, and he bears out what I've heard said about the men in America being very considerate of the women. They evidently listen to them a great deal; they don't contradict them, but it seems to me this is rather negative. There's very little gallantry in not contradicting one; and it strikes me that there are some things the men don't express. There are others on the ship whom I've noticed. It's as if they were all one's brothers or one's cousins. The extent to which one isn't in danger from them—my dear, my dear! But I promised you not to generalise, and perhaps there will be more expression when we arrive. Mr. Cockerel returns to America, after a general tour, with a renewed conviction that this is the only country. I left him on deck an hour ago looking at the coast-line with an opera-glass and saying it was the prettiest thing he had seen in all his travels. When I remarked that the coast seemed rather low he said it would be all the easier to get ashore. Mr. Leverett at any rate doesn't seem in a hurry to get ashore, he's sitting within sight of me in a corner of the saloon—writing letters, I suppose, but looking, from the way he bites his pen and rolls his eyes about, as if he were composing a sonnet and waiting for a rhyme. Perhaps the sonnet's addressed to me; but I forget that he suppresses the affections! The only person in whom mamma takes much interest is the great French critic, M. Lejaune, whom we have the honour to carry with us. We've read a few of his works, though mamma disapproves of his tendencies and thinks him a dreadful materialist. We've read them for the style; you know he's one of the new Academicians. He's a Frenchman like any other, except that he's rather more quiet; he has a grey moustache and the ribbon of the Legion of Honour. He's the first French writer of distinction who has been to

America since De Tocqueville; the French, in such matters, are not very enterprising. Also he has the air of wondering what he's doing *dans cette galère*. He has come with his *beau-frère*, who's an engineer and is looking after some mines, and he talks with scarcely any one else, as he speaks no English and appears to take for granted that no one speaks French. Mamma would be delighted to convince him of the contrary; she has never conversed with an Academician. She always makes a little vague inclination, with a smile, when he passes her, and he answers with a most respectful bow; but it goes no further, to mamma's disappointment. He's always with the *beau-frère*, a rather untidy fat bearded man—decorated too, always smoking and looking at the feet of the ladies, whom mamma (though she has very good feet) has not the courage to *aborder*. I believe M. Lejaune is going to write a book about America, and Mr. Leverett says it will be terrible. Mr. Leverett has made his acquaintance and says M. Lejaune will put him into his book; he says the movement of the French intellect is superb. As a general thing he doesn't care for Academicians, but M. Lejaune's an exception—he's so living, so remorseless, so personal.

I've asked Mr. Cockerel meanwhile what he thinks of M. Lejaune's plan of writing a book, and he answers that he doesn't see what it matters to him that a Frenchman the more should make the motions of a monkey—on that side poor Mr. Cockerel is *de cette force*. I asked him why he hadn't written a book about Europe, and he says that in the first place Europe isn't worth writing about, and that in the second if he said what he thought people would call it a joke. He says they're very superstitious about Europe over here; he wants people in America to behave as if Europe didn't exist. I told this to Mr. Leverett, and he answered that if Europe didn't exist America wouldn't, for Europe keeps us alive by buying our corn. He said also that the trouble with America in the future will be that she'll produce things in such enormous quantities that there won't be enough people in the rest of the world to buy them, and that we shall be left with our productions—most of them very hideous—on our hands. I asked him if he thought corn a hideous production, and he replied that there's nothing more unbeautiful than too much food. I think that to feed the world too well, however, will be after all a *beau rôle*. Of course I don't understand these things, and I don't believe Mr. Leverett does; but Mr. Cockerel seems to know what he's talking about, and he describes America as complete in herself. I don't know exactly what he means, but he speaks as if human affairs had somehow moved over to this side of the world. It may be a very good place for them, and heaven knows I'm extremely tired of Europe, which mamma has always insisted so on my appreciating; but I don't think I like the idea of our being so completely cut off. Mr. Cockerel says it is not we that are cut off, but Europe, and he seems to think Europe has somehow deserved it. That may be; our life over there was sometimes extremely tiresome, though mamma says it's now that our real fatigues will begin. I like to abuse those dreadful old countries myself, but I'm not sure I'm pleased when others do the same. We had some rather pretty moments there after all, and at Piacenza we certainly lived for four francs a day. Mamma's already in a terrible state of mind about the expenses here; she's frightened by what people on the ship (the few she has spoken to) have told her. There's comfort at any rate—we've spent so much money in coming that we shall have none left to get away. I'm scribbling along, as you see, to occupy me till we get news of the islands. Here comes Mr. Cockerel to bring it. Yes, they're in sight; he tells me they're lovelier than ever and that I must come up right away. I suppose you'll think I'm already beginning to use the language of the country. It's certain that at the end of the month I shall speak nothing else. I've picked up every dialect, wherever we've travelled; you've heard my Platt-Deutsch and my Neapolitan. But, *voyons un peu* the Bay! I've just called to Mr. Leverett to remind him of the islands. "The islands—the islands? Ah my dear young lady, I've seen Capri, I've seen Ischia!" Well, so have I, but that doesn't prevent . . . (*A little later.*) I've seen the islands—they're rather queer.

II

Mrs. Church in New York to Madame Galopin at Geneva

October 1880

If I felt far away from you in the middle of that deplorable Atlantic, *chère Madame,* how do I feel now, in the heart of this extraordinary city? We've arrived—we've arrived, dear friend; but I don't know whether to tell you that I consider that an advantage. If we had been given our choice of coming safely to land or going down to the bottom of the sea I should doubtless have chosen the former course; for I hold, with your noble husband and in opposition to the general tendency of modern thought, that our lives are not our own to dispose of, but a sacred trust from a higher power by whom we shall be held responsible. Nevertheless if I had foreseen more vividly some of the impressions that awaited me here I'm not sure that, for my daughter at least, I shouldn't have preferred on the spot to hand in our account. Should I not have been less (rather than more) guilty in presuming to dispose of *her* destiny than of my own? There's a nice point for dear M. Galopin to settle—one of those points I've heard him discuss in the pulpit with such elevation. We're safe, however, as I say; by which I mean we're physically safe. We've taken up the thread of our familiar pension-life, but under strikingly different conditions. We've found a refuge in a boarding-house which has been highly recommended to me and where the arrangements partake of the barbarous magnificence that in this country is the only alternative from primitive rudeness. The terms per week are as magnificent as all the rest. The landlady wears diamond ear-rings and the drawing rooms are decorated with marble statues. I should indeed be sorry to let you know how I've allowed myself to be *rançonnée;* and I should be still more sorry that it should come to the ears of any of my good friends in Geneva, who know me less well than you, and might judge me more harshly. There's no wine given for dinner, and I've vainly requested the person who conducts the establishment to garnish her table more liberally. She says I may have all the wine I want if I will order it at the merchant's and settle the matter with himself. But I've never, as you know, consented to regard our modest allowance of *eau rougie* as an extra; indeed, I remember that it's largely to your excellent advice that I've owed my habit of being firm on this point.

There are, however, greater difficulties than the question of what we shall drink for dinner, *chère Madame*. Still, I've never lost courage and I shall not lose it now. At the worst we can re-embark again and seek repose and refreshment on the shores of your beautiful lake. (There's absolutely no scenery here!) We shall not perhaps in that case have achieved what we desired, but we shall at least have made an honourable retreat. What we desire—I know it's just this that puzzles you, dear friend; I don't think you ever really comprehended my motives in taking this formidable step, though you were good enough, and your magnanimous husband was good enough, to press my hand at parting in a way that seemed to tell me you'd still be with me even were I wrong. To be very brief, I wished to put an end to the ceaseless reclamations of my daughter. Many Americans had assured her that she was wasting her *belle jeunesse* in those historic lands which it was her privilege to see so intimately, and this unfortunate conviction had taken possession of her. "Let me at least see for myself," she used to say; "if I should dislike it over there as much as you promise me, so much the better for you. In that case we'll come back and make a new arrangement at Stuttgart." The experiment's a terribly expensive one, but you know how my devotion never has shrunk from an ordeal. There's another point moreover which, from a mother to a mother, it would be affectation not to touch upon. I remember the just satisfaction with which you announced to me the *fiançailles* of your charming Cécile. You know with what earnest care my Aurora has been educated—how thoroughly she's acquainted with the principal results of modern research. We've always studied together, we've always enjoyed together. It will perhaps surprise you to hear that she makes these very advantages a reproach to me—represents them as an injury to herself. "In this country," she says, "the gentlemen have not those accomplishments; they care nothing for the results of modern research. Therefore it won't help a young person to be sought in marriage that she can give an account of the latest German presentation of Pessimism." That's possible, and I've never concealed from her that it wasn't for this country I had educated her. If she marries in the United States it's of course my intention that my son-in-law shall accompany us to Europe. But when she calls my attention more and more to these facts I feel that we're moving in a different world. This is more and more the country of the many; the few find less and less place for them; and the individual has quite ceased to be recognised. He's recognised as a voter, but he's not recognised as a gentleman—still less as a lady. My daughter and I of course can only pretend to constitute a *few!*

You know that I've never for a moment remitted my pretensions as an individual, though among the agitations of pension-life I've sometimes needed all my energy to uphold them. "Oh yes, I may be poor," I've had occasion to say, "I may be unprotected, I may be reserved, I may occupy a small apartment *au quatrième* and be unable to scatter unscrupulous bribes among the domestics; but at least I'm a *person* and have personal rights." In this country the people have rights, but the person has none. You'd have perceived that if you had come with me to make arrangements at this establishment. The very fine lady who condescends to preside over it kept me waiting twenty minutes and then came sailing in without a word of apology. I had sat very silent, with my eyes on the clock; Aurora amused herself with a false admiration of the room, a wonderful drawing-room with magenta curtains, frescoed walls and photographs of the landlady's friends—as if one cares for her friends! When this exalted personage came in she simply remarked that she had just been trying on a dress—that it took so long to get a skirt to hang. "It seems to take very long indeed!" I answered; "but I hope the skirt's right at last. You might have sent for us to come up and look at it!" She evidently didn't understand, and when I asked her to show us her rooms she handed us over to a negro as *dégingandé* as herself. While we looked at them I heard her sit down to the piano in the drawing-room; she began to sing an air from a comic opera. I felt certain we had gone quite astray; I didn't know in what house we could be, and was only reassured by seeing a Bible in every room. When we came down our musical hostess expressed no hope the rooms had pleased us, she seemed grossly indifferent to our taking them. She wouldn't consent moreover to the least diminution and was inflexible, as I told you, on the article of our common beverage. When I pushed this point she was so good as to observe that she didn't keep a cabaret. One's not in the least considered; there's no respect for one's privacy, for one's preferences, for one's reserves. The familiarity's without limits, and I've already made a dozen acquaintances, of whom I know, and wish to know, nothing. Aurora tells me she's the "belle of the boarding-house." It appears that this is a great distinction.

It brings me back to my poor child and her prospects. She takes a very critical view of them herself—she tells me I've given her a false education and that no one will marry her because she's too much of a foreigner, and no foreigner will marry her because she's too much of an American. I remind her how scarcely a day passes that a foreigner, usually of distinction, doesn't—as perversely as you will indeed —select an American bride, and she answers me that in these cases the young lady isn't married for her fine eyes. Not always, I reply; and then she declares that she'll marry no foreigner who shall not be one of the first of the first. You'll say doubtless that she should content herself with advantages that haven't been deemed insufficient for Cécile; but I'll not repeat to you the remark she made when I once employed this argument. You'll doubtless be surprised to hear that I've ceased to argue; but it's time I should confess that I've at last agreed to let her act for herself. She's to live for three months *à l'Américaine* and I'm to be a mere passive spectator. You'll feel with me that this is a cruel position for a *coeur de mère*. I count the days till our three months are over, and I know you'll join with me in my prayers. Aurora walks the streets alone; she goes out in the tramway: a *voiture de place* costs five francs for the least little *course*. (I beseech you not to let it be known that I've sometimes had the weakness.) My daughter's frequently accompanied by a gentleman—by a dozen gentlemen; she remains out for hours and her conduct excites no surprise in this establishment. I know but too well the emotions it will excite in your quiet home. If you betray us, *chère Madame*, we're lost; and why, after all, should any one know of these things in Geneva? Aurora pretends she has been able to persuade herself that she doesn't care who knows them; but there's a strange expression in her face which proves that her conscience isn't at rest. I watch her, I let her go, but I sit with my hands clasped. There's a peculiar custom in this country—I shouldn't know how to express it in Genevese: it's called "being attentive," and young girls are the object of the futile process. It hasn't necessarily anything to do with projects of marriage—though at the same time (fortunately, and this may surprise you) it has no relation to other projects. It's simply an invention by which young persons of the two sexes pass large parts of their time together with no questions asked. How shall I muster courage to tell you that Aurora now constitutes the main apparent recreation of several gentlemen? Though it has no relation to marriage the practice happily doesn't exclude it, and marriages have been known to take place in consequence (or in spite) of it. It's true that even in this country a young lady may marry but one husband at a time, whereas she may receive at once the attentions of several gentlemen, who are equally entitled "admirers." My daughter then has admirers to an indefinite number. You'll think I'm joking perhaps when I tell you that I'm unable to be exact—I who was formerly *l'exactitude même*.

Two of these gentlemen are to a certain extent old friends, having been passengers on the steamer which carried us so far from you. One of them, still young, is typical of the American character, but a respectable person and a lawyer considerably launched. Every one in this country follows a profession, but it must be admitted that the professions are more highly remunerated than *chez vous*. Mr. Cockerel, even while I write you, is in not undisputed, but temporarily triumphant, possession of my child. He called for her an hour ago in a "boghey"—a strange unsafe rickety vehicle, mounted on enormous wheels, which holds two persons very near together; and I watched her from the window take her place at his side. Then he whirled her away behind two little horses with terribly thin legs; the whole equipage—and most of all her being in it—was in the most questionable taste. But she'll return—return positively very much as she went. It's the same when she goes down to Mr. Louis Leverett, who has no vehicle and who merely comes and sits with her in the front salon. He has lived a great deal in Europe and is very fond of the arts, and though I'm not sure I agree with him in his views of the relation of art to life and life to art, and in his interpretation of some of the great works that Aurora and I have studied together, he seems to me a sufficiently serious and intelligent young man. I don't regard him as intrinsically dangerous, but on the other hand he offers absolutely no guarantees. I've no means whatever of ascertaining his pecuniary situation. There's a vagueness on these points which is extremely embarrassing, and it never occurs to young men to offer you a reference. In Geneva I shouldn't be at a loss; I should come to you, *chère Madame,* with my little enquiry, and what you shouldn't be able to tell me wouldn't be worth my knowing. But no one in New York can give me the smallest information about the *état de fortune* of Mr. Louis Leverett. It's true that he's a native of Boston, where most of his friends reside; I can't, however, go to the expense of a journey to Boston simply to learn perhaps that Mr. Leverett (the young Louis) has an income of five thousand francs. As I say indeed, he doesn't strike me as dangerous. When Aurora comes back to me after having passed an hour with him she says he has described to her his emotions on visiting the home of Shelley or discussed

some of the differences between the Boston temperament
and that of the Italians of the Renaissance. You'll not enter
into these *rapprochements,* and I can't blame you. But you
won't betray me, *chère Madame?*

III

From Miss Sturdy at Newport to Mrs. Draper at Ouchy

September 1880

I promised to tell you how I like it, but the truth is I've
gone to and fro so often that I've ceased to like and dislike.
Nothing strikes me as unexpected; I expect everything in
its order. Then too, you know, I'm not a critic; I've no talent
for keen analysis, as the magazines say; I don't go into the
reasons of things. It's true I've been for a longer time than
usual on the wrong side of the water, and I admit that I
feel a little out of training for American life. They're breaking me in very fast, however. I don't mean that they bully
me—I absolutely decline to be bullied. I say what I think,
because I believe on the whole the advantage of knowing
what I think—when I think anything; which is half the battle. Sometimes indeed I think nothing at all. They don't
like that over here; they like you to have impressions. That
they like these impressions to be favourable appears to me
perfectly natural; I don't make a crime to them of this; it
seems to me on the contrary a very amiable point. When
individuals betray it we call them sympathetic; I don't see
why we shouldn't give nations the same benefit. But there
are things I haven't the least desire to have an opinion
about. The privilege of indifference is the dearest we possess, and I hold that intelligent people are known by the
way they exercise it. Life is full of rubbish, and we have
at least our share of it over here. When you wake up in
the morning you find that during the night a cartload has
been deposited in your front garden. I decline, however, to
have any of it in my premises; there are thousands of things
I want to know nothing about. I've outlived the necessity

of being hypercritical; I've nothing to gain and everything to lose. When one's fifty years old—single stout and red in the face—one has outlived a good many necessities. They tell me over here that my increase of weight's extremely marked, and though they don't tell me I'm coarse I feel they think me so. There's very little coarseness here—not quite enough, I think—though there's plenty of vulgarity, which is a very different thing. On the whole the country becomes much more agreeable. It isn't that the people are charming, for that they always were (the best of them, I mean—it isn't true of the others), but that places and things as well recognise the possibility of pleasing. The houses are extremely good and look extraordinarily fresh and clean. Many European interiors seem in comparison musty and gritty. We have a great deal of taste; I shouldn't wonder if we should end by inventing something pretty; we only need a little time. Of course as yet it's all imitation, except, by the way, these delicious piazzas. I'm sitting on one now; I'm writing to you with my portfolio on my knees. This broad light *loggia* surrounds the house with a movement as free as the expanded wings of a bird, and the wandering airs come up from the deep sea, which murmurs on the rocks at the end of the lawn.

Newport's more charming even than you remember it; like everything else over here it has improved. It's very exquisite to-day; it's indeed, I think, in all the world the only exquisite watering-place, for I detest the whole genus. The crowd has left it now, which makes it all the better, though plenty of talkers remain in these large light luxurious houses which are planted with a kind of Dutch definiteness all over the green carpet of the cliff. This carpet's very neatly laid and wonderfully swept, and the sea, just at hand, is capable of prodigies of blue. Here and there a pretty woman strolls over one of the lawns, which all touch each other, you know, without hedges or fences; the light looks intense as it plays on her brilliant dress; her large parasol shines like a silver dome. The long lines of the far shores are soft and pure, though they are places one hasn't the least desire to visit. Altogether the effect's very delicate,

and anything that's delicate counts immensely over here;
for delicacy, I think, is as rare as coarseness. I'm talking to
you of the sea, however, without having told you a word
of my voyage. It was very comfortable and amusing; I
should like to take another next month. You know I'm almost offensively well at sea—I breast the weather and brave
the storm. We had no storm fortunately, and I had brought
with me a supply of light literature; so I passed nine days
on deck in my sea-chair with my heels up—passed them
reading Tauchnitz novels. There was a great lot of people,
but no one in particular save some fifty American girls. You
know all about the American girl, however, having been one
yourself. They're on the whole very nice, but fifty's too
many; there are always too many. There was an enquiring
Briton, a radical M.P., by name Mr. Antrobus, who enter-
tained me as much as any one else. He's an excellent man;
I even asked him to come down here and spend a couple
of days. He looked rather frightened till I told him he
shouldn't be alone with me, that the house was my brother's
and that I gave the invitation in his name. He came a week
ago; he goes everywhere; we've heard of him in a dozen
places. The English are strangely simple, or at least they
seem so over here. Their old measurements and compari-
sons desert them; they don't know whether it's all a joke
or whether it's too serious by half. We're quicker than they,
though we talk so much more slowly. We think fast, and
yet we talk as deliberately as if we were speaking a foreign
language. They toss off their sentences with an air of easy
familiarity with the tongue, and yet they misunderstand
two thirds of what people say to them. Perhaps after all it
is only *our* thoughts they think slowly; they think their own
often to a lively tune enough.

Mr. Antrobus arrived here in any case at eight o'clock in
the morning; I don't know how he managed it; it appears
to be his favourite hour; wherever we've heard of him he
has come in with the dawn. In England he would arrive at
5:30 P.M. He asks innumerable questions, but they're easy
to answer, for he has a sweet credulity. He made me rather
ashamed; he's a better American than so many of us; he

takes us more seriously than we take ourselves. He seems to think we've an oligarchy of wealth growing up which he advised me to be on guard against. I don't know exactly what I can do, but I promised him to look out. He's fearfully energetic; the energy of the people here is nothing to that of the enquiring Briton. If we should devote half the zeal to building up our institutions that they devote to obtaining information about them we should have a very satisfactory country. Mr. Antrobus seemed to think very well of us—which surprised me on the whole, since, say what one will, it's far from being so agreeable as England. It's very horrid that this should be; and it's delightful, when one thinks of it, that some things in England are after all so hateful. At the same time Mr. Antrobus appeared to be a good deal preoccupied with our dangers. I don't understand quite what they are; they seem to me so few on a Newport piazza this bright still day. Yet alas what one sees on a Newport piazza isn't America; it's only the back of Europe. I don't mean to say I haven't noticed any dangers since my return; there are two or three that seem to me very serious, but they aren't those Mr. Antrobus apprehends. One, for instance, is that we shall cease to speak the English language, which I prefer so to any other. It's less and less spoken; American's crowding it out. All the children speak American, which as a child's language is dreadfully rough. It's exclusively in use in the schools; all the magazines and newspapers are in American. Of course a people of fifty millions who have invented a new civilisation have a right to a language of their own; that's what they tell me, and I can't quarrel with it. But I wish they had made it as pretty as the mother-tongue, from which, when all's said, it's more or less derived. We ought to have invented something as noble as our country. They tell me it's more expressive, and yet some admirable things have been said in the Queen's English. There can be no question of the Queen over here of course, and American no doubt is the music of the future. Poor dear future, how "expressive" you'll be! For women and children, as I say, it strikes one as very rough; and moreover they don't speak it well, their own though it be. My small nephews, when I first came home, hadn't gone back to school, and it distressed me to see that, though they're charming children, they had the vocal inflexions of little news-boys. My niece is sixteen years old; she has the sweetest nature possible; she's extremely well-bred and is dressed to perfection. She chatters from morning till night; but its helplessness breaks my heart. These little persons are in the opposite case from so many English girls who know how to speak but don't know how to talk. My niece knows how to talk but doesn't know how to speak.

If I allude to the young people, that's our other danger; the young people are eating us up—there's nothing in America but the young people. The country's made for the rising generation; life's arranged for them; they're the destruction of society. People talk of them, consider them, defer to them, bow down to them. They're always present, and whenever they're present nothing else of the smallest interest is. They're often very pretty, and physically are wonderfully looked after; they're scoured and brushed, they wear hygienic clothes, they go every week to the dentist's. But the little boys kick your shins and the little girls offer to slap your face. There's an immense literature entirely addressed to them in which the kicking of shins and the slapping of faces carries the day. As a woman of fifty I protest, I insist on being judged by my peers. It's too late, however, for several millions of little feet are actively engaged in stamping out conversation, and I don't see how they can long fail to keep it under. The future's theirs; adult forms will evidently be at an increasing discount. Longfellow wrote a charming little poem called "The Children's Hour," but he ought to have called it "The Children's Century." And by children I naturally don't mean simple infants; I mean everything of less than twenty. The social importance of the young American increases steadily up to that age and then suddenly stops. The little girls of course are more important than the lads, but the lads are very important too. I'm struck with the way they're known and talked about; they're small celebrities; they have reputations and pretensions; they're taken very seriously. As for the little girls, as I just said, they're ever so much too many. You'll say perhaps that my fifty years and my red face are jealous of them. I don't think so, because I don't suffer; my red face doesn't frighten people away, and I always find plenty of talkers. The young things themselves, I believe, like me very much, and I delight in the young things. They're often very pretty; not so pretty as people say in the magazines, but pretty enough. The magazines rather overdo that; they make a mistake. I've seen no great beauties, but the level of prettiness is high, and occasionally one sees a woman completely handsome. (As a general thing, a pretty person here means a person with a pretty face. The figure's rarely mentioned, though there are several good ones.) The level of prettiness is high, but the level of conversation is low; that's one of the signs of its being a young ladies' country. There are a good many things young ladies can't talk about, but think of all the things they can when they are as clever as most of these. Perhaps one ought to content one's self with that measure, but it's difficult if one has lived long by a larger one. This one's decidedly narrow—I stretch it sometimes till it cracks. Then it is they call me coarse, which I undoubtedly am, thank goodness.

What it comes to, obviously, is that people's talk is much less conveniently free than in Europe; I'm struck with that wherever I go. There are certain things that are never said at all, certain allusions that are never made. There are no light stories, no *propos risqués*. I don't know exactly what people find to bite into, for the supply of scandal's small and it's little more than twaddle at that. They don't seem, however, to lack topics. The little girls are always there; they keep the gates of conversation; very little passes that's not innocent. I find we do very well without wickedness, and for myself, as I take my ease, I don't miss my liberties. You remember what I thought of the tone of your table in Florence last year, and how surprised you were when I asked you why you allowed such things. You said they were like the courses of the seasons; one couldn't prevent them; also that to change the tone of your table you'd have to

change so many other things. Of course in your house one
never saw a little girl; I was the only spinster and no one
was afraid of me. Likewise if talk's more innocent in this
country manners are so to begin with. The liberty of the
young people is the strongest proof of it. The little girls
are let loose in the world, and the world gets more good
of it than *ces demoiselles* get harm. In your world—pardon
me, but you know what I mean—this wouldn't do at all.
Your world's a sad affair—the young ladies would encounter
all sorts of horrors. Over here, considering the way they
knock about, they remain wonderfully simple, and the reason is that society protects them instead of setting them
traps. There's almost no gallantry as you understand it; the
flirtations are child's play. People have no time for making
love; the men in particular are extremely busy. I'm told
that sort of thing consumes hours; I've never had any time
for it myself. If the leisure class should increase here considerably there may possibly be a change; but I doubt it, for
the women seem to me in all essentials exceedingly reserved.
Great superficial frankness, but an extreme dread of com-
plications. The men strike me as very good fellows. I find
them at bottom better than the women, who if not invet-
erately hard haven't at least the European, the (as I heard
some one once call it) chemical softness. They're not so nice
to the men as the men are to them; I mean of course in
proportion, you know. But women aren't so nice as men
"anyway," as they say here.

The men at any rate are professional, commercial; there
are very few gentlemen pure and simple. This personage
needs to be very well done, however, to be of great utility;
and I suppose you won't pretend he's always well done in
your countries. When he's not, the less of him the better.
It's very much the same indeed with the system on which
the female young are brought up. (You see I have to come
back to the female young.) When it succeeds they're the
most charming creatures possible; when it doesn't the fail-
ure's disastrous. If a girl's a very nice girl the American
method brings her to great completeness—makes all her
graces flower; but if she isn't nice it plays the devil with

any possible compromise or *biais* in the interest of social convenience. In a word the American girl's rarely negative, and when she isn't a great success she's a great warning. In nineteen cases out of twenty, among the people who know how to live—I won't say what *their* proportion is—the results are highly satisfactory. The girls aren't shy, but I don't know why they should be, for there's really nothing here to be afraid of. Manners are very gentle, very humane; the democratic system deprives people of weapons that every one doesn't equally possess. No one's formidable; no one's on stilts; no one has great pretensions or any recognised right to be arrogant. I think there's not much wickedness, and there's certainly less human or social cruelty—less than in "good" (that is in more amusing) society. Every one can sit—no one's kept standing. One's much less liable to be snubbed, which you will say is a pity. I think it is —to a certain extent; but on the other hand folly's less fatuous in form than in your countries; and as people generally have fewer revenges to take there's less need of their being squashed in advance. The general good nature, the social equality, deprive them of triumphs on the one hand and of grievances on the other. There's extremely little impertinence, there's almost none. You'll say I'm describing a terrible world, a world without great figures or great social prizes. You've hit it, my dear—there are no great figures. (The great prize of course in Europe is the opportunity to *be* a great figure.) You'd miss these things a good deal— you who delight to recognise greatness; and my advice to you therefore is never to come back. You'd miss the small people even more than the great; every one's middle-sized, and you can never have that momentary sense of profiting by the elevation of your class which is so agreeable in Europe. I needn't add that you don't, either, languish with its depression. There are at all events no brilliant types— the most important people seem to lack dignity. They're very bourgeois; they make little jokes; on occasion they make puns; they've no form; they're too good-natured. The men have no style; the women, who are fidgety and talk too much, have it only in their *tournures,* where they have it superabundantly.

Well, I console myself—since consolation is needed—with the greater bonhomie. Have you ever arrived at an English country-house in the dusk of a winter's day? Have you ever made a call in London when you knew nobody but the hostess? People here are more expressive, more demonstrative; and it's a pleasure, when one comes back—if one happens, like me, to be no one in particular—to feel one's merely personal and unclassified value rise. They attend to you more; they have you on their mind; they talk to you; they listen to you. That is the men do; the women listen very little—not enough. They interrupt, they prattle, one feels their presence too much as importunate and untrained sound. I imagine this is partly because their wits are quick and they think of a good many things to say; not indeed that they always say such wonders! Perfect repose, after all, is not *all* self-control; it's also partly stupidity. American women, however, make too many vague exclamations—say too many indefinite things, have in short still a great deal of nature. The American order or climate or whatever gives them a nature they *can* let loose. Europe has to protect itself with more art. On the whole I find very little affectation, though we shall probably have more as we improve. As yet people haven't the assurance that carries those things off; they know too much about each other. The trouble is that over here we've all been brought up together. You'll think this a picture of a dreadfully insipid society; but I hasten to add that it's not all so tame as that. I've been speaking of the people that one meets socially, and these're the smallest part of American life. The others—those one meets on a basis of mere convenience—are much more exciting; they keep one's temper in healthy exercise. I mean the people in the shops and on the railroads; the servants, the hack-men, the labourers, the conductors; every one of whom you buy anything or have occasion to make an enquiry. With them you need all your best manners, for you must always have enough for two. If you think we're *too* democratic, taste a little of American life in these walks and you'll be reassured. This is the region of inequality, and you'll find plenty of people to make your curtsey to. You see it from below—the weight of inequality's on your own back. You asked me to tell you about prices. They're unspeakable.

IV

From the Right Hon. Edward Antrobus M.P. in Boston to the Honourable Mrs. Antrobus

November 1880

My Dear Susan

I sent you a post-card on the 13th and a native newspaper yesterday; I really have had no time to write. I sent you the newspaper partly because it contained a report—extremely incorrect—of some remarks I made at the Association of the Teachers of New England; partly because it's so curious that I thought it would interest you and the children. I cut out some portions I didn't think it well the children should go into—the passages remaining contain the most striking features. Please point out to the children the peculiar orthography, which probably will be adopted in England by the time they are grown up; the amusing oddities of expression and the like. Some of them are intentional; you'll have heard of the celebrated American humour—remind me, by the way, on my return to Thistleton, to give you a few of the examples of it that my own experience supplies. Certain other of the journalistic eccentricities I speak of are unconscious and are perhaps on that account the more diverting. Point out to the children the difference—in so far as you're sure that you yourself perceive it. You must excuse me if these lines are not very legible; I'm writing them by the light of a railway lamp which rattles above my left ear; it being only at odd moments that I can find time to extend my personal researches. You'll say this is a very odd moment indeed when I tell you I'm in bed in a sleeping-car. I occupy the upper berth

(I will explain to you the arrangement when I return) while the lower forms the couch—the jolts are fearful—of an unknown female. You'll be very anxious for my explanation, but I assure you that the circumstance I mention is the custom of the country. I myself am assured that a lady may travel in this manner all over the Union (the Union of States) without a loss of consideration. In case of her occupying the upper berth I presume it would be different, but I must make enquiries on this point. Whether it be the fact that a mysterious being of another sex has retired to rest behind the same curtains, or whether it be the swing of the train, which rushes through the air with very much the same movement as the tail of a kite, the situation is at the best so anomalous that I'm unable to sleep. A ventilator's open just over my head, and a lively draught, mingled with a drizzle of cinders, pours in through this dubious advantage. (I will describe to you its mechanism on my return.) If I had occupied the lower berth I should have had a whole window to myself, and by drawing back the blind—a safe proceeding at the dead of night —I should have been able, by the light of an extraordinary brilliant moon, to see a little better what I write. The question occurs to me, however, would the lady below me in that case have ascended to the upper berth? (You know my old taste for hypothetic questions.) I incline to think (from what I have seen) that she would simply have requested me to evacuate my own couch. (The ladies in this country ask for anything they want.) In this case, I suppose, I should have had an extensive view of the country, which, from what I saw of it before I turned in (while the sharer of my privacy was going to bed), offered a rather ragged expanse dotted with little wooden houses that resembled in the moonshine large pasteboard boxes. I've been unable to ascertain as precisely as I should wish by whom these modest residences are occupied; for they are too small to be the homes of country gentlemen, there's no peasantry here, and (in New England, for all the corn comes from the far West) there are no yeomen nor farmers. The information one receives in this country is apt to be rather conflicting, but I'm determined to sift the mystery to the bottom.

I've already noted down a multitude of facts bearing on the points that interest me most—the operation of the school-boards, the co-education of the sexes, the elevation of the tone of the lower classes, the participation of the latter in political life. Political life indeed is almost wholly confined to the lower middle class and the upper section of the lower class. In fact in some of the large towns the lowest order of all participates considerably—a very interesting phase, to which I shall give more attention. It's very gratifying to see the taste for public affairs pervading so many social strata, but the indifference of the gentry is a fact not to be lightly considered. It may be objected perhaps that there are no gentry; and it's very true that I've not yet encountered a character of the type of Lord Bottomley—a type which I'm free to confess I should be sorry to see disappear from our English system, if system it may be called where so much is the growth of blind and incoherent forces. It's nevertheless obvious that an idle and luxurious class exists in this country and that it's less exempt than in our own from the reproach of preferring inglorious ease to the furtherance of liberal ideas. It's rapidly increasing, and I'm not sure that the indefinite growth of the dilettante spirit, in connexion with large and lavishly-expended wealth, is an unmixed good even in a society in which freedom of development has obtained so many interesting triumphs. The fact that this body is not represented in the governing class is perhaps as much the result of the jealousy with which it is viewed by the more earnest workers as of its own (I dare not perhaps apply a harsher term than) levity. Such at least is the impression made on me in the Middle States and in New England; in the Southwest, the Northwest and the far West it will doubtless be liable to correction. These divisions are probably new to you; but they are the general denomination of large and flourishing communities, with which I hope to make myself at least superficially acquainted. The fatigue of traversing, as I habitually do, three or four hundred miles at a bound, is of course considerable; but there is usually much to feed the mind by the way. The conductors of the trains, with whom I freely converse, are often men of vigorous and original views and even of some social eminence. One of them a few days ago gave me a letter of introduction to his brother-in-law, who's president of a Western University. Don't have any fear therefore that I'm not in the best society!

The arrangements for travelling are as a general thing extremely ingenious, as you will probably have inferred from what I told you above; but it must at the same time be conceded that some of them are more ingenious than happy. Some of the facilities with regard to luggage, the transmission of parcels and the like are doubtless very useful when thoroughly mastered, but I've not yet succeeded in availing myself of them without disaster. There are on the other hand no cabs and no porters, and I've calculated that I've myself carried my *impedimenta*—which, you know, are somewhat numerous, and from which I can't bear to be separated—some seventy or eighty miles. I have sometimes thought it was a great mistake not to bring Plummeridge—he would have been useful on such occasions. On the other hand the startling question would have presented itself of who would have carried Plummeridge's portmanteau? He would have been useful indeed for brushing and packing my clothes and getting me my tub; I travel with a large tin one—there are none to be obtained at the inns—and the transport of this receptacle often presents the most insoluble difficulties. It is often too an object of considerable embarrassment in arriving at private houses, where the servants have less reserve of manner than in England; and to tell you the truth I'm by no means certain at the present moment that the tub has been placed in the train with me. "On board" the train is the consecrated phrase here; it's an allusion to the tossing and pitching of the concatenation of cars, so similar to that of a vessel in a storm. As I was about to enquire, however, Who would get Plummeridge *his* tub and attend to his little comforts? We couldn't very well make our appearance, on arriving for a visit, with *two* of the utensils I've named; even if as regards a single one

I have had the courage, as I may say, of a life long habit.
It would hardly be expected that we should both use the
same; though there have been occasions in my travels as
to which I see no way of blinking the fact that Plummeridge
would have had to sit down to dinner with me. Such a con-
tingency would completely have unnerved him, so that on
the whole it was doubtless the wiser part to leave him respectfully touching his hat on the tender in the Mersey.
No one touches his hat over here, and, deem this who will
the sign of a more advanced social order, I confess that
when I see poor Plummeridge again that familiar little gesture—familiar I mean only in the sense of one's immemorial
acquaintance with it—will give me a measurable satisfaction. You'll see from what I tell you that democracy is not
a mere word in this country, and I could give you many
more instances of its universal reign. This, however, is what
we come here to look at and, in so far as there appears
proper occasion, to admire; though I'm by no means sure
that we can hope to establish within an appreciable time
a corresponding change in the somewhat rigid fabric of
English manners. I'm not even inclined to believe such a
change desirable; you know this is one of the points on
which I don't as yet see my way to going so far as Lord
B. I've always held that there's a certain social ideal of inequality as well as of equality, and if I've found the people
of this country, as a general thing, quite equal to each
other, I'm not quite ready to go so far as to say that, as a
whole, they're equal to—pardon that dreadful blot! The
movement of the train and the precarious nature of the
light—it is close to my nose and most offensive—would, I
flatter myself, long since have got the better of a less resolute diarist!

What I was distinctly *not* prepared for is the very considerable body of aristocratic feeling that lurks beneath this
republican simplicity. I've on several occasions been made
the confidant of these romantic but delusive vagaries, of
which the stronghold appears to be the Empire City—a
slang name for the rich and predominant, but unprece-
dently maladministered and disillusioned New York. I was

assured in many quarters that this great desperate eternally-swindled city at least is ripe, everything else failing, for the monarchical experiment or revolution, and that if one of the Queen's sons would come over to sound the possibilities he would meet with the highest encouragement. This information was given me in strict confidence, with closed doors, as it were; it reminded me a good deal of the dreams of the old Jacobites when they whispered their messages to the king across the water. I doubt, however, whether these less excusable visionaries will be able to secure the services of a Pretender, for I fear that in such a case he would encounter a still more fatal Culloden. I have given a good deal of time, as I told you, to the educational system, and have visited no fewer than one hundred and forty-three schools and colleges. It's extraordinary the number of people who are being educated in this country; and yet at the same time the tone of the people is less scholarly than one might expect. A lady a few days since described to me her daughter as being always "on the go," which I take to be a jocular way of saying that the young lady was very fond of paying visits. Another person, the wife of a United States Senator, informed me that if I should go to Washington in January I should be quite "in the swim." I don't regard myself as slow to grasp new meanings, however whimsical; but in this case the lady's explanation made her phrase rather more than less ambiguous. To say that I'm on the go describes very accurately my own situation. I went yesterday to the Poganuc High School, to hear fifty-seven boys and girls recite in unison a most remarkable ode to the American flag, and shortly afterward attended a ladies' luncheon at which some eighty or ninety of the sex were present. There was only one individual in trousers—his trousers, by the way, though he brought several pair, begin to testify to the fury of his movements! The men in America absent themselves systematically from this meal, at which ladies assemble in large numbers to discuss religious, political and social topics.

Immense female symposia at which every delicacy is provided are one of the most striking features of American life, and would seem to prove that our sex is scarcely so indispensable in the scheme of creation as it sometimes supposes. I've been admitted on the footing of an Englishman —"just to show you some of our bright women," the hostess yesterday remarked. ("Bright" here has the meaning of *intellectually remarkable*.) I noted indeed the frequency of the predominantly cerebral—as they call it here "brainy"— type. These rather oddly invidious banquets are organised according to age, for I've also been present as an enquiring stranger at several "girls' lunches," from which married ladies are rigidly excluded, but here the fair revellers were equally numerous and equally "bright." There's a good deal I should like to tell you about my study of the educational question, but my position's now somewhat cramped, and I must dismiss the subject briefly. My leading impression is that the children are better educated (in proportion of course) than the adults. The position of a child is on the whole one of great distinction. There's a popular ballad of which the refrain, if I'm not mistaken, is "Make me a child again just for to-night!" and which seems to express the sentiment of regret for lost privileges. At all events they are a powerful and independent class, and have organs, of immense circulation, in the press. They are often extremely "bright." I've talked with a great many teachers, most of them lady-teachers, as they are here called. The phrase doesn't mean teachers of ladies, as you might suppose, but applies to the sex of the instructress, who often has large classes of young men under her control. I was lately introduced to a young woman of twenty-three who occupies the chair of Moral Philosophy and Belles-Lettres in a Western University and who told me with the utmost frankness that she's "just adored" by the undergraduates. This young woman was the daughter of a petty trader in one of the Southwestern States and had studied at Amanda College in Missourah, an institution at which young people of the two sexes pursue their education together. She was very pretty and modest, and expressed a great desire to see something of English country life, in consequence of which I made her promise to come down to Thistleton in the event

of her crossing the Atlantic. She's not the least like Gwen-
dolen or Charlotte, and I'm not prepared to say how they
would get on with her; the boys would probably do better.
Still, I think her acquaintance would be of value to dear
Miss Gulp, and the two might pass their time very pleasantly in the school-room. I grant you freely that those I
have seen here are much less comfortable than the school-
room at Thistleton. Has Charlotte, by the way, designed
any more texts for the walls? I've been extremely interested
in my visit to Philadelphia, where I saw several thousand
little red houses with white steps, occupied by intelligent
artisans and arranged (in streets) on the rectangular system. Improved cooking-stoves, rosewood pianos, gas and
hot water, aesthetic furniture and complete sets of the British Essayists. A tramway through every street; every block
of exactly equal length; blocks and houses economically let-
tered and numbered. There's absolutely no loss of time and
no need of looking for, or indeed *at,* anything. The mind
always on one's object; it's very delightful.

V

From Louis Leverett in Boston to Harvard Tremont in Paris

November 1880

The scales have turned, my sympathetic Harvard, and
the beam that has lifted you up has dropped me again on
this terribly hard spot. I'm extremely sorry to have missed
you in London, but I received your little note and took due
heed of your injunction to let you know how I got on. I
don't get on at all, my dear Harvard—I'm consumed with
the love of the further shore. I've been so long away that
I've dropped out of my place in this little Boston world
and the shallow tides of New England life have closed over
it. I'm a stranger here and find it hard to believe I ever
was a native. It's very hard, very cold, very vacant. I think
of your warm rich Paris; I think of the Boulevard Saint-
Michel on the mild spring evenings; I see the little corner

by the window (of the Café de la Jeunesse) where I used to sit: the doors are open, the soft deep breath of the great city comes in. The sense is of a supreme splendour and an incomparable arrangement, yet there's a kind of tone, of body, in the radiance; the mighty murmur of the ripest civilisation in the world comes in; the dear old *peuple de Paris,* the most interesting people in the world, pass by. I've a little book in my pocket; it's exquisitely printed, a modern Elzevir. It consists of a lyric cry from the heart of young France and is full of the sentiment of form. There's no form here, dear Harvard; I had no idea how little form there is. I don't know what I shall do; I feel so undraped, so uncurtained, so uncushioned; I feel as if I were sitting in the centre of a mighty "reflector." A terrible crude glare is over everything; the earth looks peeled and excoriated; the raw heavens seem to bleed with the quick hard light.

I've not got back my rooms in West Cedar Street; they're occupied by a mesmeric healer. I'm staying at an hotel and it's all very dreadful. Nothing for one's self, nothing for one's preferences and habits. No one to receive you when you arrive; you push in through a crowd, you edge up to a counter, you write your name in a horrible book where every one may come and stare at it and finger it. A man behind the counter stares at you in silence; his stare seems to say "What the devil do *you* want?" But after this stare he never looks at you again. He tosses down a key at you; he presses a bell; a savage Irishman arrives. "Take him away," he seems to say to the Irishman; but it's all done in silence; there's no answer to your own wild wail—"What's to be done with me, please?" "Wait and you'll see" the awful silence seems to say. There's a great crowd round you, but there's also a great stillness; every now and then you hear some one expectorate. There are a thousand people in this huge and hideous structure; they feed together in a big white-walled room. It's lighted by a thousand gasjets and heated by cast-iron screens which vomit forth torrents of scorching air. The temperature's terrible; the atmosphere's more so; the furious light and heat seem to intensify the dreadful definiteness. When things are so ugly

they shouldn't be so definite, and they're terribly ugly here.
There's no mystery in the corners, there's no light and shade
in the types. The people are haggard and joyless; they look
as if they had no passions, no tastes, no senses. They sit
feeding in silence under the dry hard light; occasionally I
hear the high firm note of a child. The servants are black
and familiar; their faces shine as they shuffle about; there
are blue tones in their dark masks. They've no manners;
they address but don't answer you; they plant themselves
at your elbow (it rubs their clothes as you eat) and watch
you as if your proceedings were strange. They deluge you
with iced water; it's the only thing they'll bring you; if you
look round to summon them they've gone for more. If you
read the newspaper—which I don't, gracious heaven, I can't!
—they hang over your shoulder and peruse it also. I always
fold it up and present it to them; the newspapers here are
indeed for an African taste.

Then there are long corridors defended by gusts of hot
air; down the middle swoops a pale little girl on parlour
skates. "Get out of my way!" she shrieks as she passes; she
has ribbons in her hair and frills on her dress; she makes
the tour of the immense hotel. I think of Puck, who put a
girdle round the earth in forty minutes, and wonder what
he said as he flitted by. A black waiter marches past me
bearing a tray that he thrusts into my spine as he goes.
It's laden with large white jugs; they tinkle as he moves,
and I recognise the unconsoling fluid. We're dying of iced
water, of hot air, of flaring gas. I sit in my room thinking
of these things—this room of mine which is a chamber of
pain. The walls are white and bare, they shine in the rays
of a horrible chandelier of imitation bronze which depends
from the middle of the ceiling. It flings a patch of shadow
on a small table covered with white marble, of which the
genial surface supports at the present moment the sheet of
paper I thus employ for you; and when I go to bed (I like
to read in bed, Harvard) it becomes an object of mockery
and torment. It dangles at inaccessible heights; it stares me
in the face; it flings the light on the covers of my book
but not upon the page—the little French Elzevir I love so

well. I rise and put out the gas—when my room becomes even lighter than before. Then a crude illumination from the hall, from the neighbouring room, pours through the glass openings that surmount the two doors of my apartment. It covers my bed, where I toss and groan; it beats in through my closed lids; it's accompanied by the most vulgar, though the most human, sounds. I spring up to call for some help, some remedy; but there's no bell and I feel desolate and weak. There's only a strange orifice in the wall, through which the traveller in distress may transmit his appeal. I fill it with incoherent sounds, and sounds more incoherent yet come back to me. I gather at last their meaning; they appear to constitute an awful enquiry. A hollow impersonal voice wishes to know what I want, and the very question paralyses me. I want everything—yet I want nothing, nothing this hard impersonality can give! I want my little corner of Paris; I want the rich, the deep, the dark Old World; I want to be out of this horrible place. Yet I can't confide all this to that mechanical tube; it would be of no use; a barbarous laugh would come up from the office. Fancy appealing in these sacred, these intimate moments to an "office"; fancy calling out into indifferent space for a candle, for a curtain! I pay incalculable sums in this dreadful house, and yet haven't a creature to assist me. I fling myself back on my couch and for a long time afterwards the orifice in the wall emits strange murmurs and rumblings. It seems unsatisfied and indignant and is evidently scolding me for my vagueness. My vagueness indeed, dear Harvard! I loathe their horrible arrangements—isn't that definite enough?

You asked me to tell you whom I see and what I think of my friends. I haven't very many; I don't feel at all *en rapport*. The people are very good, very serious, very devoted to their work; but there's a terrible absence of variety of type. Every one's Mr. Jones, Mr. Brown, and every one looks like Mr. Jones and Mr. Brown. They're thin, they're diluted in the great tepid bath of Democracy! They lack completeness of identity; they're quite without modelling. No, they're not beautiful, my poor Harvard; it must be whispered that they're not beautiful. You may say that they're as beautiful as the French, as the Germans; but I can't agree with you there. The French, the Germans, have the greatest beauty of all, the beauty of their ugliness—the beauty of the strange, the grotesque. These people are not even ugly—they're only plain. Many of the girls are pretty, but to be only pretty is (to my sense) to be plain. Yet I've had some talk. I've seen a young woman. She was on the steamer, and I afterwards saw her in New York—a mere maiden thing, yet a peculiar type, a real personality: a great deal of modelling, a great deal of colour, and withal something elusive and ambiguous. She was not, however, of this country; she was a compound of far-off things. But she was looking for something here—like me. We found each other, and for a moment that was enough. I've lost her now; I'm sorry, because she liked to listen to me. She has passed away; I shall not see her again. She liked to listen to me; she almost understood.

VI

From M. Gustave Lejaune of the French Academy in Washington to M. Adolphe Bouche in Paris

December 1880

I give you my little notes; you must make allowances for haste, for bad inns, for the perpetual scramble, for ill-humour. Everywhere the same impression—the platitude of unbalanced democracy intensified by the platitude of the spirit of commerce. Everything on an immense scale—everything illustrated by millions of examples. My brother-in-law is always busy; he has appointments, inspections, interviews, disputes. The people, it appears, are incredibly sharp in conversation, in argument; they wait for you in silence at the corner of the road and then suddenly discharge their revolver. If you fall they empty your pockets; the only chance is to shoot them first. With this no amenities, no preliminaries, no manners, no care for the appearance. I wander about while my brother's occupied; I lounge along the streets; I stop at the corners; I look into the shops; *je regarde passer les femmes.* It's an easy country to see; one sees everything there is; the civilisation's skin deep; you don't have to dig. This positive practical pushing bourgeoisie is always about its business; it lives in the street, in the hotel, in the train; one's always in a crowd—there are seventy-five people in the tramway. They sit in your lap; they stand on your toes; when they wish to pass they simply push you. Everything in silence; they know that silence is golden and they've the worship of gold. When the conductor wishes your fare he gives you a poke, very serious, without a word. As for the types—but there's only one, they're all variations of the same—the commis-voyageur *minus* the gaiety. The women are often pretty; you meet the young ones in the streets, in the trains, in search of a husband. They look at you frankly coldly judicially, to see if you'll serve; but they don't want what you might think (*du moins on me l'assure*); they only want the husband. A Frenchman may mistake; he needs to be sure he's right, and I always make sure. They begin at fifteen; the mother sends them out; it lasts all day (with an interval for dinner at a pastry-cook's); sometimes it goes on for ten years. If they haven't by that time found him they give it up; they make place for the *cadettes,* as the number of women is enormous. No salons, no society, no conversation; people don't receive at home; the young girls have to look for the husband where they can. It's no disgrace not to find him—several have never done so. They continue to go about unmarried—from the force of habit, from the love of movement, without hopes, without regrets. There's no imagination, no sensibility, no desire for the convent.

We've made several journeys—few of less than three hundred miles. Enormous trains, enormous *wagons,* with beds and lavatories, with negroes who brush you with a big broom, as if they were grooming a horse. A bounding movement, a roaring noise, a crowd of people who look horribly tired, a boy who passes up and down hurling pamphlets and sweetmeats into your face: that's an American journey. There are windows in the *wagons*—enormous like everything else; but there's nothing to see. The country's a void—no features, no objects, no details, nothing to show you that you're in one place, you're everywhere, anywhere; the train goes a hundred miles an hour. The cities are all the same; little houses ten feet high or else big ones two hundred; tramways, telegraph-poles, enormous signs, holes in the pavement, oceans of mud, commis-voyageurs, young ladies looking for the husband. On the other hand no beggars and no *cocottes*—none at least that you see. A colossal mediocrity, except (my brother-in-law tells me) in the machinery, which is magnificent. Naturally no architecture (they make houses of wood and of iron), no art, no literature, no theatre. I've opened some of the books—*ils ne se laissent pas lire.* No form, no matter, no style, no general ideas: they seem written for children and young ladies. The most successful (those they praise most) are the facetious; they sell in thousands of editions. I've looked into some of the most *vantés;* but you need to be forewarned to know they're amusing; grins through a horse-collar, burlesques of the Bible, *des plaisanteries de croquemort.* They've a novelist with pretensions to literature who writes about the chase for the husband and the adventures of the rich Americans in our corrupt old Europe, where their primeval candour puts the Europeans to shame. *C'est proprement écrit,* but it's terribly pale. What isn't pale is the newspapers—enormous, like everything else (fifty columns of advertisements), and full of the *commérages* of a continent. And such a tone, *grand Dieu!* The amenities, the personalities, the recriminations, are like so many *coups de revolver.* Headings six inches tall; correspondences from places one never heard of; telegrams from Europe about Sarah Bernhardt; little paragraphs about nothing at all—the *menu* of the neighbour's dinner; articles on the European situation *à pouffer de rire;* all the *tripotage* of local politics. The *reportage* is incredible; I'm chased up and down by interviewers. The matrimonial infelicities of M. and Madame X. (they give the name) *tout au long,* with every detail—not in six lines, discreetly veiled, with an art of insinuation, as with us; but with all the facts (or the fictions), the letters, the dates, the places, the hours. I open a paper at hazard and find *au beau milieu,* apropos of nothing, the announcement: "Miss Susan Green has the longest nose in Western New York." Miss Susan Green (*je me renseigne*) is a celebrated authoress, and the Americans have the reputation of spoiling their women. They spoil them *à coups de poing.*

We've seen few interiors (no one speaks French); but if the newspapers give an idea of the domestic *mœurs,* the *mœurs* must be curious. The passport's abolished, but they've printed my *signalement* in these sheets—perhaps for the young ladies who look for the husband. We went one night to the theatre; the piece was French (they are the only ones) but the acting American; we came out in the middle. The want of taste is incredible. An Englishman whom I met tells me that even the language corrupts itself from day to day; the Englishman ceases to understand. It encourages me to find I'm not the only one. There are things every day that one can't describe. Such is Washington, where we arrived this morning, coming from Philadelphia. My brother-in-law wishes to see the Bureau of Patents, and on our arrival he went to look at his machines while I walked about the streets and visited the Capitol! The human machine is what interests me most. I don't even care for the political—for that's what they call their Government here, "the machine." It operates very roughly and some day evidently will explode. It is true that you'd never suspect they *have* a government; this is the principal seat, but, save for three or four big buildings, most of them *affreux,* it looks like a settlement of negroes. No movement, no officials, no authority, no embodiment of the State. Enormous streets, *comme toujours,* lined with little red houses, where nothing ever passes but the tramway. The Capitol—a vast structure, false classic, white marble, iron and stucco, which has *assez grand air*—must be seen to be appreciated. The goddess of liberty on the top, dressed in a bear's skin; their liberty over here is the liberty of bears. You go into the Capitol as you would into a railway-station; you walk about as you would in the Palais Royal. No functionaries, no doorkeepers, no officers, no uniforms, no badges, no reservations, no authority—nothing but a crowd of shabby people circulating in a labyrinth of spittoons. We're too much governed perhaps in France; but at least we have a certain incarnation of the national conscience, of the national dignity. The dignity's absent here, and I'm told the public conscience is an abyss. *"L'état c'est moi"* even—I like that better than the spittoons. These implements are architectural, monumental; they're the only monuments. *En somme* the country's interesting, now that we too have the Republic; it is the biggest illustration, the biggest warning. It's the last word of democracy, and that word is—platitude. It's very big, very rich, and perfectly ugly. A Frenchman couldn't live here; for life with us, after all, at the worst, is a sort of appreciation. Here one has nothing to appreciate. As for the people, they're the English *minus* the conventions. You can fancy what remains. The women, *pourtant*, are sometimes rather well turned. There was one at Philadelphia—I made her acquaintance by accident—whom it's probable I shall see again. She's not looking for the husband; she has already got one. It was at the hotel; I think the husband doesn't matter. A Frenchman, as I've said, may mistake, and he needs to be sure he's right. *Aussi* I always make sure!

VII

From Marcellus Cockerel in Washington to Mrs. Cooler Née *Cockerel at Oakland, California*

October 1880

I ought to have written you long before this, for I've had your last excellent letter these four months in my hands. The first half of that time I was still in Europe, the last I've spent on my native soil. I think accordingly my silence is owing to the fact that over there I was too miserable to write and that here I've been too happy. I got back the 1st of September—you'll have seen it in the papers—the big familiar vulgar good-natured delightful papers, none of which has any reputation to keep up for anything but getting the news! I really think that has had as much to do as anything else with my satisfaction at getting home—the difference in what they call the "tone of the press." In Europe it's too dreary—the sapience, the solemnity, the false respectability, the verbosity, the long disquisitions on superannuated subjects. Here the newspapers are like the railroad-trains which carry everything that comes to the station and have only the religion of punctuality. As a woman, however, you probably detest them; you think they're (the great word) vulgar. I admitted it just now, and I'm very happy to have an early opportunity to announce to you that that idea has quite ceased to have any terrors for me. There are some conceptions to which the female mind can never rise. Vulgarity's a stupid superficial question-begging accusation, which has become today the easiest refuge of mediocrity. Better than anything else it saves people the trouble of thinking, and anything which does that succeeds. You must know that in these last three years in Europe I've become terribly vulgar myself; that's one service my travels have rendered me. By three years in Europe I mean three years in foreign parts altogether, for I spent several months of that time in Japan, India and the rest of the East. Do you remember when you bade me good-bye in San Francisco the night before I embarked for Yokohama? You foretold that I'd take such a fancy to foreign life that America would never see me more, and that if *you* should wish to see me (an event you were good enough to regard as possible) you'd have to make a rendezvous in Paris or in Rome. I think we made one—which you never kept; but I shall never make another for those cities. It was in Paris, however, that I got your letter; I remember the moment as well as if it were (to my honour) much more recent. You must know that among many places I dislike Paris carries the palm. I'm bored to death there; it's the home of every humbug. The life is full of that false comfort which is worse than discomfort, and the small fat irritable people give me the shivers.

I had been making these reflexions even more devoutly than usual one very tiresome evening toward the beginning of last summer when as I re-entered my hotel at ten o'clock, the little reptile of a portress handed me your gracious lines. I was in a villainous humour. I had been having an over-dressed dinner in a stuffy restaurant and had gone from there to a suffocating theatre, where by way of amusement, I saw a play in which blood and lies were the least of the horrors. The theatres over there are insupportable; the at-mosphere's pestilential. People sit with their elbows in your sides; they squeeze past you every half-hour. It was one of my bad moments—I have a great many in Europe. The con-ventional mechanical play, all in falsetto, which I seemed to have seen a thousand times; the horrible faces of the people, the pushing bullying *ouvreuse* with her false polite-ness and her real rapacity, drove me out of the place at the end of an hour; and as it was too early to go home, I sat down before a café on the Boulevard, where they served me a glass of sour watery beer. There on the Boulevard, in the summer night, life itself was even uglier than the play, and it wouldn't do for me to tell you what I saw. Besides, I was sick of the Boulevard, with its eternal gri-mace and the deadly sameness of the *article de Paris,* which pretends to be so various—the shop-windows a wilderness of rubbish and the passers-by a procession of manikins. Sud-denly it came over me that I was supposed to be amusing myself—my face was a yard long—and that you probably at that moment were saying to your husband: "He stays away so long! What a good time he must be having!" The idea was the first thing that had made me smile for a month; I got up and walked home, reflecting as I went that I was "seeing Europe" and that after all one *must* see Eu-rope. It was because I had been convinced of this that I had come out, and it's because the operation has been brought to a close that I've been so happy for the last eight weeks. I was very conscientious about it, and, though your letter that night made me abominally homesick, I held out to the end, knowing it to be once for all. I shan't trouble Europe again; I shall see America for the rest of my days.

My long delay has had the advantage that now at least I can give you my impressions—I don't mean of Europe; impressions of Europe are easy to get—but of this country as it strikes the reinstated exile. Very likely you'll think them queer; but keep my letter and twenty years hence they'll be quite commonplace. They won't even be vulgar. It was very deliberate, my going round the world. I knew that one ought to see for one's self and that I should have eternity, so to speak, to rest. I travelled energetically; I went everywhere and saw everything; took as many letters as possible and made as many acquaintances. In short I held my nose to the grindstone and here I am back.

Well, the upshot of it all is that I've got rid of a superstition. We have so many that one the less—perhaps the biggest of all—makes a real difference in one's comfort. The one in question—of course you have it—is that there's no salvation but through Europe. Our salvation is here, if we have eyes to see it, and the salvation of Europe into the bargain; that is if Europe's to be saved, which I rather doubt. Of course you'll call me a bird of freedom, a vulgar patriot, a waver of the stars and stripes; but I'm in the delightful position of not minding in the least what any one calls me. I haven't a mission; I don't want to preach; I've simply arrived at a state of mind. I've got Europe off my back. You've no idea how it simplifies things and how jolly it makes me feel. Now I can live, now I can talk. If we wretched Americans could only say once for all "Oh Europe be hanged!" we should attend much better to our proper business. We've simply to mind that business and the rest will look after itself. You'll probably enquire what it is I like better over here, and I'll answer that it's simply— life. Disagreeables for disagreeables I prefer our own. The way I've been bored and bullied in foreign parts, and the way I've had to say I found it pleasant! For a good while this appeared to be a sort of congenital obligation, but one fine day it occurred to me that there was no obligation at all and that it would ease me immensely to admit to myself that (for me at least) all those things had no importance. I mean the things they rub into you over there; the tiresome international topics, the petty politics, the stupid social customs, the baby-house scenery. The vastness and freshness of this American world, the great scale and great pace of our development, the good sense and good nature of the people, console me for there being no cathedrals and no Titians. I hear nothing about Prince Bismarck and Gambetta, about the Emperor William and the Czar of Russia, about Lord Beaconsfield and the Prince of Wales. I used to get so tired of their Mumbo-Jumbo of a Bismarck, of his secrets and surprises, his mysterious intentions and oracular words. They revile us for our party politics; but what are all the European jealousies and rivalries, their armaments and their wars, their rapacities and their mutual lies, but the intensity of the spirit of party? What question, what interest, what idea, what need of mankind, is involved in any of these things? Their big pompous armies drawn up in great silly rows, their gold lace, their salaams, their hierarchies, seem a pastime for children: there's a sense of humour and of reality over here that laughs at all that.

Yes, we're nearer the reality, nearer what they'll all have to come to. The questions of the future are social questions, which the Bismarcks and Beaconsfields are very much afraid to see settled; and the sight of a row of supercilious potentates holding their peoples like their personal property and bristling all over, to make a mutual impression, with feathers and sabres, strikes us as a mixture of the grotesque and the abominable. What do we care for the mutual impressions of potentates who amuse themselves with sitting on people? Those things are their own affair, and they ought to be shut up in a dark room to have it out together. Once one feels, over here, that the great questions of the future are social questions, that a mighty tide is sweeping the world to democracy, and that this country is the biggest stage on which the drama can be enacted, the fashionable European topics seem petty and parochial. They talk about things that we've settled ages ago, and the solemnity with which they propound to you their little domestic embarrassments makes a heavy draft on one's good nature. In England they were talking about the Hares and Rabbits

Bill, about the extension of the County Franchise, about the
Dissenters' Burials, about the Deceased Wife's Sister, about
the abolition of the House of Lords, about heaven knows
what ridiculous little measure for the propping-up of their
ridiculous little country. And they call *us* provincial! It's
hard to sit and look respectable while people discuss
the utility of the House of Lords and the beauty of a State
Church, and it's only in a dowdy civilisation that you'll find
them doing such things. The lightness and clearness of the
social air—*that's* the great relief in these parts. The gentility
of bishops, the propriety of parsons, even the impressiveness
of a restored cathedral, give less of a charm to life than that.
I used to be furious with the bishops and beadles, with the
humbuggery of the whole affair, which every one was conscious of but which people agreed not to expose because
they'd be compromised all round. The convenience of life
in our conditions, the quick and simple arrangements, the
absence of the spirit of routine, are a blessed change from
the stupid stiffness with which I struggled for two long
years. There were people with swords and cockades who
used to order me about; for the simplest operation of life
I had to kootoo to some bloated official. When it was a
question of my doing a little differently from others the
bloated official gasped as if I had given him a blow on the
stomach; he needed to take a week to think of it.

On the other hand it's impossible to take an American by
surprise; he's ashamed to confess he hasn't the wit to do a
thing another man has had the wit to think of. Besides being as good as his neighbour he must therefore be as clever
—which is an affliction only to people who are afraid he
may be cleverer. If this general efficiency and spontaneity
of the people—the union of the sense of freedom with the
love of knowledge—isn't the very essence of a high civilisation I don't know what a high civilisation is. I felt this
greater ease on my first railroad journey—felt the blessing
of sitting in a train where I could move about, where I
could stretch my legs and come and go, where I had a seat
and a window to myself, where there were chairs and tables
and food and drink. The villainous little boxes on the Eu-

ropean trains, in which you're stuck down in a corner with doubled-up knees, opposite to a row of people, often most offensive types, who stare at you for ten hours on end— these were part of my two years' ordeal. The large free way of doing things here is everywhere a pleasure. In London, at my hotel, they used to come to me on Saturday to make me order my Sunday's dinner, and when I asked for a sheet of paper they put it into the bill. The meagreness, the stinginess, the perpetual expectation of a sixpence, used to exasperate me. Of course I saw a great many people who were pleasant; but as I'm writing to you and not to one of them I may say that they were dreadfully apt to be dull. The imagination among the people I see here is more flexible, and then they have the advantage of a larger horizon. It's not bounded on the north by the British aristocracy and on the south by the *scrutin de liste*. (I mix up the countries a little, but they're not worth the keeping apart.) The absence of little conventional measurements, of little cut-and-dried judgements, is an immense refreshment. We're more analytic, more discriminating, more familiar with realities. As for manners, there are bad manners everywhere, but an aristocracy is bad manners organised. (I don't mean that they mayn't be polite among themselves, but they're rude to every one else.) The sight of all these growing millions simply minding their business is impressive to me—more so than all the gilt buttons and padded chests of the Old World; and there's a certain powerful type of "practical" American (you'll find him chiefly in the West) who doesn't "blow" as I do (I'm not practical) but who quietly feels that he has the Future in his vitals—a type that strikes me more than any I met in your favourite countries.

Of course you'll come back to the cathedrals and Titians, but there's a thought that helps one to do without them— the thought that, though we've an immense deal of pie-eating plainness, we've little misery, little squalor, little degradation. There's no regular wife-beating class, and there are none of the stultified peasants of whom it takes so many to make a European noble. The people here are more conscious of things; they invent, they act, they answer for themselves; they're not (I speak of social matters) tied up by authority and precedent. We shall have all the Titians by and by, and we shall move over a few cathedrals. You had better stay here if you want to have the best. Of course I'm a roaring Yankee; but you'll call me that if I say the least, so I may as well take my ease and say the most. Washington's a most entertaining place; and here at least, at the seat of government, one isn't overgoverned. In fact there's no government at all to speak of; it seems too good to be true. The first day I was here I went to the Capitol, and it took me ever so long to figure to myself that I had as good a right there as any one else—that the whole magnificent pile (it *is* magnificent, by the way) was in fact my own. In Europe one doesn't rise to such conceptions, and my spirit had been broken in Europe. The doors were gaping wide—I walked all about; there were no door-keepers, no officers nor flunkeys, there wasn't even a policeman to be seen. It seemed strange not to see a uniform, if only as a patch of colour. But this isn't government by livery. The absence of these things is odd at first; you seem to miss something, to fancy the machine has stopped. It hasn't, though; it only works without fire and smoke. At the end of three days this simple negative impression, the fact that there are no soldiers nor spies, nothing but plain black coats, begins to affect the imagination, becomes vivid majestic symbolic. It ends by being more impressive than the biggest review I saw in Germany. Of course I'm a roaring Yankee; but one has to take a big brush to copy a big model. The future's here of course, but it isn't only that—the present's here as well. You'll complain that I don't give you any personal news, but I'm more modest for myself than for my country. I spent a month in New York and while there saw a good deal of a rather interesting girl who came over with me in the steamer and whom for a day or two I thought I should like to marry. But I shouldn't. She has been spoiled by Europe—and yet the prime stuff struck me as so right.

VIII

From Miss Aurora Church in New York to Miss Whiteside in Paris

January 1881

I told you (after we landed) about my agreement with mamma—that I was to have my liberty for three months and that if at the end of this time I shouldn't have made a good use of it I was to give it back to her. Well, the time's up to-day, and I'm very much afraid I haven't made any use of it at all—I haven't got married, for that's what mamma meant by our little bargain. She has been trying to marry me in Europe for years, without a *dot,* and as she has never (to the best of my knowledge) even come near it, she thought at last that if she were to leave it to me I might possibly do better. I couldn't certainly do worse. Well, my dear, I've done very badly—that is I haven't done at all. I haven't even tried. I had an idea that the *coup* in question came of itself over here; but it hasn't come to *me.* I won't say I'm disappointed, for I haven't on the whole seen any one I should like to marry. When you marry people in these parts they expect you to love them, and I haven't seen any one I should like to love. I don't know what the reason is, but they're none of them what I've thought of. It may be that I've thought of the impossible; and yet I've seen people in Europe whom I should have liked to marry. It's true they were almost always married to some one else. What I *am* disappointed in is simply having to give back my liberty. I don't wish particularly to be married, and I do wish to do as I like—as I've been doing for the last month. All the same I'm sorry for poor mamma, since nothing has happened that she wished to happen. To begin with we're not appreciated, not even by the Rucks, who have disappeared in the strange way in which people over here seem to vanish from the world. We've made no sensation; my new dresses count for nothing (they all have better ones); our philological and historical studies don't show.

We've been told we might do better in Boston; but on the other hand mamma hears that in Boston the people only marry their cousins. Then mamma's out of sorts because the country's exceedingly dear and we've spent all our money. Moreover, I've neither eloped, nor been insulted, nor been talked about, nor—so far as I know—deteriorated in manners or character; so that she's wrong in all her previsions. I think she would have rather liked me to be insulted. But I've been insulted as little as I've been adored. They don't adore you over here; they only make you think they're going to.

Do you remember the two gentlemen who were on the ship and who after we arrived came to see me *à tour de rôle*? At first I never dreamed they were making love to me, though mamma was sure it must be that; then, as it went on a good while, I thought it *was* that—after which I ended by seeing it wasn't anything! It was simply conversation— and conversation a precocious child might have listened to at that. Mr. Leverett and Mr. Cockerel disappeared one fine day without the smallest pretension to having broken my heart, I'm sure—though it only depended on me to think they must have tried to. All the gentlemen are like that; you can't tell what they mean; the "passions" don't rage, the appearances don't matter—nobody believes them. Society seems oddly to consist of a sort of innocent jilting. I think on the whole I *am* a little disappointed—I don't mean about one's not marrying; I mean about the life generally. It looks so different at first that you expect it will be very exciting; and then you find that after all, when you've walked out for a week or two by yourself and driven out with a gentleman in a buggy, that's about all there is to it, as they say here. Mamma's very angry at not finding more to dislike; she admitted yesterday that, once one has got a little settled, the country hasn't even the merit of being hateful. This has evidently something to do with her suddenly proposing three days ago that we should "go West." Imagine my surprise at such an idea coming from mamma! The people in the pension—who, as usual, wish immensely to get rid of her—have talked to her about the West, and she has taken it up with a kind of desperation. You see we must do something; we can't simply remain here. We're rapidly being ruined and we're not—so to speak—getting married. Perhaps it will be easier in the West; at any rate it will be cheaper and the country will have the advantage of being more hateful. It's a question between that and returning to Europe, and for the moment mamma's balancing. I say nothing: I'm really indifferent; perhaps I shall marry a pioneer. I'm just thinking how I shall give back my liberty. It really won't be possible; I haven't got it any more; I've given it away to others. Mamma may get it back if she can from *them!* She comes in at this moment to announce that we must push further—she has decided for the West. Wonderful mamma! It appears that my real chance is for a pioneer—they've sometimes millions. But fancy us at Oshkosh!

Finley Peter Dunne

Finley Peter Dunne, one of the first and still the best of the urban humorists America has produced, was raised in the Adams Street-Desplaines Street neighborhood, on the near west side of Chicago, by middle-class, Irish-American, Catholic parents. In 1867, the year of Dunne's birth, the neighborhood was still a residential area, predominantly Irish in tone. To the east lay the business district which eventually swallowed the neighborhood; to the south lay the Archer Road neighborhood where Mr. Dooley would tend bar, largely populated by lower-class Irish, but increasingly infiltrated by other groups. As Dunne later wrote, "there was a time when Archey Road [as Mr. Dooley called it] was purely Irish. But the Huns, turned back from the Adriatic and the stock-yards and overrunning Archey Road, have nearly exhausted the original population,—not driven them out as they drove out less vigorous races, with thick clubs and short spears, but edged them out with the more biting weapons of modern civilization, —overworked and undereaten them into more languid surroundings remote from the tanks of the gashouse and the blast furnaces of the rolling-mill." Thus the speech of the Archer Road Irish, and of Martin Dooley, was inevitably neither pure Bantry Bay nor unalloyed "far-downer," but modified by Americanization and industrialization. As

Dunne observed, differences arise "from substituting cinders and sulpheretted hydrogen for soft misty air and peat smoke." Nevertheless, there is in Mr. Dooley's speech a music that is as authentically Irish as the voices in Synge's plays. No American, not even Mark Twain, ever had a better ear for dialect than Dunne.

A precociously able newspaperman, Dunne was city editor of the Chicago *Times* at the age of twenty-one, and a few years later became chief editorial writer for the Chicago *Evening Post*. When Judge Longstreet and Johnson Hooper had turned from editorializing to writing comic stories, they continued to express their political convictions, but in symbolic terms. But when Mr. Dooley speaks to his friend Hennessy, he comments directly on the issues of the day. As between the Republicans and the Democrats, the *Post* was independent and so was Mr. Dooley. If, however, Dunne's political satire was a double-edged weapon, this did not mean that the cutting edges were dull—the extent to which Mark Sullivan relied on Mr. Dooley's remarks in his history of the United States at the turn of the century is only one proof that the philosopher of Archey Road was the most penetrating political commentator of the era.

To a great extent, Dunne's Irish Catholic perspective was responsible for his incisiveness. The expansionist fever that swept America in the late 90s, climaxing in the war with Spain, was in part the result of a belief in the racial superiority of the Anglo-Saxon, a belief which contained anti-Irish and anti-Catholic overtones as well as contempt for the little brown brother of the Philippines. Dunne's recognition of the viciousness of the imperialist rationale sprang from his understanding of what Irish immigrants had been forced to endure at the hands of native xenophobes in the United States. Likewise, his satiric appreciation of the futility of amateur political reformers was based on an intimate knowledge of the social conditions that made for the power of the ward boss. Like Theodore Dreiser, another second-generation American who learned the newspaper business in Chicago in the 90s, Dunne understood that the old agrarian slogans were meaningless in an urban world.

On War Preparations

"Well," Mr. Hennessy asked, "how goes th' war?"

"Splendid, thank ye," said Mr. Dooley. "Fine, fine. It makes me hear-rt throb with pride that I'm a citizen iv th' Sixth Wa-ard."

"Has th' ar-rmy started f'r Cuba yet?"

"Wan ar-rmy, says ye? Twinty! Las' Choosdah an advance ar-rmy iv wan hundherd an' twinty thousand men landed fr'm th' Gussie, with tin thousand cannons hurlin' projick-tyles weighin' eight hundherd pounds sivinteen miles. Winsdah night a second ar-rmy iv injineers, miners, plumbers, an' lawn tinnis experts, numberin' in all four hundherd an' eighty thousan' men, ar-rmed with death-dealin' canned goods, was hurried to Havana to storm th' city.

"Thursdah mornin' three thousand full rigimints acrost to Matoonzas, an' afther a spirited battle captured th' Rainy Christiny golf links, two up an' hell to play, an' will hold thim again all comers. Th' same afthernoon th' reg'lar cavalry, consistin' iv four hundherd an' eight thousan' well-mounted men, was loaded aboord th' tug *Lucy J.*, and departed on their earned iv death amidst th' cheers iv eight millyon sojers left behind at Chickamaha. These cav'lry'll co-operate with Commodore Schlow; an' whin he desthroys th' Spanish fleet, as he does ivry Sundah an' holy day except in Lent, an' finds out where they ar-re an' desthroys thim, afther batterin' down th' forts where they ar-re con-cealed so that he can't see thim, but thinks they ar-re on their way f'r to fight Cousin George Dooley, th' cav'lry will make a dash back to Tampa, where Gin'ral Miles is preparin' to desthroy th' Spanish at wan blow,—an' he's th' boy to blow.

"The gin'ral arrived th' other day, fully prepared f'r th' bloody wurruk iv war. He had his intire fam'ly with him. He r-rode recklessly into camp, mounted on a superb

specyal ca-ar. As himsilf an' Uncle Mike Miles, an' Cousin
Hennery Miles, an' Master Miles, aged eight years, dismounted fr'm th' specyal train, they were received with
wild cheers be eight millyon iv th' bravest sojers that iver
give up their lives f'r their counthry. Th' press cinchorship
is so pow'rful that no news is allowed to go out; but I have
it fr'm th' specyal corryspondint iv Mesilf, Clancy th'
Butcher, Mike Casey, an' th' City Direchtry that Gin'ral
Miles instantly repaired himsilf to th' hotel, where he made
his plans f'r cr-rushin' th' Spanyards at wan blow. He will
equip th' ar-my with blow-guns at wanst. His uniforms ar-re
comin' down in specyal steel protected bullyon trains fr'm
th' mint, where they've been kept f'r a year. He has or-
dhered out th' gold resarve f'r to equip his staff, numberin'
eight thousan' men, manny iv whom ar-re clubmen; an' as
soon as he can have his pitchers took, he will cr-rush th'
Spanish with wan blow. Th' pur-pose iv th' gin'ral is to permit no delay. Decisive action is demanded be th' people.
An', whin th' hot air masheens has been sint to th' front,
Gin'ral Miles will strike wan blow that'll be th' damdest
blow since th' year iv th' big wind in Ireland.

"Iv coorse, they'se dissinsions in th' cabinet; but they
don't amount to nawthin'. Th' Sicrety iv War is in favor iv
sawin' th' Spanish ar-rmy into two-be-four joists. Th' Sicrety
iv th' Threeasury has a scheme f'r roonin' thim be lindin'
thim money. Th' Sicrety iv th' Navy wants to sue thim befure th' Mattsachusetts Supreme Coort. I've heerd that th'
Prisident is arrangin' a knee dhrill, with th' idee iv prayin'
th' villyans to th' divvil. But these diff'rences don't count.
We're all wan people, an' we look to Gin'ral Miles to desthroy th' Spanish with wan blow. Whin it comes, trees
will be lifted out be th' roots. Morro Castle'll cave in, an'
th' air'll be full iv Spanish whiskers. A long blow, a sthrong
blow, an' a blow all together."

"We're a gr-reat people," said Mr. Hennessy, earnestly.

"We ar-re," said Mr. Dooley. "We ar-re that. An' th' best
iv it is, we know we ar-re."

On His Cousin George

"Well," said Mr. Hennessy, in tones of chastened joy: "Dewey didn't do a thing to thim. I hope th' poor la-ad ain't cooped up there in Minneapolis."

"Niver fear," said Mr. Dooley, calmly. "Cousin George is all r-right."

"Cousin George?" Mr. Hennessy exclaimed.

"Sure," said Mr. Dooley. "Dewey or Dooley, 'tis all th' same. We dhrop a letter here an' there, except th' haitches, —we niver dhrop thim,—but we're th' same breed iv fightin' men. Georgy has th' thraits iv th' family. Me uncle Mike, that was a handy man, was tol' wanst he'd be sint to hell f'r his manny sins, an' he desarved it; f'r, lavin' out th' wan sin iv runnin' away fr'm annywan, he was booked f'r ivrything from murdher to missin' mass. 'Well,' he says, 'anny place I can get into,' he says, 'I can get out iv,' he says. 'Ye bet on that,' he says.

"So it is with Cousin George. He knew th' way in, an' it's th' same way out. He didn't go in be th' fam'ly inthrance, sneakin' along with th' can undher his coat. He left Ding Dong, or whativer 'tis ye call it, an' says he, 'Thank Gawd,' he says, 'I'm where no man can give me his idees iv how to r-run a quiltin' party, an' call it war,' he says. An' so he sint a man down in a divin' shute, an' cut th' cables, so's Mack cudden't chat with him. Thin he prances up to th' Spanish forts, an' hands thim a few oranges. Tosses thim out like a man throwin' handbills f'r a circus. 'Take that,' he says, 'an' raymimber th' *Maine*,' he says. An' he goes into th' harbor, where Admiral What-th'-'ell is, an', says he, 'Surrinder,' he says. 'Niver,' says th' Dago. 'Well,' says Cousin George, 'I'll just have to push ye ar-round,' he says. An' he tosses a few slugs at th' Spanyards. Th' Spanish admiral shoots at him with a bow an' arrow, an' goes over an' writes a cable. 'This mornin' we was attackted,' he says. 'An',' he says, 'we fought the inimy with great courage,' he says. 'Our victhry is complete,' he says. 'We have lost ivrything we had,' he says. 'Th' threacherous foe,' he says, 'afther desthroyin' us, sought refuge behind a mudscow,' he says; 'but nawthin' daunted us. What boats we cudden't r-run ashore we surrindered,' he says. 'I cannot write no more,' he says, 'as me coat-tails are afire,' he says; 'an' I am bravely but rapidly leapin' fr'm wan vessel to another, followed be me valiant crew with a fire-engine,' he says. 'If I can save me coat-tails,' he says, 'they'll be no kick comin',' he says. 'Long live Spain, long live mesilf.'

"Well, sir, in twenty-eight minyits be th' clock Dewey he had all th' Spanish boats sunk, an' that there harbor lookin' like a Spanish stew. Thin he r-run down th' bay, an' handed a few war-rm wans into th' town. He set it on fire, an' thin wint ashore to war-rm his poor hands an' feet. It chills th' blood not to have annything to do f'r an hour or more."

"Thin why don't he write something?" Mr. Hennessy demanded.

"Write?" echoed Mr. Dooley. "Write? Why shud he write? D'ye think Cousin George ain't got nawthin' to do but to set down with a fountain pen, an' write: 'Dear Mack, —At 8 o'clock I begun a peaceful blockade iv this town. Ye can see th' pieces ivrywhere. I hope ye're injyin' th' same gr-reat blessin'. So no more at prisint. Fr'm ye'ers thruly, George Dooley.' He ain't that kind. 'Tis a nice day, an' he's there smokin' a good tin-cint see-gar, an' throwin' dice f'r th' dhrinks. He don't care whether we know what he's done or not. I'll bet ye, whin we come to find out about him, we'll hear he's ilicted himsilf king iv th' F'lip-ine Islands. Dooley th' Wanst. He'll be settin' up there undher a pa'm-three with naygurs fannin' him an' a dhrop iv licker in th' hollow iv his ar-rm, an' hootchy-kootchy girls dancin' befure him, an' ivry tin or twinty minyits some wan bringin' a prisoner in. 'Who's this?' says King Dooley. 'A Spanish gin'ral,' says th' copper. 'Give him a typewriter an' set him to wurruk,' says th' king. 'On with th' dance,' he says. An' afther awhile, whin he gits tired iv th' game, he'll write home an' say he's got the islands; an' he'll tur-rn thim over to th' gover'mint

an' go back to his ship, an' Mark Hanna'll organize th'
F'lip-ine Islands Jute an' Cider Comp'ny, an' th' rivolutchin-
ists'll wish they hadn't. That's whatt'll happen. Mark me
wurrud."

On Reform Candidates

"That frind iv ye'ers, Dugan, is an intilligent man," said
Mr. Dooley. "All he needs is an index an' a few illustrations
to make him a bicyclopedja iv useless information."

"Well," said Mr. Hennessy, judiciously, "he ain't no Socrates an' he ain't no answers-to-questions colum; but he's
a good man that goes to his jooty, an' as handy with a pick
as some people are with a cocktail spoon. What's he been
doin' again ye?"

"Nawthin'," said Mr. Dooley, "but he was in here Choos-
day. 'Did ye vote?' says I. 'I did,' says he. 'Which wan iv
th' distinguished bunko steerers got ye'er invalu'ble suf-
frage?' says I. 'I didn't have none with me,' says he, 'but
I voted f'r Charter Haitch,' says he. 'I've been with him in
six ilictions,' says he, 'an' he's a good man,' he says. 'D'ye
think ye're votin' f'r th' best?' says I. 'Why, man alive,' I
says, 'Charter Haitch was assassinated three years ago,' I
says. 'Was he?' says Dugan. 'Ah, well, he's lived that down
be this time. He was a good man,' he says.

"Ye see, that's what thim rayform lads wint up again.
If I liked rayformers, Hinnissy, an' wanted f'r to see thim
win out wanst in their lifetime, I'd buy thim each a suit
iv chilled steel, ar-rm thim with raypeatin' rifles, an' take
thim east iv State Sthreet an' south iv Jackson Bullyvard.
At prisint th' opinion that pre-vails in th' ranks iv th' glory-
ous ar-rmy iv ray-form is that there ain't annything worth
seein' in this lar-rge an' commodyous desert but th' pest-
house an' the bridewell. Me frind Willum J. O'Brien is no
rayformer. But Willum J. undherstands that there's a few
hundherds iv thousands iv people livin' in a part iv th' town

that looks like nawthin' but smoke fr'm th' roof iv th' Onion
League Club that have on'y two pleasures in life, to wurruk an' to vote, both iv which they do at th' uniform rate iv
wan dollar an' a half a day. That's why Willum J. O'Brien
is now a sinitor an' will be an aldherman afther next Thursdah, an' it's why other people are sinding him flowers.

"This is th' way a rayform candydate is ilicted. Th' boys
down town had heerd that things ain't goin' r-right somehow. Franchises is bein' handed out to none iv thim; an'
wanst in a while a mimber iv th' club, comin' home a little
late an' thryin' to riconcile a pair iv r-round feet with an
embroidered sidewalk, meets a sthrong ar-rm boy that
pushes in his face an' takes away all his marbles. It begins
to be talked that th' time has come f'r good citizens f'r to
brace up an' do somethin', an' they agree to nomynate a
candydate f'r aldherman. 'Who'll we put up?' says they.
'How's Clarence Doolittle?' says wan. 'He's laid up with a
coupon thumb, an' can't r-run.' 'An' how about Arthur
Doheny?' 'I swore an oath whin I came out iv colledge I'd
niver vote f'r a man that wore a made tie.' 'Well, thin, let's
thry Willie Boye.' 'Good,' says th' comity. 'He's jus' th' man
f'r our money.' An' Willie Boye, after thinkin' it over, goes
to his tailor an' ordhers three dozen pairs iv pants, an' decides f'r to be th' sthandard-bearer iv th' people. Musin'
over his fried eyesthers an' asparagus an' his champagne,
he bets a polo pony again a box of golf-balls he'll be ilicted
unanimous; an' all th' good citizens make a vow f'r to set
th' alar-rm clock f'r half-past three on th' arfthernoon iv
iliction day, so's to be up in time to vote f'r th' riprisintitive
iv pure gover'mint.

" 'Tis some time befure they comprehind that there ar-re
other candydates in th' field. But th' other candydates know
it. Th' sthrongest iv thim—his name is Flannigan, an' he's
a re-tail dealer in wines an' liquors, an' he lives over his
establishment. Flannigan was nomynated enthusyastically
at a prim'ry held in his bar-rn; an' befure Willie Boye had
picked out pants that wud match th' color iv th' Austhree-
lyan ballot this here Flannigan had put a man on th' day
watch, tol' him to speak gently to anny raygistered voter

that wint to sleep behind th' sthove, an' was out that night visitin' his frinds. Who was it carrid th' pall? Flannigan. Who was it sthud up at th' christening? Flannigan. Whose ca-ards did th' grievin' widow, th' blushin' bridegroom, or th' happy father find in th' hack? Flannigan's. Ye bet ye'er life. Ye see Flannigan wasn't out f'r th' good iv th' community. Flannigan was out f'r Flannigan an' th' stuff.

"Well, iliction day come around; an' all th' imminent frinds iv good gover'mint had special wires sthrung into th' club, an' waited f'r th' returns. Th' first precin't showed 28 votes f'r Willie Boye to 14 f'r Flannigan. 'That's my pre-cin't,' says Willie. 'I wondher who voted thim fourteen?' 'Coachmen,' says Clarence Doolittle. 'There are thirty-five precin'ts in this ward,' says th' leader iv th' rayform ilimint. 'At this rate, I'm sure iv 440 meejority. Gossoon,' he says, 'put a keg iv sherry wine on th' ice,' he says. 'Well,' he says, 'at last th' community is relieved fr'm misrule,' he says. 'To-morrah I will start in arrangin' amindmints to th' tariff schedool an' th' ar-bitration threety,' he says. 'We must be up an' doin',' he says. 'Hol' on there,' says wan iv th' com-ity. 'There must be some mistake in this fr'm th' sixth pre-cin't,' he says. 'Where's the sixth precin't?' says Clarence. 'Over be th' dumps,' says Willie. 'I told me futman to see to that. He lives at th' cor-ner iv Desplaines an' Bloo Island Av'noo on Goose's Island,' he says. 'What does it show?' 'Flannigan, three hundherd an' eighty-five; Hansen, forty-eight; Schwartz, twinty; O'Malley, sivinteen; Casey, ten; O'Day, eight; Larsen, five; O'Rourke, three; Mulcahy, two; Schmitt, two; Moloney, two; Riordan, two; O'Malley, two; Willie Boye, wan.' 'Gintlemin,' says Willie Boye, arisin' with a stern look in his eyes, 'th' rascal has bethrayed me. Wait-her, take th' sherry wine off th' ice. They'se no hope f'r sound financial legislation this year. I'm goin' home.'

"An', as he goes down th' sthreet, he hears a band play an' sees a procission headed be a calceem light; an', in a carredge, with his plug hat in his hand an' his di'mond makin' th' calceem look like a piece iv punk in a smoke-house, is Flannigan, payin' his first visit this side iv th' thracks."

Expansion

"Whin we plant what Hogan calls th' starry banner iv Freedom in th' Ph'lippeens," said Mr. Dooley, "an' give th' sacred blessin' iv liberty to the poor, downtrodden people iv thim unfortunate isles,—dam thim!—we'll larn thim a lesson."

"Sure," said Mr. Hennessy, sadly, "we have a thing or two to larn oursilves."

"But it isn't f'r thim to larn us," said Mr. Dooley. "'Tis not f'r thim wretched an' degraded crathers, without a mind or a shirt iv their own, f'r to give lessons in politeness an' liberty to a nation that manny-facthers more dhressed beef than anny other imperyal nation in th' wurruld. We say to thim: 'Naygurs,' we say, 'poor, dissolute, uncovered wretches,' says we, 'whin th' crool hand iv Spain forged man'cles f'r ye'er limbs, as Hogan says, who was it crossed th' say an' sthruck off th' comealongs? We did,—by dad, we did. An' now, ye mis'rable childish-minded apes, we propose f'r to larn ye th' uses iv liberty. In ivry city in this unfair land we will erect school-houses an' packin' houses an' houses iv correction; an' we'll larn ye our language, because 'tis aisier to larn ye ours than to larn oursilves yours. An' we'll give ye clothes, if ye pay f'r thim; an', if ye don't, ye can go without. An', whin ye're hungry, ye can go to th' morgue—we mane th' resth'rant—an' ate a good square meal iv ar-rmy beef. An' we'll sind th' gr-reat Gin'ral Eagan over f'r to larn ye etiquette, an' Andhrew Carnegie to larn ye pathriteism with blow-holes into it, an' Gin'ral Alger to larn ye to hould onto a job; an', whin ye've become edy-cated an' have all th' blessin's iv civilization that we don't want, that'll count ye one. We can't give ye anny votes, because we haven't more thin enough to go round now; but we'll threat ye th' way a father shud threat his childher if we have to break ivry bone in ye'er bodies. So come to our ar-rms,' says we.

"But glory be, 'tis more like a rasslin' match than a father's embrace. Up gets this little monkey iv an' Aggynaldoo, an' says he, 'Not for us,' he says. 'We thank ye kindly; but we believe,' he says, 'in pathronizin' home industhries,' he says. 'An',' he says, 'I have on hand,' he says, 'an' f'r sale,' he says, 'a very superyor brand iv home-made liberty, like ye'er mother used to make,' he says. ''Tis a long way fr'm ye'er plant to here,' he says, 'an' be th' time a cargo iv liberty,' he says, 'got out here an' was handled be th' middlemen,' he says, 'it might spoil,' he says. 'We don't want anny col' storage or embalmed liberty,' he says. 'What we want an' what th' ol' reliable house iv Aggynaldoo,' he says, 'supplies to th' thrade,' he says, 'is fr-esh liberty r-right off th' far-rm,' he says. 'I can't do annything with ye'er proposition,' he says. 'I can't give up,' he says, 'th' rights f'r which f'r five years I've fought an' bled ivry wan I cud reach,' he says. 'Onless,' he says, 'ye'd feel like buyin' out th' whole business,' he says. 'I'm a pathrite,' he says; 'but I'm no bigot,' he says.

"An' there it stands, Hinnissy, with th' indulgent parent kneelin' on th' stomach iv his adopted child, while a dillygation fr'm Boston bastes him with an umbrella. There it stands, an' how will it come out I dinnaw. I'm not much iv an expansionist mesilf. F'r th' las' tin years I've been thryin' to decide whether 'twud be good policy an' thrue to me thraditions to make this here bar two or three feet longer, an manny's th' night I've laid awake tryin' to puzzle it out. But I don't know what to do with th' Ph'lippeens anny more thin I did las' summer, befure I heerd tell iv thim. We can't give thim to anny wan without makin' th' wan that gets thim feel th' way Doherty felt to Clancy whin Clancy med a frindly call an' give Doherty's childher th' measles. We can't sell thim, we can't ate thim, an' we can't throw thim into th' alley whin no wan is lookin'. An' 'twud be a disgrace f'r to lave befure we've pounded these frindless an' ongrateful people into insinsibility. So I suppose, Hinnissy, we'll have to stay an' do th' best we can, an' lave Andhrew Carnegie secede fr'm th' Union. They'se wan consolation; an' that is, if th' American people can govern thimsilves, they can govern annything that walks."

"An' what 'd ye do with Aggy—what-d'ye-call-him?" asked Mr. Hennessy.

"Well," Mr. Dooley replied, with brightening eyes, "I know what they'd do with him in this ward. They'd give that pathrite what he asks, an' thin they'd throw him down an' take it away fr'm him."

A Book Review

"Well sir," said Mr. Dooley, "I jus' got hold iv a book, Hinnissy, that suits me up to th' handle, a gran' book, th' grandest iver seen. Ye know I'm not much troubled be lithrachoor, havin' manny worries iv me own, but I'm not prejudiced again' books. I am not. Whin a rale good book comes along I'm as quick as anny wan to say it isn't so bad, an' this here book is fine. I tell ye 'tis fine."

"What is it?" Mr. Hennessy asked languidly.

" 'Tis 'Th' Biography iv a Hero be Wan who Knows.' 'Tis 'Th' Darin' Exploits iv a Brave Man be an Actual Eye Witness.' 'Tis 'Th' Acoount iv th' Desthruction iv Spanish Power in th' Ant Hills,' as it fell fr'm th' lips iv Tiddy Rosenfelt an' was took down be his own hands. Ye see 'twas this way, Hinnissy, as I r-read th' book. Whin Tiddy was blowed up in th' harbor iv Havana he instantly con-cluded they must be war. He debated th' question long an' earnestly an' fin'lly passed a jint resolution declarin' war. So far so good. But there was no wan to carry it on. What shud he do? I will lave th' janial author tell th' story in his own wurruds.

" 'Th' sicrety iv war had offered me,' he says, 'th' command of a rig'mint,' he says, 'but I cud not consint to remain in Tampa while perhaps less audacious heroes was at th' front,' he says. 'Besides,' he says, 'I felt I was incompetent f'r to command a rig'mint raised be another,' he says. 'I determined to raise wan iv me own,' he says. 'I selected fr'm me acquaintances in th' West,' he says, 'men that had thravelled with me acrost th' desert an' th' storm-wreathed mountain,' he says, 'sharin' me burdens an' at times con-

frontin' perils almost as gr-reat as anny that beset me path,'
he says. 'Together we had faced th' turrors iv th' large but
vilent West,' he says, 'an' these brave men had seen me
with me trusty rifle shootin' down th' buffalo, th' elk, th'
moose, th' grizzly bear, th' mountain goat,' he says, 'th' silver man, an' other ferocious beasts iv thim parts,' he says.
'An' they niver flinched,' he says. 'In a few days I had thim
perfectly tamed,' he says, 'an' ready to go annywhere I led,'
he says. 'On th' transport goi'n to Cubia,' he says, 'I wud
stand beside wan iv these r-rough men threatin' him as a
akel, which he was in ivrything but birth, education, rank
an' courage, an' together we wud look up at th' admirable
stars iv that tolerable southern sky an' quote th' bible fr'm
Walt Whitman,' he says. 'Honest, loyal, thrue-hearted la-
ads, how kind I was to thim,' he says.

" 'We had no sooner landed in Cubia than it become
nicessry f'r me to take command iv th' ar-rmy which I did
at wanst. A number of days was spint be me in recon-
noitring, attinded on'y be me brave an' fluent body guard,
Richard Harding Davis. I discovered that th' inimy was
heavily inthrenched on th' top iv San Joon hill immejiately
in front iv me. At this time it become apparent that I was
handicapped be th' prisence iv th' ar-rmy,' he says. 'Wan
day whin I was about to charge a block house sturdily de-
finded be an ar-rmy corps undher Gin'ral Tamale, th' brave
Castile that I afthwards killed with a small ink-eraser that
I always carry, I r-ran into th' entire military force iv th'
United States lying on its stomach. "If ye won't fight," says
I, "let me go through," I says. "Who ar-re ye?" says they.
"Colonel Rosenfelt," says I. "Oh, excuse me," says the gin'ral
in command (if me mimry serves me thrue it was Miles)
r-risin' to his knees an' salutin'. This showed me 'twud be
impossible f'r to carry th' war to a successful con-clusion
unless I was free, so I sint th' ar-rmy home an' attackted
San Joon hill. Ar-rmed on'y with a small thirty-two which
I used in th' West to shoot th' fleet prairie dog, I climbed
that precipitous ascent in th' face iv th' most gallin' fire I
iver knew or heerd iv. But I had a few r-rounds iv gall
mesilf an' what cared I? I dashed madly on cheerin' as I
wint. Th' Spanish throops was dhrawn up in a long line

in th' formation known among military men as a long line. I fired at th' man nearest to me an' I knew be th' expression iv his face that th' trusty bullet wint home. It passed through his frame, he fell, an' wan little home in far-off Catalonia was made happy be th' thought that their rip-risintative had been kilt be th' future governor iv New York. Th' bullet sped on its mad flight an' passed through th' intire line fin'lly imbeddin' itself in th' abdomen iv th' Arrchbishop iv Santiago eight miles away. This ended th' war.'

"'They has been some discussion as to who was th' first man to r-reach th' summit iv San Joon hill. I will not attempt to dispute th' merits iv th' manny gallant sojers, statesmen, corryspondints an' kinetoscope men who claim th' distinction. They ar-re all brave men an' if they wish to wear my laurels they may. I have so manny annyhow that it keeps me broke havin' thim blocked an' irned. But I will say f'r th' binifit iv Posterity that I was th' on'y man I see. An' I had a tillyscope.'"

"I have thried, Hinnissy," Mr. Dooley continued, "to give you a fair idee iv th' contints iv this remarkable book, but what I've tol' ye is on'y what Hogan calls an outline iv th' principal pints. Ye'll have to r-read th' book ye'ersilf to get a thrue conciption. I haven't time f'r to tell ye th' wurruk Tiddy did in ar-rmin' an' equippin' himself, how he fed himsilf, how he steadied himsilf in battle an' encouraged himsilf with a few well-chosen wurruds whin th' sky was darkest. Ye'll have to take a squint into th' book ye'ersilf to l'arn thim things."

"I won't do it," said Mr. Hennessy. "I think Tiddy Rosenfelt is all r-right an' if he wants to blow his hor-rn lave him do it."

"Thrue f'r ye," said Mr. Dooley, "an' if his valliant deeds didn't get into this book 'twud be a long time befure they appeared in Shafter's histhry iv th' war. No man that bears a gredge again' himsilf 'll iver be governor iv a state. An' if Tiddy done it all he ought to say so an' relieve th' suspinse. But if I was him I'd call th' book 'Alone in Cubia.'"

AMERICAN LITERATURE
IN NORTON AND LIVERIGHT PAPERBACK

Sherwood Anderson *Beyond Desire* • *Dark Laughter*

Kate Chopin *The Awakening* NCE

Samuel L. Clemens *Adventures of Huckleberry Finn* NCE (2d Ed.)
  • *Pudd'nhead Wilson* and *Those Extraordinary Twins* NCE

Stephen Crane *Maggie: A Girl of the Streets* (1893 ed.) NCE • *The Red
    Badge of Courage* NCE (2d Ed.)

E. E. Cummings *The Enormous Room* • *Him, a Play*

Theodore Dreiser *Sister Carrie* NCE

William Faulkner *Soldiers' Pay*

Ernest Gaines *Bloodline* • *Of Love and Dust*

Ronald Gottesman et al., Eds. *The Norton Anthology of American
            Literature*

Nathaniel Hawthorne *The Blithedale Romance* • *The Blithedale
        Romance* NCE • *The House of the Seven
        Gables* NCE • *The Scarlet Letter* NCE (2d Ed.)

Henry James *The Ambassadors* NCE • *The American* NCE • *Eight Tales
    from the Major Phase: "In the Cage" and Others* • *The
    Portrait of a Lady* NCE • *The Turn of the Screw* NCE • *The
    Wings of the Dove* NCE

Sarah Orne Jewett *"The Country of the Pointed Firs" and Other Stories*

Kenneth S. Lynn, Ed. *The Comic Tradition in America*

Herman Melville *The Confidence-Man* NCE • *Moby-Dick* NCE • *The
        Shorter Novels (Benito Cereno, Bartleby the Scrivener,
        The Encantadas, Billy Budd)*

Frank Norris *McTeague* NCE

William Saroyan *Chance Meetings*

Gertrude Stein *Gertrude Stein's America* • *Paris France*

Henry David Thoreau *Walden* and *Civil Disobedience* NCE

Jean Toomer *Cane*

Walt Whitman *Leaves of Grass* NCE

NCE Norton Critical Edition